# THE INVISIBLE CAMORRA

# The Invisible Camorra

Neapolitan Crime Families
across Europe

**Felia Allum**

CORNELL UNIVERSITY PRESS   ITHACA AND LONDON

Copyright © 2016 by Cornell University

All rights reserved. Except for brief quotations in a review, this book, or parts thereof, must not be reproduced in any form without permission in writing from the publisher. For information, address Cornell University Press, Sage House, 512 East State Street, Ithaca, New York 14850.

First published 2016 by Cornell University Press
Printed in the United States of America

Library of Congress Cataloging-in-Publication Data

Names: Allum, Felia, 1971– author
Title: The invisible Camorra : Neapolitan crime families at work in Europe / Felia Allum.
Description: Ithaca ; London : Cornell University Press, 2016. | Includes bibliographical references and index.
Identifiers: LCCN 2016021196 | ISBN 9781501702457 (cloth : alk. paper)
Subjects: LCSH: Camorra. | Organized crime—Social aspects—Europe.
Classification: LCC HV6453.I83 C2895 2016 | DDC 364.106089/5104—dc23
LC record available at https://lccn.loc.gov/2016021196

Cornell University Press strives to use environmentally responsible suppliers and materials to the fullest extent possible in the publishing of its books. Such materials include vegetable-based, low-VOC inks and acid-free papers that are recycled, totally chlorine-free, or partly composed of nonwood fibers. For further information, visit our website at www.cornellpress.cornell.edu.

Cloth printing                10  9  8  7  6  5  4  3  2  1

*For Mirabelle and Amadis*

## Contents

| | |
|---|---|
| Acknowledgments | ix |
| Glossary | xiii |
| Acronyms | xvii |
| | |
| Introduction | 1 |
| **1.** Local Motives, Global Choices | 16 |
| **2.** Functional Mobility | 40 |
| **3.** Camorra Clans in Germany and the Netherlands: Hof, Hamburg, and Amsterdam | 64 |
| **4.** Camorra Clans in France: La Seyne-sur-Mer, Paris, and Villeneuve-Loubet | 105 |
| **5.** Camorra Clans in Spain: Granada, Tarragona, and Tenerife | 136 |
| **6.** Camorra Clans in the United Kingdom: Preston, London, and Aberdeen | 180 |
| Conclusion | 212 |
| | |
| Notes | 231 |
| Works Cited | 243 |
| Index | 261 |

## Acknowledgments

This book is the result of both an academic and a personal journey, at times lonely, at times full of joy, but always full of questions. Along the way were many encounters and exchanges, some planned and others fortuitous. There were people who looked at me and passed by without stopping, and there were those who looked at me and stopped and took an interest. It is some of them I would like to thank here, for their support, kindness, and friendship.

I thank the University of Bath for the sabbatical that I was given in 2010–2011 and also the two Knowledge Transfer grants (2012) that allowed me to organize workshops with practitioners, policymakers, and academics. In particular, in May 2012 I was able to invite an antimafia judge and put him face-to-face with the British police. Sabbaticals are essential to any researcher, especially those who have to go into the field. They also make us better teachers, as we can present our research firsthand to our students. After eight years at Bath, that sabbatical year allowed me to return to studying the Camorra close-up.

I am particularly grateful to Roger Eatwell and Sue Milner, who believed in me and my research project right from the start despite attempts to block it by others. I thank Adalgisa Giorgio, who has also been the most supportive, efficient, and caring of colleagues. She looked after me and protected me while tirelessly giving herself to her research, students, and university. I also thank my undergraduate and postgraduate students who have since 2011 listened to my explanations, stories, and analysis. They have been patient and engaging.

In collecting material across Europe, I encountered many obstacles but I also came across some caring interlocutors, in particular Charles Duchaine, Nicolas Bessone, Solange Moracchini, Ursula Toettel, Jose Daniel Baena Sanchez, Joan Queralt Domenech, Stephan Pruss, and Laura Requena Espada. In the United Kingdom, Stan Gilmour has been a constant and helpful listener and adviser. I also thank Tim Gray, Lewis Benjamin, and Jon Murray, who made time for me. I thank Simon Erkins (Fladgate LLP) for his legal advice and Felicity McMahon for her thorough libel read of my text.

The last twenty-four years has seen a new wave of antimafia activism, especially in relation to the Camorra, where everyone is an expert. I rarely came across antimafia protagonists but I do know of silent heroes: the hardworking antimafia judges, the busy flying squad and conscientious Guardia di Finanza in Naples who work body and soul to fight the Camorra, often with few resources. Sincere thanks to them and their staff: Sergio Amato, Federico Cafiero de Raho, Stefania Castaldi, Luigi Alberto Cannavale, Rosario Cantelmo, Rosamaria D'Antonio, Marco Del Gaudio, Michele Del Prete, Vincenzo D'Onofrio, Pierpaolo Filippelli, Fulvio Filocamo, Luigi Landolfi, Piero Lupi, Raffaello Magi, Paolo Mancuso, Catello Maresca, Alessandro Pennasilico, Vittorio Pisani, Barbara Sargente, Luca Semeraro, Maurizio Vallone and Mariella Vecchi. The time they gave me and the discussions we had have been invaluable in helping me to understand different aspects of this criminal phenomenon. I also thank the five state witnesses who agreed to be interviewed by me in Italy. Their time and clarifications helped me in my thinking process.

Armando D'Alterio and Franco Roberti have always answered my questions with care and attention, and I thank them very much for their time. Special mention also of Carmine Iuliano, Sergio Bergamasco, Emilio Fiora, and Tommaso Solazzo, who were helpful, kind, and attentive to my nonstop barrage of questions. There are also two passionate unassuming judges whose constant professionalism and great dedication I came to admire. Their encouragement during this research was invaluable. I thank Giuseppe Borrelli, whose time and documents were invaluable at critical junctures, and Filippo Beatrice, whose interest, enthusiasm, and critical observations kept me on my toes. Because of him I was able to make my own sense of it all and "walk alone"; without him the project would have been much more problematic and challenging than it already was . . . thank you. Colleagues, friends, and family have provided time, support, and laughs along the way: Susan Carrée, Isaia Sales, Alan Pearce, Marisa Iorio, Annarita Criscitiello, Luigi di Prisco, Katrina and Mike Sartorius, Justine Wittenberger, and Rex Jackson-Coombs. I also thank Anna Hamilton, Aviva Mirels, Mario Lauria, and Antonella Giustino, but more specifically, Fabrice Allum and Andrea Lauria who helped me escape from my traveling *camorristi*, from time to time, by taking me to watch Reading, l' Olympique de Marseille, and S.S.C Napoli play football. My deepest thanks to my parents and Matilde Lauria for their constant support and love.

Alessandro Colletti has been a reliable friend who always responded to my requests. I am extremely grateful to him for all his help and that of Gianna Caratelli, who produced the social network graphs in his book.

Adele Lauria and Julia Molinari have in different ways kept me going and feeling positive in moments of self-doubt: Adele, on my many trips to Naples, where she looked after me and my girls; Julia during our many summers on the beach discussing academic English, qualitative methodologies, and the psychology of traveling *camorristi*.

Some of my ideas have been presented in earlier publications: "Italian Organized Crime in the UK," *Policing* 6, no. 4 (2012): 354–359; "Italian Organized

Crime in the UK: Continuing the Debate," *Policing* 7, no. 2 (2013): 227–232; "Understanding Criminal Mobility: The Case of the Neapolitan Camorra," *Journal of Modern Italian Studies* 19, no. 5 (2014): 583–602.

I thank Roger Haydon for believing in this project and Emily Powers, Karen Laun, and Susan C. Barnett for being so efficient. I would also like to thank Mary Petrusewicz for her sterling editorial work and rendering my text readable.

Lastly, I thank Mimi, Ami, and Stasha for their patience, support, and love over the last five years. In particular, Mimi and Ami for indulging me in my relationship with Naples, the Camorra, and Italy. They too have become mafia experts and, aged eleven and nine, they can explain the Camorra to anyone. Thanks to Stasha for just being there.

Since this text analyzes what appears to be criminal behavior, I have sought to change names and identities and used initials to designate certain individuals in order to tell their story. It is in no way my intention to harm the reputation or accuse individuals of criminal behavior, rather it is to tell the story of various Camorra clans and their presence and activities in Europe. It would have been easier to systematically change all the names of clans and individuals and would have given me greater freedom to tell their stories. But I decided against this approach because I hope that this analysis will contribute to the historical understanding of Camorra clans in Naples, Campania, and Europe. All the individuals referred to in this text as criminals have been convicted in the first instance, *primo grado*, by the Italian judicial system. However, in many cases their final appeals have not yet been heard and so their convictions have not yet been confirmed at the highest level, *terzo grado*, and therefore, they must be considered innocent.

In addition, please note that the use of the term *accomplice* is to be understood in a more academic sense rather than implying blameworthy (and potentially criminal) conduct. In other words, by accomplices, I am interested in identifying the type of people who offer help to clans and the nature of this assistance. This has been defined as "complicit," "collusive," and "compenetrative" (Sciarrone, 2014). It varies in shape and form and is still relatively understudied. In this book, it is about what they could have exchanged with clans and the nature of that relationship, it is not about implying blame but understanding the general dynamics, if there are any. In other words, in this book, individuals' involvement or contact with *camorristi* and their associates does not necessarily imply guilt and should not do so. I have made my best endeavor to ensure that all ethical guidelines were respected and that URLs for external websites are correct and active at the time of going to press. A note about translations: all foreign-language texts have been translated by the author and double-checked by a qualified translator.

The approximate currency exchange rates during the time of my research were as follows: 1 dollar: 1,500–1,800 lire, 1 pound sterling: 1,784–3,115 lire, 1 dollar: 1.220–0.6254 euros, 1 pound sterling: 1.7510–1.0219 euros. For lire these are the minimum and maximum values of the exchange rate between 1980 and 2000; for euros these are the minimum and maximum values of the exchange rate between 2000 and 2013.

# Glossary

| | |
|---|---|
| blitz | a police raid |
| borghesia camorristica | Camorra middle class |
| Camorra war | a war between Camorra clans. In the 1980s, there were two: First Camorra war (1978–83) and Second Camorra war (1984–88). |
| contrabbandieri | individuals who smuggle cigarettes into Naples/Italy |
| carabineri | National military police of Italy |
| casa madre | the headquarters (of a clan) |
| cassa comune | the common fund of the clan |
| Eurojust | European Union Agency that deals with judicial co-operation in criminal matters |
| Europol | European Union's law-enforcement agency |
| faida | long-drawn out feud |
| faida di Scampia | the feud of Scampia (2004–2005) |
| girati | a group of *camorristi* who turned against their leader |
| guappo/guappi | old-fashioned criminal/s |
| Guardia di Finanza | Italian financial police |
| "made in Italy" | the concept of specific designs being made by Italian artisans with Italian materials |
| magliaro/magliari | door-to-door salesman/men |
| mafia association | a group of people who belong to a mafia clan/the crime of belonging to a mafia clan (art. 416-bis) |
| maxi | important/big |
| maxi processo | a trial with an important number of defendants |
| mesata | a monthly salary paid to clan members. |
| Mezzogiorno | southern Italy |
| 'ndrine | a clan part of the Calabrian 'Ndrangheta |
| Nuova Camorra Organizzata (NCO) | Camorra alliance led by Raffaele Cutolo |
| Nuova Famiglia (NF) | Camorra alliance that countered the NCO. Made up of many different groups, close to the Sicilian Mafia. |
| omertà | the law of silence |
| outilleurs napolitains | Neapolitan street sellers |
| paranza (colloquial) | a Camorra group/team |

| | |
|---|---|
| pentito/pentiti) | a *camorrista* who becomes a state witness |
| Polizia di Stato | Italian National Police |
| pizzo | the extortion tax |
| puntate | an investment in a batch of drugs |
| latitante | a fugitive from the law |
| Legge Rognoni-La Torre | Italian law (648/1982) that established "mafia association" as a crime. |
| libro paga | the clan's general account/ledger that registers incoming and outgoing expenses |
| sistema | Camorra system |
| Spagnoli | Spaniards |
| staffetta | a relay team of drug couriers |
| uno scippo | a predatory crime/bag/purse/watch snatching |
| vicolizzazione | importance of the street |

**LEGAL TERMS**

| | |
|---|---|
| Primo grado | first level of judgment |
| Secondo grado | second level of judgment (Appeal Court) |
| Terzo grado (Cassazione) | Court of Cassation |
| Ordinanza di custodia cautelare in carcere | pre-trial arrest warrant |
| Ordinanza di custodia cautelare agli arresti domiciliari | pre-trial house arrest |
| Misure cautelari personali | pre-trial measures that limit the personal freedom of individuals who are suspected to have committed serious crimes in order to stop them from contaminating the evidence, absconding, or repeating the crime |
| Misure di prevenzione patrimoniali | nonconviction-based confiscation of assets |
| Obbligo di soggiorno Soggiorno obbligato | obligatory residence order "internal exile" whereby a person was forced to live in a specific location/commune with restricted movement because they were considered "socially dangerous" to society at large (now abolished) |
| Divieto di soggiorno | forbidden from living in one or another commune or province |
| Libertà vigilata | post-trial: "under surveillance": not a form of punishment but a measure that consists of conceding freedoms to the |

|  |  |
|---|---|
|  | condemned/prisoner who remains under police surveillance and benefits from support and assistance from social services |
| Libertà controllata | "conditional freedom": an alternative to a prison term, the condemned is freed but must respect certain conditions and rules |
| Semi-libertà | "partial freedom": an alternative to a prison term, the condemned leaves the prison to work but returns in the evening |

**NICKNAMES**

| | |
|---|---|
| 'A Scigna | Monkey |
| Faccia d'angelo | Angel Face |
| Francesco di Carlantonio | Francesco, son of Carlo Antonio |
| 'O Calabrese | The Calabrian |
| 'O Carusiello | The Young Boy |
| 'O Giallo | The Yellow One |
| 'O Fantasma | The Ghost |
| 'O Fuggiasco | The Runaway |
| 'O Romano | The Roman |
| 'O Pazzo | The Mad Man/One |
| 'O Lupo | The Wolf |
| 'O Zio Antonio | Uncle Antonio |
| Peppe 'O Barone | Giuseppe the Baron |
| Peppe Showman | Giuseppe the Showman |
| Rosario 'O Biondo | Rosario, the Blond One |

# Acronyms

| | |
|---|---|
| BKA | Bundeskriminalamt (German Federal Police). |
| Criminalpol | Direzione Centrale Della Polizia Criminale (Criminal Police Central Directorate) |
| DCSA | Direzione Centrale per i Servizi Antidroga (The Office of National Drug Control Policy) |
| DDA | Direzione Distrettuale Antimafia (Local Antimafia Prosecution Service) |
| DEA | The American Drug Enforcement Administration |
| DIA | Direzione Investigativa Antimafia (Antimafia Investigation Directorate) |
| DNA | Direzione Nazionale Antimafia (e Antiterrorismo) (National Antimafia (and counterterrorism) Directorate) |
| EAW | European arrest warrant |
| EU | European Union |
| ICT | Information and Communication Technologies |
| IPC | Intellectual Property Crime |
| NCO | Nuova Camorra Organizzata (New Organized Camorra) |
| NF | Nuova Famiglia (New Family) |
| PACA | Provence-Alpes-Côte d'Azur region (south of France) |
| SEPBLAC | Servicio Ejecutivo de la Comisión de Prevención del Blanqueo de Capitales e Infracciones Monetarias (Executive Service of the Commission for Monitoring Exchange Control Offences) |
| UniFab | Union des Fabricants Français |

# THE INVISIBLE CAMORRA

# Introduction

"The Camorra is a puzzle and should be studied as such."
"It is a line that cuts through us at times without us even noticing" (FB)

When the sociologist Sudhir Venkatesh hung out with members of the Black Kings street gang from the Robert Taylor Homes in Chicago during the 1990s, he knew he was frequenting some of the most deprived parts of the city where gang members controlled many illegal deals and scams: extortion, gambling, prostitution, selling stolen property, and countless other activities. It was clear "outlaw capitalism" (2008:37).

However, if he had hung around Nunzio De Falco or Michele Zaza during the late 1980s when they lived in Spain and France, he would not have realized who they were. On the face of it, they were respectable, law-abiding citizens. Nunzio came from the Casertano region and lived in the north of Italy near Como for many years; he moved to Granada in the south of Spain in 1986.[1] There, he became the manager of an Italian restaurant, lived in a villa on via Pedro Antonio Alarcon, and had many friends among the immigrant Italian community. Michele and his family moved to Villeneuve-Loubet, near Nice, in the south of France, in 1988.[2] There, he was a retired businessman who enjoyed his fortune and visited many French and Italian friends. On closer inspection, however, these Neapolitans were not the hardworking Italian immigrants or cosmopolitan businessmen they might first appear to be. They were in fact alleged bosses of the Neapolitan Mafia, the Camorra, who had moved to Europe and were continuing their criminal activities in a new setting. But is this proof of the criminal migration of the Camorra?

By February 1992, alarm bells had started to ring. The Italian national police directorate, Criminalpol, had already acknowledged the existence of Camorra groups abroad, some of whom engaged in drug trafficking and money laundering, and now started to draw attention to the fact that they were expanding across borders. France, the United Kingdom, Austria, Portugal, Holland, and even Scotland were all identified as host countries where "drugs and recycling [of money] also signify the need to reinvest capital and have unsuspecting front names: pizzerias, restaurants, pubs, clothes shops," and where there was an "attempt to infiltrate the economy and business at other levels."[3]

In 1993, the Italian Ministry of the Interior elaborated on Camorra expansion across borders, noting that drug-trafficking Camorra groups had "specialized in large-scale money laundering activities and had chosen European regions with a high circulation of capital as their operating bases (for example, Switzerland and the Côte d'Azur)." The Ministry highlighted "a more recent phenomenon, the implantation of new Camorra settlements in Europe" (MI1: 291). In 1994, it made a distinction between Western Europe, with its drug-trafficking routes, and Eastern Europe, where "the Camorra's occupation of illegal markets . . . (in particular in the Czech Republic) tends to assume features of criminal 'colonization,' developing not only illegal traffics but also controlling prostitution and the sale of counterfeit goods" (MI2: 109).

More than twenty years later, the true extent of the Camorra's presence in Europe is still unclear. Has there been a much "feared 'mafia-on-the-march'"? Are there more than just thinly spread "mafia-bridgeheads" (Van Duyne, 1997: 202) in Europe? Paoli and Fijnaut in 2006 argued that the "fear of the expansion of the Italian mafia to the whole of Europe and its becoming a model for others . . . [has] proved to be unfounded" (304). They believed that Italian mafia groups may have "representatives and, less often, branches only in those countries—Germany, Belgium and France—that attracted consistent migration flows from southern Italy since at least the 1950s. In no European country except Italy—nor in northern or central Italy itself—do Italian mafia groups control a significant portion of local illegal economies or exercise a systematic influence over the legal economy or political system" (305). They concluded that Italian mafias had not infiltrated civil society, the economy, or political systems beyond southern Italy.

Today there is evidence to suggest that during the postwar period, Italian mafias have moved out of their territory of origin, even the Camorra (see Sciarrone, 2014). In the 1980s, the boss Antonio Bardellino was believed to be living in Brazil. In December 2006, the French daily *Libération* reported that ninety drug traffickers had been arrested across Europe: "According to Madrid, this network's principal aim was to supply clans trafficking in Italy" and was "composed of representatives of the most important Neapolitan clans, Colombians, Spaniards, Marseillais, and Bulgarians." The operation recovered more than six tons of hashish and one ton of cocaine.⁴

In 2011, a European Parliament report suggested that "transnational organised crime in Europe" is not "the expression of the transplantation of foreign mafias" (EP1: 14). It argued that "it is not because a diaspora exists in a country that this diaspora will automatically serve as 'soldiers of crime' of a mafia and it is not because drug trafficking exists that we can infer a mafia exists" (15). It concluded that "the evidence suggests that the migration of some mafia-type groups can take place, but that it is *rare* and *highly localised*" (14; my emphasis). The academic literature has also analyzed the presence of the mafias abroad, labeling it "diffusion" and "contagion" (Sciarrone, 1998), "colonization" (Massari, 2001: 15), "entrenchment" and "expansion" (Armao, 2003), "transplantation" and "expansion" (Varese, 2011), "cosmopolitanism" and not "localization" or "immobility" (Morselli, Turcotte, and Tenti, 2011), "functional diversification" (Campana, 2011), "settlement-infiltration-imitation-hybridisation" of Italian mafias (Sciarrone and Storti, 2014), and "criminal expatriates" (Soudijn and Huisman, 2010). But are these terms helpful in explaining the Camorra's migration in Europe?

The main focus of this book is to examine the so-called criminal migration of the Neapolitan Camorra. What exactly does the Camorra look like when it moves abroad? How do *camorristi* behave? Do they move abroad because they want to become legitimate or do they play a waiting game until it is safe to return home? What illegal and legal activities are they involved in? What tactics do they employ?

I answer these questions by presenting original research on the presence of *camorristi* in Europe. I analyze and compare the behavior of various types of *camorristi* who travel abroad and I touch on the nature of this movement: the organizational structures, members, strategies, activities, roles of women, and relationships with other criminal groups; the support systems that clans develop; and finally, the international response to this transnational phenomenon.

This study is located in political sociology and a wider multidisciplinary context where I seek to examine the local and global dynamics of criminal migration. I have three aims: First, to analyze why, how, and what Camorra clans, associates, and *camorristi* have been doing when they move to the United Kingdom, France, Germany, the Netherlands, and Spain between 1980 and 2015.⁵ Second, to explain the nature of the Camorra's mobility between Naples and Europe. Lastly, to emphasize the complexity of the phenomenon and the apparent lack of information about Italian mafias abroad, which often lead to exaggeration or underestimation by the authorities and the media.

Roberto Saviano in his novel *Gomorrah* (2008) gave the Neapolitan Camorra international recognition as a mafia to be reckoned with. Previously, it had lived in the shadows of the Sicilian Cosa Nostra and the ferocious Calabrian 'Ndrangheta. The Camorra is the third-largest Italian mafia and is predominately active in Naples and the Campania region. A "mafia"[6] can be defined as a criminal association interested in social, economic, and political power. It combines elements of both a traditional secret society and an efficient business (Sciarrone, 1998), which makes it difficult to define and explain.

The secret-society dimension lies in the way clans seek physical control over their local territory, developing a criminal ideology by exploiting cultural values (including violence) and using their social capital for their moneymaking agenda. They establish a clearly defined Camorra value system, which must be respected and they seek to govern civil society, the local economy, and the political system. The business dimension is observable in the Camorra's organizational structure as an "enterprise" that allows it to operate in legal and illegal markets (see Sciarrone, 1998; 2014). In the words of Paoli, mafias are "functionally diffuse" entities (2003: 143) because they have social, economic, and political power.

The term "Camorra" is the specific label given to describe the many different Neapolitan criminal families, clans, alliances, and confederations active in Naples and Campania (Sales, 1988). In 2010, it was believed that there were roughly 32 clans in the city, and 45 in the province of Naples (QN13). In 2014, it was estimated that there were over 160 clans in Campania[7], with over 50 clans in Naples city alone (DIAc: 102–126[8]).

A brief history shows how the Camorra differs from the other two mafias in its origins, historical development, and organizational structures, but resembles them in its criminal activities and its relationship with civil society, the legitimate economy, and politicians. In the postwar period, the Camorra radically changed. Beginning in the 1950s, there were unsophisticated, arrogant, independent criminals, *guappi*, who commanded their city districts and in the hinterland there were agricultural mediators and cow thieves.[9] By the 1990s, they had become efficient criminal entrepreneurs who were present both in the illegal and legal economies (see Sales, 1988; Behan, 1996; Allum, 2006). Today, the Camorra has become a powerful criminal force capable of controlling sectors of the European and Italian drug, counterfeit, cigarette, and waste-management markets as well as investing in many legitimate businesses in Naples, Italy, and Europe and winning many local and national public contracts.

The influence of the Sicilian Mafia has been fundamental in this economic transformation, but the Camorra has remained a visible, violent, and territorial criminal association, as several conflicts have demonstrated: from the first Camorra war (1978–1983) between Raffaele Cutolo's *Nuova Camorra Organizzata* (NCO) and the *Nuova Famiglia* (NF), an alliance of Sicilian-sponsored criminal families[10] (see CD1; Behan, 1996; Allum, 2006), to the more recent *faida di*

*Scampia* (2004–2005) between the Di Lauro clan and the Amato-Pagano families, and in 2012–2013, the war between the followers of the Di Lauro clan and a splinter group, the Vanelli-Grassi group (*i girati*).[11]

Today each clan is a small loyal family unit held together by its Camorra value system and a common fund that pays members a regular salary,[12] creates social cohesion, and supports a collective sense of identity and belonging. Each clan physically controls a specific local territory and, by doing so, governs the illegal and legal economic activities. To accomplish this, it seeks relations with local businessmen and politicians and alliances with other rival clans to guarantee complete hegemony over its territory. Clans are by nature territorial and have deeply embedded roots in the local community, which produces their inherent strength and power base.

Compared with Cosa Nostra and the 'Ndrangheta, the Camorra has always been considered less dangerous because it is more visible, territorial, and amateurish. Indeed, the Sicilian state witness Tommaso Buscetta once remarked, "the Camorra, I don't even want to talk about it, I don't deal with buffoons who are so stupid they even enrol policemen" (Falcone and Padovani, 1993: 99).

And yet when *camorristi* move abroad, things change: they become less attached to a specific territory and focus purely on economic activities. They do not migrate as clans but as individuals who manage to "camouflage" (Beatrice, 2009: 478) themselves so efficiently that it becomes difficult to recognize them as a threat to foreign societies and economies. In our changing globalized world, where trade, travel, and communication are based on velocity and borders dissolve, nation-states are having trouble keeping up with the growing internationalization of people's lives and businesses. As a result, legal, judicial, and police loopholes, financial gaps, and loose international communities appear that are being exploited by skillful mafia groups.

The danger may not be as visible as violent mafia murders, frenzied shoot-outs, and puddles of blood on the pavement, but the virtual invisibility of *camorristi* stems from their capacity to hide their origin and invest their illegal cash in legal European economies. Their presence abroad distorts national economies and legitimizes their native criminal activities without their being identified by European authorities for who and what they are. Camouflage allows these *camorristi* to exploit and manipulate the existing differences between countries, systems, and cultures in the new global economy. As Robinson pointed out, "criminals create wealth by purposely functioning beyond sovereign reach" (2000: 18).

Franco Roberti, Italy's chief antimafia prosecutor, has always insisted that in order to understand the Camorra today, it is fundamental to analyze the link that clans cultivate "between the global and the local," as it is this which "expresses the true face of the modern Camorra" (2012: 241). An analysis of that relationship structures this book and explains why my approach encompasses Camorra activities both local and global.

My analysis is based on the notion of globalization and the interdependency it creates. The era of "modernity"[13] we live in "is inherently globalising" and "universalising," writes Giddens (1990: 63, 175), who goes on to define the term "globalisation" as "the intensification of worldwide social relations which link distant localities in such a way that local happenings are shaped by events occurring many miles away and vice versa" (64).

The world has become a smaller place. Modernity and globalization have introduced changes that have increased opportunities for citizens to improve their lives. But a darker, more somber and obscure side has also multiplied the opportunities for skillful businessmen and criminals. Within this context, the Schengen agreement, the single currency, sophisticated technology, cheap travel, flexible banking regulations, a market for luxury goods at cheap prices, and a demand for drugs are all transformations that have created a greater interdependency—an interdependency that the Camorra exploits.

Three recurring notions encapsulate the Camorra's main features abroad: "functionality," "liquidity," and "invisibility." These three concepts, which I analyze throughout this book, highlight how, within the context of globalization,[14] the Camorra has had the capacity to learn, adapt, and manipulate situations to its advantage. The Camorra does not migrate unchanged, but becomes functional, liquid, and invisible abroad. As I discovered, its structures, values, and tactics depend on its location and markets. But the link, the "umbilical cord" (Bianchi and Rio, 2013: 26[15]), between Naples and these new territories remains fixed at all times, there are no peripheral branches or independent enterprises abroad. In simple terms, clans outside Naples, rather than migrating and becoming independent, interconnect their territories in a functional cycle. Like many international organizations, there exists a great interdependency between territories.

Let me preview some of my findings to explain what I have identified. First, the motives for the movement of Camorra bosses and their top associates[16] were never purely economic. My findings confirm the main literature in this area showing clear common "push" and "pull" factors (Sciarrone, 1998; 2014; Varese, 2011). However, I did observe a hierarchy in the importance of "pull" factors. The presence of an immigrant community or friends living abroad determines the initial choice of location. This is very different from other criminal groups, such as Albanian organized crime members, who do not move as active criminal entrepreneurs but develop into them once they are in a new setting (see Arsovska, 2015).

Second, clans have different configurations depending on their setting, while retaining the same overarching organization. It is not the activities that radically change but the internal organizational structures and behavior. Apart from extortion rackets, reserved so far exclusively for their local territory, the majority of Camorra activities are a continuation of their illegal Neapolitan operations. Camorra clans might be compared with multinational corporations or NGOs because of their extensive international presence, but they cannot be compared in terms of organizational structures and operational strategies.

In Naples, the Camorra is a "family crime enterprise"; in Europe it extends and becomes a "network enterprise" (Castells, 2000a: 171). Its presence reflects its interaction with its new environment: a context of "light capitalism" (Bauman, 2000: 126) that transforms it into an invisible liquid.[17] For example, the Piccirillo clan was compact in Naples, whereas in England it became a loose team. The same can be said of the larger Nuvoletta, Polverino, and Amato-Pagano clans in Spain: same clan, different internal organizational structures.

Abroad, clans become pragmatic and mobile network enterprises. They adopt fluid "network enterprise" structures, have volatile identities, and functional and disengaged values that focus on precise economic strategies in relation to their activities and needs at home. For example, there is no need for one hierarchical leader, but rather a group of councilors who make decisions, and its business logic is based on profit maximization, rational calculations, short-termism, and a quick turnover of personnel. Clans are no longer interested in the means (violence, intimidation, extortion), but rather in the ends, seeking profit at all cost. This produces flexible, fluid, and adaptable operational structures.

Visible power and territorial control become less vital because "for all practical purposes, power has become truly *extraterritorial*, no longer bound, not even slowed down, by the resistance of space" (Bauman, 2000: 11). The Camorra "is unpredictable and moves following different paths . . . seeking only to make money, without losing time to think about the modalities to adopt" (FB). This method of operation is different from other organized crime groups such as the Calabrian 'Ndrangheta and Chinese groups. To colonize a territory would "imply capital-intensive, cumbersome and unprofitable chores of administration and policing, responsibilities, commitments—and, above all, cast considerable constraint on one's future freedom to move" (Bauman, 2000: 188).

The Camorra's family crime enterprise becomes a network enterprise abroad; thus they are the same overarching organization with different internal operational structures. However, this network abroad cannot be analyzed as a Camorra franchise, an off-shoot, or a semi-independent branch reproducing traditional Camorra activities and behavior such as extortion rackets or intimidation. No clan has set up its own headquarters abroad, cutting itself off completely from its Neapolitan home territory and recruiting foreigners. *Camorristi* abroad are an extension of the Neapolitan operation, not an unimportant periphery or merely "criminal expatriates" (Soudijn and Huisman, 2010). They should be analyzed as fully integrated bases involved in the necessary economic and criminal activities of their clan in Naples. In addition, no independent Camorra branch exists that motivates Neapolitan criminals to leave Naples,[18] nor are there yet second-generation Neapolitans being raised abroad who become *camorristi*.[19] The interdependency of territories is the new dimension I identified and is indispensable to our understanding of the Camorra abroad.

Third, rather than criminal migration, Camorra clans do something different. By moving abroad, they engage in a form of continuous mobility between their territories without establishing constrained settlements or moving away permanently, as criminal expatriates may do. I call this "functional mobility" because clans develop their criminal activities by connecting their center of operations, Naples, the *casa madre*, with different territories in a regular and functional commercial cycle. There is a clear interdependence between territories connected by fluid organizational structures. The *pentito* Michele Siciliano described this as "a continuous loop" (MS) between home and host territories where there was a feedback effect: an ongoing, two-way, reciprocal exchange of members, goods, and money between Camorra territories. In this way, clans connect their territories functionally as opposed to one-way expansionist mobility. They seek not to deplete the new territory of its resources but to set up a continuous two-way functional exchange for the long-term benefit of the clan. The host territory is used for the functional needs of the clan in Naples.

Lastly, for Camorra clans to have a persistent presence abroad they need to have at their disposal accomplices, professional facilitators, and enablers.[20] They form part of a "gray undefined zone" because "to take advantage of the Camorra means to belong to the Camorra" (LGv, 19/3/2003: 40). This support system in situ is quasi-invisible, undertakes a multitude of jobs, and has varying responsibilities. They may or may not be aware of the criminal projects of those they help. Sciarrone's notions of "complicit," "collusive," or "compenetrative" accomplices are very useful (2011: 35–37). Moreover, Ruggiero add that transnational "alliances and networks may well be an important matter for concern, less because they foster the growth of organized crime internationally than because they encourage partnerships between organized and white collar criminals" (2000: 197). The exchange of skill sets is an intrinsic aspect of the Camorra's existence and still requires considerable research because they are so invisible.

This brief summary makes it clear that the Camorra in its foreign skin is an intricate criminal animal that does not easily fit into existing academic categories: there was no "exportation" or "transplantation" of one clan from one territory to another abroad, nor was there a "colonization" or a total "delocalization." Rather,

Camorra clans infiltrated themselves into different European illegal and legal sectors as a functional, liquid, invisible transnational criminal network.

Finding data has been an arduous task because of the cross-border nature of the phenomenon, the problems of representativeness of the sample, and the difficult access to local, national, and international material. I limit my study to five West European states—Germany, the Netherlands, France, Spain, and the United Kingdom—between 1980 and 2015. Most of the data was collected between 2010 and 2015.[21] I decided to adopt a qualitative, mixed-method approach, as this would allow me to put together the most comprehensive picture possible.

I started out by requesting information from national authorities, looking for confirmation of the validity of existing theories and for concrete data to use. This proved problematic because in the majority of the five countries a Camorra presence was not identified. In 2009, when I first started to slowly collect material, I remember finding myself in the office of a prosecuting judge in Marseille, waiting for him to tell me that a Camorra clan had colonized a district and transplanted itself to the city. But this was not the case. Yes, there were traces of the Camorra, but they could not be described in those terms, and there existed very little documentary evidence. I received the same answer later that year in the United Kingdom when I interviewed the Association of Chief Police Officers Lead on Organised Crime (JM). Yes, there were traces of Italian mafias, but they had not colonized districts, cities, or regions in the United Kingdom. Even Aberdeen, the city of the notorious La Torre clan in Scotland, could not be described as the transplantation of a Camorra clan. There were no official British documents identifying it as a mafia in the United Kingdom. It soon became clear that there was a serious problem, an information gap, in the existing police and judicial material in the different countries. So much so that trying to locate material in Europe on Camorra associates has been challenging and at times demoralizing!

The lack of any antimafia association legislation in our five countries made it nearly impossible to identify clans without adopting an Italian perspective based on Italian police and judicial investigations. For example, until 2010, only one case in France identified and prosecuted a *camorrista* without the case being initiated by the Italian authorities; more recently in Spain, there have been two other such cases. Indeed, some European authorities did not want to talk openly about the threat posed by Italian mafias or identify what the Camorra might be doing in their country. A Transcrime project on Italian mafias (2013)[22] encountered similar difficulties and thus decided to limit its analysis to the official reports of the Italian Direzione Nazionale Antimafia (DNA) and Direzione Investigativa Antimafia (DIA) between 2000 and 2011.

I had to change tactic because relying on open primary sources from the five European countries would have produced very few documents and nearly no analysis. I therefore tried another approach: I decided to follow the *camorristi* from Naples to Europe using Italian documents, but persisted in my mixed-method approach. I used predominantly primary sources,[23] with some secondary data collected between 2006 and 2015. A variety of rich primary material should allow both a bottom-up and a top-down perspective, both a European and a Neapolitan perspective.

To identify concrete cases, I then looked for Camorra-related groups or individuals in the five host countries. The sample cases were selected on the basis of the clan's activities abroad and the quality of the material available. I soon noticed that clans were systematically targeting four criminal markets in each of our five host countries. In general, these were: (1) acquisitive crime, (2) the production and selling of counterfeit goods, (3) drug trafficking, and (4) money laundering. I built a sample of sixteen clans present abroad that varied greatly in terms of geographical location and number of members (see table I.1).[24] Only fourteen of those sixteen clans are analyzed here (see maps 1 and 2).

The majority of my cases were then constructed around individuals, groups, and associates with a criminal record in Naples who later appear in Western Europe. Clearly my approach was heavily influenced by the narratives of Neapolitan judges, but this was out of necessity rather than choice. To counter this influence, I tried to consistently triangulate the judicial material with other sources (in-depth interviews, state witness statements, newspaper articles, statistics). I have studied over thirty *camorristi* in particular detail: their roles include top bosses, lieutenants, advisers, soldiers, women, and enablers. A social network software (Netdraw software; Borgatti, 2002) was used to produce a picture of the organizational structures of some of these clans in order to provide a quick overview of where members were located and what they are doing. This is to help visualize Camorra mobility in terms of space and time.

To build as complete a picture as possible, I gathered material on Italian mafias in the five countries and specific information on my sixteen selected cases (see table I.2). In Europe, I managed to collect primary material from different national police forces and judiciaries,[25] various Italian liaison magistrates and police officers,[26] ministries of the interior,[27] and international bodies.[28] In Italy, I collected material in Naples from the local Antimafia Prosecution Service (DDA); the Polizia di Stato, the DIA, Naples branch; the Guardia di Finanza, Naples branch; and in Rome from the DNA and the DIA that oversee national and international judicial and police investigations.

For each case chosen, I used at least two sources[29] to confirm the validity of the judicial information. Often, these were in-depth interviews, judicial documents, police data, and newspaper articles that I found in Naples and abroad. The material I could access was often limited because there exists no clear open police and judicial archive in the Naples Tribunal. As the majority of my cases were recent, I was

**TABLE I.1** Choice of cases: Period, origin, host country, and number of members

| CLANS | PERIOD | HOST COUNTRY | CITY | HINTERLAND | 1988/MEMBERS[1] | 1994/M[2] | 1997/M[3] | 2011/M[4] | 2013/M[5] |
|---|---|---|---|---|---|---|---|---|---|
| Amato-Pagano clan[6] | 2000s | Spain | Yes | No | — | — | — | — | — |
| Annunziata-Aquino family | 2000s | Holland/Germany | N | Y | — | 18 | 24 | 25 | — |
| Bardellino/De Falco clan | 1990s | Spain | N | Y | 484 | 179 | — | — | — |
| Caldarelli clan | 2000s | United Kingdom | Y | N | n/a | — | — | — | — |
| La Torre clan | 1990s | United Kingdom | N | Y | — | 96 | — | — | — |
| Licciardi clan/Secondigliano alliance | 1990s | Germany, France, Spain, United Kingdom | Y | N | Contini: 15; Mallardo: 4 | Contini: 89, (335 [1993]); Mallardo:29; Licciardi: 55 | Contini: 255; Mallardo: 86; Licciardi: 315 | Contini: 220; Mallardo: 110; Licciardi: 75 | Contini: 136; Licciardi: 14 |
| Mazzarella clan/city clans | 2000s | All | Y | N | — | 199 | — | 100 | 316 |
| Misso clan/De Tommaso team | 2000s | Spain | Y | Y | 141 | 54 | 50 | 120 | 34 |
| Nuvoletta/Gala cell | 1990s | Holland | N | Y | 141 | — | — | — | — |
| Polverino clan | 2005–12 | Spain | N | Y | — | — | 295 | — | 150 |
| Nuvoletta clan | 1995–2010 | Spain | Y | N | 141 | — | — | 120 | — |
| De Sena group | 2000s | France | N | Y | 22 | 31 | 60 | — | — |
| Piccirillo clan | 2000s | United Kingdom | Y | N | — | — | 12 | 100 | 23 |
| Rinaldi clan | 1990–2000s | Germany | Y | N | — | 62 | 195 | 110 (Altamura-Reale) | 26 |
| Stolder clan[6] | 1990s | Holland | Y | N | — | 45 | 59 | — | 16 |
| Zaza clan | 1980–1990s | France | Y | N | 216 | 179 | 255 | — | — |

[1] AC1–1 and AC1–2 in Allum, 2000: appendix six. For a general indication.
[2] 'Provincie di Napoli, Caserta e Salerno, Situazione dei clan, 1993–1994', in Allum, 2000:406–408; 411–412.
[3] Scribani 1997. Il Mattino, 9/7/1997, "Sappiamo chi sono: Ora staniamoli, ecco gli uomini della Camorra," 23.
[4] QN13.
[5] QN14.
[6] Not analyzed in this study.

**TABLE I.2**  Use of material/country for specific cases

| MATERIAL | ITALY | SPAIN | UNITED KINGDOM | GERMANY | FRANCE | NETHERLANDS |
| --- | --- | --- | --- | --- | --- | --- |
| Police data, local | Y | N | Y | Y | N | N |
| Police data, national | Y | Y | Y | Y | N | Y |
| Judicial files | Y | N | N | N | Y | N |
| Ministry information | Y | Y | Y | N | Y | N |
| Newspaper articles | Y | Y | Y | Y | Y | Y |
| Parliamentary documents | Y | Y | Y | N | Y | N |
| Interviews, police officers (local and national) | Y | Y | Y | Y | N | Y |
| Interviews, Italian police liaison officers | n/a | Y | Y | N | Y | N |
| Interviews, judges | Y | N | N | N | Y | N |
| Interviews, journalists | Y | Y | Y | N | Y | N |
| Interviews, state witnesses | Y | n/a | n/a | n/a | n/a | n/a |
| Interviews, academics | Y | Y | Y | N | N | N |

generally able to identify the Neapolitan investigating magistrate who had dealt with the case, so I could interview officials and collect the relevant documents. This produced a clear judicial narrative, but as Kelly states: "a bias permeates the bulk of the writing on organized crime from which most social scientists draw information" (1982: 220–221).

To counter this bias, I actively sought to interview other protagonists and experts (in particular, police officers, academics, and journalists) who dealt with my specific cases. All these records and accounts had an in-built subjectivity. An additional difficulty was to recuperate material for the older cases on Michele Zaza (1980–94) and Nunzio De Falco (1980–2003) because there are no general police or judicial archives in Naples from that time. However, with luck and tenacity I was able to obtain the 1989–1991 court files from the Tribunal of Marseille (France), the Questura di Roma (QR1), and the Guardia di Finanza files for Zaza in addition to interviewing the police officers (SG and PZ) who followed the De Falco case when he was arrested in Granada and extradited back to Italy.

Of paramount importance for me was to interview former *camorristi*, now state witnesses, who had spent time abroad, especially in the United Kingdom. Between 2010 and 2013, I interviewed five state witnesses.[30] Two had spent time in the United Kingdom, one was the boss of a member who had spent time in France, and two were Camorra women. While some argue that an interview "can create as many problems as it solves" because "the extent to which an informant is prepared to divulge information is usually determined by external and

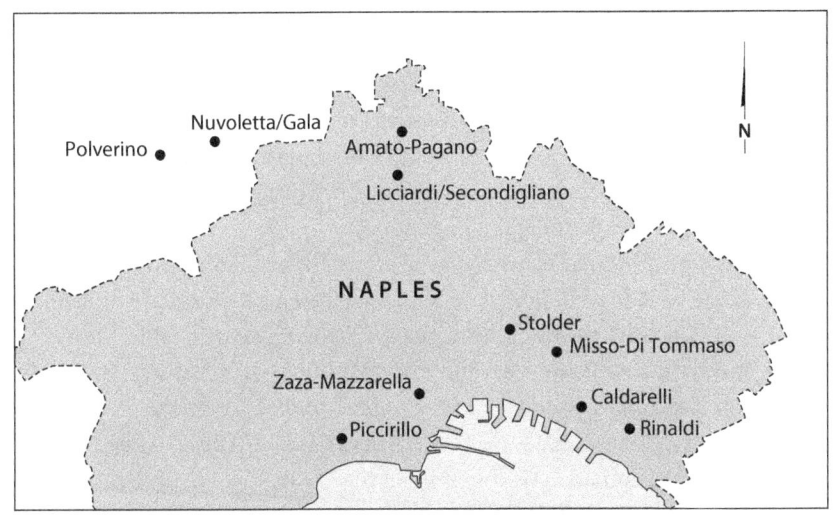

**MAP 1** Case studies of groups of clans from the urban Naples area

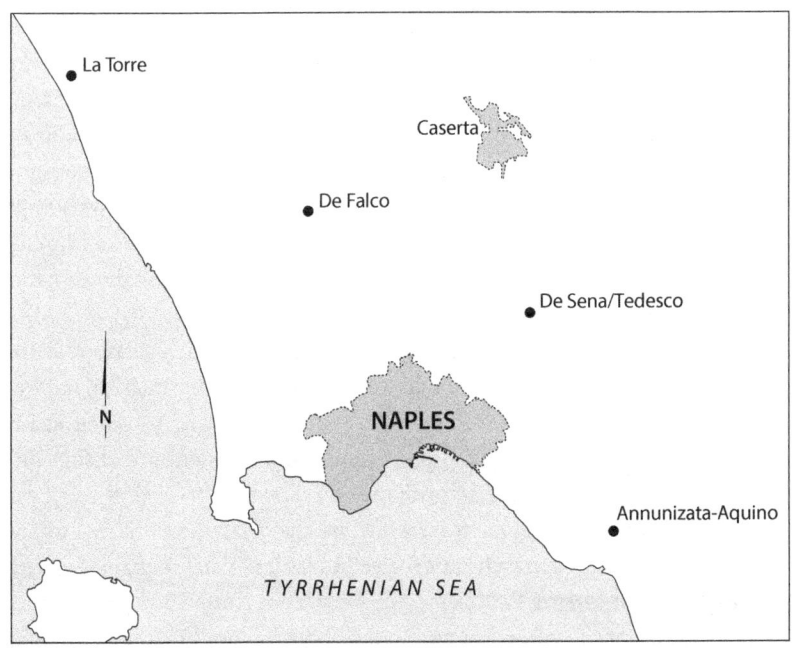

**MAP 2** Case studies of groups of clans from outside the Naples area

internal constraints based on cultural, psychological and professional factors" (Rawlinson, 2000: 357), the advantage of having interviewed state witnesses in this particular study was that it provided specialist insight into criminal mobility, detailed accounts of behavior, structures, and activities of *camorristi* abroad, as well as explanations of Camorra mentality, codes and values at home. The added value was that they confirmed events described in police and judicial documents while analyzing and explaining the finer details.

These heavily protected discussions, held in dark and anonymous police stations in Rome or judicial buildings in Naples, helped me confirm my hunch that Camorra mobility differed from the depiction in the existing literature. They also put me face-to-face with *camorristi* and their real-life experiences. So although the information has come from the extensive judicial and police material I have collected, the analysis is mine and comes with all the limitations of qualitative research.

I used conversation analysis of my interviews with state witnesses and their interrogations by judges but also of my in-depth interviews with judges, police officers, and trial transcriptions. In terms of validation, I have double-checked the interpretation presented in the transcripts—the dates, facts, events (see Perakyla, 1997)—with other records. I have also consulted newspaper articles and have referenced them where possible, although in some cases this was not possible. In some places, dates might be incorrect, which may be due to different sources. In addition, in 2010–2011 I visited with the Naples flying squad the different districts of the clans examined in this study in order to understand them and their local physical territory better. The research is one-sided (as all academic research is), in this case because the majority of documents provide an Italian perspective. I have done everything I can to collect diverse documentation to produce a balanced account, but the narrated version of events is my interpretation and my analysis. Also, I should note that in some places the analysis might seem vague. This is not to confuse the reader but rather to protect the author. On occasion to avoid questions of libel and implicating certain individuals, names have been changed and initials used as a further precaution.

A brief note about ethnicity. This study is not about an alien conspiracy theory, nor do I seek to fall into the ethnicity trap. I do look at one particular ethnic group and its movement abroad: Neapolitan Italian *camorristi* and their associates. Once I was accused of facilitating a right-wing agenda by focusing on a specific ethnic community, but this is not the case. I decided to look at this group not because I believe all Neapolitans were and are criminals but because I wanted to build on my previous research experience in Naples. As Nicaso and Lamothe (2005) made clear in *Angels, Mobsters and Narco-Terrorism*, "the subject of ethnicity or national origin often has to be dealt with in any book about mafias, triads, or cartels." I do not "intend to smear the reputation of the hundreds of thousands—or millions—of law abiding people of the country in which a criminal organization operates; the focus is only on the very, very, few people who engage in organized criminal activity. This is fair and honest" (4). In this book, I tell the story of Neapolitan *camorristi* in Europe.

Rather than organize the material thematically, which might have seemed a logical approach, it eventually made more sense to organize the material as a journey through Europe, like the journey I had accomplished for this research. Chapter 1 seeks to explain the motives for Camorra mobility, chapter 2 details how these groups move around, and chapters 3–6 analyze the Camorra's presence in Germany, the Netherlands, France, Spain, and the United Kingdom. This presentation allows me to highlight diverse histories, geographical locations, markets, judicial regimes, civic cultures, immigrant communities, and the sustained relationship with Naples. In the end, everything comes back to Naples.

# 1
# LOCAL MOTIVES, GLOBAL CHOICES

"Why do *camorristi* move abroad?" We often assume they do so as part of an economic strategy to expand their businesses and increase their profits. And yet the evidence is not that straightforward; there may be other social, emotional, or psychological motives. Moreover, moving abroad is an expensive and risky business, not an option open to all.

Can we identify the motives of *camorristi* who traveled abroad? This is not easy, and in practical terms we can analyze the motives only of those bosses and their lieutenants who were wanted and who migrated. Individuals close to the Camorra who leave Naples without being on the run are more difficult to identify; they become invisible in Europe and their motives cannot be studied here. In this chapter, therefore, I concentrate on the motives for criminal mobility, from Naples to Europe, of more than fifteen Camorra bosses and their associates between 1980 and 2015. I adopt a two-level approach, identifying both local push factors and global pull factors and how they interacted to determine the final destination. Overall, my analysis allows me to draw out some general trends; in particular, it is clear that the desire to make money cannot explain everything.

## Overview of Camorra Mobility

Camorra mobility is not a recent phenomenon, but is very different from the movement of the Calabrian 'Ndrangheta. During the 1950s whole communities from close-knit villages left Calabria and moved to towns and cities in the north of Italy, Northern Europe, and across the world in search of work and a better life. In these immigrant communities there were criminal elements and sometimes even small 'Ndrangheta clans, 'ndrine (Cicionte, 1992; Forgione, 2009). That these uprooted criminal elements put down roots in new host environments meant that, when necessary, they could be activated as useful links and a significant support system for instructions or projects coming out of Calabria. This was especially apparent during the early 1990s when the 'Ndrangheta turned to these contacts to organize their drug-trafficking operations. Immigrant communities have been particularly instrumental in the 'Ndrangheta's colonization of northern Italy and Germany.

The Camorra has been different. The places in Campania from which Neapolitans have emigrated (places such as Benevento, the Avellinese, and the Cilento) are not natural Camorra strongholds (IS), and migration from Camorra bastions such as Naples city and the Casertano region has not been systematic or widespread. There may be fewer criminal elements in the permanent Neapolitan community abroad than in the Calabrian, which may explain why Camorra mobility appears to have different dynamics. Neapolitan movement has been fluid, with less visible fixed structures and settlements abroad because of the absence of emigrant support. Local variables are extremely important as we try to understand the international picture of mafia mobility.

I have compiled a list of fugitive *camorristi* who have moved abroad (see tables 1.1, 1.2, and 1.3) from a variety of sources, as not one Italian law-enforcement agency was able to provide comprehensive figures. These data are not official and may contain inconsistencies, but I believe they provide a useful overview.

From these tables we can make four tentative observations about general Camorra mobility. The first concerns the numbers of *camorristi* moving abroad. The picture between 1950 and 1982 is practically nonexistent because the data do not exist (the same might be said about mafias in European Union member states today.) Indeed, I detect almost no visible movement during the 1970s, with the exception of Aniello Nuvoletta, a suspected member of the Nuvoletta clan, who left Marano in 1975 and was arrested in Switzerland in 1984 for drug trafficking,[1] and the alleged NCO member Corrado Iacolare, who in the early 1980s escaped to South America.[2] Only after 1982 does the movement of suspected *camorristi* become visible and can be monitored because in that year the Italian parliament introduced the new Antimafia Rognoni-La Torre law (law 646/1982). This law made membership in a mafia-like criminal association ("mafia association") a crime.[3] Anyone wanted or convicted in Italy for this crime and who traveled abroad became more discernible and visible for the Italian authorities.

The decades between 1982 and 2015 witnessed relatively persistent Camorra movement. Although the 1990s may appear to be a period of relative calm

**TABLE 1.1** Individuals arrested abroad for crimes committed in Italy during the 1970–1980s

| NAME | CLAN | COUNTRY | WANTED SINCE | ARRESTED IN | WANTED FOR |
|---|---|---|---|---|---|
| Aniello Nuvoletta | Nuvoletta clan | Switzerland | 1975 | 1984 | Int. drug t. |
| Corrado Iacolare | NCO | Uruguay | 1980s | 1989 | Murder |
| Rolando Tortora | NCO | France | 1982 | 1988 | Mafia ass. |
| Antonio Bardellino | Casalesi clan | Spain | 1983 | 1983 | Mafia ass. |
| Antonio Bardellino | Casalesi clan | Brazil | 1983 | Murdered May 1988 | Mafia ass. |
| Antonio La Torre | La Torre clan | United Kingdom | 1984 | 1996 | Mafia ass. |
| Michele Zaza | Zaza clan | Paris, France | 1984 | 1984 | Mafia ass. |
| Nunzio Barbarossa | Zaza clan | Paris, France | 1984 | 1984 | Mafia ass. |
| Umberto Ammaturo | Ammaturo clan | Peru | 1987 | 1993 | Int. drug t. Mafia ass. |
| Francesco Schiavone | Casalesi clan | Lyon, France | — | May 1989 | Mafia ass. |
| Mario Fabbrocino | Fabbrocino clan | Argentina | 1988 | 1997 | Murder |
| Giuseppe Autorino | Alfieri clan | Venezuela | 1988 | 1994 | — |
| Nunzio De Falco | Casalesi clan | Granada, Spain | 1988 | 1997 | Mafia ass. |
| Michele Zaza | Zaza clan | Nice, France | 1991 | 1994 Died 1994 | Mafia ass. |
| Nunzio Barbarossa | Zaza clan | Nice, France | 1989 | Died 1989 | — |
| Mario Iovine | Casalesi clan | Toulon, France | 1989 | July, 1989 | Mafia ass. |
| Mario Iovine | Casalesi clan | Portugal/Brazil | — | Murdered 1991 | Mafia ass. |

compared with the 1980s, a closer look reveals the movement of some important bosses (see table 1.1). By the mid-1980s, thanks to the Rognoni-La Torre law, around fifteen suspected bosses had been arrested abroad, and in the 2000s, thirty suspected bosses and advisers were arrested. By the early 2000s, based on evidence in judicial and police documents, it appears that at least one associate of each of the main Camorra clans involved in counterfeit goods (Di Lauro, Mazzarella, Licciardi, Contini) was resident and active abroad: from Europe to South America, Africa, North America, and Australia.

From our data (see tables 1.1, 1.2, and 1.3), movement appears regular and cannot be explained simply in terms of economic rationality. It cannot be that all *camorristi* are rushing abroad to open local branches of their traditional criminal operations, or there would be numerous and visible permanent settlements abroad. Explanations must include other factors: for example, changes in the law, sentimental relationships, or a shift in the criminal equilibrium in Naples,

**TABLE 1.2** Individuals arrested abroad for crimes committed in Italy during the 1990s

| NAME | CLAN | COUNTRY | WANTED SINCE | ARRESTED ON | WANTED FOR |
| --- | --- | --- | --- | --- | --- |
| Paolo Pesce | Mariano clan | Fuengirola, Spain | 1991 | 17/12/08 | Murder |
| Ciro Mazzarella | Mazzarella clan | Lugano, Switzerland | 1992 | 23/9/1993 | Mafia ass. |
| Raffaele Caldarelli | Caldarelli clan | London, UK | 1995 | 5/9/06 | Int. drug. t., Mafia ass. |
| Gaetano De Lorenzo | Casalesi clan | Spain | 1996 | 9/12/02 | Mafia ass., extortion |
| Pietro Licciardi | Licciardi clan | Germany/Czech Republic | 1998 | 1999 | Mafia ass., murder |
| Vincenzo Mazzarella / Ciro Giovanni Spirito | Mazzarella clan | Nice, France | — | 3/7/1999 | Mafia ass., murder |
| Gennaro Mazzarella | Mazzarella clan | Porto Banus, Marbella, Spain | 1998 | 1998 | Mafia ass. |

The local context is a good place to start. At the same time, it is important to note that some clans cannot and will not move abroad—and their lack of mobility can also be explained by the local context: perhaps an absence of emigrant roots or inadequate criminal power, resources, or social capital. For example, smaller clans with a younger leadership, such as those from Santa Lucia, the Pallonetto, and the Sanità districts or the Marcinese region, have not yet been spotted abroad. The strength of a clan at home may determine its potential abroad, although sometimes even the boss of a small clan can travel abroad thanks to a few loyal friends.

Second, the type of *camorrista* who is mobile appears to have changed over time, perhaps as legislation has begun to target all members. Initially, during the 1980s, it was predominately leaders who traveled and escaped from Campania. For example, during the 1980s, many of the NF leadership moved abroad, such as Umberto Ammaturo, Antonio Bardellino, and Michele Zaza. During the 2000s, criminal mobility was no longer exclusive to bosses, though bosses still made up the majority of travelers (for example, Giuseppe Polverino and Paolo Di Mauro from the Contini clan, both arrested in Spain). In more recent years we also find mobility among some middle-ranking members who manage criminal activities (drug trafficking, counterfeit goods, etc.) as well as among those in charge of money-laundering operations. For example, AW was arrested in Spain in early 2000 for allegedly organizing money laundering for the Nuvoletta clan. So,

**TABLE 1.3**  Individuals arrested abroad for crimes committed in Italy during the 2000s

| NAME | CLAN | COUNTRY | WANTED SINCE | ARRESTED ON | WANTED FOR |
|---|---|---|---|---|---|
| Domenico Verde | Polverino clan | Taranjao, Spain | 2000 | 03/9/12 | Int. drug t. |
| Fabio Allegro | Polverino clan | Estepona, Spain | 2006 | 10/9/10 | Int. drug t. |
| Francesco Schiavone | Casalesi clan | Poland | 2002 | 13/3/04 | Mafia ass. |
| Raffaele A. Ligato | Casalesi clan | Berlin, Germany | 2003 | 26/1/05 | Murder |
| Gennaro Panzuto | Piccirillo clan | Preston, UK | 2004 | 2007 | Int. drug t. |
| Raffaele Amato | Amato-Pagano clan | Barcelona, Spain | 12/2004 | 23/2/05 | Murder Int. drug t. |
| Vincenzo Mazzarella | Mazzarella clan | Paris, France | 2004 | 17/12/04 | Mafia ass. |
| Paolo Di Mauro | Contini clan | Barcelona, Spain | 2005 | 27/1/10 | Mafia ass. |
| Luigi Mocerino | Contini clan | Barcelona, Spain | — | 27/1/10 | Mafia ass. |
| Patrizio Bosti | Secondigliano alliance | Girona, Spain | 2005 | 10/8/08 | Murder |
| Raffaele Amato | Amato-Pagano clan | Barcelona, Spain | 2006 | 17/5/09 | Murder Int. drug t. |
| Vincenzo D'Avino | Giuliano clan | Madrid, Spain | 2001, 2006 | 17/10/09 | Int. drug t. |
| Antonio Caiazzo | Caiazzo clan | Majadahonda, Spain | 3/2007 | 28/1/09 | Mafia ass. |
| Raffaele Laurenti | Frizzero clan | Spain | 2007 | 10/9/08 | Mafia ass., extortion |
| Ciro Mazzarella | Mazzarella clan | Santo Domengo, Dominican Republic | 2007 | 10/2/09 | Int. drug t. |
| Salvatore D'Avino | Giuliano clan | Marbella, Spain | 2007 | 23/8/11 | Int. drug t. |
| Mario Assegnati | Nico clan | Spain | — | 18/12/08 | Int. drug t. |
| Francesco Simeoli | Caiazzo clan | Majadahonda, Spain | 6/2007 | 28/1/09 | Mafia ass. |
| Salvatore Zazo | Mazzarella clan | Barcelona, Spain | 2008 | 18/1/09 | Int. drug t. |
| Giuseppe Persico | Mazzarella clan | Faro, Portugal | — | 10/08 | Int. drug t. |
| Pasquale Mazzarella | Mazzarella clan | Marbella, Spain | 2009 | 4/1/12 | Mafia ass. |
| Ettore Sabatino | Sabatino clan | Dortmund, Germany | 2009 | 15/7/09 | Murder |
| Antonio Lo Russo | Lo Russo clan | Nice, France | 2010 | 15/4/14 | Mafia ass. Int. drug t. |
| Vincenzo Cesarano | Cesarano clan | Bucharest, Romania | 2011 | 16/5/14 | Extortion |
| Clemente Amodio | Mazzarella clan | Marbella, Spain | 2/2011 | 4/1/12 | Mafia ass. |
| Vincenzo Nettuno | Nuvoletta clan | Marbella, Spain | 7/2012 | 12/11/15 | Int. drug t. |

although we cannot observe the mobility of individuals with no criminal past, we can see a slow increase in the emigration of Camorra managers as well as bosses.

Third, destinations change compared with the 1980s. As an Italian Ministry of the Interior document noted in 1993, during the 1980s bosses were attracted by both the lure of South America and the proximity of Europe (MI1). South

America, because of its inefficient policies against organized crime and its flourishing business opportunities, was perhaps particularly attractive, given the clans' developing involvement with drug importation and their partnerships with the Sicilian and American mafias. Many NF Camorra bosses, Umberto Ammaturo and Mario Fabbrocino, for example, were arrested in South America in the 1990s, having been on the run since the 1980s. It is believed that the boss Antonio Bardellino was murdered in Buzios, Rio de Janeiro, in May 1988. However, by the 1990s and 2000s (see tables 1.2 and 1.3), Europe became the favored destination.[4] The attraction of Europe may be because of its proximity to Italy, the existing support networks already there and new economic opportunities, in particular in Spain but also in East European countries. New market opportunities perhaps lured *camorristi* to the east, but Spain's wholesale market for drugs remains an important consideration.

Lastly, there appears to exist an invisible community made up of helpful individuals who become a support network for *camorristi* on the run. This community cannot be measured or seen, but it seems to play a fundamental role in Camorra movement, enabling those *camorristi* unfamiliar with the new host country to move abroad without hassle and benefit from all kinds of logistical support. Such support may not be criminal nor Neapolitan, but it is vital for *camorristis'* travel and movement abroad. This community may consist of friends, relatives, or acquaintances who want to (or are forced to) help.

Do these helpers move because of their relationship with the clan, which would be a strategic decision, or do they link up with the clan because they are part of an Italian migrant community abroad that is called on to help? For example, one man moved from Casal di Principe to the Lazio region, where he lived for twenty-five years and is believed by the judiciary to be an associate of the Casalesi clan—helping fugitives on the run and with other financial activities—but to the outside world he presented himself as "a legitimate businessman."[5] Did he initially leave Campania to pursue clan projects in that region? Can the same be said for other associates abroad?

## Explaining Camorra Mobility (1980–2015)

Many studies that have considered *mafiosi* motives for criminal movement abroad stress the strategic, rational, and economic logic behind these decisions. My evidence will not allow me to claim that all *camorristi* want to leave Naples to open new Camorra branches or outlets abroad. If this were the case, would not all *camorristi* move abroad and choose the same host environment to make the most profit? It "is easier said than done" (Morselli, Turcotte, and Tenti,

2011: 184). We tend to forget the social, emotional, and economic costs involved in criminal migration. Explanations for Camorra mobility are subtler than pure economic rational choice.

In general, *camorristi* who operate abroad seek to avoid a heavy material investment in a new territory. They want to remain light in order to facilitate easy movement from one place to another. Looking at our different cases, we see a delicate interplay of local variables and global structural factors; there are no monocausal explanations for Camorra movement. As in all forms of migration, there are factors that will push criminal migrants away from a territory and those that will pull them to a new territory.[6]

*Camorristi* decide when to leave and where to go in a three-stage process: first, local push factors propel them to leave Naples, then two phases of global pull factors influence their choice of destination. Push factors are individual and personal, emanating from the local context: being wanted by the judiciary and the police, thus forcing "the escape" (Sciarrone, 1998: 78; Varese, 2011: 27), and a fear of gang warfare and being murdered by a criminal rival. It was clear from the evidence that local motives for bosses and their close associates did not stem from spontaneous personal desire. Neither was it always the case that they were sent or transplanted to a new territory by the clan or were only following up a new business opportunity. If anything, it was the judicial reality of survival combined with personal agency in the specific criminal context of Naples. The importance of the local territory is crucial in explaining the push factors.

Pull factors are structural circumstances that influenced *camorristi's* exact choice of destination. If a Camorra boss *did* move away from Naples and needed to spend time in a particular location, he would have specific motives for choosing his destination. Three global-structural factors were initially identified: familiar networks, profitable markets, and vulnerable law-enforcement regimes (see figure 1.1).

However, there appears to be an explicit hierarchy of factors. One pull factor influences the majority of our cases: familiar networks. This is the second phase in the decision-making process. All Camorra bosses identified familiar networks that determined their future location. Accessing such a familiar network in the destination country is an essential and determining pull factor that explains the choice of destination. Without such a support system, what Von Lampe calls "niches of familiarity" (2012: 189), to facilitate the criminal's stay in the new territory and guarantee logistical support, *camorristi* would have difficulty moving abroad. It remains a basic requirement for all traveling *camorristi*; they go where there are already established Neapolitans, Italians, or friends whom they know. Not one of the people I tracked went to a location where there was not an existing contact.

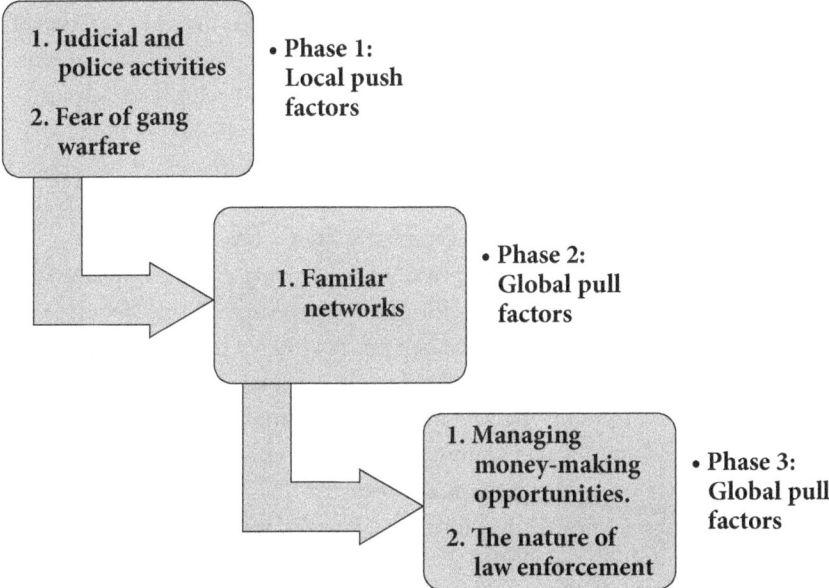

**FIGURE 1.1** Motives for leaving Naples: A three-phase decision-making process

The third phase involves a final choice based on the other two remaining pull factors; the precise location is pinpointed, but only after familiar networks have been identified. Two further pull factors are important: economic opportunities and the perceived weak law-enforcement regime (in particular, toward mafia association). As Gennaro Panzuto, a former member of the Piccirillo clan, argued: "England is attractive because of its laws. It is a free port because of these laws" (GP).

In the analysis that follows I untangle the push and pull factors in different cases of *camorristi* who were active abroad in order to highlight how local and global factors interact and explain the motives for their mobility.

## Local Push Factor (1): Judicial and Police Activity

The majority of the Camorra bosses found abroad are there because they are on the run from Italian law; in effect, they "escape" to a new setting (FR). Police investigations, possible arrest warrants, and even special pre-trial measures for mafia suspects (such as special police surveillance, house arrest, or an obligatory residence order) are a great concern for bosses, as these measures restrain their criminal movement, activities, and projects and prompt them to leave. Such special police measures under antimafia legislation are for individuals who, the police believe, based on solid evidence, belong to a mafia-type criminal association. But police measures can also be applied to individuals who, because of their criminal lifestyles, are simply considered as "socially dangerous to public security." Such special measures, considered by many to be controversial, are applied regardless of whether a criminal trial has taken place. They can, however, be nullified before a court if the evidence is considered not robust enough.

In the case of a pending criminal trial or even during preliminary investigations by the police and judicial authorities, the Italian criminal code allows for the arrest of an individual when the court believes that there exists enough evidence to warrant arrest, even simply if that person is considered "socially dangerous for public security." Reasons that would warrant arrest or restrict an individual's freedom of movement include committing a crime, concerns over interference with the evidence or a substantial flight risk. The Italian state has used these measures extensively in its fight against the Camorra, which has indeed had the unintended consequence of forcing *camorristi* abroad (MV).

When the Italian judicial authority issues a pre-trial arrest warrant (an *ordinanza di custodia cautelare in carcere*) on the basis of collected evidence and ongoing investigations and wants to prosecute an alleged *camorrista*, instead of waiting for trial, the *camorrista* will often abscond and go abroad, knowing that there he can become invisible, as judicial asymmetries and a lack of awareness of the mafia phenomenon create a safer environment for him. As Jamieson explains: "For Italian criminality, overseas expansion has not only offered economic benefits but has become an important means of avoiding arrest and imprisonment" (2000: 228). Indeed, it has become a fundamental means of avoiding prosecution. More recently, efficient anti-money-laundering legislation (in particular, *misure di prevenzione patrimoniali*, nonconviction-based asset confiscation of business activities and properties) has also forced criminals and their assets abroad. As a French judicial document explained about a suspected Camorra associate, he "left Italy after the judicial authorities seized his assets because of his involvement in the Camorra" (PM1: 5).

A closer look shows that between 1980 and 2015, *camorristi* from all clans, whether from the provinces or the city, have been given this motive to leave (see table 1.4). Identifying the main judicial trials and police investigations can explain the different waves of Camorra mobility as well as decisions to violate the resulting legal punishment (for example, *divieto di soggiorno*—banned from living in specific locations, *semi-libertà*—partial freedom of movement, or *libertà vigilata*—being under surveillance). These events provided the push factors for the main NCO and NF bosses during the 1980s when the judiciary and police clamped down on their activities. The 1980s saw a number of key *maxi processi* (maxi trials) against emerging clans: the boss Antonio Bardellino and his group were convicted in the first instance in November 1983, and there was a *maxi blitz* against his rivals, the NCO, in June 1983 and a trial in 1984, with other sentences in 1983, 1985, and 1986 (see CASMCV1, DIA1). During the 1990s, the Alfieri confederation, the Nuvoletta clan, and the Casalesi confederation were all targeted by the judiciary, which was using new antimafia laws to challenge their economic and political power (see table 1.4). These were key incentives and push factors for Camorra bosses.

The boss Antonio Bardellino from the Caserta region, who was once described as embodying the "Camorra, politics and business" (Capacchione, 2008: 1), left Italy because he was wanted in Naples. He was arrested in Barcelona, Spain, on 2 November 1983, only a few weeks before being found guilty in the first instance (*primo grado*) on 17 November in Naples for mafia association.[7] However, he had a great capacity for both escaping capture and for absconding from prison. He had already been on the run since 1982, avoiding the initial pre-trial arrest warrant. It was believed that "before hiding out in Spain, Bardellino had spent a long time in Brazil, even being able to escape abroad to Rio de Janeiro" (PN4: 30). Although arrested in Spain and wanted in Italy, he was given "conditional freedom"[8] by the Spanish judge and jumped bail (PN4: 33).

Vincenzo De Falco was one of Bardellino's close lieutenants. His older brother, Nunzio, whom we have already met, and who had until recently lived in the north of Italy, but continued to have problems with the law, decided to leave the Italian territory in July 1986. A later police document noted: "Indeed, there was information about the probable presence of Nunzio in the city of Granada (Spain),

**TABLE 1.4** Main police blitz and judicial acts against Camorra clans (1983–1995)

| DATES | POLICE BLITZ AND JUDICIAL ACTS |
| --- | --- |
| 17/6/83 | Maxi blitz against NCO (850 arrests) |
| 17/11/83 | Sentence against NF |
| 17/8/84 | Maxi trial against NCO (640 defendants) |
| 30/3/85 | Sentence (1) against NCO |
| 20/3/86 | Sentence against Nuvoletta clan |
| 29/4/86 | Sentence (1) against Antonio Bardellino and his group |
| 15/9/86 | Sentence (2) against NCO |
| 09/5/87 | Sentence (2) against Antonio Bardellino and his group |
| 16/12/87 | Sentence against Cosa Nostra (maxi trial) in Palermo, including A. Bardellino and L. Nuvoletta |
| 19/9/94 | Pre-trial arrest warrants against Alfieri clan ("Maglio"[1]) |
| 10/10/95 | Pre-trial arrest warrants against Nuvoletta clan |
| 05/12/95 | Maxi blitz (called "Spartacus") against Casalesi clan (157 arrests). |

[1] Name of the judicial operation.

who at that time was the object of an arrest warrant [325/A/88 of 10/7/89] issued by the Tribunal of S. Maria Capua Vetere for 'mafia association' and the 'illegal carrying of arms'" (QC1: 25). Vincenzo also went abroad to avoid capture by the police. He spent time in the south of France because he had relatives living there, but ultimately "decided to escape to Spain after the arrest of [his boss] Mario Iovine in France; he was the object of a pre-trial arrest warrant for 'mafia association,' 'murder,' and 'hiding a dead body'" (ibid.). Spain he chose because his brother was based there.

Antonio La Torre,[9] of the La Torre clan, is another case in point. He was the older brother of the boss Augusto, whose clan from Mondragone was an ally of the larger Bardellino-Iovine confederation. But when Antonio was charged with "mafia association" in 1985 (*ordinanza* 269/A/84 of 10/5/85) and denounced by the flying squad of Caserta in November 1985, he had already left Italy rather than face investigation and trial,[10] and he ended up in Scotland (TN16). His cousins, Michele Siciliano and Tiberio La Torre, also fled to Aberdeen because they were wanted. Siciliano explains: "In 1991, on 11 January, there was a blitz in Mondragone at my parents' house in via Santa Lucia. I had just left their house 4–5 minutes before, and I was now considered on the run [and wanted]." He confirms the same dynamics for Tiberio: "[He] was another fugitive. In 1991, he was arrested.... In 1995, he was released, but the judgment would have become final sooner or later. So he left the country ... and came to Aberdeen" (MS).

There are also examples where bosses have fled punishment. The drugs baron and NF boss Umberto Ammaturo was sentenced to seventeen years for mafia association and drug trafficking in 1987. He was sent to Mondovì (Cueno, northern Italy) as part of his parole[11] but decided to leave Italy and go on the run. First he went to Brazil and then settled in Peru before being arrested in 1993.

About fifteen years later, the same pattern reappears for *camorristi* based both in the province of Naples and in the city center—suggesting that these are long-lasting and resilient motivations. Giuseppe Polverino,[12] the leader of the Polverino clan from Quarto, moved to Spain permanently in 2006 to manage his clan's drug activities directly. He decided to remove himself from Italian law because he felt the police were monitoring his activities: "he absconded, fleeing from the workhouse in Pisa" (TN23: 57). In doing so, he violated his parole, *semi-libertà*, and by leaving his designated residence, he became a *latitante*, a wanted man. In Spain he joined his associates who were importing hashish. These associates were no ordinary citizens, as they too were on the run from Italian police: Domenico Verde, who "had for some years avoided being found by the Italian authorities and had decided to live in Spain" (ibid: 56), or one of his colleagues, AF, who was also wanted by the Italian police and had quietly disappeared, seeking refuge in Spain.[13]

Gennaro Panzuto, a member of the Piccirillo clan from the city-center district of La Torretta, fled to the United Kingdom to avoid arrest in 2006. He was in the middle of a bloody feud with rivals and was a marked man, but left Naples because he was the target of a pre-trial arrest warrant: "I then went to the UK because I was on the run."[14] In his own words: "In 2006, there was a blitz and all my clan was arrested, even my allies. As I am always a bit forward-looking, I knew a blitz was in the air. When the police came to my place, they didn't find me. Immediately, within fifteen days, I planned my departure, documents, and so on, and I went there [Preston, UK]" (GP). SD, a local, recalls: "I remember that at the time, it was said that Gennaro Panzuto, . . . was a *latitante* and hiding in the UK" (QN11: 3). Newspapers also reported that "he had fled to the UK in 2006 following a bloody turf war in Naples and was wanted for over four murders."[15] A criminal acquaintance of Panzuto, AS, who also spent time in the United Kingdom, was finally arrested in Portugal in 2008 because he was wanted in Italy for drug trafficking.

Pietro Licciardi,[16] a key leader of the Secondigliano alliance during the 1990s, did not, as one might imagine, leave Naples to expand business across Europe, but rather because he was wanted by the Italian authorities. In particular, they were looking for him in connection with "a bomb attack in the Sanità district" of the city (QN1, QN4: 1: 158). The same motives explain Raffaele Caldarelli's[17] move to London. The boss of the Case Nuove district of Naples, was arrested in September 2006 because he was wanted in Naples: "On the first of June 2002, Raffaele Caldarelli went on the run to avoid being remanded in prison" (GF4: 8). Salvatore and Gennaro Rinaldi, bosses of the Rione Villa in the San Giovanni a Teduccio district, moved to Hamburg on two occasions. The motive for their second stay during the 2000s was determined by judicial concerns. Gennaro Rinaldi went on the run in 2006 and was arrested in October 2007 because he was sentenced in Italy to eight years in prison for extortion. His younger brother, Salvatore, was arrested in Hamburg in February 2010. He was wanted after having been sentenced to six years and ten months in prison for extortion using mafia methods (AC3).

Di Mauro, believed to be a top member of the Contini city clan by the judiciary and involved in international drug trafficking, relocated permanently to Spain in 2008. This move was a direct result of being wanted by the Italian authorities. Once in Spain, he continued to organize his group's importation of hashish—directly via sea from Morocco—and its exportation to Italy (see PN17). Previously, he had been based in Naples and had traveled regularly to Spain, but in becoming a fugitive, he made Spain his permanent residence while still traveling extensively for business purposes.[18] Another international drug trafficker close to the Mazzarella clan adopted the same logic. Before his arrest warrant was issued, he traveled back and forth with a close colleague to manage his drug trafficking activities across Europe (PN10). But in 2006, after the Italian authorities issued a pre-trial arrest warrant for his arrest, he moved permanently to Spain, until the Italian police caught up with him in January 2009. These cases highlight the unintended consequences of police and judicial activities and how they influence the decisions of *camorristi*.

## Local Push Factor (2): Fear of Gang Warfare

The second significant push factor is the fear of violence: possible attacks and reprisals from rivals, a direct result of local Camorra dynamics. Strange as it may seem, violence and the possibility of death are major preoccupations for *camorristi*, even as they themselves rely on these resources so frequently. Evidence shows that Camorra bosses leave Naples to protect themselves and their families. Since the 1970s there have been several internecine Camorra wars in Naples, particularly during the 1980s and 2000s (see figure 1.2). Even after a war has officially ended, there lingers a perpetual atmosphere of violence, intimidation, and threats, which can motivate anyone to leave.

Although in general the number of Camorra murders in Naples and Campania is in decline, the region still remains very violent and the years of bloodshed have had a direct psychological effect, motivating criminals to leave their district. It pushes them away from their local territory, especially during vicious wars. The first Camorra war between the NCO and the NF in 1978–1983 produced between eight hundred and fifteen hundred murders (see CD1), and more recently, during the *faida di Scampia* in 2004–2005, some of the most atrocious attacks of brutality one could imagine were carried out, with more than seventy murders in a year and many innocent victims.[19] The last thirty years of Camorra history have been marked by constant violence (see figure 1.2), and this undoubtedly has been a concrete motive for *camorristi* to leave Naples.

Fear of violence and a sense of self-preservation are thus strong motivating factors for *camorristi* to leave. Michele Zaza was a renowned cigarette smuggler who had been co-opted into the Sicilian Mafia along with the Nuvoletta brothers and Antonio Bardellino. He had a heart condition that made him feel rather vulnerable, probably producing in him a heightened sense of mortality. For example, when his brother Ciro died in a mysterious car crash in 1978, he handed himself in to the police, although he was on the run.[20] During the first Camorra war, together with, among others, Luigi Giuliano, Lorenzo Nuvoletta, Antonio Bardellino, and Umberto Ammaturo, he became one of the leaders of the NF.

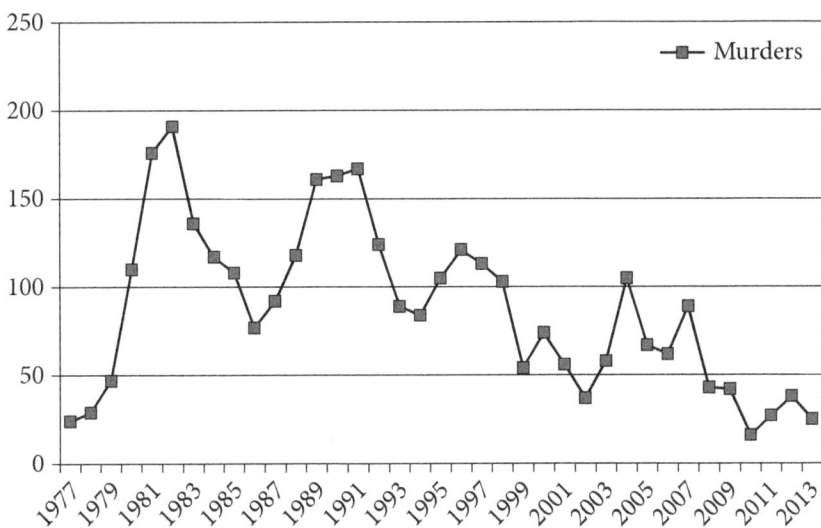

**FIGURE 1.2** Camorra murders in Naples and its province (1977–2013)

But toward the end of this war in 1982, he was rarely seen in Naples, often staying away in Rome, Paris, or Los Angeles to avoid the extreme barbarity of his NCO rivals and his NF allies. Raffaele Cutolo of the NCO had wanted him out of Naples and so did the emerging young NF leaders: they resented his successful criminal activities and international contacts. They perceived him as a *passé* godfather and saw in him a possible obstacle to their new criminal ventures: "the ambitions of the Zaza-Mazzarella family could not but clash with the equally expansionist intentions of the Secondigliano families, the families from Naples city and the Nuvoletta, Mallardo groups" (PN5: 68). Both the NCO and his own allies sought to impose "heavy taxes on his traffics" (TN1: 4) and systematically tried to eliminate him and his relatives.

A local newspaper reported that Zaza's elder brother, "Salvatore, managed to escape a fearsome attempt on his life on 24 January 1983 when a squad of killers charged into a Neapolitan clinic to massacre him."[21] A Guardia di Finanza document gives further details: "On 24 January 1983, an armed commando made up of twelve people broke into the clinic Villa del Sole in Naples, via Manzoni, with the objective of physically eliminating Salvatore Zaza, who was there for health reasons. This criminal act failed miserably in that Zaza had been released a few days previously" (GF1: 4).

Paolo Mancuso, who investigated Michele Zaza during the 1980s–1990s, suggests that this attempted murder of his brother had an important psychological effect on Michele: It "scared him. . . . His brother was no longer involved in organized crime, and when they go and get him [Salvatore, in 1982–1983], this is something that scares him" (PM). Then, in 1984, Michele's father-in-law, Giuseppe Liguori, was the target of gunshots (TN1: 11). This constant threat of violence became an acute fear for Michele Zaza and may well explain his decision to leave Naples and transfer his family to Rome once and for all. A judicial document concluded: "On this point, it can be noted that the permanent move of Zaza to Rome, . . . as he himself declared when questioned, was motivated by his need for security and with the intention of enjoying in peace his gains without being bothered by other Camorra clans" (CApN1: 3–4). As Judge Paolo Mancuso suggested, "he didn't want to face counterviolence. In other words, he did not want to be the target of an attack" (PM).

In another example, in 1996 an internal war broke out between two city clans, the Mazzarella and the Rinaldi. This forced some members of the Rinaldi group to leave Naples and go into hiding in Hamburg, Germany. A police report indicated that "such a violent attack by the Mazzarella clan inevitably forced members of the Rinaldi family to leave their district, the Villa district, to take refuge outside of Naples. Some members of the Rinaldi family violated their remand conditions "in fear of being targets of violent attacks from their rivals" (AC3: 3). In 1997, when the situation had calmed down, the leaders returned from Germany to regain control over their home territory.

Raffaele Amato was a drug manager for the Di Lauro clan from Scampia and oversaw the clan's importing of drugs into Naples from Spain. However, in 2003, when Cosimo Di Lauro, son of the boss, became leader and reorganized the clan's internal structure, he told Amato "to leave Naples, making it clear that he would kill him if he did not do so. . . . Amato reluctantly accepted and moved away" (TN21: 33). This disagreement led to the *faida di Scampia* in 2004 because Amato did not simply roll over. He was not going to stop importing drugs and hand over all his contacts, markets, and expertise to Cosimo. He thus sought refuge in Spain, moving there more or less permanently for a year to organize his group's counterattack, its survival, and its drugs operations. This is why the Amato-Pagano clan became known as *gli Spagnoli*, the Spaniards.

Acerra, a small town on the outskirts of Naples, provides us with another example of this innate fear of violence. DTS[22] was the right-hand man of Giovanni Messina, one of the emerging bosses of the De Sena clan, and when Messina was imprisoned, DTS sought to become a boss in his own right. In 2007, DTS moved to La Seyne in the south of France because life in Acerra had become too dangerous for him. "He was at war with everyone, creating confusion . . . irritating his rivals, who would no doubt seek revenge" (TNv1). Indeed, although DTS was also on the run, it appears to have been more this fear that motivated his move to France. As one observer recalled, he "left Italy because some members of the Italian Mafia were looking for him in order to kill him" (CAAP4, 2: 3).

The local newspaper described how DTS became the regular target of his rivals, the De Falco clan, once even being touched "by numerous bullets that did not pass through [his] bulletproof jacket. . . . A few months later, there was another ambush, again it failed" (*Il Mattino*, 15/2/2008). A French friend suggests that he "arrived in France because he had become 'undesirable' in Acerra. He had to leave the town because his life was in danger there. I know that he had been imprisoned for murder; I think that his departure from Italy was related to those events" (CAAP4, 3: 4–19). It could be said that "Acerra was a place where horrible things happened" (TNv4: 7) and it was better for him to move away if he wanted to stay alive.

## Global Pull Factor (1): Familiar Networks

The presence of friends, acquaintances, and associates plays *the* key role in determining where *camorristi* choose to go. Rare are those *camorristi* who moved abroad without any help from contacts already established in the host country. These contacts were always either friends or friends of friends or people from the same town. Compared with the 'Ndrangheta, who already had active criminal elements in the foreign social fabric, the *camorristi* use and target these familiar contacts and transform them into a reliable support system. As Williams and Godson have argued, "ethnic communities can be an important resource for transnational criminal enterprises, providing recruitment opportunities, cover and support" (2002: 331).

Familiar contacts enable "foraging criminals" to cross borders and establish themselves in host countries: "migrant communities are often highlighted as an important support infrastructure for transnational offenders" (Von Lampe, 2012: 189). These communities not only provide support on arrival but also, once a *camorrista* is established locally, become a protective web or a barrier against authorities. They are "difficult to penetrate since they have inbuilt defense mechanisms provided by their language and culture. These barriers are often strengthened by ties of kinship, and inherent suspicion of authority" (Williams and Godson, 2002: 331). Note in particular the "shielding effects of cultural and language differences" (Von Lampe, 2012: 190).

The Camorra's support system, its niche of familiarity abroad, has three different components (and is rarely criminal to start with):

1. Blood relatives or extended family based in the host country who speak the language and are integrated into the local host community. They have

immigrated to the new location and are in no way criminal or involved in crime.
2. Neapolitan immigrant communities, and also general Italian immigrant communities, who moved to the region in the postwar period or recent past but are not related to the *camorristi*. They are friends and associates of *camorristi*, who are trusted and loyal.
3. Professional business associates who might be Neapolitans, Italians, or natives.

Relatives and extended family, but also friendly, open, and available immigrant communities embedded in the local social fabric, seem to have played a determining role in the *camorristi's* choice of destination. This niche of familiarity is an invisible but fundamental support system, a latent community of constant help, advice, and complicity that is not necessarily criminal.

Family members are a reliable, constant support system and may be from the host country or have lived there for a considerable amount of time. In both of the locations to which Michele Zaza attempted to move (the United States and France), he had a support system at his disposal. Although his move to Los Angeles in 1984 was aborted, there he could count on American relatives who were respectable members of the local community and who could provide extensive help and advice (QR1: 388). When he moved to France in 1988 he took a loyal associate as well as a trusted gatekeeper who helped him settle into the local community. His new base was about 45 minutes from Ventimiglia and the Italian border, and only three and a half hours from Milan.

Antonio La Torre's choice of the United Kingdom, and specifically Aberdeen, was made for family reasons. In 1982, he had married a Scottish woman and "went to live in Scotland" (TN16: 686). He was never an isolated immigrant, and in turn could provide the same support for his cousins, Michele Siciliano and Tiberio La Torre, when they turned up in Aberdeen in 1991.

DTS's decision to move to La Seyne in 2007 was probably determined by the presence of one of his childhood friends there. GE was half French by his mother, whom he followed when she decided to return to the south of France. He became DTS's gatekeeper: "I have known him [GE] for many years because he lived in the same district as me (in Acerra). I know that [he] has lived in France for several years, certainly before 2007. I think he lives in Toulon, he had a ... shop" (CAAP4, 4: 1).

His friendship and resulting support played a determining role in DTS's choice of destination, as GE explained: "We saw each other again in 2006, 2007 when I returned to Acerra. . . . He wanted to come to France to see whether he could work and live here. He arrived at the beginning of 2007, he stayed a week, . . . but we saw each other every day. On his return [to France] he rented a flat at La Seyne-sur-Mer and paid 450 euros a month. He worked part time as a painter in the construction business" (CAAP4, 5: 3). Because GE was an integrated member of this French community, the support enjoyed by DTS was not purely Neapolitan, but rather a mixture of Italian and French: a traveling Italian companion and criminal, childhood friends originally from Acerra, Italian immigrants, and French nationals (CAAP4). Familiar contacts are not natural criminals, though when called on to help, they may do what they can.

Trusted and loyal associates can also determine the choice of destination. When Nunzio De Falco decided to move to Granada, Spain, in 1986, there was already an existing community of Italians who had moved there some time before, in particular, some Calabrian brothers. Their presence in Granada determined his initial choice of destination and meant that he was not a lost Neapolitan immigrant. The lifestyle he adopted and the organization of his personal safety shows that he had a strong support system: "the Spanish police made clear that De Falco lived in a 'bunker' villa built in the suburbs of Granada" (QC1: 18), and guarded by Italians and Spaniards who were probably in possession of sophisticated armaments and looked after his security using special walkie-talkies (QC1; TN4). Within this system, a gatekeeper provides access to the new local host community—someone who is familiar with the host country, who understands its culture, language, and legal system, but who also knows the *camorrista's* context of origin, thus helping the transition to the new environment.

Associates already involved in illicit trafficking can determine the destination too. For drug-trafficking clans, for example, the choice of Spain appears an obvious one, since they already have a business infrastructure that they can transform into a support system. Spain was the natural choice both for Raffaele Amato and Giuseppe Polverino. Amato already had a drug-importation network in place in different Spanish cities, all he had to do was use this network differently. As one *pentito* explained: when the main leaders of the clan lived in Spain in 2004–2005, "the Amato and Pagano families had at their disposal logistical support" (TN21: 97). If, on the other hand, the Amato-Pagano clan had chosen to move to France, this support would have been much more complicated to secure. Giuseppe Polverino knew that he already had a potential support system in Spain. In Spain, he was reunited with four to five permanent Neapolitan members of his clan who lived in different cities and managed drug-trafficking operations. Most of them were on the run from the Italian authorities. Having lived in Spain for a couple of years, they were very familiar with the local culture, language, institutions, and rituals. They provided good local knowledge and support.

For the counterfeit sector, the organizational structure abroad is less helpful because it is more fluid, more transnational, and not necessarily fixed in one location. However, it still offers help for *camorristi* and determines their destination. Pietro Licciardi moved where he could enjoy the most support: to the German part of the counterfeit operations. This support system enabled him to travel abroad more easily and to feel secure about his movements and activities. His support system was mainly made up of Neapolitan residents in Germany and traveling members of the clan who managed his hideout, with some local German help, in particular from women. For example, one Neapolitan resident in Chemnitz who was related to a clan member managed the boss's stay and activities while he was in Germany (QN4, 3: 74). The Bundeskriminalamt identified five to six Neapolitans permanently based in Germany, plus a girlfriend who made up this niche of familiarity. This support was not exclusive to Germany and must have existed in other countries; in 2001 the nephew of Licciardi hid in the United Kingdom. It was the Neapolitan support system that provided help: there "was a *magliaro*" who "had friends and support that allowed him to offer assistance" to the fugitive (QN4, 1: 172).

The Rinaldi clan chose Hamburg in Germany because they had some Italians contacts there. The police acknowledged that the Rinaldi clan was located in Hamburg because "it had the support of trusted people" and "it enjoyed solid logistical and economic support, to such a point as to guarantee their hiding." In particular, a house was made available and "'a fictitious tenant" tried to cover up their presence (AC3: 7, 8).

Associates were not necessarily Italian and could be from the host country, although this was rare. The case of Gennaro Panzuto is a good example and perhaps an indication of how things might develop in the future. He went on the run in the United Kingdom but did not have a family or an Italian immigrant support system. His niche of familiarity was a group of British associates he had met through a friend and who were keen for him to move to Preston. They would provide him with all that he required: "Everything you need, they said." This included "driving around in a Rolls-Royce, living in a villa with a swimming pool, going out in the evening to the best places in Preston" (GP). So in the United Kingdom Panzuto had a fully English support system made up of locals.

It is important to differentiate this niche of familiarity from the group of professional accomplices, enablers, or facilitators that Camorra groups may use abroad. Professional accomplices may form part of the support system, but they are different because they are an integral part of the criminal project, whereas the relatives, friends, and immigrant communities help out of friendship, loyalty, a common past, or even coercion, rather than as part of a common criminal project. This invisible community may remain latent for long periods of time and be activated by *camorristi* when they require assistance. Such individuals are very difficult to identify.

## Global Pull Factor (2): Managing Moneymaking Opportunities

Economic considerations are not the main pull factor. They are, nevertheless, important and form part of the third decision-making phase (see figure 1.1). They influence decisions only after a reliable contact has been identified in the new host country. And they matter when *camorristi* look at their options and calculate the best place to migrate to. The opportunity to manage their moneymaking activities, access flourishing markets, and make easy profits are significant secondary considerations that help to determine specific geographical location. As one judge noted regarding the months the small-time *camorrista* DTS spent abroad, "the French stay, although imposed by the necessity to escape the rage [of his rivals] ..., was wisely spent exploiting the possibility of developing the illegal traffic of stolen cars and arms" (TN20: 429).

Michele Zaza, having chosen France as his destination, had to decide whether he would settle in Paris, where he had some economic interests, or the south of France. We can only assume that he decided on the south of France because of its easy access to various locations where he could develop his deals. Nice was a strategic position with easy access to France (Marseille), Italy (Milan), and Switzerland (Zurich)—ideal for his contraband activities. Antonio Bardellino also looked for economic opportunities in new host countries: "At a certain point in time, Bardellino thought about moving away from Brazil, where he had invested money, and to take it from there, ... and invest it in San Domingo" (CSv, in CASMCV1: 793–794).

For Antonio La Torre, Scotland was a good economic opportunity, and that must have been a consideration when he decided to move. Before moving there permanently in 1982–1983 he had "visited it more and more frequently" (CSv, 11/1/94, in TN4: 290) to study the possibilities. Perhaps an Italian restaurant? "Yes, he ... initially opened a restaurant" (TN16: 686). The local police explained his logic: "I think that if you were looking for somewhere to go and open up an Italian restaurant and to break into a new market. I think this was an appeal as well, because Aberdeen wasn't multicultural. It is very much an outpost and very traditional. I think there would have been an opportunity there" (GramP). La Torre saw a gap that he could fill by representing the demand for a new market, which Varese (2011) argues is so fundamental for "transplantation." However, it was not really a new market and was not the defining factor for his move;

rather, it provided a way to develop the clan's existing money-laundering activities, interconnecting its territories in a functional cycle.

Drug-trafficking clans chose either Spain or the Netherlands as a base for their drug-importing business. De Falco chose Spain because of the numerous business opportunities it also offered him, not only for his illegal activities but for his legal activities too. He saw opportunities there to develop the drug-trafficking network with which he was already involved in the north of Italy. This would not be a new market for him, but one he could manage directly. As a representative of the Bardellino-Iovine confederation, he became an important player in its drugs network and money-laundering activities primarily through the routes, contacts, and opportunities offered by the new location.

When Raffaele Amato considered his migration options, Spain was the obvious choice because from there he could also manage his drug-importing activities directly. He was already familiar with the place and its culture. By living in Spain and carrying on his drug-importation business, he made it very difficult for his Neapolitan rivals to gain access to suppliers and thus reinforced his new clan's power. Giuseppe Polverino's choice to move to Spain was clearly motivated by economic considerations: he already had a good understanding of the international hashish market, contacts, and networks, so it made sense to manage this moneymaking activity directly in Spain. Another renowned drug trafficker, Alfonso Annunziata[23] from Boscoreale, moved to the Netherlands, where he could better manage his operations hands-on.

## Global Pull Factor (3): The Nature of the Law-Enforcement Regime

The last pull factor is perhaps less influential than the power of money, but nevertheless it plays a role in determining the destination of some *camorristi*: the nature of the law-enforcement regime in the new host environment. *Camorristi* look at and study whether the law-enforcement agencies of a specific country are alert to "mafia association" in terms of legislation and perception. The disparity between the ways law-enforcement regimes tackle organized crime might be a consideration for some *camorristi* who need to move abroad. They undertake a process of "regime shopping," comparing countries in terms of potential punishment if they are caught.

Maurizio Vallone emphasizes how Italian antimafia laws now strike at the heart of mafia power: "We have some very efficient instruments to fight organized crime that not only tackle the military branch of the clans but also, if not predominantly, seek to confiscate their financial empires. We have very strong laws, laws that are very aggressive toward mafia-owned properties in terms of confiscating and seizing them. These laws, however, are exclusively Italian laws. This permits very strong action against these individuals, but there is no equivalent in foreign laws" (MV). *Camorristi* do think about the legal system they are about to move to. They do think about the anti-organized-crime regime and whether the local police have a trained eye for mafia-style organizations and activities.

Not all EU member states recognize mafia association as a crime. As a consequence, these countries, particularly the United Kingdom and Spain, are seen as a "soft touch" regarding organized crime and mafias. Moreover, proving mafia membership and pre-crime activities are considered problematic by many states, although this is slowly starting to change. The Italian police use wire and telephone taps extensively to prove membership, and such evidence is also used in court. British courts do not use this type of evidence.

Legal differences make extradition a challenge. In the past, when Italy sought extradition for *mafiosi*, the British authorities would not automatically hand over the accused. A clear case was Michele Siciliano, a member of the La Torre clan, who was arrested in Woking in 1995. After his arrest, he spent six weeks in a cell before an extradition hearing at the Bow Street Magistrates' Court.[24] However, since he was wanted in Italy for mafia association and this was not a recognized crime in the United Kingdom, the British judge freed him. In his own words: "Initially we had only faint ideas about law 416-bis not being recognized, but this was the confirmation. I was arrested and then released after a month" (MS). He returned to Aberdeen and, through his local businesses, continued recycling illegal money made from drugs in Mondragone.

Since the introduction of the European Arrest Warrant (EAW) in 2003 it has become easier for the Italian authorities to pursue *camorristi* who go abroad, but it is still difficult to extradite Italians wanted for "mafia association." The United Kingdom is still perceived as a soft touch. The difficult experiences of Antonio La Torre, Tiberio Francesco La Torre, and Raffaele Caldarelli have compounded matters. More recently, the case of Domenico Rancadore in 2014 shows that the Italian state must be particularly insistent if it is to get *mafiosi* back to Italy to face charges. As the British tabloid *The Mirror* noted in 2007: "They are the suburban Sopranos—Italian gangsters who settle in the UK to escape justice in their homeland."[25]

When Gennaro Panzuto arrived in the United Kingdom, his English accomplices said to him: "You know the Italian law includes 'Camorra association'? Well, we don't have it as a crime in our law. If you are on the run now for 'mafia association,' no one can extradite you because, here, 'association' as a crime doesn't exist" (GP). In other words, his presence and activities were invisible to the British authorities. He could feel safe. As one newspaper pointed out, "Last night Lancashire police took the unusual step of appealing for information on the Camorra suspects—who may have used budget airlines to 'slip off the radar' as they travelled to the UK."[26] Local police in Aberdeen pointed out that because the United Kingdom had different tools to investigate and punish organized mafia crime, the activities of Antonio La Torre were "invisible to us." They were unaware of his activities: "He wasn't really committing a crime. He's not the sort of guy that's going to come to the attention of law enforcement, routinely, other than for minor driving or drink related matters and those sorts of things, but he's not going to get into trouble and really mingle with it" (GramP).

The EAW was introduced to facilitate procedures but has also produced further opportunities for delay and for undermining differences in legal systems. For example, Raffaele Caldarelli was arrested in London in September 2006 on such a warrant. He was extradited to Italy only after three years of legal battle, as the British authorities sought to understand the legitimacy of the crime he was wanted for ("mafia association"), what it meant, how it was reached, and the terms of his arrest warrant (see HCJ1 and HCJ2), all of which he challenged on technicalities and procedures. He even took his case to the House of Lords as a dilatory tactic because of the differences in legal systems. The Italian judges responded by renewing the request for extradition each time.

In addition, the nature of the prison regime faced by *mafiosi* in Italy (so-called harsh prison conditions) is also questioned by other EU member states in relation to human rights. Since *mafiosi* have long been able to carry on their activities from prison undisturbed, prison conditions (article 41 bis) were tightened in 1992, including restrictions in family visits and the use of solitary confinement, which are now the norm. Some believe these stricter conditions violate human rights; the European Court of Human Rights has been outspoken on this subject (see ECHR1). However, it could also be argued that ruthless terms and harsh conditions (including being tried in absentia) are necessary to counter such pervasive criminal organizations.

Spain is particularly perceived by *camorristi* to be a preferred location for arrest and serving time because its legal instruments are not attuned to organized crime. Maurizio Presteri recalled: "Prison is very hard, especially in Italy. We hope to be detained in Spain. Over there, once a month, if you behave properly you can spend time with a woman and there are also some gyms (*salles de sport*) and activities in prison. If you say to me 'ten years in Spain or five years in Poggioreale [Naples prison],' I answer, 'ten years in Spain'" (Saviano, 2012: 188–189). In Spain, officials have also been seen by *camorristi* as perhaps easier to manipulate and corrupt, although only in relation to their criminal activities and, as yet, not politics. Indeed, Antonio Bardellino was released in Spain, which allowed

**TABLE 1.5** Overview of main Camorra wars (1970–2013)

| DATES | WAR BETWEEN | WINNERS |
|---|---|---|
| 1978–1983 | NCO vs. NF | NF |
| 1984–1988 | Nuvoletta-Gionta alliance vs. Bardellino-Alfieri confederation | Alfieri confederation |
| 1991–1995 | Schiavone-Bidognetti alliance vs. De Falco-Caterino-Di Simone alliance | Schiavone-Bidognetti alliance |
| 1997–2000 | Alliance of Secondigliano vs. Mazzarella-Misso-Sarno cartel | Alliance of Secondigliano |
| 2004–2005 | Di Lauro clan vs. Amato-Pagano clan | Amato-Pagano clan |
| 2012–2013 | Vanella-Grassi clans vs. Abbinante-Notturno-Mennella clans | Still ongoing |

**TABLE 1.6** Italian citizens living abroad, any ethnicity (2007)

| COUNTRY | POPULATION |
|---|---|
| Italians in Germany | 582,111 |
| Italians in Argentina | 527,570 |
| Italians in France | 348,722 |
| Italians in Belgium | 235,673 |
| Italians in Brazil | 229,746 |
| Italians in the United States | 200,560 |
| Italians in the United Kingdom | 170,927 |
| Italians in Canada | 131,775 |
| Italians in Australia | 120,239 |
| Italians in Venezuela | 94,704 |
| Italians in Spain | 83,924 |
| Italians in Uruguay | 71,115 |
| Italians in the Netherlands | 17,000–18,000 |

*Source:* MI6; Dutch figures from http://www.italiansinfuga.com/2015/09/03/46-il-numero-di-italiani-in-olanda-dal-2007/ (accessed 21/3/2016).

him to disappear when he should have remained in prison. It is also alleged that the Amato-Pagano clan tried to pay a police official to deconfiscate one of their high-speed boats in Spain.

The motives for the mobility of Camorra bosses and their associates are complicated. As we have seen, there is more to encourage and motivate them abroad than just the opportunity to make or invest money. We need to understand a combination of factors, both in the local context of Naples and in the broader markets of Europe.

# 2
# FUNCTIONAL MOBILITY

To fully identify the Camorra in its foreign skin, it has to be analyzed in its original form in its local setting. Otherwise, it cannot really be understood as a global actor. Sales argues that the Camorra "moulds its illegal interests on the conditions it finds in society" (1995: 44), in other words, the local Neapolitan territory. The evidence shows how these clans branch out and link their local conditions to new territories abroad. Consequently, clans in the north of Italy or abroad have not yet become involved in activities that are completely unrelated to their home territory.

In this chapter, I look at the different economic sectors in which clans are active abroad to show how they connect their territories, move between them, and make them highly interdependent. This process I call "functional mobility" because *camorristi* do not migrate or move away, never to return, but are constantly traveling back and forth between territories in Naples and abroad.[1]

## Functional Mobility

What emerges from my research on Camorra clans in five West European countries is a picture of *camorristi* exploiting new territories and opportunities in relation to their home territory. Locations abroad were not close enough for easy "expansion," "contamination," or "multiplication," which is what happened, according to Brancaccio and Martone (2014), in the lower Lazio region. Instead, clans change behavior, values, and modi operandi while remaining the same overarching organization. It is the specific operational structures that change according to the territory abroad: in Naples, they remain a family crime enterprise, but abroad, they become business network enterprises with a strong hub and spoke structure.² These networks of various sizes are adaptable, with Naples remaining at the center of clan operations. They are not loose, ad hoc international networks with no clear headquarters, but rather function within a larger Camorra organization. Mobility is based on locating resources and markets in order to help the clan survive, thrive, and prosper at home.

This movement I call "functional mobility" because *camorristi*, once forced abroad, travel constantly between their different territories in pursuit of a commercial project, for which their foreign territories become paramount. They and their associates interlink local districts with new territories in a continuous two-way exchange, with people, resources, and money moving in both directions. This movement is mainly based on the identity, needs, and activities of the clan in Naples, but also on what *camorristi* can actually do. They use their existing skill sets, markets, and contacts to continue their criminal activities in local and global contexts; in sum, they adopt a functional approach.³

Evidence suggests that Camorra clans in Europe do not diversify but continue those criminal activities they are familiar with and in which they have expert knowledge. Rarely are they new commercial ventures. Extortion is uncommon because, as the antimafia judge Anna Canepa made clear when referring to mafias in the north of Italy: "they are *not* interested in dominating the territory [as would be the case with extortion], they *are* interested in dominating markets" (ACap). *Camorristi* seek not to govern or colonize a new territory but to do what makes sense in the context of their legal and illegal commercial plans.

Being present in two locations means that clans develop a dual identity while remaining the same organization: In Naples, they control, govern, steal, trade, and invest in legal and illegal markets. Abroad, they become transnational entrepreneurs among "trading communities" (Van Duyne, 1993: 119) who steal, buy, trade, and invest. They import goods into their home markets, export other goods abroad, and invest their illegally made profits in new money-laundering ventures across Europe. Globalization facilitates the development of this dual identity: solid in Naples and liquid abroad, but more important, invisible abroad because foreign authorities do not perceive the harm they do, their criminal origin, or their potential. New territories are not second-rate peripheries; they are an integral part of the "modern Camorra" (Roberti, 2012).

Because of the Camorra's capacity to exploit opportunities, it now has "a firm European vision" (MdG). In 1996, Behan suggested that moving abroad was "a step backwards in a *camorrista's* criminal career" (128). This is no longer the case, if ever it was. The former director of the DIA in Naples, Maurizio Vallone, describes the movement of *camorristi* as a form of "transhumance" (MV); once abroad, *camorristi* always look for better pastures for their activities while some members remain at home.

## Functional Mobility in Europe

A brief overview of our five chosen countries shows that each country has specific conditions that clans exploit, within the general context of EU integration and globalization. These include geographical, cultural, and linguistic similarities, the presence of important Italian immigrant communities, flourishing economic opportunities for the Italian market, lenient banking regulations, different legal institutions, and consolidating political institutions (see table 2.1).

All these factors have contributed to successful Camorra mobility in that clans consciously manipulate such conditions in the interests of their criminal projects. For example, EU integration has significantly eased their activities. The signing of the Schengen agreement in 1985 and its implementation into EU law in 1995 greatly simplified cross-border movements (of goods, people, and euros) for all. This may change as a reaction against the Paris terrorist attacks in 2015, but internal movement will still remain easy for EU nationals, and criminals always have access to fake documents if necessary. It is not only market opportunities, by-products of ongoing globalization, that are attractive but also other factors such as local culture, laws, proximity to Italy, and immigrant communities.

What we must remember in relation to these new host countries, however, is that the *camorristi* and their associates develop illegal and legal activities that connect specifically to their markets in Naples. To a large extent their economic activities depend on their activities in Naples, and our evidence shows continuous liquidity, flexibility, invisibility, adaptability, and interconnectivity between both territories.

**TABLE 2.1** Overview of attractive conditions for the Camorra clan in host countries (1980–2015)

| | JUDICIAL SYSTEM | IMMIGRANT COMMUNITY | POLICE AWARENESS | TRAVEL RESTRICTION | BUSINESS OPPORTUNITY | DRUGS HUB | GEOGRAPHICAL PROXIMITY |
|---|---|---|---|---|---|---|---|
| Germany | Y | some | Y | N | Y | N | Y |
| France | Y | some | slight | N | Y | N | Y |
| Spain | Y | some | slight | N | Y | Y | N |
| Netherlands | Y | some | slight | N | Y | Y | N |
| United Kingdom | Y | some | slight | slight | Y | N | N |

**TABLE 2.2** The four main identified criminal sectors of Camorra clans in Europe (1980–2015)

| | CORE ACTIVITIES |
|---|---|
| **NAPLES** | **ABROAD** |
| Extortion | Acquisitive crime<br>—Simple crime<br>—Commercial sector<br>—Predatory |
| Production and control of fake goods markets | Production and control of fake goods markets<br>—Organized crime<br>—Productive and commercial sectors<br>—Parasitic<br>—*The counterfeit market* |
| Distribution of drugs | Drug trafficking/contraband<br>—Organized crime<br>—Production and commercial sectors<br>—Parasitic<br>—*The drugs economy* |
| Money laundering/recycling | Money laundering/recycling<br>—Financial crime<br>—Financial sector<br>—Symbiotic |

Between 1980 and 2015, Camorra involvement in four specific economic and criminal sectors was identified as its main foreign activities. These were: (1) acquisitive crime, (2) production and selling of counterfeit goods, (3) drug trafficking (with some firearms trafficking), and (4) money laundering—recycling and investment (see table 2.2). These sectors are analyzed here to illustrate how *camorristi* undertake functional mobility in Europe.

## Acquisitive Crime

In all cities around the world, there exists ad hoc, random, casual, unsystematic acquisitive crime.[4] By acquisitive crime, I mean snatch theft, robbery, aggravated assault, burglary, car theft, arson, property crime,[5] and frauds, as opposed to smaller misdemeanors (also labeled "petty crime") such as shoplifting, traffic violations, pickpocketing, all activities undertaken by petty criminals. Acquisitive crimes are predatory crimes: the victims suffer loss or damage to their property and/or suffer physical pain or harm. They include harm to companies and businesses. Acquisitive crime can be organized, ad hoc, or spontaneous and undertaken by an individual or by a gang. But what distinguishes it from mafia-type crime is that it lacks a solid organization, a set territory, and an ideology based on social, economic, and political power.

Italian national crime statistics provide us with a very broad overview of the general trends in crime in Italy (MI5), but do not help us tell the story of the Camorra's relationship with the local petty-crime community. They offer a snapshot view of Italian crime in terms of geographical distribution and trends for specific crimes. For example, they show how bag snatching, a pure predatory crime (*uno scippo*), is in decline after having peaked in 1990–1991 (MI5: 10). They tell us how, in the center-north, there are more pickpockets and apartment burglaries compared with the south, where violent muggings and bag snatching have been more common. And they highlight the differences between the center-north and the south, which may be explained not by victim reports but by the lifestyles and activities of the population (MI5: 10–14).

These statistics emphasize that bag snatching and robberies are particularly high in Campania (ISTAT: 134): it is "historically the region where the highest level of bag snatching is reported" (MI5, 1: 43) and where robberies peaked in 1990 with 173 for every 100,000 inhabitants (M15: 13). In the general Mezzogiorno region there were 35.7 bags snatched per 100,000 inhabitants (ISTAT: 136), whereas robberies of shops were also very frequent in Campania and Sicily, which may be linked to the presence of mafia groups (MI5: 14). These general trends show that there is a potential labor force for a criminal group looking to recruit foot soldiers.

Acquisitive crime is not representative of core Camorra activities in Naples. Unlike traditional Camorra activities such as extortion rackets, these sorts of crimes tend not to be undertaken by an organized criminal association but by the criminal underclass of petty criminals. However, there is a clear relationship between the two: many top bosses start out as young ambitious petty criminals, others make up the core of the clans' army of loyal foot soldiers. For example, analysis of the main members of the two most important Camorra city clans in a 1998 police document (QN2) suggests that the majority of these members started their criminal careers early, usually in acquisitive crime (see table 2.3), in contrast to leaders of the clans in the provinces, who were more likely to start out in extortion and other economic activities. Here, the average age of the first crime was twenty-three and all had long criminal records as well as a history of being stopped and searched by the police.

Thus the behavior of petty criminals *can* overlap with that of *camorristi* in Naples, as many petty criminals aspire to become one of them. Indeed, the majority of respected *camorristi*, before progressing into positions of power, start out as small-timers who aspire to become part of *il sistema*, the system. Apart from family networks, it is mainly in this petty-crime community that Camorra clans find future

**TABLE 2.3** Age of first arrest, first crime, number of crimes on criminal record, and number of contacts with police of the main members of two important Camorra city clans (1998)

| NAME | DOB | FIRST ARRESTED | CRIME | CRIMES IN CRIMINAL RECORD/POLICE CONTACT-SEARCHES |
|---|---|---|---|---|
| BI | 1956 | 13 | Criminal association, armed robbery | Criminal record |
| LC | 1958 | 15 | Theft | Criminal record |
| AZ | 1961 | 33 | Extortion | (7)/(6) |
| MN | 1954 | 26 | Armed robbery, burglary, arms | (10)/(3) |
| OP | 1952 | 32 | Criminal association, theft, arms, etc. | (7)/(4) |
| WE | 1957 | 19 | Car theft | (12)/(1) |
| AU | 1951 | 34 | Robbery and arms | (7)/(9) |
| FF | 1938 | 51 | Having and selling drugs | (2)/(7) |
| QR | 1959 | 23 | Armed robbery of a car | (6)/(7) |
| KY | 1971 | 18 | Drugs holding/selling | (5)/(14) |
| TR | 1969 | 13 | Armed robbery/apartment | (29)/(10) |
| ZR | 1944 | 40 | Abetting | (**)/(6) |
| UI | 1958 | 33 | Drugs | (**)/(3) |
| OK | 1971 | 16 | Threatening behavior | (13)/(3) |
| DS | 1973 | 18 | Armed robbery | (4)/(8) |
| TY | 1974 | 19 | Carrying arms | (4)/(9) |
| FX | 1976 | 14 | Robbery of moped | (4)/(6) |
| DE | 1979 | 17 | n/a | (**)/(7) |
| BP | 1964 | 23 | Armed robbery | (12)/(1) |
| JK | 1976 | 18 | Robbery and arms | (7)/(9) |
| DW | 1963 | 21 | Using and having illegal poker machines | (2)/(7) |
| IE | 1978 | 17 | Betting | (6)/(7) |
| **Mean age** | | 23.31818182 | | |
| **Median age** | | 19 | | |
| **Mode age** | | 18 | | |

*Source:* QN2, chapter 23.

foot soldiers and lieutenants. Joining a criminal family takes petty criminals out of their narrow, isolated, and marginalized ghetto and into a welcoming and caring structured organization. Acceptance into the clan is not automatic and many *pentiti* have explained that recruitment is either through blood ties or exceptional skills at petty crime that catch the eye of an established member.

Abadinsky suggests that "a potential recruit must exhibit a recognition of the authority of the organization and a willingness to perform various criminal and non-criminal activities (usually minor at first) with skill and daring and without asking questions" (1990: 34). A would-be recruit might attract attention by committing some acquisitive crimes. Ianni explains that a "linkage develops when an experienced criminal in the neighborhood sees that a young boy (or gang of young boys) possess talent and recruits him into organized crime ventures" (1974: 275).

During the 1980s, Michele Zaza recruited young petty criminals into his clan. FL was one such delinquent who became a *camorrista* in this way. According to boss Luigi Giuliano, FL "was simply a street urchin, a thief who would steal with me." Then thanks to Zaza, "he made a true and real quantum leap" (LGv, 12/2/2003: 5). The Amato-Pagano clan from Scampia-Melito has also recruited minors extensively: "a petty criminal, for whom obviously the existence of the *scissionisti* [Amato-Pagano] clan and the membership of PG was common knowledge, turned to him and expressed his desire to become a member of the clan" (TN21: 60). Before becoming a full-time member of the Camorra, the eager petty criminals usually have to go through a "criminal apprenticeship" (Ianni, 1974: 275). For example, the Polverino clan always set a test before members could join to make sure that they would be up to it (DVv, 22/1/2010: 10).

Why mention acquisitive crime and petty criminals here? In Naples criminals were involved in the Camorra, but abroad I found a small number of them involved in these unstructured criminal activities. It would appear that some *camorristi* resort to these basic skills and in any location, especially abroad. Acquisitive crime has been labeled by Dutch police as "mobile banditism" (DP1: 141) in reference to East European groups.

I identified three specific types of Camorra involvement in cross-border acquisitive crime in Europe: (1) Former Camorra associates who live abroad and undertake petty crime with no apparent relation to Camorra clans based in Italy, but who might provide logistical support to members if they come to visit. This is casual behavior. (2) Control by Camorra associates in Naples of the stolen-goods market, including goods stolen by gangs of petty criminals (in particular Rolex watches), and also low-level *camorristi* in the north of Italy and Europe. This is a watch-snatching, predatory, "mafia-less" crime. (3) Individuals who, in Naples, gravitate around *camorristi* or were themselves *camorristi* and who change their behavior once in Europe. They resort to their basic skill set and undertake acquisitive crimes when nothing more sophisticated is possible or when criminal deals fell through.

The first category is former Camorra associates who permanently live abroad and are involved in acquisitive crime. They no longer have regular contact with the Camorra apart from playing host to traveling members. They remain criminals even if they are no longer involved with their clan in Naples (CSv, 1993). This could be analyzed as a form of transplantation or independent settlement although they do not undertake Camorra activities. I found little information about them apart from the fact that they were isolated individuals whose only connection with the Camorra was their past. They exist but very little is known about them, as they and their activities remain invisible.

The second category is made up of unrelated gangs (who may or may not frequent *camorristi*) who sell their stolen goods to Camorra associates and representatives or who are organized by them. Europol has started to acknowledge this as a problem (Europol1), and so have the Spanish (Gómez-Céspedes, 2012) and Dutch authorities. Not all countries make the link between acquisitive crime and organized criminal gangs—in effect, criminal travelers. It may suggest a link between crimes and ethnicity, but as this phenomenon is still understudied, one cannot automatically assume a relationship. Moreover, there is little systematic evidence about the exact nature and extent of these gangs' acquisitive crimes and of indirect Camorra involvement. However, some evidence can be interpreted in relation to the Camorra and these gangs.

Several accounts assert the existence of gangs of Neapolitans who traveled to host countries to snatch and steal jewelry and Rolex watches or organize bank robberies. They did not target one particular country; Neapolitan petty criminals visited pretty much all European countries. A connection between them and the organized structure of the Camorra may prove difficult to detect. The *pentito*, Gennaro Panzuto makes the link, however: "Before becoming a *camorrista*, . . . we are almost all robbers. I started very young. I was thirteen when I started. I say robberies, . . . it's rather bag snatching. I used to steal watches, Rolex . . . not in Naples. Always outside. Initially I used to rob in Milan, Florence, Viareggio, Bologna, almost the whole country, but always up north. I used to go and get watches, like a watch salesperson going into jewelry shops with their bag. Once a week, I would take a bag and, during the week, I stole watches." And they made a healthy profit: "Do you know how much money I made when I was stealing in Spain? But I am talking at the time of Italian lira. I earned 50 to 60 million a week [in 1993]."[6] Because so many young Neapolitans were involved, this activity was called "made in Naples" (GP).

During the 1980s, associates close to clans saw the potential of this type of crime and turned it into a Camorra-sponsored activity. Neighboring European countries are used by young *camorristi* and associates as a mass market where goods are snatched or stolen and then sold to dealers or sellers of illegal goods. These Camorra-sponsored associates, connected to city-center clans such as the Giuliano and Misso clans, bought stolen goods from anywhere, even abroad, because "the Camorra is not necessarily interested in the regularity of the criminal act, all it is interested in is to find the possible illegal channels to make money, even if this involves an ad hoc activity undertaken by nonmembers" (FB).

This form of crime was a simple way of exploiting host countries: goods stolen abroad were taken back to Camorra associates in Naples who paid the Camorra a cut, and the profits made from the sale of these goods were reinvested in Camorra activities. The organization required was basic, as Gennaro Panzuto reiterates: "At the lower level, there were the *paranze*, the teams, three, four guys who rob and steal certain things. Then there were the managers in the various European cities. The Mazzarella clan had the idea of putting a person there, managing the *paranze* of thieves. However, thieves don't steal because the Mazzarella clan says they can steal. They steal because they know how to get rid of the goods easily. The Mazzarella clan says: 'I am here. I am here in Barcelona. You are a thief here. Whatever you steal, you have to [sell to us]'" (GP). Evidence of this activity in Germany, France, and Spain was discovered.

The third category is the direct involvement of established *camorristi* in acquisitive crime. When they go abroad, in the absence of contacts and networks, they resort to core skills such as violence, stealing, and basic fraud. DTS, a *camorristi* from Acerra, is a good example. In France he sold stolen cars picked up in Italy. It is precisely because these *camorristi* undertake simpler and less sophisticated forms of crime that they remain below the radar in Europe. Those involved in these crimes tend to belong to the smaller and more tumultuous clans, which may be why their members are not involved in more elaborate, Camorra-related activities.

The role of the Camorra in acquisitive crime abroad was surprising. It took either an ad hoc form in order to survive or a more organized form in order to sell its stolen goods, with Naples still the central location. It is possible to see how *camorristi* and their associates adapt their criminal strategies to use Europe to their advantage.

## The Counterfeit Market

The Camorra's presence is also noted in the European counterfeit market. I had some vague notion of the Camorra's involvement in this market but not how extensive it was. My findings underline once again the Camorra's capacity to have a modern business vision that is ahead of its time in exploiting the opportunities globalization presents. Clans clearly identified opportunities, as they did with the fall of the Berlin Wall in 1989, which they could exploit by interconnecting their different territories, resources, and markets. They understood how a low investment could bring a high return, and that a poor understanding of mafia activity abroad resulted in low detection rates across Europe.

What is the counterfeit market? There exists neither a "universally recognized definition" (ISFPI) nor an EU-wide definition of counterfeit goods or piracy.

Each EU member state has a different definition, which means that the harm done by the counterfeit goods market is perceived inconsistently. In 2010, the Union des Fabricants Français, or UniFab, defined each country's situation as a "catastrophic result" (UniFab2: 16) because of the absence of political will and coordinated action to combat these crimes.[7]

In 2007, the European Commission estimated that counterfeit goods represented "5–7% total of the world's legal commerce" (UNCRI: 2). In 2011, the original value of seized counterfeit goods in the EU was more than 1.2 billion euros (MSE2: 10), which suggests the amount of money not going back into the legal economy. In 2012, it was estimated that by 2015 the worldwide value of counterfeit goods would be $1,700 billion (MSE2: 3). More precisely, in 2012 it was estimated that without counterfeit goods Italy would enjoy 110,000 more jobs, 1.7 billion euros more in revenue for the treasury, and a market worth 13.7 billion euros.[8] Under current circumstances all this money is going directly into the pockets of criminal gangs, and in Italy into the bank accounts of the Neapolitan Camorra. As the boss Luigi Giuliano explained, "such profits . . . are greater than those made from drug trafficking" (LGv, 5/2/2003: 4), and the counterfeit goods sector has become the Camorra's "exclusive domain" (QN10: 7). Europe is one of its main markets.

Definitions diverge. The Italian authorities consider "producing and selling counterfeit goods" to mean "the intent to use a fake label that creates confusion about the authentic origin of the product, and the possible deception of the consumer. 'Alteration,' however, should consist in the partial modification of a genuine brand."[9] The French also focus on the idea of creating "confusion" for the buyer between the original and fake product (UniFab1: 4), whereas the British authorities concentrate on "the infringement of trademark and copyrights" (IP1: 7). The terms "counterfeiting," "piracy," or "intellectual property crime" can thus be defined as the copying and production of items identical to trademarked goods with the intention of fooling customers into thinking the goods are the genuine article, but without any of the guarantees of a certified product. The items are cheaper but of poorer quality, and as a consequence, often dangerous.

The impact of the counterfeit market on Italy has become more visible: in 2010 it was reported by the DNA that counterfeit goods had a 22.2 percent negative impact on small- and medium-sized companies in terms of competitiveness (DNA1: 291). A police document explained the impact on the economy in more detail: "Although they do not create dangerous situations for the police, and do not have a direct impact on the social fabric, thus producing less social harm, [these crimes] have a tendency to considerably influence and damage the national economic system by limiting the development of productive factors through the development of a parallel market of fake goods" (QN10: 4).

But counterfeiting is not perceived, either by academics or by European law-enforcement agencies, as an obvious, traditional, or core Camorra activity. It is believed that Camorra clans have been involved in this activity since the early 1980s both in Italy and abroad (BRIF), and there is evidence that Neapolitans have been involved during the whole of the postwar period, with *camorristi* keeping a close eye on it (Brancaccio, 2015). UniFab argues that the production and selling of counterfeit goods is Italy's "Trojan horse" (UniFab2: 26). For example, in 1993 it was reported that one of the smaller activities undertaken by the boss Michele Zaza to finance his drug-importing business was "importation into France from Milan, using Tunisian couriers, of fake designer labels."[10] We now know that, by the 2000s, Camorra city clans, in particular, the Mazzarella clan, Michele Zaza's nephews, had become fully involved in these activities and was an emerging European leader in this sector.

Between the 1990s and 2012, the Camorra's presence in this market evolved from being fully involved in all aspects of the operations to becoming a silent partner with close associates who use their import-export companies to manage importation and distribution in Europe (see chapter 5). Clans are less directly involved but are still investing extensively in this sector (see MSE1), as it remains a vital moneymaking activity. Compared with the past, the Camorra's new strategy of invisibility might be an even wiser form of involvement that avoids detection.

Clans now place fake goods in legal shops and continue to use street-sellers (whether Neapolitans in Europe or Senegalese in Italy). They use all of their contacts and resources (whether local factories or Chinese associates) and also cooperate with other networks. They do not remain ethnically bound. They have many accomplices, which explains how many items can be made and how they can invest their profits into other activities. Their involvement is characterized by short-term, temporary, diffuse, loose networks that work from deal to deal with various partners. The enterprise network structure that clans adopt is a strong hub and spoke network with Naples at the center of its operations and profits returning systematically to Naples. This allows for flexibility but also reinforces the clan's power in its home territory.

By 2013, the European market had perhaps become saturated, whereas South America was a new flourishing market for clans. Yet the European market will remain important. Camorra activities there shows how crafty and ingenious *camorristi* can be, always looking for new and original ways to make money.

Counterfeiting is a suitable crime for a criminal association with international aspirations. In the 1990s, Europe represented a massive, open, and easy market for many reasons. First, detection was limited. Detecting counterfeit activities is complex, as criminals use various techniques, accomplices, and forms of transport to smuggle goods across borders. Initially it was believed that counterfeited goods were only luxury goods, but this is not the case. In the beginning, counterfeit goods were largely fake and imitation clothing labels (leather jackets, sportswear, etc.). Now, however, everything and anything can be counterfeited, from luxury products, clothing, handbags, perfumes, makeup, watches, DVDs, CDs, and software, to electronic goods, medicines, industrial equipment, car spares, wines, spirits, food, and building materials—anything that customers are willing to buy, especially in a time of austerity.

Second, this crime is perceived as "a victimless crime" because no victims are being physically hurt. But counterfeiting is damaging to society in a more subtle way: It distorts the economy by diverting money from the legal economy into the illegal one. It can also harm citizens with substandard products and can involve violent mafia-style methods to deal with the army of street-sellers. In the words of the United Nations, counterfeit goods "undermine licit trade and endanger lives" (UNODC2: ii).

Third, the general understanding of counterfeiting activities outside Italy remains limited and inconsistent. It is not an activity that law-abiding citizens normally associate with mafia-like organizations, added to which it is still not considered dangerous or harmful by European law-enforcement agencies or the general public. For example, the Dutch police believed that in 2008 "the expectation is that ICT [Information and Communication Technologies] Piracy will be of no *specific threat* (my emphasis) in the next four years" (DP1: 195),[11] and the British analyzed counterfeit goods in relation to illegal immigration, identity fraud, counterfeit currency, and pharmaceuticals and internet developments (see SOCA), never considering it as a crime undertaken by Italian mafias working as coherent network enterprises abroad.

A good example of public perception comes from France. When some Neapolitans were arrested for selling fake agricultural equipment near Toulouse—part of the *Outilleurs Napolitains* scam—(see chapter 4), readers of *La Dépêche*, the local newspaper, reacted by saying:

> Mafia? Here we go again. The Neapolitan Camorra does not launch itself into such nonlucrative activities, compared with, say, investing in real estate, which they can do in Italy; we simply arrest a few stooges from Naples (Naples is the capital of trafficking of all types, which is not surprising). In any case, the methods employed here demonstrate amateurism and not the mafia. Indeed, the illegal selling of cigarettes there (in front of everyone) is more profitable without having to decamp abroad. I cannot imagine these crooks belonging to the mafia (*"grand banditisme"*).[12]

As a consequence of this narrow perception, producing and selling counterfeit goods as a crime still incurs comparatively light punishments (such as fines or suspended sentences). And yet "counterfeiting is a threat not only to the global information economy, but also to public safety and national security" (Treverton et al., 2009: xiv).

Various reasons explain the Camorra's specific interest in the counterfeit sector. First, the risks are low and the profits high. For example, in 2007 the difference in profit between 1 gram of cannabis and 1 counterfeit computer program was 34.32 euros (UNCRI: 5).[13] Second, this was an economic sector that remained poorly regulated and policed. There was also no sense of harm or urgency. Host countries in Europe offered favorable conditions. The fact that victims were unaware of the crime and that they did not see themselves as victims was helpful. European police forces also had little knowledge of Italian mafias and their activities, which meant that these countries appeared to the Camorra as spaces where they were immune. The absence of the category "mafia association" as a crime in many countries reinforced this sense of impunity.

The nature of the counterfeit market is also important. The European market had great potential: it was a virgin market and seen as a gold mine because it could replenish the clan's funds as well as provide a mechanism for recycling already made illegal profits. The *pentito* GG explained: "These shops guarantee important sums of cash made from the sale of clothes. As these shops are all controlled by the Licciardi clan, they represent a continuous source of funds for them, in the sense that through these shops important sums of ready cash can be made quickly and used as needed" (GGv4, 14/1/1999: 4). Treverton also made this point when he argued that "counterfeit is widely used to generate cash for diverse criminal organizations. In the case of DVD film piracy, criminal groups are moving to control the entire supply chains, from manufacture to distribution to street sales, consolidating power over this lucrative black market and building substantial wealth and influence in virtually every part of the globe" (Treverton et al., 2009: xii).

Third, the use of containers to ship goods allows the products to be easily hidden. There are so many containers coming into European ports daily that it becomes problematic for port authorities to keep a check on them, especially when they then move to another destination. One example is the importation of electronic goods. Clans controlled key access to European ports for containers from China, ports such as Naples, Barcelona, Nice, Malaga, and Rotterdam. Families close to the Camorra, such as the Redde family in Barcelona and the Bluae family in Malaga, owned import companies based in these ports (BRIF). It has also been suggested that Camorra clans have associates in situ in China overseeing the production of electronic goods.

Lastly, counterfeiting is an activity that requires contacts, knowledge, and flexible organization. The Camorra and its associates have always been close to the *magliari* community (see Brancaccio, 2015), so it came to this sector well prepared: apart from the necessary strategy, it also had the appropriate products and the right contacts to take over this market. Associates close to the clan already worked in textiles and leather. They had factories in Naples and Italy that produced different types of fake goods, while other associates, who had invested in production activities in China, were able to import electronic goods into Europe for the clans. In addition, the door-to-door salesmen were Neapolitan *magliari* or "spiders," as defined by the British authorities. They were "not connected directly to the whole operation but are brought in to facilitate the higher-risk element of the crime, the sale and delivery of fake items" (IP1: 15). There would have been no need to organize from scratch, but only to take over and control the existing network. Indeed, the Camorra had the right contacts.

Many *magliari* and individuals in this sector were also related to, or close to, Camorra members. When the clan decided to invest in this sector it already had available personnel who had specialized knowledge of the market and its different dynamics. These combined factors meant that the clans could easily take over the market and labor force knowing the state of play, but also how they would need to act, using violence toward the *magliari* network and its producers when necessary.

Italian mafias have always had a good nose for business: they have been able to identify opportunities even before they appeared. This has happened with smuggled cigarettes, drugs, and waste management. The Camorra's appearance in the counterfeit sector is another good example of its adaptability and responsiveness, identifying a demand for products at cheaper prices. In Europe counterfeiting was not a new market but one the Camorra expanded from Italy because clans recognized its moneymaking potential and existing labor force. It was also a good cover for fugitives, as local law-enforcement agencies were not necessarily looking for Italian criminals on the run.

The counterfeit sector has always been an ideal fit for Camorra clans, so much so that they have become synonymous with it. The notion of "functional mobility" explains how clans use both local and foreign territories for their interests: Naples was the center of operations where decisions were made. Host countries provided the market in which to sell the goods as well as an already existing workforce in the *magliari* network. Clans made use of host countries in a two-way relationship between territories. Their success and systematic presence also suggests that Neapolitan criminal groups will continue to have the upper hand in this sector, which needs further research and better cross-border police strategies.

## International Drug Trafficking

In 1987, Aldo Vessia, the general prosecutor in Naples, reiterated a United Nations statement to the effect that "drugs are the most disastrous plague of the world, which continues not only to subsist but also to increase its trafficking and consumption" (Vessia, 1988: 42). This remains the case, but there still exists a problem in understanding the overall picture: "the main challenges continue to be the availability and reporting of data on different aspects of illicit drug demand and supply in member states" (UNODC4: 3). This lack of clarity plays directly into the hands of the Neapolitan Camorra, avid to make a profit wherever and however it can. Little is substantially known about the involvement of Camorra clans in international drug trafficking into Italy and Campania. Our understanding of the Camorra's involvement remains partial and is probably just the tip of the iceberg.

Direct drug importation (cocaine, hashish, heroin, and synthetic drugs) and selling is the most lucrative business that any criminal gang can be involved in today. They are profitable activities for all aspiring criminal organizations because Europe remains a vibrant market for drugs consumption. When cocaine consumption declined in the United States, it grew in Europe: "From 1998 to 2007 cocaine prevalence declined in the United States and expanded in Europe, particularly in Spain and the United Kingdom" (EC2: 12). In 2011, "the five dominant national markets of the UK, Spain, Italy, Germany and France ... represent more than 80% of European cocaine consumption" (UNODC3: 58). Italy is the third-largest West European market for the consumption of both cocaine, 19 percent in 2008, and heroin, 20 percent in 2008 (UNODC1: 18, 21).

Why is it so attractive? The risks of being caught might be higher than for other illegal activities, such as the production and distribution of counterfeit goods, but the returns are also higher in a shorter amount of time. Italian mafias have enjoyed such returns. Since the 1970s, Camorra clans have been a consistent partner and ally of Cosa Nostra and the 'Ndrangheta in drug-trafficking activities, but they have always seemed less organized and international. Today the Camorra is both present and active on its own terms. Philip Willian estimated in 2005 that Camorra revenue from drugs was $21 billion annually, and its estimated annual gross revenue from all activities was $33 billion (2005: 42).

Camorra clans that wanted to survive have all progressively turned to drug trafficking over the last twenty years. As a UN document made clear, "as of 2007, the Camorra, located in Naples, was reported to have begun trafficking cocaine to Italy from Spain, as well as directly from South America." It noted that "more recently, the Sicilian Mafia has also got involved, getting support from the 'Ndrangheta and the Camorra to bring cocaine into the areas it controls"

(UNODC3: 40). South America (Colombia, Peru, and Bolivia) is the main continent for the production of the entire supply of cocaine and thus presents a geographically convenient location for importation into Europe.

Three phases of Camorra involvement in drug trafficking reflect different eras and strategies: (1) during the 1970 and 1980s, based on earlier cigarette smuggling operations, *camorristi* were involved with Sicilian and American mafia networks; (2) during the 1990s, Camorra clans sought to become more autonomous; and (3) by the 2000s, Camorra clans were independent drug clans and recognized international drug players. Since the early 2000s, there has also been the emergence of brokers who mediate between the sellers in South America and Camorra clans in Campania.

Camorra clans are now fully integrated into the international drug-trafficking community, with all the larger clans directly involved in importing drugs. The constant demand and dynamic that the drug market presents in Italy and Naples implies necessary mobility for clans out of their territory of origin to buy goods directly. Clans need to link the territory of origin with host countries. There is a functional interaction between territories, resources, and people according to their needs, which is fundamental to success in this sector.

Italy is at the geographical crossroads of these different routes, has many ports, and is close to countries with major criminal groups. Although law-enforcement agencies have become more efficient at detecting drug importation, mafias adapt and are always one step ahead: they "innovate, seeking novel ways of getting their product to the consumer," they modify "their techniques," and find "new methods" (UNODC3: 6), and were thus well placed and had all the necessary skills to become involved in these markets.

The DNA's 2010 annual report made clear that supplies of cocaine came from Colombia, transiting principally via Mexico, Spain, the Netherlands, Brazil, and the Dominican Republic; supplies of heroin came from Afghanistan, transiting through Greece and Turkey; supplies of hashish came from Morocco via Spain and France; and synthetic drugs and supplies of marijuana came from the Netherlands. Cocaine is the highest-trafficked drug and the main groups are the 'Ndrangheta, Camorra, Colombian, Albanian, Dominican, Moroccan, and Spanish; and for heroin the main groups are Sicilian, Puglisi, Neapolitan, Turkish, Moroccan, Tunisian, and Albanian (DNA1: 341).

For the last twenty-five years, since the early 1990s, Camorra clans have imported cocaine and hashish, their preferred drug markets, but some clans also traffic heroin. The main cocaine supply countries, through which the drugs enter Europe, remain Spain and the Netherlands,[14] although there is also a route directly from South America into the port of Naples.[15] A judicial document in 2006 highlighted the different routes used: "From the areas of production, drugs enter Europe, especially through the Atlantic, in containers into the ports of Spain, the Netherlands, and Portugal, but also by air parcels, suitcases, and 'mules'" (TN13: 44). But groups change and adapt. Since 2008, sea transport has become the main mode of importation for cocaine, whereas previously it had been through airports (PCM: 42).

Heroin appears to have been less systematically trafficked; it was often riskier and had greater social stigma attached to it.[16] The nationalities of people arrested in Italy for heroin trafficking in 2000–2008 also reflect the lack of Italian involvement (only 10 percent), leaving the market to other groups (Albanian 32 percent, Turkish 13 percent, and other Balkan groups 13 percent) who have the networks, contacts, and geographical know-how (UNODC1: 58). Some groups have dabbled in the importing of heroin and pills (the Annunziata family), or the importing of ecstasy (the De Falco or Frizzero clans). However, cocaine remains the Camorra's preferred drug commodity; 60 percent of those arrested in Italy for cocaine trafficking are Italian (UNODC3: 40).

The majority of Camorra clans are in one way or another involved in local drug distribution and they do not exclusively traffic in one drug; they will traffic and deal in several drugs as the opportunity arises. This was the case for the La Torre and De Falco clans, both of which trafficked in cocaine, hashish (coming in from North Africa), and heroin (from the Baltic route). But, as Becucci has pointed out, local organized crime groups in Campania can extend their "control not only over large trafficking operations but also street dealing" (2004: 274).

What evidence is visible shows that Neapolitan drug networks so far have remained ethnic based, although in cooperation with other criminal groups: "Drug trafficking epitomises the new networked structure of organised crime.... Drug trafficking conspiracies, both domestically and internationally, are generally made up of a network of individuals and groups, each of which specialises in one or more aspects of the trade, such as supplying the raw material or processed product; arranging financing; brokering the purchase, transportation, or distribution; physically transporting the goods; or storing, wholesaling and retailing the product" (Schneider, 2009: 345). Members of the Polverino clan did not hesitate to buy from Moroccans, become involved with Polish couriers, or hire Spanish help when necessary; the Amato-Pagano clan and the Annunziata-Aquino network all dealt with South Americans in Spain (TN24; TN22; TN12).

I identified four types of Camorra involvement and mobility in relations to drug trafficking: (1) Camorra clans become drug networks, (2) Camorra clans employ foreign or Italian brokers to buy and transport drugs into Campania for them, (3) Camorra clans buy from independent drug importers/traffickers in Campania, and (4) Camorra clans buy locally from other clans. Unlike the 'Ndrangheta and previous Camorra leaders who went to South America to source

**TABLE 2.4** Camorra clan involvement in international drug trafficking

| WHO | ROLE IN DRUG TRAFFICKING | NEAPOLITAN CAMORRA CLANS |
| --- | --- | --- |
| Camorra clan | Camorra bosses transform their clan into drug importation businesses | Amato-Pagano, Annunziata-Aquino, Gallo, Zazo, Polverino clans |
| Brokers | Individuals: mediators who organize the transactions, transportation, and delivery of drugs to specific clans in Campania | La Torre, Nuvoletta, Limelli-Vagone, Casalesi, Fabbrocino, Falanga-Mennella, Pagnozzi, Mazzarella, Reale clans |
| Independent traffickers | Individuals who sell to clans in Campania | Amato-Pagano, Contini clans |
| No one | Limited to distribution of production in Naples and the hinterland. Buy from other clans. No travel or involvement with international drug trafficking rings. | Misso, Piccirillo, Licciardi, Contini, Giuliano clans |

drugs directly, today the majority of Camorra groups do not systematically do so. Camorra bosses transform part of their organization into a drug-business network and travel to wholesale countries (Spain and the Netherlands) to buy drugs, which they then import into their home market. This is the classic scenario; different clans are involved in this form of mobility.

There now exists a community of brokers and independent drug importers who sell directly to Camorra clans; they form part of an international community of drug specialists. Brokers have a more focused role and are close to some clan members. They act as "mediators between international groups that sell and the local clans that manage the distribution of drugs across the territory" (TN14: 44). They have a certain amount of autonomy, but their main clients are specific Camorra clans. Thus a relationship of sorts develops that can become a regular one. For example, "BCL, who was an important player in the international drugs panorama ... had the role of mediator between the Colombian cartels and Maghrebin producers of the drugs, guaranteeing their introduction into member states." On one occasion, "some of his merchandise was destined for the capital of Campania ... where he had developed an alliance with a local criminal clan from the San Giovanni a Teduccio district" (GF3: 3). Independent drug traffickers differ slightly, they supply drugs to many clans in Campania. "They get drugs whatever way possible. They are not subordinate to one specific clan but are free agents who deal with whomever they wish, sell to whomever they want, have contacts with more than one criminal organization" (DVv, 29/1/2010, in TN23). They deal on their own terms.

The Camorra clans involved in international drug importation show the features of functional mobility, and in particular, continuous communication and exchange between Naples and territories abroad within the Schengen space, which has made this traffic relatively easy. But what are the main features of the drug clans' functional mobility? The clans are continuously active and present in both locations. In Naples, clans would sell the goods; abroad, they became liquid business networks. Abroad, members of the clans or trusted contacts negotiated with wholesalers or brokers. These contacts could be: (1) a clan member resident in the host country or a traveling member with residency abroad, (2) traveling brokers, and (3) South American contacts (up until now usually from the Colombian cartels). Some of the more specialized bosses had direct contacts in Colombia, as was the case for Raffaele Amato. Others had contacts with representatives of the cartels or South Americans based in Europe who sold to organized crime groups, as was the case for the Annunziata-Aquino family.

One of the Polverino clan's drug managers explained the extensive organization required in both locations: It needs "the investment of important capital, the use of couriers and modes of transport, the involvement of a number of highly specialized individuals who are close to the world of organized crime or who are at least in contact with people who count in that sector. It is for this reason that drug trafficking is normally undertaken by powerful mafia clans or by individuals who are not members of one particular Camorra mafia group but who nevertheless have contacts with more than one criminal organization" (DVv, 29/1/2010, TN23: 163).

Clans require a readily available army of mobile couriers, vehicles, and containers that deliver the goods from the host country to their market. Money to pay for the goods is also transported via road. For the criminal organization, drug trafficking is not considered logistically or operationally complex once the right contacts have been established: low levels of skill are required, and thus unskilled laborers are used and easily replaced. Compared with the fake-goods market, there is a less structured organization, but the manpower is considerable and needs to be easily replaceable when members are arrested, which is often.

Couriers and the transportation of drugs from Spain into Italy have evolved rapidly. In the last five to ten years it has become much more professional, with a stable horde of couriers fully aware, integrated, and involved in the criminal project. They always seek to avoid detection, as one courier explained, who "travels with wife and children," as this raises less suspicion, and there was also "good pay" (PN8: 60–63). Previously, a clan would threaten individuals or force them to become couriers as a way of paying back debt or dues to the clan. There have been examples of Neapolitans arrested in France for drug importation who were not members or involved in a clan (see chapter 4). Operations have become more organized: traffickers can use container ships from Barcelona (as was the case for the Polverino clan) as well as couriers (the Amato-Pagano clan). To avoid detection, they use a *staffetta* system—a relay—whereby two cars travel together to look out for each other. Once back in Italy, the goods are deposited safely and then the local clans look after their commercialization. Clans distribute their merchandise to their own trusted distributors and *piazzas* (TN13), as well as to other Camorra groups. The importation system requires various trips and journeys across Europe and an efficient transport system that functions in both directions, with money coming out of Naples and drugs traveling into Naples. Camorra drug organizations are fluid networks with members and goods continuously moving around. They are not necessarily "flat" networks, because there are clear elements of leadership and hierarchy.

The same can be said for their financial investments. The initial start-up money in drug-trafficking activities comes directly from the local territory: money principally made from extortion rackets. The investment is clan or alliance based, with members investing *puntate* (a stake, a portion of the operation). As a clan member explained, "the system of 'stakes' was that each of us invested in the journeys to Spain to finance the [drugs] operation" (TN13: 29). The money was then transported to Spain, the Netherlands, or Germany by couriers who would hand it over to their contacts in exchange for the drugs. Money was thus continuously transported back and forth across Europe. In some cases the profit from the drug operations was then transported back to Europe to invest in real estate and other commercial ventures.

Drug importation into Italy and Naples allowed Camorra clans to become international players. It is not just a matter of Camorra members moving away from Naples to organize drug trafficking unrelated to the clan. Naples remains the center for the collection of the money, its investment, and the mass market in which the product is sold to clients. Host countries are the entry points for the goods into the European Union but also the meeting points for business contacts. Both contexts interact to produce profitable activities for the clan in its territory of origin. If clans want to be involved in drug importation, members must be mobile to manage the economic activity, they cannot do this from Naples alone. Those clans who do not travel abroad to buy their goods directly from foreign importers can still sell locally by buying from other importing clans or brokers, but they do not make the substantial profits the others do.

## Money-Laundering Activities

The last sector in which I found Camorra members active was in financial crime, specifically in money-laundering activities across borders. In 1999 Mueller argued that "the true dimensions of money laundering are largely unknown" (1999: 6).

In 2015 there is still no real understanding of the amounts laundered; as Moran noted, "there is a great deal of disagreement . . . as to the true extent of money laundering" (2008: 34–35). And in a globalized cross-border context, this paucity of knowledge becomes a problem for law-enforcement agencies that cannot pay attention to all the different transactions and activities that are going through various jurisdictions (Keh and Farrell, 1997: 107). Until more research is undertaken, the true extent of the damage caused by the recycling and investment of the mafia's "dirty capital into the 'clean' economy" (Arlacchi, 1988: 103) will never be fully understood. Camorra clans now invest locally, nationally, and internationally, and the amounts they launder are not small. In Italy such activities are targeted and confiscated; in an international context, they remain hidden and invisible.

Money laundering is often presented as a separate crime undertaken by organized crime groups. This is wrong. For mafias, money laundering is an integral part of their activities: it is the invisible conclusion of their money cycle, the output of their illegal activities, and their fundamental raison d'être. It becomes their "lifeblood" (Robinson, 1994: 3). More precisely, in the words of Moran, money laundering is "the act of making illicit funds appear to be legitimate sources of revenue." He goes on to explain: "Probably the most widely used method of money laundering is the transfer of money out of the country in which the money was made (by air, sea, land or the Internet). This cash is then deposited abroad. Next, there are a series of international money transfers until it is virtually impossible to track the trail of money. What is generally agreed upon is that money-laundering activities have an effect on the international economy" (2008: 34–35). To launder money the mafia requires either a certain amount of mobility—traveling members—or accomplices in situ.

If mafias did not launder money, they would not be able to use their money in the legitimate economy and would remain deeply anchored in the underground economy. Castells calls this "the matrix of global crime": "the whole criminal system only makes business sense if the profits generated can be used and reinvested in the legal economy" (2000b: 178). Money laundering serves a specific and necessary criminal purpose and is particularly related to high-profit activities such as drug trafficking—and also for counterfeit goods and the shops that deal in them: they "are often managed by front names but in reality they are used to recycle money made from illegal activities" (GGv, 14/6/99: 4). Money laundering is the stepping-stone from the illegal underworld to the legal economy, where it becomes more and more difficult to detect the presence of mafias because they no longer purely undertake business transactions but in effect become the business enterprise itself.

Camorra families launder money in many varied ways, from small local investments to large international building projects. The *pentito* Pasquale Avagliano explained how clans invest their "hot" money in small commercial activities locally. One example is friendly, available car dealerships: "I know that there are a number of car dealers that are 'available' to the clans of Secondigliano.... This is widespread in Naples: Camorra groups that have cash at their disposal need to invest it and do it in financial-commercial activities that are already well established; in this way, they become stronger" (PAv, 23/10/2003: 6). It is clear that not all clans recycle, invest, or reinvest their dirty money into commercial activities, as Raffaele Giuliano (RGv, 6/4/1999) has made clear, but it is a necessity for all ambitious clans in order to survive and expand their criminal activities. The larger and more organized clans have, according to Roberti, "sought to evolve through investment diversification, breaking out of the limited area of the construction sector and public works' contracts. Today, the profits of the mother firm are invested in other legal activities.... In short, the primary criminal firm, by means of various 'clean' companies, is then transformed into formally legal activity" (2008: 47).

As a consequence, clans have developed intricate techniques to launder their money in the official economy, making it nearly impossible to detect them. They do not do this alone but thanks to an extensive web of accomplices from the business community who are "above suspicion": "the effectiveness of such an operation depends on the strength of its 'cover,' so as to reduce as far as possible the probability that from the reinvestment of the legal activity one can trace the illegal source of the sums invested" (Roberti, 2008: 47). Accomplices, facilitators, and enablers make up the grey area because mafias cannot carry out these activities on their own. Here accomplices are crucial. Clans have an extensive community of accomplices at their disposal in Naples. Blood relatives act as front names for car ownership, properties, companies, and luxury goods, but so do different white-collar professionals and businessmen: people who have either been forced into complying or who identify with the Camorra's criminal interests. They are subordinate businessmen who are open to illegality and corrupt values.

Can the same be said for the Camorra abroad? When clans started to make significant sums of money from contraband cigarettes and drugs, many invested locally and nationally in Italy: Antonio Bardellino and Lorenzo Nuvoletta in the 1970s invested in cement companies in the Caserta region, and the La Torre clan invested in local companies in Mondragone. However, with the expansion into drug importation in the 1980s, some of those *camorristi* who started to travel abroad also started to invest there too. For example, it is believed that Antonio Bardellino invested in San Domingo, whereas Michele Zaza invested in Paris and the south of France.

During the 1990s, with the introduction of harsh confiscation and asset-seizure measures in Italy and more flexible banking regulations abroad, clans sought new opportunities to launder money abroad (MV). There was a clear change of focus. European host countries now provided the ideal opportunity to recycle and invest in the legal sector: some experts even suggest that "when money was invested in other countries, this often could be explained by close personal contacts or the logistics of criminal activities" (OCM1: 173). Those clans that invested abroad did so because they were familiar with the available opportunities and because it was easier to invest abroad than in Italy. Some bosses also employed third parties without physically moving abroad, as for example some associates of the Contini clan (see PN17).

One Italian judge working in Europe explained how clans employ experts to give advice about their money-laundering activities abroad: "First of all, they do not move around randomly because, even if they appear to be of humble origins and to be uneducated, they are surrounded by consultants who advise them in their businesses decisions. . . . These professional, financial advisers know the system, especially the loopholes, and so they are able to give advice on all kinds of transactions" (IJ). Giovanni Falcone explained: "Because the financial operations necessary to launder drug money cannot be carried out by the organisations themselves—they lack the technical knowhow—the task is given to international finance experts, the so-called 'white collars' who act on behalf of organised crime to transfer illegal capital to more hospitable countries, the notorious 'tax havens.' It is always difficult to find traces of such operations" (Falcone and Padovani, 1993: 129).

In the sixteen cases I analyzed, there was evidence of many different forms of money laundering. The patterns I found were: (1) many drugs clans exported money from Naples to be laundered in the host country (such as the La Torre, Amato-Pagano and Polverino clans); (2) a few clans immediately invested their profits in the host country, not necessarily returning them to Naples (such as the Rinaldi clan); and (3) some clans used advisers to invest their money through credit institutions, or white-collar professionals (such as solicitors) based abroad, or invested abroad using Italian-based advisers (see Contini clan, PN17). The Amato-Pagano clan is interesting because it employed financial advisers in credit institutions to buy land in Spain. In this way, the clan was able to move money across borders and accounts in various transactions without ever being identified as the client (see PN9). Clans are always looking for new methods and techniques to avoid being traced because for them money is what counts.

Money laundering is an excellent example of functional mobility. It acts as a clear loop between territories. Money made in Naples from illegal activities is laundered abroad, while money made from counterfeit goods abroad is sent back to Naples for the common fund. Europe is a great investment opportunity, and the lack of public awareness and implementation of financial regulations on money laundering by European governments and banks makes it an ideal location. Some banking systems appear more flexible and relaxed, with fewer regulations, which make them even easier to use. Moreover, there is generally less understanding of the possible money-laundering activities of mafia groups and the harm they do to the local and international economies. This means more passivity in civil society, among law-enforcement agencies, and government. This activity of the Camorra is likely to continue to develop abroad.

# 3
# CAMORRA CLANS IN GERMANY AND THE NETHERLANDS
Hof, Hamburg, and Amsterdam

Our journey begins in Germany and the Netherlands. These two North European countries have strong civic cultures, flourishing economies, and effective political institutions—a far cry from the purportedly backward Mezzogiorno region with its mafias. And yet there have been traces of Italian mafias present in Germany since the 1960s (Reski, 2015[1]) and in the Netherlands since the 1990s (Fijnaut et al., 1998: 81).

In 2000, the German police identified 63 Italian mafia groups active in their country; this figure went down to 26 in 2013, with an average of 29.79 groups per year for the period 2000–2013 (BKA-NS).[2] The Camorra was not considered the most active mafia compared with the 'Ndrangheta,[3] but it was nevertheless present: 79 *camorristi* were arrested between 1997 and 2012, just over 5 a year. Information about the situation in the Netherlands was unavailable, although in the late 1990s, a Dutch study did recognize the presence of the Camorra but noted that this "mafia does not have much power in the Netherlands" (Fijnaut et al., 1998: 81). However, in 1990, a Camorra clan appears to have been involved in the import-export of flowers with international Dutch companies (see PN2), but no judicial action was ever taken. So, it is there.

In this chapter I analyze four clans in these two countries. Between 1980 and 2015, Camorra clans were active in acquisitive crime, drug trafficking, and the counterfeit market (see table 3.1). Money-laundering activities were less easy to identify because of the limited material available. The stories here demonstrate how clans have solid roots in Naples and, by developing activities abroad, how they interconnect their territories in order to pursue their economic agenda. The

**TABLE 3.1**  Camorra case studies in Germany and the Netherlands (1988–2013)

| CLAN | DATES | LOCATION/ITALY | LOCATION/ABROAD | CRIME |
|---|---|---|---|---|
| Stolder clan* | 1988–90 | Maddalena, Naples city | Amsterdam | Drug T. |
| Annunziata-Aquino group | 2000–2012 | Boscoreale, Naples province | Kassel, Fuessen, Freiburg / Amsterdam | Drug T. |
| Nuvoletta / Gala cell | 1995–98 | Marano, Naples province | Amsterdam | Drug T. |
| Secondigliano alliance / Licciardi clan | 1990–2002 | Secondigliano, Piazza Garibaldi-Naples, Giuliano—Naples province | Chemnitz, Berlin. | CF |
| Rinaldi clan | 1996–2009 | S. Giovanni a Teduccio, Naples city | Hamburg | CF |

*This clan was not discussed in this study.

spatial/territorial dimension underlines the clans' vibrancy and how they manipulate local and global conditions, territories, and markets.

## Acquisitive Crime

Some *pentiti* have mentioned, in passing, that former *camorristi* or their associates have undertaken acquisitive crimes in Germany and the Netherlands. But information from German, Dutch, and Italian police on mobile petty Neapolitan criminals present is patchy at best. For example, figures provided by the BKA for 1987–1990 show that on average per year 20,805 Italians were accused of committing crimes in Germany, of which 1,121 were for drug dealing and trafficking, 4,529 for forgery, 3,348 for fraud, and 52 for extortion. In addition, on average per year 78 Italians were accused of what the BKA terms "illegal import of drugs in no small quantities" (see BKAa). This does not shed much light on Italians involved in acquisitive crime. I use the limited material from Italian judicial documents to provide a general overview.

Three forms of acquisitive crime were identified. First, there was some evidence of former *camorristi* permanently moving to Germany and being involved in acquisitive crime (CSv, 30/4/1997: 3). They also appear to provide support for *camorristi* who travel abroad—but without the proper tools to monitor their activities, no general comment can be made. Second, there was evidence of *camorristi* who traveled abroad and, unrelated to their clan's criminal agenda, undertook acquisitive crime, mostly robberies and bag snatchings. The state witness GG explained in 1999: "Among the other criminals-*camorristi* that have committed crimes in Germany,

I would like to name TS, who belongs to the Licciardi clan, and in Germany the most important robberies are done by him. He has a lover in Germany and when he goes there he lives with her.... I would like to add that [this] person ... was part of AZK's group and participated with him when he committed robberies in Germany" (GGv, 14/1/1999: 6). This type of activity does not appear to be connected to the clan in the same way as functional mobility; although organized, it was much more random, and individuals committed crimes when they felt like it. They appear to have relied on a community or pool of Neapolitan immigrants permanently resident in Germany who, when called on, acted as a logistical support system. As the *pentito* Carmine Schiavone suggests, "DL remains a *mafioso* and I do not exclude that he could have provided mafia members with a base" (CSv, 30/4/1997: 3).

Third, the functional mobility of petty criminals was detected. The boss Raffaele Giuliano explains how, in Germany, a group of Neapolitans undertook acquisitive crimes such as jewelry robberies and burglaries. Goods were then returned to Naples to sell to the coordinator of the stolen jewelry market, an associate of the Misso clan (see ch. 5):

> In that period, there was a burglary on a jewelry representative in Cologne; I remember how they punctured one of his car wheels while he was traveling to force him to stop.... The support was given by SC. They stole diamonds worth 400–500 million lire, money that was made once the goods were sold in Naples. The goods were bought by Peppe [De Tommaso],[4] who owned a jewelry shop.... A similar burglary ... was undertaken in Paris, always against jewelry representatives. The group acted in the same way ... the modalities of the burglary were identical to that in Cologne.... The stolen goods from Paris were sold to Peppe [De Tommaso]. They made 1 billion lire selling these goods. (RGv, 14/6/2000: 5)

Criminal tourism is a type of Camorra presence in Europe, even if it is not in a traditional form. There was no Camorra settlement here, but forms of acquisitive crime that were linked to it in various ways, and in particular, the management of stolen goods. We see how even nontraditional Camorra activities are linked to Naples and how European countries were targeted by *camorristi* for resources while remaining bound to Naples.

## The Counterfeit Market

In 2002 German police estimated that 4.2 percent of crimes undertaken by non-Germans were related to the sale of fake goods (BKA-NS, 2003: 10), and by 2012 this had risen to 6.3 percent (BKA-NS, 2012: 7). Unlike other European police forces, the BKA discovered, by chance after a tip-off, the production and distribution of counterfeit goods by Camorra clans in November 1990. Germany appears to have been one of the first countries to be targeted by the expansion of the Secondigliano alliance, although for the whole postwar period *camorristi* have been close to those involved in the clothes trade and to street-sellers (see Brancaccio, 2015).

In 1993, the German and Italian Ministries of the Interior established close bilateral agreements and subsequently an "Italo-German task force" to jointly monitor and investigate cross-border activities (DIAb). As a result, they were able to ascertain what was happening in the counterfeit market relatively quickly. The German authorities tackled this criminal activity at the EU level by focusing on it during their European Presidency and at the G8 summit in 2007 (EC1: 5). The Dutch police, on the other hand, have not linked this crime to mafias even though Rotterdam is the biggest port for counterfeit items entering the EU. This activity has clearly been thriving; 65 million counterfeit articles were seized in 2008 in the Netherlands alone (UNODC2: 177).[5]

In 2002, the Neapolitan judiciary officially identified what they describe as a "holding company" operating internationally, extensively involved in the counterfeit market and managed directly by the Secondigliano alliance (QN4, 1: 32–33). This was the first identified Camorra group to enter this sector and establish an internal counterfeit division. Different Camorra city groups have since become greatly involved in this sector—not just one clan but the two main city alliances and their allied partners as well: the Secondigliano alliance (and the smaller Di Lauro clan) and the Mazzarella-Misso cartel (with its allies, the Caldarelli clan).

With the fall of the Berlin Wall in 1989, the Secondigliano alliance targeted German and East European markets with fake leather jackets, a compulsory fashion item for all youngsters. They produced the goods in Italy and then distributed them around Europe, usually by car inland, although other goods (such as electronic items from China) were shipped via containers. The German counterfeit market has remained a reliable market for the Camorra, as clans are familiar with it; the risks are perceived as low, and the profits high.

The situation in Germany during the 1990s was probably representative of what was taking place in other European countries, but little is known about the Netherlands. However, given its geographical proximity to Germany and its reputation for lax law enforcement among *camorristi*, there may have been activity there. During an interrogation in 1999, the *pentito* GG claimed that in the Netherlands an associate of the Secondigliano alliance ran a shop selling false Rolex watches and fake leather jackets, which he used as a cover for his drug-trafficking operations (TN11: 50). But the lack of Dutch investigations[6] means that this claim cannot be verified, and it remains difficult to assess the true extent of the Camorra's presence in the Netherlands.

Although the counterfeit scenario in Europe today has evolved considerably, these cases highlight how clans develop business opportunities, use host countries to further their interests, adapt their organizational structures and internal codes to ensure invisibility, and acquire the necessary facilitators to do so. The case of the Secondigliano alliance illustrates the first phase of the Camorra's involvement in this market, whereas the Rinaldi clan shows how clans perpetually imitate each other.

## The Counterfeit Market, the Secondigliano Alliance, and the Rinaldi Clan

This is the story of the Secondigliano alliance[7] from the northern Neapolitan suburbs of Scampia, Secondigliano, Case Rose, Poggioreale, Piazza Garibaldi, and Giugliano, and the Rinaldi clan from the district of Rione Nuova Villa in San Giovanni a Teduccio. Both were active in the international counterfeit market, controlling and recruiting Neapolitan door-to-door sellers to hawk their imitation goods in Germany, Europe, and beyond.[8] The former was active from the late 1980s onward and behaved as an international company—let's call it the Secondigliano counterfeit company—whereas the latter was active during 2009 and operated more like a traditional small family business.

By the early 1990s the powerful Secondigliano alliance had developed an extensive economic structure and geographical presence that transcended national borders and expanded into the international counterfeit market. Its company-like structure was a division within the alliance that specialized in the importing, production, and selling of counterfeit goods. It functioned as a mutable network with members located abroad, but it was intrinsically linked back to its permanent headquarters in Italy. Thus our analysis is as much about its organization in Naples as it is about its presence in Germany. Starting in Hof, it expanded its economic activities around the world, even taking over and reorganizing the American counterfeit market in 2000 (see QN4, 1: 55) and Latin America, where it is still believed to be present today. The Rinaldi clan, on the other hand, was a smaller outfit. Its leaders had repeatedly fled to Hamburg in 1996 and again in 2009, where they set up a counterfeit operation. This was a new business venture for them because in Naples they specialized in drugs.

The stories recounted here are not about Camorra clans moving out of Naples to settle a colony abroad or convert the Neapolitan immigrant community to their ways. Rather, they are about the economic strategies of clans that sought to exploit opportunities in host countries by infiltrating a foreign illegal sector.

## THE CLANS: THEIR MEMBERS AND TERRITORIES

The Secondigliano alliance was a confederation made up of the Licciardi, Contini, and Mallardo families. In 2011, it was estimated that there were 75 members in the Licciardi clan, 220 in the Contini clan, and 110 in the Mallardo clan (QN13), compared with 15 in the Contini clan in 1988 and only 4 in the Mallardo clan (AC1–1 in Allum, 2000: 374, 385). These figures do not reflect the true power of this alliance, its extensive membership, and deep roots in the local community. The Rinaldi clan, by contrast, was smaller and always perceived as more compact. In 1994, it was estimated that under Vincenzo Rinaldi, it had 62 members (Allum, 2000: 408), and by 2011, together with its allies, the Altamura-Reale clans, it had 110 members[9] and had become an ally of the Secondigliano alliance (QN13).

Towards the end of the first Camorra war in the early 1980s, some even say later, between 1988 and 1989 (CAv, 29/3/94: 1), the Secondigliano alliance emerged as the dominant criminal force in the city. Its three main clans had all been members of the anti-Cutolo fraternity, the NF.[10] Initially, this alliance was a strategic marriage of convenience: the three main criminal families were "one thing" (CVv, in TN19: 8), and became a strong and homogenous alliance across Naples between 1989 and 1996. They had immense power and "were an important stable, powerful organization" that had "a continuous structure" (LGv, 20/3/2003: 8), unlike other more fragile clans.

The criminal equilibrium to the east of the city after the end of the first Camorra war was in a state of flux because of the "continuous games of alliances and clashes between clans" (FAv, 12/6/1997, in QN3, 1: 176). These districts were controlled by a myriad of clans that reflected the NCO versus NF ideological divide. The Formidable-Altamura clans close to the NCO were on one side, and the Rinaldi clan on the other, under the protection of the larger NF-Mazzarella family. The Rinaldi family became a clan in its own right between 1989 and 1992 (QN3), having previously carried out burglaries and sold smuggled cigarettes for its alma mater (AC3: 1).

To be an efficient international organization functioning in more than one location, strong leadership is indispensable. Leaders provide direction, foresight, and strategy. In return, they demand respect because "authoritarian leadership, which is autocratic, aims at obedience" (Rowan, 1976: 70). The historical leaders of the Secondigliano alliance were the three charismatic leaders of the individual families: Gennaro Licciardi (a Scigna'),[11] Eduardo Contini (Faccia d'Angelo or "O Romano"), and Francesco Mallardo (Ciccio di Carloantonio). They were connected by blood: three sisters were married to Mallardo, Contini, and Patrizio Bosti, one of the leaders of the Licciardi clan (PN5: 16, 29). Family and intermarriages were an essential binding mechanism for Neapolitan criminal alliances, producing stable roots in the local community.[12]

It was the Licciardi clan that came to manage the counterfeit company. Growing up in a large family,[13] Gennaro Licciardi, the leader of the alliance until his death in 1994, had undertaken his criminal apprenticeship under the boss Luigi Giuliano, becoming one of his lieutenants. Eager and criminally intelligent, he soon established his own independent clan in his home district of Secondigliano. He was considered "reliable, charismatic" (CAv, in PN5: 12), and "humble" (GP), the "'true' criminal mastermind behind the Secondigliano alliance and its internal counterfeit division" (GGv, 14/1999: 5),[14] and the "supreme controller" of the Secondigliano district and surrounding areas (PN5: 23).

In the beginning, it was solely blood ties that designated leadership roles in the alliance, but this soon evolved to a looser confederation model in which leadership became multidimensional, rotating, and reactive. Compared with other criminal groups such as the Sicilian Mafia, there no longer existed one constant leader or a fixed trio of leaders, but rather representatives from the most powerful families. All were on equal terms, with smaller peripheral clans showing them total obedience. This meant that "clans interlinked their competences across a vast territory that is Secondigliano, using criminal control that extends across the whole of the city and through alliances and representatives that extend across the province and the Casertano region" (PN5: 25). This powerful, coordinated Neapolitan leadership was strong and respected in the local community because it provided jobs, salaries, stability, and imposed law and order. The drawback was that it became vulnerable to challenges from emerging bosses who contested the existing order. This criminal leadership and alliance did reproduce itself abroad, but not its subordinate relationships with the minor gangs (GP, see chapter 6).

Antonio Rinaldi ('O Giallo), was the first leader of the Rinaldi clan to break free from Mazzarella control. He was charismatic, had remarkable criminal ability (see QN3), and it was suggested that he was very keen to achieve his own independence and autonomy like many other up and coming young *camorristi*. This raw hunger resulted in the elimination of Antonio and his brother Vincenzo because their former patrons did not accept their search for freedom. Indeed, "popular rumor at the time was that 'the Yellow One' had become bigger than Vincenzo Mazzarella, and this was the motive for his murder" (AFv, in QN3, 1: 22), why he was physically eliminate[d]" in December 1989 (QN3, 1: 26). Vincenzo was duly murdered in 1996 after an escalation in violence between both clans.

Pietro Licciardi ('O Fantasma), the younger brother of Gennaro, was a leader of the criminal alliance who in 1982 became an executive managing director of the Secondigliano counterfeit company. Initially, he was not perceived as a natural-born leader because, although he had been a small-time criminal, having been arrested at the age fifteen for theft, he "had never [really] been on the streets" (PN5: 24) and lacked the necessary criminal skills. But in time he was able to assert his authority, becoming both "the most powerful leader" (PN5: 28) and a respected executive managing director because he combined experience with competence. He had gained good firsthand knowledge of the *magliari* network during the early 1980s in the north of Italy with his friends and on visits to Germany while he was developing as a criminal (QN4; PN5).

A constant physical presence in Secondigliano, where the clan was criminally active, was essential to reinforce its headquarters. This territorial presence, and its resulting local recognition and power, were fundamental for clan leaders to guarantee social consensus and profit. For example, in 2001 Pietro's sister, Maria, and her husband represented her two brothers in the local day-to-day running of the clan and the alliance's criminal activities while they were in prison (see TN15). Without this stable territorial presence, the leaders would have been unable to uphold their power in the local community.

It was no different for the management of the counterfeit company, which also required local coordination and a hands-on approach. Most decisions about the company's activities were systematically made in Naples, where the company held its informal board meetings to discuss business. One area manager based in Germany was told that "the instructions had come from Naples and it was to Naples that [he] had to request any form of change" (QN4, 1: 127). Thus no decisions were made autonomously by area managers. This was made clear by one local manager who affirmed: "they have decided this in Naples, I cannot do anything about it" (QN4, 1: 46). Once taken, decisions were relayed to the different levels of the network across Europe, either face-to-face or over the telephone. The telephone was often used to issue instructions, orders, and threats, demonstrating how even intimidation could become mobile if necessary.

But when physical presence was needed, and to remedy the potential loss of local power, a loyal representative was handpicked to carry messages across Europe. When Pietro was forced to move to Prague and Chemnitz between March 1998 and June 1999, where he worked in a clothes shop,[15] his trusted lieutenant acted as a true "ambassador" (QN4, 1: 168) and commuted between Prague and Naples, the company's headquarters. He was a shuttle, bringing the boss's instructions back to the board of directors' meetings in Naples, where they were discussed and approved. These arrangements developed perhaps out of necessity or perhaps because of the nature of the counterfeit market, but proved to be a flexible system of decision making and a real collaborative effort. But, the boss would always have the last word. The Secondigliano company's board of directors had no intention of moving its headquarters away from Naples or of managing its counterfeit activities independently from Germany.

The leaders of the Rinaldi clan were also determined by strong blood ties. After Antonio's murder in 1989, it was his older and more charismatic brother, Vincenzo, who took over (see QN3). And when Vincenzo was murdered in 1996, their older brother, Gennaro Rinaldi ('O Leone), became the boss. Their leadership style was conventional, forceful, and imposing, but to avoid extermination they left Naples with their families (QN3, 1: 174) and regrouped in Germany. This absence created a local vacuum, rendering them fragile as rival clans contested their territorial supremacy in San Giovanni. No matter how charismatic or intelligent a leader, if he is not physically present in the home territory, the clan becomes vulnerable. Because of this, in 2009 their loyal foot soldiers and the organizers of counterfeit activities remained in San Giovanni a Teduccio as a necessary physical presence while the leaders relocated to Hamburg.

The confederation structure of the Secondigliano alliance had two local organizational levels: a clan level in individual districts and an alliance level across the region. The criminal configuration of the Licciardi clan was that of a "generational family" made up of brothers, sisters, and in-laws (PGv, in TN19: 43). This inner core based on blood ties continually reinforced the existing solidity; their kinship ties and daily interaction produced criminal stability. These relationships were based on traditional values such as respect, loyalty, security, obedience, commitment, confidence, dignity, and courtesy, but these could also be interpreted as constraints. The outer core was made up of reliable foot soldiers who often had a special bond with individual leaders; they worked for their family on a day-to-day basis, looking after their physical welfare (even on holiday), protecting them in their home territory, while also working in the illegal department, such as XC, who "had a trusted role in the family" and was "completely trusted by the leader" (TN19: 231–32). These faithful lackeys had indispensable jobs in the local territory, to protect the leaders. They never moved to host countries, nor were they involved in the counterfeit division in Naples.

The second level contained the main partners of the alliance: the inner core, the leaders and brothers-in-law, Eduardo Contini and Francesco Mallardo, and their relatives. These solid family ties were the underpinning of the criminal alliance in Naples (see PN17), but abroad this level manifested itself as local area managers representing their specific clan's interests in the counterfeit company. Forming the outer core of this level of the alliance were subordinate strategic satellite clans, such as the Piccirillo clan from the Torretta or the Calone clan from Posillipo, smaller groups described as the "ribs" of the Licciardi clan

(TN19: 11). These faithful allies were located across the city and acted as supporters, assistants, and foot soldiers who were all paid a regular salary and looked after by the alliance. These two organizational levels were based on traditional criminal values, regular salaries, and social consensus; they remained deeply embedded in Naples and never moved abroad.

During the 1980s, much of the alliance's internal structure was ad hoc and disorganized, with many members multitasking or overlapping in their roles, although profits were distributed according to a quota system among the three main alliance families.[16] By the late 1990s, a major rationalization had been introduced in many clans. The clans now resembled "crime enterprises," which were corporate-like with criminal activities efficiently organized into two departments: (1) the illegal department (made up of different divisions dedicated to a set territorial activity: extortion rackets, drug trafficking and selling, illegal lottery, counterfeit) and (2) the legal department (made up of a recycling and investments division).

Each division operated separately but communicated with others at the clan and alliance level. Each division had different methods; some had international structures whereas others remained local. For example, the Contini clan's drug division focused mainly on importation and left distribution to other organizations and individuals. Members' tasks, roles, responsibilities, and duties were all related to their division. For example, members in the extortion division did not travel abroad, but those in the drugs division did. Parallel to work in the various divisions, members also specialized in the use of violence so they could undertake military duties if commissioned: either in their divisions or if called on by the leadership for specific murders or violent acts. Some members could be both killers and involved in the extortion or drugs divisions.

Although each clan had its own divisions, it also had common projects. The Secondigliano counterfeit company was one such project. It is believed that this company was established in 1982 when the alliance invested money in certain producers of fake goods. This common division operated as a traditional holding company with a pan-European structure. Its headquarters were located in Naples and had two managing directors and a stable board of directors (see figure 3.1). The managing directors were not outsiders, but the boss, Pietro Licciardi, and his business acquaintance, Zinzi. Zinzi, a local boy from Secondigliano, already owned a company that produced imitation clothes as well as importing and exporting them (TN11, TN15).

The board of directors assisted the managing directors, both financially and logistically (QN4, 1: 38–41). At this top decision-making level the economic entity fused with the criminal agenda: *camorristi* and businessmen came together to make decisions about the company and direct general operations. They

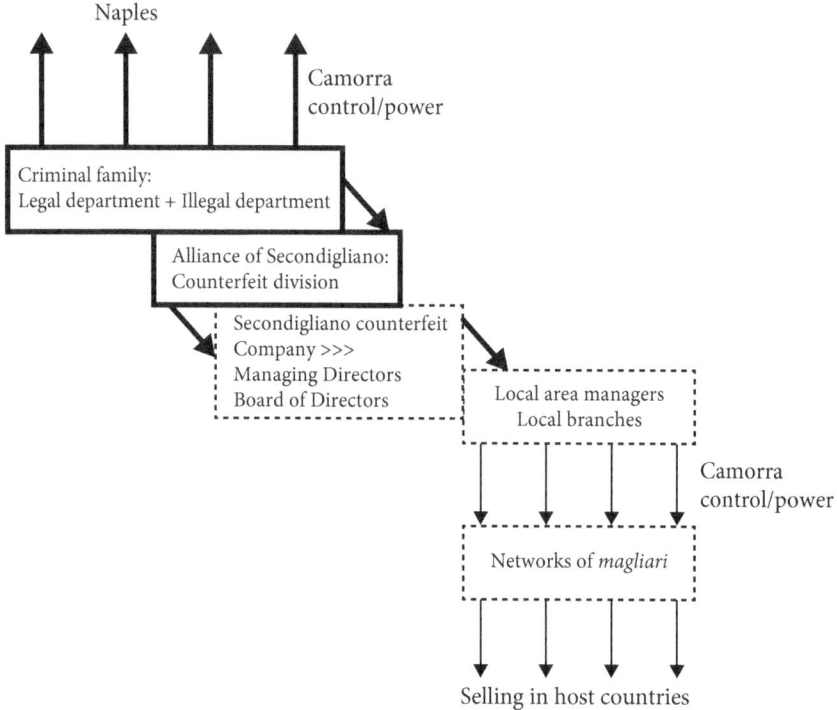

**FIGURE 3.1** Organizational structure of the Secondigliano alliance (1990–2001)

coordinated the local activities: managed the transport of goods, did the accounting, and took care of the financial investments (QN4, 2: 2). In particular, they managed the personnel based abroad, which included local area managers, who administered the warehouses in situ, and the door-to-door salesmen, the *magliari* network.

These activities in Europe were managed by shady businessmen of Neapolitan origin, some of whom had settled abroad and had dubious pasts; they "were chosen and appointed by those who in Naples managed the whole organization" (QN4, 3: 1). They were handpicked because of their friendship with the leaders, but also because of their detailed knowledge of the counterfeit sector. These associates lived abroad and managed operations for the alliance, but regularly traveled back to Naples to receive instructions. As one associate in Germany said to another, "I have been in touch with Naples to know what I should do" (QN4, 3: 78). When the company took over the German market in 1990, "the whole operation took place following precise instructions from Pietro Licciardi" (QN4, 1: 124), who was based in Naples. This board of directors can be described as a permanent "floating community" (Venkatesh, 2013: 53).

The lowest level of the company was the workforce: the existing *magliari* network. These were Neapolitan door-to-door salesmen who traveled around Europe and were close to *camorristi* (Brancaccio, 2015). Francesco Rosi's 1959 film, *I Magliari*, depicts their activities well. Previously, these street-sellers were independent and worked alone as freelancers. Now the Camorra company reorganized their activities and forced them into becoming its employees. Confronted with such violence, they became the counterfeit company's extensive workforce, selling Camorra-produced fake goods at its prices.

This was not a Camorra clan but a counterfeit network. Made up of about ninety-seven members including the board of directors and local managers as well as producers and *magliari*, it was mainly composed (88 percent) of men (see PN6, TN11). The women (12 percent) were either related to the board of directors or used as front names. The average age was roughly forty-one years, the range being seventeen to seventy-three (TN11). Some members were residents in Canada, Australia, Switzerland, Germany (Hof, Chemnitz, Berlin), France (Paris), and Greece (Athens). Of the ninety-seven members, all but two were born in Campania: one was born in Australia but lived in Campania, the other was a Greek citizen born and bred in Greece. Of the seven members of the board of directors, only two lived abroad, in Berlin, and of the whole network, another five were residents abroad. Thus this network was predominately Neapolitan, although open to Neapolitans living abroad, with one foreign collaborator. They were all Italian speakers.

Figure 3.2 highlights a solid Camorra alliance in Naples; part of it became a fluid business network between territories, the Secondigliano company. This network, owing to the nature of its economic activities, includes members from different clans and non-Camorra members. Overall, we note how many members of the network do not work in one specific territory but are constantly connecting different geographical locations (white), whereas those who are permanently based abroad are not members of the clan (black). We also note a group that is peripheral to the business network and permanently located in Naples (grey): they are all clan members and have leadership positions in the Secondigliano

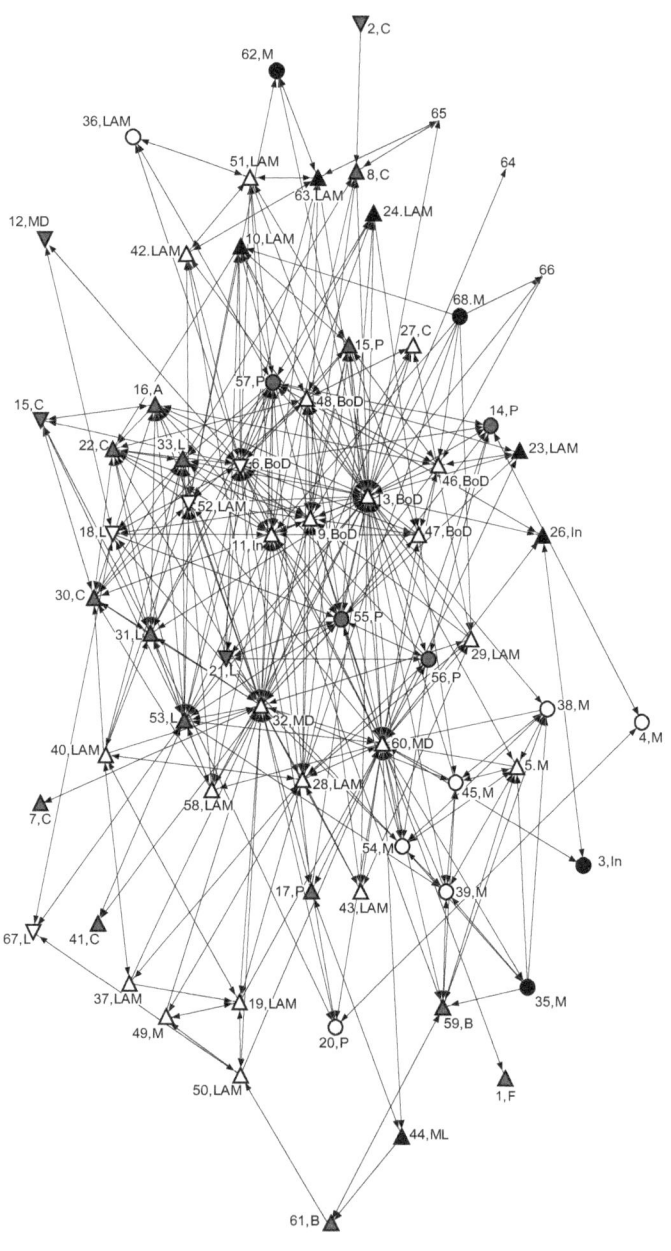

**Key**

Colors: grey (Naples/Italy), black (abroad), white (travels)

Shapes: △ = clan member  ○ = non-clan member  ▽ = other clan

Roles: businessmen (B), managing director (MD), producer (P), *magliaro* (M), member (C), local area manager (LAM), board of directors (BoD), leader (L), investor (In), accomplice (A), front name (F), money launderer (ML)

**FIGURE 3.2** The Secondigliano counterfeit company across Europe (1990–2001)

*Note:* This network was constructed using the flying squad's three police volumes (QN4), whereas the counterfeit network information was taken from TN11.

alliance. Only three individuals (nodes 3, 62, 68) are not members but have leadership roles in the counterfeit network. It is for this reason that both executive managers, the most active elements of the network (32 and 60, the top managers), connect the main actors of the networks: at one level, the *magliari* (4, 5, 35, 39, 38, 45, 49, 54, 62, 68), at another, the producers (14, 20, 56, 55, 57, 16) and investors (326, 11), even though they may not have been in the same country.

A closer comparative look at the composition of the Licciardi clan and the counterfeit company (see TN11, QN4) demonstrates that whereas the gender difference is the same, the average age of clan members was younger and the company's members were more widely located. According to a judicial investigation of the two main rival city alliances in 1997, the average age of members[17] was thirty-two, with 3.5 percent women (PN5). By 2009, the core Licciardi clan's average age was still thirty-six, with 11 percent women (see TN19).

The Rinaldi clan was also an intimate criminal group based on a generational family. Its leadership revolved around five siblings and their cousins, and as such, there was no elaborate internal structure. Compared with the Secondigliano company, it adopted a simpler business structure, a basic network with members in different locations: in Naples, those who organized the production of fake clothes, and in Hamburg, a loose coordination of activities by the leader, who imposed his products and conditions on Neapolitan *magliari*. No intermediary structures, no board of directors or local area managers, but a tight family network with wives and friends involved in counterfeit activities across Europe. The clan connected its local and host territories into a simple business cycle. The lack of sophistication is exemplified by the clan's choice of ordinary courier service for transportation of their fake goods (AC3: 4).

Although more rudimentary, according to a 2009 police document it nevertheless involved about thirty-two people, with the majority of them located abroad (see figure 3.3). The main nucleus of the leadership was Neapolitan, but living in Hamburg (nodes 1, 2) with their families (3–7), whereas about 41 percent of the network were made up of traveling *magliari* (16–28), and 44 percent were Italians involved in semilegal activities based in Germany and Switzerland (11, 12, 14, 29, 30, 31). The average age was forty-two, and 16 percent of the network were women (4, 5, 6, 7, 9) who also traveled. This was a very simple hierarchical clan (the network has the shape of a star), including not only the counterfeit structure but also trusted Italian businessmen. The different locations show this was a highly mobile network in which Naples played a less central role than in other cases because money did not systematically return there.

Both organizational structures are at odds with the existing literature (see Van Duyne, 1993: 99); these were not just flexible networks but were linked to a solid alliance permanently fixed in Naples, with mobile managers who organized

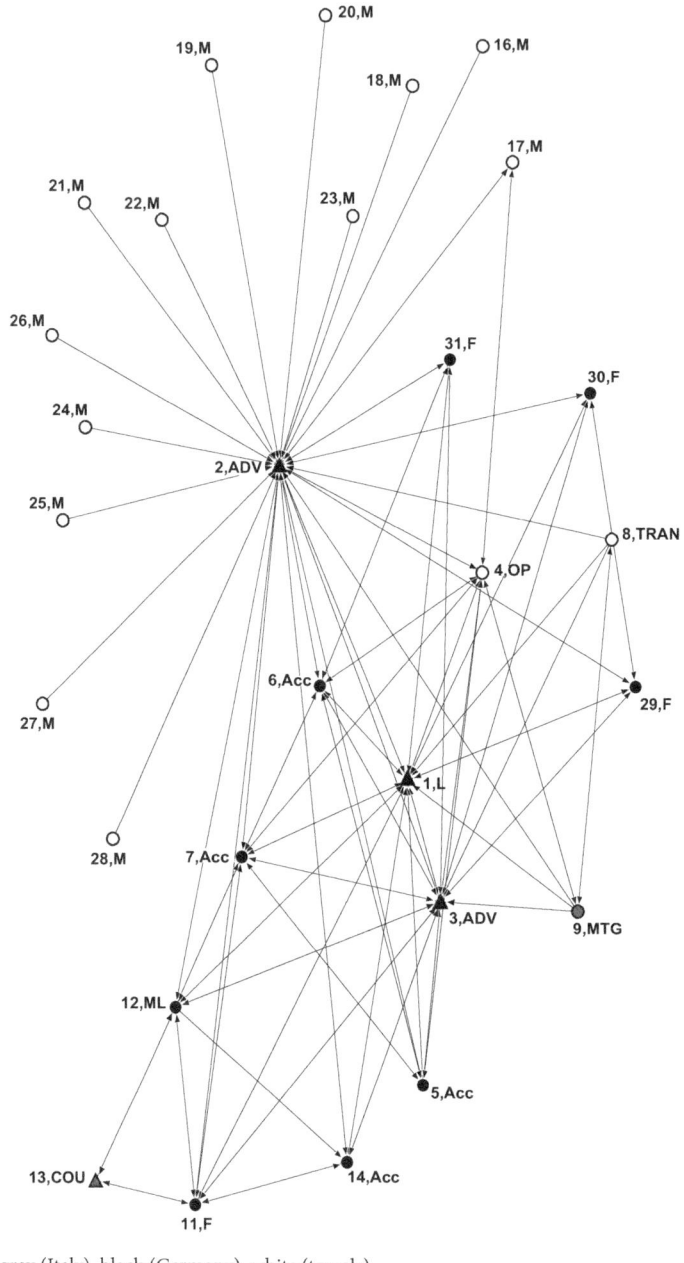

**Key**

Colors: grey (Italy), black (Germany), white (travels)

Shapes: △ = clan member   ○ = non-clan member   ▽ = other clan

Roles: Camorra leader (L), Camorra adviser (ADV), organizer of production (OP), organizer of transport (TRAN), accomplice (Acc), money launderer (ML), manager of transport (MTG), front name (F), accountant/clan (COU), *magliaro* (M)

**FIGURE 3.3** The Rinaldi clan and its counterfeit network in Hamburg (2009)

warehouses in the main trading countries. In other words, a Camorra group in Naples became a business network structure as it moved out of Italy.

Women are a clear element of stability. In the Secondigliano alliance they have always been particularly active and vocal, as GG made clear in 1998: "women (wives, sisters, or mothers of the leaders) have had an important, not a secondary, role in many decisions" (GGv, 28/10/98: 3–4). Women were involved in drug selling and the general welfare of the clan (surveillance, looking after guns, accounting, etc.), but one woman has been particularly significant. A former member recalls: "Maria Licciardi ... is known as a leader of the clan whom her brother Gennaro asked for advice before taking pivotal decisions; she is considered to be a clever criminal strategist" (TN19: 41). The boss, Carmine Alfieri, had already noted her presence in the 1990s: "I know that Gennaro Licciardi had a sister who was involved with the clan's activities" (PN5: 49); she was "the real confidante of her brother" (GGv, 28/10/98: 3–4) and "someone to be reckoned with" (PGv, in TN19: 46). Her importance can be deduced from the fact that "she was also accompanied in her movements by a bodyguard and patrol" (PN5: 49).

Out of the four Licciardi sisters, Maria was the oldest and was emblematic of strong, influential, and active Camorra women (see QN1), although it is unclear whether she was allowed to take on this role because she was related to the leaders or because of her own specific skills. She replaced her brothers while they were in prison and managed various divisions in the illegal department. She made decisions, developed strategies, gave advice, and managed the clan's accounts (TN19; see also QN4). We know, for example, that on one occasion she decided to give money to a prisoner in the same cell as another member (QN4, 1: 18–19). To be taken as seriously as her brothers she had to demonstrate the brutality and ruthlessness of a man. Thus many considered her vindictive—the evil spirit of Camorra women (TN19: 36–70), with her "cruelty," her "determination," and "her spirit of revenge" (GPv, in TN19: 16).

She was also the only woman to have an active role in the counterfeit company. Not a formal member of the board, she was fully involved in its management and accounts, but never traveled abroad to organize the *magliari* workforce. She assisted her brother Pietro greatly. Luigi Giuliano explained that in the 1990s, "it was Maria Licciardi who was in charge and who managed the leather jackets sector" (LGv, 5/2/2003). Others have argued that she was one of its "cashier[s] ... she was the brain behind this operation" (TN15: 22). She demonstrates the flexible nature of management roles in the company, forever changing when necessary.

Women in the Rinaldi clan were also present, but compared with Maria they appear to have been less active. In 2009, they appear to participate in counterfeit operations in Naples, perhaps because they were considered to be above suspicion, perhaps because they were freer to do so. In particular, they managed the production and transportation of fake goods to Hamburg. It was the women who would "look after the transfer of the parcels that contained jackets, tracksuits, and other counterfeit clothes from Naples to Germany. They would also have the specific task of identifying the factories producing the goods in Naples and choosing the type of clothes to sell," as well as paying the couriers who sent the parcels to Germany (AC3: 6). Without their efficient participation this criminal activity would have been more problematic.

Recruiting the right kind of people into any organization is crucial, especially for an illegal company or criminal clan that exists in two locations. In Naples, both clans recruited their foot soldiers using the normal criminal channels: either from family or from the pool of local petty criminals. However, the recruitment policy employed for counterfeit activities by the Secondigliano company was more transnational, whereas the Rinaldi clan recruited Neapolitans directly in Germany. For both organizations, there was no overlap between foot soldiers and *magliari*.

For the Secondigliano counterfeit company, the alliance recruited for two types of jobs: the board of directors and local area managers, and the *magliari* network. The directors were co-opted into the criminal project through their contacts with the leaders, whereas the local managers were recruited for their knowledge and because of their marriages with relatives of the Secondigliano alliance (see Brancaccio, 2011a). These positions were versatile and had frequent personnel turnover. To recruit *magliari*, the company used two techniques. First, it used violence to enroll the existing Neapolitan *magliari* in Europe. This is where the Camorra remains true to its local roots: it used threats and violence to take control of their activities, shops, and products. This *magliari* community was terrorized by Camorra representatives into becoming their employees, and as they recognized Camorra power and threats, which native citizens might not, they soon gave in.

The case of Vincenzo Orsini and his associate, Pasquale Silvestro, in Hof are emblematic of the methods used to recruit *magliari*. Orsini became the "object of special attention by [a criminal] organization that wanted to take over his business" (QN4, 1: 42). He was ordered to close his shop; that order "had come from Naples" (QN4, 1: 42, 44). The criminal clan duly got its way, as a police report made clear: "the following [day] 18/11/1990, PV [member of the board of directors] took possession of Orsini's shop in Hof" (QN4, 1: 42). Once the company took over the existing supply chain and distribution warehouses of individual *magliari* based in various European cities, it effectively controlled the previously independent *magliari* network.

The second recruitment method was local in Naples: leaders enrolled new *magliari* to sell their counterfeit goods in Europe. The unemployed Raffaele

Pascarella explains his job interview: "A certain Pietro (of about forty to forty-five years of age) asked me whether I wanted to sell fake leather jackets for the company, [called] CCC. I agreed. Then they told me that if I sold abroad, I could make more money, selling the jackets at double the price. In 1994, l bought two thousand jackets from the CCC company. I sold many jackets, which allowed me to make about 14,000 lire a month (TN11: 543–544). Judging from this evidence, the counterfeit company never engaged native *magliari* in host countries, they were always Neapolitans recruited in Naples.

The Rinaldi clan, on the other hand, was able to enroll young Neapolitans as *magliari* in Germany. SE is a case in point. Unemployed, he left Italy to seek work in Germany, but was recruited as a door-to-door salesman by the clan. He became involved in its counterfeit fraud and sold fake clothes to at least thirty-one old-age pensioners in Germany: "he would have sold poor-quality leather items at expensive prices, paying a percentage of his profit as a tax to the Neapolitan clan."[18] This fraud targeted frail and elderly Germans and was not directly linked to its traditional Camorra activities.

In Naples, both organizations had strong internal value systems[19] that determined their *modi operandi*, their rules, regulations, and codes of behavior. It is perhaps easier to document the alliance's system because its power was more pervasive, its membership more extensive, and its use of violence more visible than that of the smaller Rinaldi clan. However, both are less easy to trace in Europe. In Naples the value system was based on cultural and criminal values (Allum, 2006), such as *omertà*, violence, respect, and traditional ways of life, which the alliance used to impose its rules over both its members and civil society in order to produce social consensus. In Germany, the company did not impose these values on civil society but merely sold its goods, usually to unsuspecting vulnerable pensioners, because being violent and imposing *omertà* would have only drawn attention.

Violence and vendettas were frequently used in Naples to protect the alliance's existence and had the symbolic value of showing who was boss. Abroad, the Secondigliano counterfeit company did use violence and intimidation, but not against its German clients, as the investigating magistrate, Filippo Beatrice, made clear: "you can understand from the telephone intercepts that conflicts to conquer markets took place but not against Americans or French citizens, only against Neapolitans" (FB). Even in 2009, violence still appeared to be used (PN17). It sought to impose its power over, and retain obedience from, the *magliari*, Neapolitan immigrants living abroad, and rival Camorra counterfeit clans, especially if they resisted. Local German police had difficulty seeing this violence; as an officer explained, "because of their established subculture as well as the *omertà*, it is very difficult to recognize this organization [the Camorra] and therefore to fight it" (BKA2: 2).

This logic ruled in Naples for everyone: those who did not respect the boss's demands were punished. One *magliaro* was beaten on orders of the boss behind the Ausonia Theatre, Rione Amicizia, because he no longer wanted to sell their goods and wanted to be independent (TN11: 69). Similar violence and threats were used against Neapolitan producers if they did not do as they were told. But the board of directors always sought a peaceful solution because reckless violence abroad could damage their commercial activities long term (TN15).

Territorial control was also imposed through extortion, which became an essential tool to maintain hegemony. In Germany, however, this manifested itself only as an economic presence whereby local area managers controlled the type of goods and the prices of door-to-door sellers. Panzuto has also suggested that the *magliari* were the eyes and ears of the Secondigliano alliance in Europe, which could be interpreted as a form of territorial control, a way for the criminal group to know what was going on and identify new opportunities.

Lastly, the central value binding Camorra members together is money. A salary system is replenished from the common fund, which since 1985, has developed in parallel with its business structures to become a fixed value for the clan: "the system of salaries is not exclusive to the Licciardi clan but is common to all criminal organizations that more or less have a large number of members and supporters . . . there exists an organized system of distribution of monthly salaries to members, supporters, and friends" (QN4, 1: 21).

In Secondigliano, the salary system created a sense of identity around the clan, but it was never replicated in Germany, as members and *magliari* earned their money through the profits they made in selling goods. The same pattern appears for the Rinaldi clan: it was operative in Naples, whereas in Germany it was unnecessary because there were so few members. It is interesting that the Secondigliano company's profits made abroad were systematically sent back to Naples to the common fund. This was less obvious for the Rinaldi clan. The larger criminal clans thus became dependent on their economic system abroad to sustain the Neapolitan salary system.

## THE CLANS: THEIR ACTIVITIES

Both groups undertook traditional Camorra activities in Italy and abroad became an economic presence. Between 1990 and 2000, the Secondigliano alliance dominated criminal activities in Naples: "it controlled the city districts and the extortion rackets, the distribution of drugs and clandestine gambling in that territory" (QN12: 4), and became key players in the international counterfeit sector, having established operations both in Italy (Naples, Lago di Garda, and between the Veneto and Brescia regions) and abroad. The Rinaldi family business was not directly involved in counterfeit activities in Naples.

The Rinaldi clan in Naples was involved in a myriad of criminal activities, including managing an illegal lottery, armed robberies, extortion rackets, and selling heroin and cocaine, but not counterfeiting. It focused on drugs, which it bought from "suppliers belonging to various international cartels to sell across its territory," as drug trafficking had always been its main illegal activity (QN3, 1: 37). It also undertook extortion rackets against local businesses and was considered an extortion company, a holding *del pizzo*: Silvana Fucito, the owner of a paint shop in San Giovanni a Teduccio, refused to pay the clan's racket money and had her shop burned down on 19 September 2002.[20]

These criminal activities were fundamentally linked to the clan's territorial control. In this sense, the clan not only governed activities but also traded in many different goods. In Hamburg, none of these activities were reproduced; there the clan was purely involved in selling counterfeit goods and reinvesting its profit locally. It was not interested in physical control over the territory. Although in Naples the clan had little involvement with professionals, in Hamburg it had support from businessmen based in Germany and Switzerland (AC3).

The two main activities of the Licciardi clan and the Secondigliano alliance have always been extortion rackets and drug importation and distribution, which is why two specific internal organizational divisions emerged in their illegal department. The Licciardi clan undertook an array of extortions, from small local shopkeepers and the cleaning contract of the cemetery of Secondigliano to big building contractors (TN15). More subtle forms of extortion included clan members taking goods from shops without or only partially paying for them (see TN19). Extortion rackets were territorial and there is no direct evidence of the alliance undertaking them in Germany, or at least none have been openly reported. In addition to extortions, the alliance took over the Giuliano clan's illegal lottery system. This was a smaller, less profit-orientated activity, but its infrastructure had deep roots in the community, providing essential jobs that reinforced the alliance's local power base.

Clans in the alliance have always been involved in drug trafficking—the Contini clan in particular was considered the most active member, as the arrest of the boss Di Mauro in Barcelona, Spain, in January 2010 testifies (see PN17). In 1993, however, it could be suggested that the Licciardi clan took less of an interest in directly importing drugs (see TN19). Perhaps because it became involved in more lucrative activities that it was able to control more fully, perhaps the counterfeit market. Nevertheless, the clan remained involved in the local distribution of cocaine and heroin across the city, providing local employment and keeping its roots in the community. The alliance also sold drugs to smaller clans and was a constant supplier even when other clans, such as the Amato-Pagano clan, came to dominate imports during the early 2000s. Both the regular income and the territorial presence drug trafficking produced were the lifeblood of the clan and the alliance.

These territorial activities produced funds that needed cleaning and recycling by the legal department. More important, they produced the start-up funds for the alliance's new counterfeit division. Members laundered money through the legal department. The boss Carmine Alfieri explained: "I know that the Licciardi-Mallardo-Contini group recycled their enormous profits made from drug trafficking by using a 'medieval' system. They would threaten legitimate businesses and would gain exclusive control of them . . . thus, with as little hassle as possible, these activities maintained their appearance of belonging to their original owners" (CAv, in PN5: 17) while having dirty money pumped into them. More straightforward methods were also used. Clan members extensively bought watches, cars, and real estate registered under front names, as in the case of Pietro Licciardi, who would put properties in the name of family members who clearly did not have the financial means to buy them (TN19).

In short, the alliance's core activities were intrinsically territorial and its natural resources were exploited to produce power. The roots of the organization were sturdy and were characterized as much by the ends as by the means. Money was only the end product, but the means to generate this end product—Mafia methods and, specifically, the use of violence—were just as important. The alliance's activities abroad were different, more market orientated in nature with profit maximization as the prime motive camouflaging its criminal origin and rendering it invisible.

Although *camorristi* have always been close to *magliari*, investigators believe Germany was the first foreign country targeted by the counterfeit company in its move into the international counterfeit market. Guglielmo Giuliano recounts:

> After the fall of the Berlin wall, the organization led by Licciardi, Contini, and Mallardo started to operate in Eastern Europe, and in particular in East Germany. Using preexisting networks established by Neapolitans who were already present in Germany, they started a true and real monopoly in the commercialization of clothes, [and] false leather that was sold as real leather. They are specific types of clothes that are rather in demand in Eastern Europe, and Licciardi, Contini, and Mallardo forbade other criminal organizations to extend their own economic interests in Germany. . . . I also believe that the Secondigliano families had a monopoly on the selling of electric drills in Germany (TN11: 56).

This expansion went from concentrating purely on production to the commercialization of products. When the alliance went too far to the east and started to impinge on the markets of groups such as the Russian Mafia, it backtracked to avoid conflict (QN4, 1: 36). The company did not enter into an international alliance, but respected other criminal groups' territory and activities.

Until 1990, production and commercialization were separate activities; then the alliance decided to take over the commercialization phase too. The alliance concentrated on foreign markets and on controlling the whole process: producing and imposing fake items, dictating retail prices, and selecting markets for the *magliari* and demanding from them a percentage of their profits. As a result, the company took over strategic distribution warehouses and shops in Hof, Chemnitz, Prague, Paris, Lyon, London, Madrid, Athens, and Berlin, and placed their representatives as local area managers in these key locations.

Three things help explain this strategic commercial choice: First, the clans were familiar with the market and products, and were already investing in the production of fake goods in Italy, but not in the selling process. All the alliance had to do was to take control of the *magliari* network. Pietro Licciardi already knew this sector and had the right contacts. Second, all the structures of this new economic operation already existed. All the necessary personnel were already present in Germany: a Neapolitan community of *magliari* who could be beaten into obedience and an established infrastructure of friendly Neapolitan immigrant businessmen who could become local managers. PV and PG, members of the board of directors, are two good examples. PV lived in Germany between 1974 and 1982 and had been involved in some violent criminal acts there and was familiar with the country (QN4, 1: 44), whereas PG was related to the clan and had lived in Germany between 1983 and 1985; he not only knew the setting well but also the *magliari* network because "in Karlsruhe, he had legitimately sold leather items" (QN4, 1: 52[21]). Third, as already noted, Germany represented an extensive, virgin market for fake leather jackets, and there was a huge demand for this "must have" fashion item in Eastern Europe. These were all elements that would help ease the alliance's takeover of this market.

The five-stage business plan of the company did not follow the traditional pattern (see table 3.2). In Germany, the alliance used "its Camorra method," its systematic recourse to violence, to control the process. By analyzing the company's business development, it is possible to see how the local and host environments depended on each other, how they interacted between tasks and regions to the benefit of the local territory and the clans in Naples.

During pre-phase one, the basis of the operation was the knowledge that by using violence the company could impose its will and methods without any competition. This was decisive and would guarantee success. *Magliari* were not

**TABLE 3.2** The Secondigliano counterfeit company's development

| PHASES | TRADITIONAL ACTIVITIES | SECONDIGLIANO ALLIANCE BUSINESS ACTIVITIES |
|---|---|---|
| Pre-Phase One: | | Mafia methods |
| Phase One: | Initial investment | Initial investment from illegal profits (drugs, extortion in Naples) |
| Phase Two: | Production | Illegal factories in Campania / Production in China |
| Phase Three: | Transport | Transport via roads by *magliari* |
| Phase Four: | Commercialization | Impose products and materials on *magliari* network |
| Phase Five: | Reinvestment of profits | Return of money to Italy and investment in illegal and legal activities |

protected by the company, but had to adhere to its criminal project whether they accepted it or not. And if they did not agree, they were either beaten up, had their shops appropriated starting with shops in Hof, or were run out of town.

Once the company had gained control of the different *magliari* networks, placing its associates as local area managers, it then imposed its terms of business. Three conditions were imposed: First, *magliari* could use and buy goods only from Camorra suppliers. One *magliaro* explained, "I always had to buy the jackets from the organization" (see TN11: 547). Second, local area managers in Italy had to pay a fee (5 marks) per item sold (see QN4, 1: 47, 130), and so did the *magliari* who worked directly for the company: "They told me I could sell at whatever price I wanted but I had to give them 30,000 lire per jacket" sold (see TN11: 543). This bought permission to undertake commercial activity in Germany, but no protection was provided in return. And lastly, *magliari* had to sell their goods where the local manager had instructed.

Intimidation was also used to manage producers in Naples if they disobeyed orders. On one occasion, the alliance "threatened the Neapolitan factories and blocked them from sending their goods abroad" (QN4, 1: 61) because they were not respecting its instructions. Intimidation was characterized more by its ends than its means: the ends, the profits, were more important than the violence used to impose the criminal agenda.

Phase one, which can be dated at around 1990 and before, was the start-up phase. The accumulated funds made from the illegal department in Naples, in particular from drugs, were invested to establish a counterfeit division within the alliance. More precisely, the initial investment—illicit funds from local criminal activities—was made when the Licciardis gave money to a business associate to start up "a company-like structure" (TN11: 421; QN4, 1: 38). This became the Secondigliano counterfeit company, and it would manage the production and sale of Camorra counterfeit goods. As Luigi Giuliano clarified: "naturally the money invested in these activities comes from the illegal profits made from the crimes, which I have spoken of before [drugs, extortion rackets]" (LGv, 5/2/2003: 4). In other words, the profits made from drug dealing in Naples formed the economic foundation for the counterfeit company abroad.

The second phase was the production of goods. The importance of Naples becomes explicit in this phase. The choice of specific production method adopted depended on the clan, its contacts, and its access to resources. Some fake goods were produced in Italy, some in China. An artisanal method, initially preferred by the Secondigliano alliance, produced fake leather jackets and clothes, employing its local business contacts in Campania with factories in Secondigliano, Arziano, Casoria, Melito, and Como, northern Italy.[22] These contacts were factory owners, shop owners, producers, and company directors who adapted their resources to production for the alliance. Not every clan could become involved in this activity because basic machinery, financial resources, business networks, and planning skills were required.

Individuals close to the Contini clan developed a second approach as they concentrated on the production of electronic goods such as drills, cameras, and Bosch washing machines: the mass production method. Bosti, one of Contini's lieutenants, through contacts who had factories in the Far East, imported mass-produced fake goods via containers into the port of Naples (see TN15). The technique was to import the goods and then add fake labels once they had legally arrived in Naples. This is the predominant method today. A strategic decision was made by the Contini clan to invest in electronic goods to avoid direct competition with the Licciardi clan.

Phase three saw the transportation of products from Naples by car across Europe to Germany either by the local area managers or the *magliari*. Local area managers transported goods to their wholesale outlets and deposits so that *magliari* could come and stock up. Alternatively, *magliari* bought directly in Naples. As one recounted, "The last time I went to Austria was about nineteen days ago with my car, a Lancia Thema. I went on my own, and when I entered Austria I brought with me about thirty leather jackets" (TN11: 544).

Commercialization of fake goods was phase four. During the postwar period, *magliari* sold their goods in open-air markets or door-to-door. They were skillful and reliable sellers who had the gift of the gab. One *magliaro* explained his technique: "How did I sell the jackets? I invented a story about sales at the end of a fair. I sell the jackets from the car and I speak with people on the street. I sell about six jackets a day. When I sell on the street, I do not say that they are fakes. If I am asked, I say that they are fake leather jackets. If they ask me, I answer that they are made in an economic way, I do not say that they are real leather" (TN11: 544-45). The *magliari* were the last level of this commercial network. Their work was precarious, uncertain, ad hoc, and risky, with the potential for violence if they did not follow the strict instructions they received.

The fifth phase was the reinvestment of profits, which were "considerable" and "superior to those made from drugs" (LGv, 5/2/2003: 4), although this might not seem obvious. Traditionally, it is believed that the Camorra reinvests abroad, and there is evidence that the drug clans do this, as in the case of the Amato-Pagano, Nuvoletta, and Polverino clans. But the counterfeit company operated differently; the majority of the money was returned to Naples and into the clan's common fund. There were five main methods: First, via bank transfers just under the accepted limit for anti-money-laundering laws in order not to raise alarms in the bank (in particular, from the United States and Brazil). *Magliari* would transfer money back to relatives and friends. Second, money was physically returned to Naples by *magliari* traveling by car or plane or by people traveling by train. Third, some money was returned by post. Fourth, money transfers were used to return money from Switzerland. And lastly, one of the members of the board of directors would gamble money in a Venice casino to recycle it (QN4, 2:114). Whereas in other cases the investment phase dealt mainly with the investment of leaders' money, the money here was used for the clan's common fund. This reinvestment phase underlines how dependent the two territories were on each other.

Three different uses were identified for money returning to the local territory in Naples: First, it was mainly distributed according to the quota system for different alliance groups. Each clan received its share, which it used for internal clan business—the common fund paid salaries and legal assistance. The second use was to keep the counterfeit division afloat. The money paid for the production chain, in particular the factories and the raw materials. Once these two demands were satisfied, the remaining money was distributed among leaders and recycled into the legal economy with the complicity of accomplices who acted as front names or set up shell companies. Some examples of investments made by the Licciardi family include: "70 properties, including villas, deposits, industrial sites, the extensive industrial grounds of 22 companies, 15 factories producing and distributing clothes, 1 travel agent, 1 estate agent, and 1 gym" (QN12: 3).

The activities chosen by the Rinaldi clan abroad were new and unconnected to their criminal activities in Naples. In Hamburg, although members seemed to be involved in an Italian restaurant, they imitated the Secondigliano alliance's choice of counterfeiting activities. However, theirs was a very basic counterfeiting network that imported and sold clothes, leather jackets, and tracksuits as they identified gaps in the market. The German authorities described this as "frauds experienced by the unsuspecting elderly, who having bought leather garments, complained about the poor quality and packaging in relation to the price paid"

(AC3: 4). The clan became a loose network adopting an elementary business strategy based on the production and importation of counterfeit goods from Naples to Hamburg.

THE CLANS: THEIR ACCOMPLICES

Accomplices are essential to the Camorra's success; they are the backbone of the association, legitimizing its existence and connecting it to the rest of society. This is particularly true in the counterfeit market because of the need for sellers, producers, and investors. Accomplices helped the clans in various ways; they were not innocent bystanders or victims, but fully involved participants with an interest at heart. The community from which accomplices were sought here was a small self-interested business community with no scruples, often individuals who had a common past, experience, and values with the Camorra; a blurring of lines existed between legality and illegality and there was an exchange of contacts, knowledge, and skills. For example, in general many Camorra bosses have enjoyed support in Spain, on the Costa del Sol, where a community of Neapolitan businessmen has property and business interests.[23]

Not everyone feared the Secondigliano alliance, and some accomplices were able to engage with them as equals. One example was a local businessman who was a front name and who allowed members to buy precious watches, fast cars, and launder illegal profits in real estate. But he also had his own agenda and benefited financially, increasing his own profits by buying new properties (see TN19). He always kept his distance and his complicity remained ambiguous. It was not the overriding interests of the clan that predominated, but those of the individual partners; this businessman gave as much as he received.

The Secondigliano counterfeit company had many facilitators in Naples and Europe who were predominately Neapolitan and Italian; the Rinaldi clan, on the other hand, had a more restricted group based permanently in Hamburg and Switzerland. In Naples, with limited social capital, it had fewer accomplices, whereas abroad it had managed to identify some useful Neapolitan contacts in Hamburg who provided a logistical base, financial lay out, and cover, in particular, work in a pizzeria. Another businessman living in Switzerland provided organizational support. He was believed to manage, organize, and oversee counterfeit activity (AC3). Back in Naples, the producers of the fake goods were not co-opted and were probably unaware of the bigger criminal project.

Because the Secondigliano alliance leadership had social capital in Naples, the company benefitted from the help of useful accomplices with different roles and agendas. They were all "complicit," "collusive," or "compenetrative" (Sciarrone,

2011b), voluntarily participating in a criminal project, and by doing so exchanging skills and resources with *camorristi*. They were professional businessmen, not natural and automatic allies of the Camorra, who initially had no direct contact with the Neapolitan criminal underworld, but who in time became accomplices of the Camorra and the Secondigliano alliance in particular (TN15). There is, however, little evidence of the alliance's involvement with German businessmen.

VCT was the owner of a clothes company that produced fake leather jackets in factories based in Arzano, Campania. He had always worked closely with leaders of the Secondigliano alliance and "provided them with fake leather jackets that were sold all over the world" (QN4, 1: 58). He saw himself as "separate" from the alliance, although he was completely aware of its criminal status. He made his position clear when he stated: "I am the businessman." It is "the others" who "have always come to me" (ibid). He was a shrewd businessman with a strong sense of self, showed no loyalty to a specific clan, and was independent-minded. He did not come into direct contact with the executive managers or the *magliari*, but dealt solely with members of the board, and his behavior was that of someone who understood that he was vital to their commercial activities. A police document noted that he "is a producer who for his own activities uses the mediation of those who control the market. . . . The distinction in reality is very subtle because he is aware and conscious of operating next to a *camorrista*, not violating his authority but using it to increase his own production and profit" (ibid). Indeed, once he felt that he was no longer getting anything out of this partnership, he moved on and sought to do business with the rival Di Lauro clan. His engagement with Camorra clans was always on a temporary basis, and if conditions deteriorated he would not hesitate to change sponsors. His relationship with the clans can be defined as "instrumental" because he sought to maximize his own profit and not that of the criminal association; he was complicit.

MF lived in Paris and in 1986 became a member of the French Chamber of Commerce because he owned a clothes, fabric, and lingerie company. He also had various factories in Campania and businesses in Braunschweig (Germany) that sold fabric. Once close to Michele Zaza, he was "an old fashioned *magliaro*" (TN15: 22) who was now close to the Contini clan. During the 1980–1990s, he was the local manager who oversaw French operations. He owned a commercial warehouse, which was used as a wholesale outlet from where he organized the French *magliari* network, buying and selling them fake goods. But he also traveled frequently to his factories in Campania (Arzano, Casoria, and Melito), which produced leather jackets for the company (QN4, 1).

In 1998, he became an official employee of the Tatt Company when GA, Contini's representative, became the owner of different shops in Paris and Lyon (QN4,

3: 56). From that date onward, MF concentrated on making the French market a success. In this way, he became part of the Contini operation and assisted GA by obediently doing the accounts and taking orders. He also covered and protected him on one occasion, even hiding documents that the police were looking for. He fully colluded but did not pursue his own personal economic agenda. As a result, he was an important part of the chain, loyal and fully committed to the company without a sense of self, and he put his resources and skills at its disposal.

BC co-owned with a board member a clothes company (TN15) that produced leather jackets and clothes and sold cameras and drills (QN4, 1: 39). He became a member of the company before 1994 and often managed the financial interests of his friend the boss Vincenzo Licciardi as well as his own interests (QN4, 1: 78; TN15). His relationship with the alliance was completely different from that of VCT, whom he sought to replace when he distanced himself from the company. It was based on genuine friendship and financial investments, so he not only acted as a front name and money launderer but did what friends do: for example, he gave his brother's passport to Pietro Licciardi to go on the run to Prague in 1999 (QN4, 1: 39). This act demonstrates great devotion and a team spirit. But it is the emotive language he uses that clearly accentuates his attachment to the Camorra group: when the clan was undergoing a difficult moment, he stated: "*We*, instead, are always here" (QN4, 1: 81). His use of the expression "we," as in "we, the clan," indicates his strong sense of loyalty and shows that he did not consider himself an outsider.

## International Drug Trafficking

Germany and the Netherlands are important strategic countries for Neapolitan drug traffickers, but for different reasons. As the IMF noted in 2010: "Germany is not a significant drug cultivation or production country. However, Germany's location at the center of Europe and its well-developed infrastructure make it a major transit hub" (IMF: 22). Although Hamburg is an important harbor, in general Germany has been used by *camorristi* as a transit country rather than an entry point for drugs. The Netherlands, on the other hand, has since the 1980s become one of the main European wholesale drug markets.

The general involvement of Neapolitan clans in drug trafficking into Europe over the last forty years has fluctuated. During the 1980s Germany was perceived by *camorristi* as a "light touch" because of its law-enforcement regime. Some *pentiti* explained why Antonio Bardellino's organization, like Alfieri's and Nuvoletta's, had different bases in Germany: "The traffic of drugs and firearms passed through Germany because it was common knowledge that its laws protected civil liberties more and thus there were less controls than in Italy" (CSv, 30/4/1997: 3).

It was suggested that this group of Camorra bosses was involved in drug trafficking because they had the right contacts and, as GG seems to indicate, they did not prioritize the Italian market: "They were part of the group that operated for my brother, Nunzio, and their activity consisted in trafficking cocaine between Paris, Monaco, and Berlin" (GGv, 14/1/99: 7). In other words, only certain elite groups could traffic and sell drugs from different locations. But by the mid-1990s, many of the contraband Camorra clans had turned to drug importation because it became the must-engage-in business for them. The risks were high, but so then were the returns. In 2015, 20 percent of Camorra clans (and counting) were involved in direct drug importation; a true democratization of this activity has started.

The routes, methods, and strategies of Neapolitan drug traffickers in Germany and the Netherlands still remain unclear. Neapolitan traffickers have systematically traveled back down from Amsterdam to Italy via Germany. This route is, for example, reflected in the percentage of Italians arrested for importing cocaine into Germany in 2008: 4 percent (UNODC1, fig. 58, p. 91). But over the last three decades the BKA has worked hard to deter Italians from crossing into its country. The Netherlands, on the other hand, is a wholesale hub for Neapolitans, where they go to buy drugs because it is a major European entry point for cocaine from South America. It is also perceived as a more permissive society with a relaxed law-enforcement regime. The cases that follow highlight the interdependent nature of Camorra activities abroad and the continuous communication between both territories.

## Drug Trafficking, the Annunziata–Aquino Group, and the Gala Subgroup

The focus now turns to Alfonso Annunziata ('O Calabrese or "Zio Alfonso"), and Giuseppe Gala ("Peppe Showman"). Both men were involved in importing drugs from the Netherlands[24] and Germany (wholesaler and transit countries) into Italy (market and customers) between the 1980s and 2000s, although their organizations and strategies were intrinsically different in Naples and abroad. Alfonso Annunziata was believed to be "one of the most important Italian drug traffickers"[25] who imported and sold cocaine and skunk in Boscoreale (Naples province), whereas Giuseppe Gala managed one of the supply drug networks for the larger Nuvoletta clan in Marano. Both cases emphasize the fluidity of the organizational configurations, the various phases of drug trafficking, and the types of clans involved. They underline how each group has a different modus operandi, how it undertakes a form of organized crime abroad, how it becomes a network structure to do so—and how vital this extraterritorial activity is for clans, connecting their local territory with global markets.

## THE GROUPS: THEIR TERRITORIES AND ACTIVITIES

Alfonso Annunziata was the charismatic leader of a drug trafficking group from Boscoreale, based in the hinterland of Naples, in the "Scampia of the Vesuvius."[26] This group has been defined by local police as "predominant" (QN13) because it only wanted to dominate its own territory and had no expansionist aspirations. It was purely interested in selling drugs to its neighbors, which could be explained by the fact that it first started out as a drugs network that slowly put down local roots, in time becoming a more established criminal family that used violence. This network imported cocaine regularly, either buying it directly from Peru via Germany or in the Netherlands, whereas Giuseppe Gala and his smaller team were "an operating arm" of the larger Nuvoletta clan (MTv, 10/4/1999) that imported hashish, ecstasy, pills, and cocaine from the Netherlands to Marano in Campania.

Although a drug importer, Giuseppe Gala was different from Alfonso because drug importation was only one of his many illegal activities. He was an ordinary businessman who officially sold computers (GB) but who had criminal aspirations and developed a "compenetrative" relationship with the local Nuvoletta clan. He represents a class of ambitious, unscrupulous, and corruptible businessmen, an accomplice-turned-criminal who fluctuates between the legal and illegal worlds and orbits around *camorristi*.

Clan members described him as "a person of great value" because of his international activities, which gave "him a turnover of 100–200 million lire a month" (TN8: 108). Locally, for the Nuvoletta clan, he carried out extortions, perhaps did a few murders, and was a front name. He not only managed the importation of drugs but also laundered money through many financial frauds and scams in Marano (see GV, 29/9/1999: 73, in TN8). One judicial document noted, "there is no doubt that Gala was regularly involved in business activities... that involved the Nuvoletta family's interests" (TN8: 74). But rather than develop the clan's interests, he sought to further his own, and ultimately his dubious activities proved too dangerous: "in 2003, he was murdered, burned, and disposed of in the trunk of a car."[27]

Initially, Alfonso Annunziata was purely interested in drugs and firearms trafficking into Italy, specializing in cocaine. During the 1980s, he managed a small drug-trafficking network from the Netherlands and Germany into Campania and northern Italy, while across his local territory, Boscoreale, during the 1990s, his network slowly established solid roots, and more traditional criminal activities. It became "the system" (PF). As leader, he oversaw activities with a stern gravity, imposing his rules, approach, and ideas. And he was often seen positively by the local population: "Alfonso Annunziata was described by bystanders as a benefactor, a man able, with due force, to multiply profit from illegal activities and distribute it to members" (TN12: 237).

Gala's group, on the other hand, was able to operate only thanks to the special sponsorship of the clan from Marano: "the subgroups the Nuvoletta clan employed for the importation of drugs were the Verde[28] and Gala families" (SIv, 1/10/2002: 69). Giuseppe Gala took orders from and was subordinate to the Nuvoletta leadership. But he was difficult with his collaborators and bothered his superiors, often acting openly confrontational as he defrauded them. His ambition was to have his own criminal clan: "he sought to increase his criminal prestige by becoming independent" (TMv, 21/4/1999). As a result, he was often alienated by members but was still kept in the clan because he had useful contacts with other criminal groups, including the Secondigliano alliance (TMv, 6/12/1999). In the end, rather than being available to the entire Nuvoletta leadership, he remained a peripheral player who worked exclusively for one of the high-ranking members, managing a small team.

Alfonso Annunziata was more his own man. He was a bright, elegant, "calm, laid back, gentle, and amiable" criminal (TNI1: 276). By the age of twenty-four, he was already extensively involved in a variety of acquisitive crimes (frauds, robberies, theft, receiving and selling stolen goods, and carrying arms), and then he became a drug trafficker. This he made clear in November 2000 during the Maglio trial[29] when he stated "I am a drug trafficker" (AA) to explain why he could not be part of the Alfieri confederation, who was morally against drug traffickers and would punish them (see TN2). In the mid-1990s, the disappearance of this Camorra confederation from the criminal landscape in the Nola region gave him space to develop his own activities. The membership of his circle gradually grew from eighteen members in 1993 (Allum, 2000: 406) to sixty in 2013 (PF).[30]

Between 1984 and 2004, Annunziata regularly spent time in prison for drugs and firearms trafficking, and between 2004 and 2006 was on the run. It has been suggested that he lived in Amsterdam, Germany, and Spain (TNI1), although he afforded himself the luxury of returning home to Boscoreale from time to time, as was the case during Christmas 2002. In 2006 he was arrested in Amsterdam on an EAW issued by the Italian authorities.

Since the 1980s, Annunziata had, on his own, organized an efficient drugs network in Europe: he spent "a long time in the Netherlands and developed drug routes that flooded the Neapolitan region with hashish and cocaine."[31] He was constantly negotiating business deals with other Italian and foreign criminal groups. As a result, he was not frightened of leaving Boscoreale to tend to his international operations, which is why he traveled frequently and lived for long periods abroad (TNI1). As leader of a drugs network, he was less attached to his local territory than were other Camorra bosses. Newspapers often described him as "a ghost"[32] because of this dual presence in Boscoreale and in Amsterdam.[33]

Giuseppe Gala was one of four brothers and the leader of a subgroup of the larger Nuvoletta clan, which had until its decline in 2001 a considerable membership. For example, in 1988 it was estimated to have 141 members (AC1–1: 16–20), and in 1994 the number was 199 (Allum, 2000: 408). The Gala team between 1996 and 1997 was made up of three intimate family units, similar to the Annunziata group but smaller, with only ten interrelated core members (MTv, 10/4/1999). They were the Gala brothers, the Napolano brothers, and the Del Prete-Tipaldi cousins.

A former member, Tipaldi, explained the Gala team's organizational structure. It had three levels of membership: (1) the hierarchical leader Giuseppe Gala and his brothers, who managed the drug-importation (hashish, cocaine, and ecstasy) network (SIv, 1/6/2002); (2) an inner core made up of the leader's most trusted relatives, often cousins; and (3) an outer core made up of "other people who were used for the execution of orders and who did not have the opportunity of having privileged contact with Gala, they were thus at an inferior level to that of the leadership of the subgroup" (MTv, 21/4/1999). The team was essentially a generational family based on four brothers. It functioned as a network abroad, but its local blood ties gave it a reliable base. Gala "trusted them [his core members] blindly because of their family connection," and one of his members stated, "I was like a son to him" (MTv, in TN8: 71).

In Marano, Gala did not manage to develop a collective identity in his small team because he was unable to set up a permanent salary system. Members remained satisfied, however, as they received a percentage from each individual drug deal and extortion racket. His members sometimes used violence to impose themselves among the local community because they were part of the Camorra, but it was not systematic. Indeed, this subgroup was an ad hoc family business, quite unprofessional and inefficient at times.

Not one member of the team lived permanently in the Netherlands to oversee its drugs operations. They behaved as criminal tourists, regularly traveling back and forth across Europe to negotiate drug deals with foreign criminal groups. They bought from Italian, Dutch, and South American wholesalers in Amsterdam and they organized couriers. This system changed from deal to deal and was temporary in nature. Reliable couriers or team members were employed to transport drugs from the Netherlands.[34] This team became a loose ad hoc drugs network, not a local Nuvoletta branch with a franchise in the Netherlands.

Alfonso Annunziata was from a large traditional family with seven siblings, which produced during the 1990s the organizational base of his drugs network. In time, this network put down roots in Boscoreale and became a small criminal family: the Annunziata-Aquinos. The family was led by Alfonso, who was supported by his young nephews, the Aquino brothers-in-law Carmine and Raffaele. An intergenerational model of leadership materialized as Alfonso and Carmine, the son of one of Alfonso's sisters, became the leaders of the emerging group and were its key decision makers. Carmine assisted the older Alfonso both in the management of his regular drugs network and his new structure in Boscoreale. They were also assisted by five subordinate, interrelated family units that were all involved in the drugs network and became the stable organizational base of the group locally. This base was founded on traditional values and blood ties. Indeed, marriage provided loyal and trustworthy lieutenants. The main families intermarried, and there were also marriages with other local criminal families from across the region.

However, the organization of the drugs network fundamentally changed in 2002. Carmine Aquino wanted to impose "firmly his leadership position in order to show that he was able to take over the leadership of the organization" (see QN5). A complex dual structure appeared: in Boscoreale, one tight criminal family that all members belonged to, that had one supreme leader, Alfonso; and abroad, the drugs network had two parallel branches that coexisted within the same family.

The internal structure of the Annunziata-Aquino family in Boscoreale was simple and not as developed as in other clans, as it had emanated from Alfonso's 1990s drugs network. It did not have rational departments and divisions and was more ad hoc. This can be seen in the many different duties, tasks, and roles members had both in the drugs network and family. Whereas in larger clans there was a distinction between the drugs-importing group and the distribution teams, that was not the case here; members' tasks and activities overlapped, demonstrating the lack of numbers needed to perform the various jobs.

Members ranged from petty criminals to white-collar professionals. Many also had respectable jobs: there were bar owners, bike shop owners, tomato factory workers, managers of a transport company, and a hauler. But there were also petty criminals. For example, one small-time criminal who needed money after his release from prison asked a friend for help. His friend introduced him to the criminal group and he soon started selling drugs for it (see TNI1). Some members were couriers, transporters, sellers, bodyguards, and negotiators concurrently. For example, XA was both a drug seller and money collector for each trip, as well as an enforcer. LL bought and sold the drugs and organized courier trips and the transfer of money and cocaine. Another member organized the boss's meetings when he was on the run (TN17; PN10).

Members were predominantly Neapolitan, although some had lived abroad: YC, "who had experience living abroad," acted as a mediator and negotiator with other foreign criminal groups because "he had lived for many years in Germany and the Netherlands" (TN10: 33). Some were based in northern Italy: associates and financers of the Aquino drugs branch were identified in Verona, Brescia, and Turin—locations not chosen strategically but more because of who lived there. For example, BP was a member of the Aquino drugs network based in Verona and was connected to the clan through his father-in-law, who lived in Boscoreale. He was a drug trafficker, and it is believed that Carmine Aquino preferred working with him because he had experience, know-how, and a reputation. Indeed, in the 1990s "[Giuseppe] Gala was known to have contact with BP, [who was] known to the Dutch police as a drug trafficker" (TN8: 23). BP was not a member of the criminal family, nor a member of a Camorra settlement, nor an autonomous trafficker, but rather a member of the Aquino drugs network that operated in the Netherlands, Germany, and the north of Italy.

Three judicial documents give us an overview of the composition of the different drug branches: One in 2001 identified sixty-one members of the Aquino branch, with an average age of thirty-five and the majority based in Campania, although some were strategically located in Avellino, Turin, Florence, Verona, and Holland (PN10). Another in 2004 was composed of forty-three members—thirty-seven men and six women, with an average age of thirty-six (TN12), and members across Italy and one member in the Netherlands. Another investigation in 2002 identified the international link of Annunziata's drugs network, with 28 percent being born abroad (Colombia, Argentina, Germany, Morocco, Panama) and the majority not based in Boscoreale (TN7). These documents demonstrate the flexibility of the different networks to engage with other nationals and extend beyond their territory of origin for business.

Women were fully involved. Older women in the Annunziata-Aquino family, in particular, were more present in the local territory than in the drugs network, compared with women in the Gala subgroup, who were visible mainly in the drugs network abroad. They participated by collecting *pizzo* money and became the spokesperson for their men in prison. This gave them "undisputed criminal prestige," as a result of which they were often offered "gifts" and "money made from illegal activities" (TN12: 333). They managed the social funds of the family; there appeared to exist a system in which members were "expected" to make a financial contribution from their illegal activities for members in prison (TN12: 406; 463).

In the drugs network, women cut up the doses, sold them, and found customers as well as accompanying couriers on trips, so the couples transporting the drugs would be "above suspicion." Girlfriends and offspring were often present in the car during journeys abroad in order "to limit the controls by the police" (TN12: 442). They would seem "less suspicious in a car near the borders if the family were present" (TN12: 506). Moreover, women related to the two bosses played crucial mediating roles between the two emerging and competing drug networks (see TN12: 270–282) and intervened in delicate situations to sort out tensions between the two. They could do so because they were related and respected.

The Gala subgroup's internal value system in Naples was part of the larger Nuvoletta's system and difficult to differentiate. Like many *camorristi*, Gala imposed his power through his illegal and legal activities rather than seeking traditional territorial control. He was a sly, calculating, and opportunistic character who was not a team player; he was an "ambiguous subject" because he "worked also to look after his own interests" (MTv, 10/4/99). But his recognized membership in the Nuvoletta clan gave him respect and power vis-à-vis civil society. In the Netherlands, this was not the case. He did not impose his values on the local community, but managed a drug trafficking network, purely negotiating business deals and having an economic presence.

Since the Annunziata-Aquino family was first a drugs network that then developed into an organization that resembled a Camorra clan, it has been difficult to identify its internal value system. The behavior of members in Italy differed from their behavior in Germany and the Netherlands. In Boscoreale, members behaved in an arrogant, self-important, overconfident, and violent manner in favor of the family's interests or individual members. One example of this bullish behavior was their attitude toward one of their "'friendly' building constructors: "one member bought tiles from him that were more or less worth 30,000 thousand lire per square meter, paying him only 5,000 lire" (TN10: 24). Generally, they controlled territory by imposing their values, criminal activities, and social consensus, often using violence. Firearms were used to regulate members and enforce rules. Leaders were keen to inflict sanctions on those who did not respect their rules or who did not repay their debts. On one occasion, Alfonso did not react very kindly when he realized that a member of his family was not respecting his orders, and he asked other members to threaten the insubordinate.

These social roots did not exist abroad. Network members behaved in a civil and business-like manner toward German and Dutch citizens because they were simply carrying out business transactions. There were no visible acts of violence against German or Dutch citizens, no physical harm. If violence was deployed, it was only toward other Neapolitans and criminals who understood the value system and codes. There is some suggestion of a murder of a Neapolitan in Mainz in 1986 that related to the family, but it has not been proven.[35] Another example is the Stolder clan, which imported drugs from the Netherlands during the 1980s–1990s. In 1990, one of its leaders did not hesitate to shoot a Slavic drugs broker in Amsterdam because he had not respected their deal,[36] and since European law-enforcement agencies were not looking at this as a mafia-related crime, they did not analyze it as the spread of mafia violence across its borders (CAN2).

Unlike larger clans, the Annunziata-Aquino family did not have an established salary system in Boscoreale during the 2000s, but it had a voluntary mutual assistance system (see TTA1). Tensions arose when members were reluctant to help others (see TN12; TTA1). However, the leader expected members to respect the rule of mutual assistance when necessary and contribute from their own profits (TN12: 268). For example, in 2002 when one of the couriers was arrested in Germany on his way back to Italy with drugs hidden in his car, the boss insisted that all members support this family while the arrested was facing judicial procedures and economic hardship (see TN12: 270).

## THE ACTIVITIES OF THE ANNUNZIATA-AQUINO FAMILY AND THE GALA SUBGROUP

The drug-trafficking activities of the Gala subgroup and the Annunziata–Aquino networks connected their home markets with host wholesale countries in order to maximize profit. It was estimated that in 2001–2002 Alfonso Annunziata's drug network alone imported 5 kilos of drugs every month (TTA1: 35) and that his preferred source market was Amsterdam. However, for a short period of time in 2002, he switched to Germany.

In the early 1980s, Alfonso Annunziata set himself up as a drug trafficker (AA), and in 1985, his nephew became his subordinate "business partner" (TNI: 181). Alfonso traveled directly to the Netherlands, where containers arrived from South America, and there, he negotiated with his Dutch, Italian, and South American contacts who sold him cocaine. Drugs were then imported and sold in his home territory,[37] to other local clans (in particular, the Ascione clan of Ercolano), and to other retail contacts in Verona and Turin. By regularly importing drugs, his network became part of a fluid drugs trading community both in the Netherlands and Germany.

Over the years, the Annunziata drugs network had developed stable contacts with representatives from Colombian cartels based in the Netherlands: a Panamanian-Dutch national who owned a restaurant and two Colombian brothers. Between 2002 and 2003, the importation was to Germany, via Hamburg, because of problems in the Netherlands, but as couriers were getting caught more regularly, and in particular in 2002 when couriers were stopped with 30 kilos of cocaine,[38] the whole organization switched back to Amsterdam. In effect, this police crackdown resulted in the split of the Annunziata drugs network: two parallel and competing branches emerged within the same drugs network (see TN12).

For Alfonso Annunziata, there should have been only *one* channel of importation into Italy. But the younger generation, the Aquino brothers-in-law, had different ideas. They basically copied the established operations of the Annunziata branch: they negotiated with the same sellers, they employed the same members to import drugs, and their products were destined for the same markets in the province of Naples. They decided to go it alone because they wanted to make more money, quicker. For example, on one occasion, they bought 1 kilo of cocaine for 36,000 euros and were able to sell it for 43,000 euros (TN12: 360).

These two branches cohabited within the same drugs network but were united as a criminal family. After their German difficulties, both moved quickly to seek safer markets and collection points in order to guarantee continued success. They "switched . . . operations back to the Netherlands" (see PN7) to "avoid transiting via Germany" (PN7: 119). The new route now went through Luxembourg, Belgium, and France via Ventimiglia and Bardonecchia, and then down to Boscoreale.

Alfonso, violating his parole conditions, moved back to live in the Netherlands to retain control over his operations, while the Aquino branch (one in hospital prison in Turin, the other free) used trusted lieutenants to undertake negotiations with South American wholesalers. This new parallel branch had groups located in Brescia, Turin, and Boscoreale, all involved in financing the so-called *puntate*, or investments into drug deals, as well as distributing drugs locally. The new branch challenged Alfonso's traditional model in every aspect and created a free for all for everyone involved.

Another reactive change was to switch from cars to trucks because couriers using cars were being caught too frequently. Trucks would be less suspicious: Aquino told his South American supplier that they had hired a road hauler because they believed that this would prove more successful (TN12: 113). And to avoid losses they increased their prices to make up the money: "Aquino, in discussing the price of the drugs, which was believed to be more than the interlocutor was willing to pay, explained that, after his registered losses, he was constrained to intensify the importing of drugs and at the same time he would have to keep the price that high at least until the Christmas period" (TN12: 62).

Several steps in the process of drug acquisition and its sale in Italy undertaken by the two branches highlight the dependency on both territories and the flow between them. In order to negotiate a transaction, the managers, Alfonso or Carmine, contacted the European cartel representatives active in Germany and the

Netherlands (see PN7). They would then seek the financial backing of various buyers, financiers, and shareholders in Italy and organize the handover of the money in Germany and the Netherlands. Then came the collection of the drugs and their transportation to Italy. During acquisition and transport a guarantor[39] was usually present to ensure the agreement. Last came the handing over of the goods to the buyers in Italy, who would then prepare them for street distribution (see TN12).

Organization was crucial and there were three main jobs: (1) locating the financial backers in Italy, (2) identifying trustworthy couriers (some were found locally in Boscoreale, others in Piedmont), and (3) collecting the money to pay for the drugs, negotiating the prices, organizing the exchange of the goods for money, and overseeing the transportation. Flexibility also meant a lack of rules, and this allowed the couriers to double deal: importing drugs both for separate branches as well as for themselves without informing the leaders.

Couriers used this fluid organizational structure to their advantage, as they were the ones running the highest risks. They concealed the goods in the trunks of cars, trucks, and road haulers. For the Annunziata branch, couriers tended to be members from Boscoreale, whereas the Aquino branch also employed some of the contacts of a northern associate (PN7). Both branches used these couriers, but the leaders were not necessarily aware of this, which suggests that the couriers manipulated the system to make money for themselves as well as for the various leaders. GX and the Y brothers, for instance, couriered for both branches concurrently and at the same time sold drugs themselves. These double-dealing activities, the zealous interest in money over tradition, and a declining respect for leaders shows the capitalist features of this emerging criminal family.

Although the younger generation relied on Alfonso's contacts, they moved away from his hands-on approach. Alfonso used a few old trusted members, whereas Raffaele widened his group and made it more sophisticated, including associates based outside Campania. Alfonso had one supplier of cocaine, who worked both in Germany and the Netherlands, and when he was in trouble, he would seek out drugs in Peru and negotiate directly with sellers there. The Aquino branch delegated to their known brokers. They also used modern technology more frequently, to avoid detection and also because they could not travel extensively: "They used services offered by the Internet, which provided a good degree of anonymity and meant that it was very difficult for the police to intercept them" (TN12: 345). "As we have already shown, during the investigations there was an extensive exchange of e-mails between the two" (TN12: 132).

By 2001, in Boscoreale Alfonso's network had become a "crime family" enterprise, particularly in its local activities, though not necessarily as intensely as other clans who already had demonstrated a collective criminal project that went beyond the sale of drugs. This family developed core activities based in Boscoreale, producing a value system with a collective identity among members. Traditional activities such as extortion rackets, loan-sharking, and controlling installations of video poker games[40] were all imposed using violence across the territory.

The extortion tax, *il pizzo*, for example, was a central activity and created deep roots in the community, but it was also important for members because it was a further source of income. Another regular activity was loan-sharking: "the profit made from the various illegal activities are even invested in loan-sharking to traders and businessmen in financial difficulty" (TN12: 269). The group provided cash to businesses in financial difficulties at a set interest rate: the leader—and in his absence, his family—acted like a central bank, and members as individual small banks (see TN12: 258). Loan-sharking was a smaller activity that might have appeared unorganized, but was coordinated by Annunziata, who had set rules and was careful to set a level of interest low enough to avoid being reported to the police (TN12: 265). One activity linked to the other. Members did not belong to separate organizations with different activities, but one organization which developed various interlinking activities. Here, the extraterritorial activities provided a foundation for the territorial activities.

Giuseppe Gala represented the Nuvoletta clan—he was *un homme à tout faire*, a factotum. During the 1990s he was part of the Nuvoletta's drug division: he led a team that was involved in importing drugs (cocaine, hashish, ecstasy) into Italy and Campania from the Netherlands and Spain. A former member explained that the Nuvoletta clan employed two specific importation methods: first, the paying of *puntate*: "the paying of a stake into a general [drugs] importing round organized and managed by other clans or brokers," and second, the direct importation of drugs—although it is suggested that the Gala subgroup was one of the last groups to do so (SIv, 1/10/2002, in TN8).

Gala's setup was simple. As part of a larger organization, he furnished drugs for his sponsors so they could sell them exclusively across their territory. He organized couriers to buy from representatives of the South American cartels or his contacts located in Amsterdam and then transported the drugs back to Marano. Once in Marano, he controlled their distribution: "they were put in deposits that were managed by Giuseppe Gala" (GCv, 14/2/2003: 146, in TN8). Then "the selling and distribution of drugs in Marano was controlled by the [Nuvoletta] organization; no one from outside could come and sell drugs here, or at least no one could sell drugs that had not been bought [imported] by the *Maranesi*" (MTv, 10/4/1999).

By the late 1990s, Gala had become more involved in financial scams, as he became the administrator of a company that managed the distribution of Parmalat products (dairy products, drinks, food, etc.) in Marano and Ponticelli.

As the clan had invested in this company, he became the main manager, but acted through a front name (TN8). It was his job to distribute Parmalat products in Marano, which he did by imposing them on shopkeepers using threats of violence. He and his men also had an arrangement with the local representative of Bauli Spa. Unbeknown to the national company, during festive periods his men would impose Panetone cake and sparkling wine, Spumante, on businesses at their price: "The businesses in Marano had no choice, they understood that to have an easy life, they had to pay what we asked. It became a consolidated practice at festive times" (MTv, 21/4/1999, in TN8). The Panetone cost 50,000 lire, but the businesses would pay 100,000 lire without questions asked. They did the same for Spumante. This fraud produced considerable sums of money that was used to provide for clan members in prison (TN8).

In addition to the food sector, Gala had an interest in the construction industry (especially building without permits), and it is believed that he invested greatly in real estate in Marano and other regions. He also bought ongoing commercial concerns, such as a local discotheque (MTv, 6/71999, in TN8: 78), in the name of a holding company in which various associates and clan members had shares. Gala's business activities highlight that he was unscrupulous and pushed his own agenda in a dangerous criminal environment.

Giuseppe Gala was not involved in financial scams or money laundering in the Netherlands, but only in managing the importation of drugs. (It is believed that the Nuvoletta clan did invest in Spain, but through other associates.) Gala's team offered services only to its sponsoring Camorra clan. These subgroups were mobile, but not independent, and were subordinate to the clan. Their activities connected the home territory with territories abroad, where goods, money, and people traveled back and forth. The emerging Polverino clan would refine this model of organization (see chapter 5).

## ACCOMPLICES OF THE ANNUNZIATA-AQUINO FAMILY AND THE GALA SUBGROUP

Accomplices for drug-trafficking networks lurk at the margins of these trading communities. The nature of accomplices in these networks is not obvious—indeed they are barely visible because of the illegality involved. Thus it is not clear where the legitimate accomplice would have a role except at the point of recycling money from drug-trafficking activities.

The Annunziata-Aquino family may or may not have invested money in the Netherlands; this is difficult to make out. But it is possible to gauge the nature of some of the accomplices who assisted this network in Europe. Neapolitan and Italian relatives and friends who had emigrated long ago and had become integrated into local communities offered help. They were fully integrated into host countries, having businesses in Germany and in the Netherlands (see TNI1), and appear complicit in the sense that their involvement may have been one-off arrangements that may not have even been economic but merely providing logistical support for a loved one without being aware of their criminal project.

Giuseppe Gala had accomplices in Marano for his various shady deals, but since his team acted as a business in foreign territories, did not need them so extensively abroad. In Marano, he interacted with many legitimate businessmen who became complicit in his frauds, especially his Bauli Spa and Parmalat scams. They probably took a cut and could be considered more collusive than complicit because they were aware of Gala's Camorra links. But they did not seek to develop the clan's interests; it was a matter of short-term self-interest.

In Germany, as we have seen, *camorristi* tended to buy drugs from South Americans, transit through the country with their Dutch-bought goods, and sell their counterfeit clothes. There were also traces of involvement in acquisitive crime and financial investments. In the Netherlands, they were more focused on buying from the specialized drugs wholesale market for their home markets. In both cases, they exploited the lack of understanding of the mafia phenomenon among civil society and law-enforcement agencies, and also the lack of international police and judicial cooperation. They also took advantage of the readily available resources in the new environment for their home markets.

# 4

# CAMORRA CLANS IN FRANCE
La Seyne-sur-Mer, Paris, and Villeneuve-Loubet

Closer to Italy than Germany and the Netherlands in terms of culture, language, and history, France is and has been the home of Italian *mafiosi* (Calvi, 1993). Some even suggest that Italian mafias have "colonized" the Midi region in the south of France (Bianchini, 1995). And the arrests of the alleged NCO member Rolando Tortora in Nice in 1988, of the Casertano boss Mario Iovine in Toulon in 1989, of the Sicilian Giuseppe Falsone in Marseille in 2010,[1] of the Calabrian Roberto Cima in Golfe-Juan in 2010,[2] of the alleged Calabrian boss Giovanni Franco in November 2013,[3] or even of the Neapolitan Antonio Lo Russo in Nice in 2014,[4] might confirm this.

French magazines such as *Historia*, *L'Express*, and *Le Point*[5] regularly publish special reportage claiming that foreign mafias are "invading." These journalists present a coherent narrative of a rational takeover, but their portrayal is unfair. French MPs who examined this question in the 1990s concluded that "Italian mafias have not implanted themselves extensively across the French territory, although there have been some clear attempts. Instead, our country is used as a route for their trafficking and a place to hide" (D'Aubert, in AN1: 44). More recently, in 2011 a French Ministry of the Interior report suggested that their presence "was discrete and stable" because they had clearly adopted a strategy of invisibility in order to "fit in" (MIF: 1).

From the limited material available, I have reconstructed a few stories of *camorristi* in France since the 1980s. What emerges is a picture of varied and chaotic criminal organizations that highlights how the new setting and the clan in Naples contribute to Camorra behavior in France. The cases analyzed range

**TABLE 4.1**  Camorra cases in France (1980–2014)

| CLAN | DATES | LOCATION/ITALY | LOCATION/ABROAD | CRIME |
|---|---|---|---|---|
| De Sena clan | 2007–2008 | Acerra, Naples province | La Seyne-sur-Mer, Toulon | Acquisitive crime |
| Zaza clan | 1980–1995 | Santa Lucia, Naples | Nice | Contraband, ML |
| City clans, Mazzarella, Contini | 2004–2013 | Naples city districts | Toulouse, Lyon, etc. | CF |
| Secondigliano alliance | 1998–2001 | Secondigliano, Piazza Garibaldi—Naples, Giuliano—Naples province | Paris, Lyon | CF |

from Michele Zaza ('O Pazzo), "the king of contraband cigarettes," in the 1980s to the counterfeit activities of various Camorra city clans, *outilleurs napolitains*, in 2000s (see table 4.1). Other activities such as the trafficking of waste management alluded to by Pietro Grasso in 2011 and the production of fake coins[6] are also mentioned.

Camorra clans have been present in France since the early 1980s, but it would be misleading to define this presence as a form of "exportation" or "transplantation." Rather, clans have operating cells when and where they can; these are flexible, irregular, and haphazard because "the Camorra is interested in everything: it seeks to make money from activities that do not appear at first as criminal, they are into everything, whatever" (CD). The Camorra has a ubiquitous presence.

## Acquisitive Crime

Is there a link between the Camorra in Naples and the Neapolitans who violently steal jewelry in the south of France? Regularly during the summer, young Neapolitan men are arrested in Nice or Cannes for stealing Rolex watches. They have no previous criminal record, no direct relationship with a Camorra clan, and they justify their acts by arguing that in Italy they have no work and they do this to make money to support their families.[7] Moreover, Aubry noted a general variation in figures for armed robberies ("*vols à main armée*"), but a new phenomenon has emerged: the targeting of jewelry in armed raids by Balkan groups (2009: 33). Some of these less structured forms of organized crime may also be undertaken by Neapolitan groups.

There is also evidence of *camorristi* who resort to their basic criminal skills when they travel abroad. Clearly these are not Camorra activities; they are acquisitive forms of crime, which may be organized and may or may not be linked back to Naples. The number of people involved is small, but a pattern across Europe emerges, suggesting that members of minor clans, perhaps with less personnel, resources, and contacts, tend to resort to acquisitive crime when abroad as part of their strategic functional mobility. The following cases demonstrate how *camorristi* adapt to their new settings; they show the ease with which disorganized *camorristi* can access France, its social communities and its economic fabric.

## Acquisitive Crime and the De Sena Clan

In September 2008, French gendarmes in Toulon received an anonymous tip-off that there was a stash of dangerous firearms in a garden in the seaside town of La Seyne-sur-Mer. This led to the identification of DTS, a former member of the De Sena clan from Acerra, who had moved there. His presence, with an Italian friend, is not evidence of a Camorra settlement, as he did not transfer his whole criminal group to France. But he did live there permanently for a year, regularly traveling between Acerra and La Seyne to manage his various scams. His activities, at times sporadic, at times organized, linked his territories in a continuous traffic of cars (and firearms).

### THE DE SENA CLAN: ITS MEMBERS AND TERRITORIES

Camorra clans in the town of Acerra, located northeast of Naples with about fifty-five thousand inhabitants, are considered to be a specific form of Camorra with "a complex territory" (VdO). Compared with other clans, they are "independent, ruthless, and violent," systematically on the defensive to resist being colonized by the bigger city clans. On one occasion, a local clan planted a hand bomb under the car of a clinic administrator to intimidate him as part of an extortion racket.[8] This Camorra was "one of the most capable . . . of adapting to new situations" and switching allegiances to survive, but remained "archaic" and "ragged" because its financial operations were less organized (VdO).

During the early 2000s, the criminal equilibrium in Acerra was delicately balanced, with several clans coexisting and many leading members in prison. The main alliance was based on an axis between the De Falco and Di Fiore families against the Crimaldi and De Sena-Mariniello families. The De Sena clan was historically the oldest criminal family still active across the territory because Mario De Sena, its leader, had been close to Nicola Nuzzo ('O Carusiello), the local NCO Camorra boss in the 1980s.

DTS, our young traveling criminal, was neither a Camorra leader nor a core member of the inner De Sena clan. He was the trusted lieutenant of De Sena's right-hand man, Giovanni Messina, who explained that DTS "killed people and attempted to murder rivals with me. He participated with me directly" (GM). DTS was thus an emerging *camorrista* trying to make a name for himself in a criminal vacuum, especially after his boss, Messina, was arrested in 2004. In an act of pure arrogance, DTS decided to take over extortions in Acerra and establish his own clan without his mentor's approval. The rival clans reacted violently to this provocation by ambushing him and his father.[9] Messina confirmed that DTS "clashed with the other clans," and, according to a local newspaper, is believed to have been involved in the murder of a rival, Raffaele D'Urso Caterino, on 16 May 2006.[10] DTS became an isolated figure, and as he never had the social capital of a boss, his best option was to take time out and run away rather than try to organize a clan in Acerra to fight back. He moved to La Seyne-sur-Mer in May–June 2007.

In France, DTS contacted one of his childhood friends, GE, who lived in Ollioules, near Toulon. GE was a petty criminal who lived at the margins of legality. He was born in Acerra to a French mother and in his twenties returned to France to be close to his family. He was no traditional immigrant, in that he traveled regularly back to Acerra, kept himself informed of criminal events in the town, and trafficked all sorts of things between both locations (CAAP4: 7). He became DTS's gatekeeper to French society and crime.

DTS was in France as part of a survival strategy, not sent by the De Sena leadership to export and expand its business activities. In Italy, the De Sena group was not a traditional Camorra family based on blood ties (GM), but rather a very loose group centered around one leader and his loyal followers with their neighborhood alliances. This indistinct organizational structure replicated itself in France: there was no organized clan or criminal family, only an isolated *camorrista* who surrounded himself with a petty-crime network. DTS participated in their small-time cross-border criminal activities, such as car trafficking. But as a *camorrista*, he was vulnerable, weak, and lost. To counter this feeling, he regularly returned to his home territory and was in constant contact with his local associates, who acted as his eyes, so that he could remain informed about the evolving local criminal situation.

GE had a shop in Toulon and was able to offer his friend logistical support and more. Because he had all the backup he needed, DTS was not interested in recruiting French locals, or indeed GE, into his clan. Instead, he wanted to engage in joint criminal ventures, as there existed a strong complicity between both men (GM). They became partners in crime. GE as a petty criminal did not turn to crime because of his Neapolitan friend, but was already involved in his own murky world of trafficking. He was considered to be "an arms seller" for [Camorra] clans [in Acerra] . . . , but since 2004 had sold firearms exclusively to DTS (CAAP4: 4).

In Acerra, members of the De Sena clan were variously small-time crooks, ambitious criminals, and older, more experienced *camorristi* who had grown up during the first Camorra war. Each member collected associates, friends, and followers who were not necessarily members of a specific clan. For example, DTS had five or six youngsters working with him who were not clan members, nor his close relatives, but who occasionally engaged with the clan. The family unit still played a role, in that each member enjoyed support and protection from relatives who provided a base for developing criminal ambitions. However, the lack of tight kinship meant that there existed greater flexibility among and between clan members, with little trust and no duty-bound behavior.

In France, DTS's car-trafficking team was a basic star-shaped network (see figure 4.1), which could be said to reflect the simple organizational structure of the Camorra in Acerra. There were set roles, but the locations could vary between France (nodes 3, 4, 6, 7, 9, 10, 14, 18, 24, 25, 27, 28, 29, 30, 33, 34, 35, 36, 37, 38) and Italy (nodes 11, 15, 17, 16, 19, 39, 20, 21, 22, 23, 40, 41, 42). The core network was ethnically diverse and made up of four players: two French (nodes 2, 3) and two Italian (nodes 1, 5) in their twenties; one being a *camorrista*. They all lived in France but traveled when necessary. Having said this, even in Acerra, there was more organization than in the new location because there was still one main leader supported by loyal *camorristi* and surrounded by a group of trusted foot soldiers who helped control the local territory, however spasmodically.

Between 2006 and 2008, DTS was continuously traveling to Italy; he commuted back and forth between La Seyne and Acerra, almost daily, like a shuttle (TNv1). This spatial element of movement between the countries in which *camorristi* are active appears to be a common trait in our cases: they rush, dash, and hurtle back and forth. *Camorristi* never cut themselves off from their roots and remain constantly in contact with their territory while becoming light and extraterritorial. In the end, they always returned to their power base.

Women also play a role in this story (nodes 3, 4, 6, 9, 10, 14 in figure 4.1). They were neither passive nor indifferent, but fully active both in Italy and France. In Acerra, mothers, sisters, and aunts frequently participated in the criminal activities of their men, helping out whenever they could, especially when the men were in prison. Inevitably, they filled the criminal vacuum. One mother in Acerra insisted on taking over her imprisoned husband's criminal activities because she felt that her son did "not appear to have the qualities or experience to substitute his father" (TN20: 245). Surprisingly, the women in France also engaged in their men's criminal scams and provided vigorous support. For example, GE's partner fully participated in the car fraud, doing all the paperwork, while his lover responded to his requests. Their lawyers argued that both women acted in this way "out of love and they did not know anything. They were

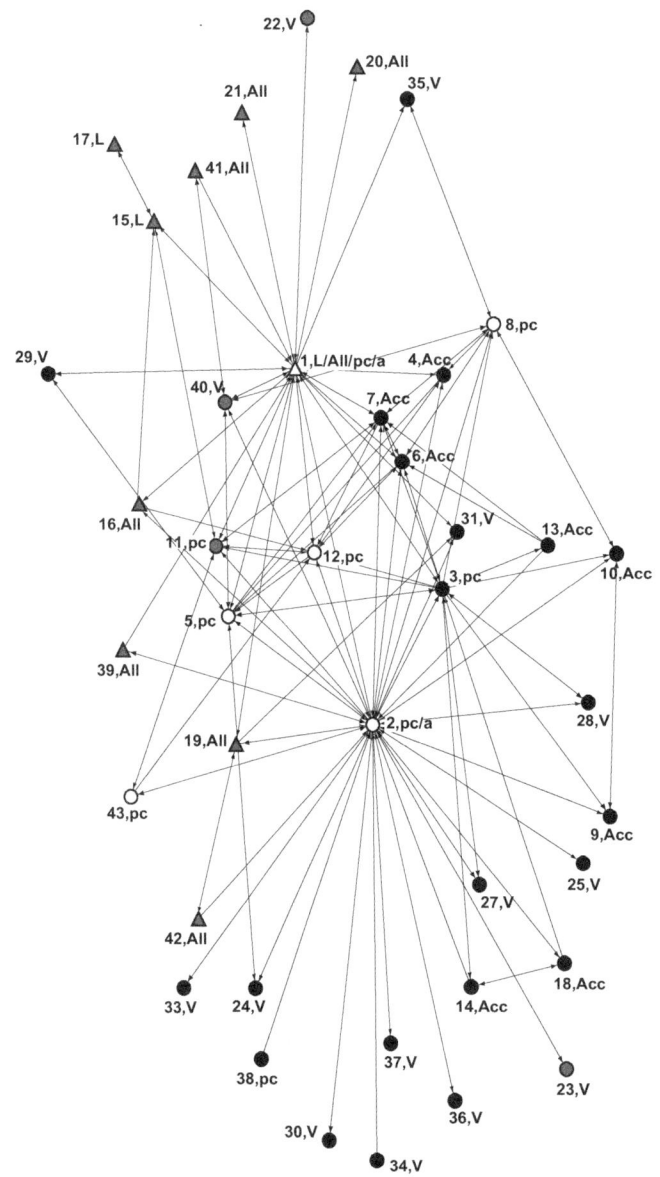

**Key**

Colors: grey (Acerra/Italy), black (abroad), white (travels)

Shapes: △ = clan member   ○ = non-clan member   ▽ = other clan

Roles: leader (L), accomplice (Acc), petty crime (pc), victim (V), all Camorra activities (All), arms (a). (By all Camorra activities, I mean all local teritorial activities such as extortion, loan sharking, drug dealing, etc.)

**FIGURE 4.1** DTS and his car fraud network (2006–2008)

completely in love."[11] They nevertheless went to prison for their involvement in GE's criminal activities.

Although this Camorra was "ragged," it nonetheless had a distinct value system (*omertà*, honor, and vendetta) and an internal modus operandi, with a set code of conduct and a specific salary system. The clan physically controlled the Acerran territory with lookouts ready to warn members of police patrols, and imposed traditional values to do so. Violence was a key characteristic of the Camorra's behavior in Acerra. Membership and a career in the clan were often linked to one's capacity to be violent; "you had to kill someone to be someone" (GM). The clan used violence regularly to impose its values, to control its territory, to manage civil society, to avoid police capture, and to eliminate rivals. On one occasion a foot soldier was asked to viciously beat an individual, "to give them a lesson" because they had insulted the family. To have true value, the beating had to take place in the clan's district and would serve as a "public example to all" (TN20: 382). Symbols were constantly used to impose power, but were not needed in France.

DTS's reputation was acknowledged by the locals in France; they all knew who he was and what he did. But there was never any need for him to replicate his Camorra values. It was unnecessary because his gang was a loose network and not a criminal clan with a collective identity. Consequently, DTS and GE behaved differently in both locations: DTS in France abandoned his violent and threatening behavior and acted as a regular law-abiding citizen. He exploited the low perception of Italian mafias in France and accepted that his power was not transnational. GE, on the other hand, was more arrogant, self-righteous, and often used threatening behavior when he returned to Acerra (TN20: 437).

The traditional salary system existed locally and was "for prisoners, expenses, to buy weapons, [and] to do all these things" (GM). It was not reproduced in France. For a time, DTS managed the salary system in Acerra and was considered fair with hard-working members while excluding those less deserving (TN20: 371). In France, no members required paying and there was no need for money to be sent back to Acerra.

In early 2008, DTS returned to Italy, as French investigators began closing in on his illicit trafficking, and was arrested in March for attempted murder. In La Seyne he did not open a local branch of his Camorra activities but adapted to a new setting, resorting to what he knew best: organizing acquisitive crime. It was neither settlement nor infiltration, neither imitation nor hybridization (as defined by Sciarrone and Storti, 2014), but something else. He managed a small gang that connected La Seyne to Acerra through the trafficking of cars and arms, with no link to a Camorra clan. This activity demanded speed and swiftness of action, but no visible violence.

## DE SENA CLAN ACTIVITIES

The De Sena clan in Acerra carried out traditional Camorra activities: extortion rackets, drug distribution, and firearms trafficking. Leaders made decisions and directed their members in these activities. DTS was one such member who worked as the *bras fort* of the clan. For example, he collected extortion payments, as "extortions in our territory are automatic. Anybody coming to undertake public works here, any company wanting to build flats, public works, any type of work, already knows that they must speak to the clan. . . . There was a building boom, not only in my town but also in Casalnuovo, near Acerra. We would do extortions every half hour. At least [a] hundred people were paying. . . . DTS was someone dealing precisely with extortions" (GM).

The inconsistent nature of these clans meant that members could carve out space for their own autonomous criminal deals. DTS duly filled this space. The leadership allowed him to undertake criminal activities that may not have been directly related to the common fund. As Messina explained: He "had his own market. All of us had something on the side. . . . He had his own market with many young people selling drugs for him. It was his personal small system" (GM).

In France, DTS did not replicate or extend these core activities. He did not deal drugs, but fully participated in joint criminal ventures with GE, which saw an exchange of goods and resources between territories: "He wasn't there permanently. Therefore he had some business, business both in Acerra and France; otherwise, there is no reason to go back and forth" (GM). These activities were, specifically, car fraud and firearms trafficking. They were carried out solely between the south of France and Acerra. They took place on a regular basis but were self-contained, therefore there was no need to engage with other foreign criminal groups.

It was estimated that between 2007 and 2008 this small network undertook seventeen car scams, earning up to 10,000 euros per car. The fraud consisted of stealing or otherwise procuring cars in Acerra, fixing their insurance papers, and selling them in France to unsuspecting drivers or restealing them. On one occasion in 2007, GE sold a Porsche 996 previously belonging to his uncle to an unsuspecting buyer. Once the 35,000 euros went into a bank account, the network stole the car from the new owner, having kept a set of keys, and then reregistered it in Italy (CAAP4). This was an adaptable and successful scam, but difficult to detect.

The trafficking of firearms, although only half uncovered by French investigators, was a two-way exchange: "from Italy 'implicated firearms' were exported to France, and from France, firearms bought there were sent to Italy" (CAAP4–1: 1). The shifting of these arms had to be rapid and smooth in order that no trace be left.

DTS's behavior and activities changed from those of an emerging *camorrista* to those of a petty criminal. These activities demonstrate one of the simpler forms of functional mobility: a pure exchange of resources, goods, and people across borders and activities that are malleable depending on the territory and individuals involved.

### DE SENA CLAN ACCOMPLICES

What is striking about this story is the nature of DTS's relationship with accomplices in France. The social presence of this *camorrista* in France was hardly visible because he adopted a strategy of invisibility. His presence, therefore, did not ring alarm bells in the local community, which embraced him because he had friends there. These accomplices were not businessmen, as in other cases, but French citizens and Italian immigrants. They acted not out of self-interest, but out of friendship; they were collusive accomplices. The Italian judiciary noted this special relationship and deduced that there existed a "tight exchange" between such French citizens (CAAP4–1: 98), although it was unclear what they were doing together. Some were even identified in Acerra. Whereas in other cases the enablers become insiders, here the French facilitators remained outsiders and provided help, expertise, and a variety of resources.

GE's role was essential, for his accomplices extended to his Neapolitan associate. Since GE was fully integrated into French society, he made DTS feel "completely safe in the French territory, where he found himself" (CAAP4–1: 65). Thanks to this, DTS "had at his disposal a real and true operative and logistical 'pillar,' able to assure him refuge in case of problems as well as guaranteeing self-financing through lucrative illegal activities undertaken there" (CAAP4–1: 1). GE legitimized DTS, and his friends accepted DTS without being worried or asking questions. They knew of DTS's mafia reputation, but this did not stop them from interacting and helping him when required. The loyalty of GE's friends was not negligible and shows how even French people can become involved in illicit activities or in covering up illegal activities out of friendship (CAAP4: 20). Is this contagion, colonization, or sympathy?

DTS's time in France highlights some unpredictable aspects of *camorristi* abroad, the varied nature of criminal mobility, the transformation of a *camorrista* into a petty criminal, and the spatial use of territory to make money. It shows the limited resources of a single *camorrista* abroad, his determination to survive and adapt: he takes up acquisitive crime and rushes everywhere, undertaking different forms of trafficking to survive. This case is more reminiscent of general organized crime than of the Camorra and underlines why we need to understand the phenomenon in its different contexts and guises.

## The Counterfeit Market

Between 2000 and 2010, there was an explosion in the counterfeit sector, matched by a clear attempt by the authorities to improve their understanding in order to control the phenomenon. Indeed, over the last fifteen years French Customs and Excise has been engaged in a strong anticounterfeit policy, demonstrating that it is sensitive to the problem. However, France remains a stable market: in 2008, 6.5 million articles were intercepted, up 41.3 percent from the previous year (UniFab2: 28). One in two French businesses admitted to being a victim in 2001 (UniFab2: 11). The activity is often not perceived as a crime. In 2010, the main counterfeit goods that arrived in France were either from China (70 percent) or Africa (17 percent). In addition, goods are no longer sold only face to face, there has been an increase in the use the Internet as a means of selling and distributing fake goods (UniFab2: 65).

Evidence suggests the presence of Camorra interests in the counterfeit sector in France. Involvement of the main city clans is emblematic of the Camorra's new versatility. The structures, activities, and capital investment by these groups are extraterritorial, light, and unencumbered: there is perpetual movement and they "cannot easily hold their shape" (Bauman, 2000: 2). Both the Secondigliano counterfeit company in 2001 and a whole variety of door-to-door sellers organized by local area managers close to city Camorra clans (Mazzarella, Contini, Stolder, among others) were identified in France.

### The Counterfeit Market and the Secondigliano Alliance (1998–2001)

During the 1990s in France two Camorra counterfeit organizations competed with each other. The Secondigliano counterfeit company had local branches in Paris and Lyon (QN4, 2: 27), and so did the smaller Di Lauro clan, which "had a network of shops in Europe and more than one factory in Italy. . . . One of these shops is based in Paris and is managed by ST, who is still with Di Lauro" (GGv, 26/11/98, in QN4, 1: 70). In Paris, the Secondigliano company's shop, located in the twelfth arrondissement, opened in 1999. It sold clothes, electrical goods, and cameras, and bought its goods ("cloths, material, confectionary, underwear"; see QN4, 1) from its warehouse in a small building in Lyon. Previously managed by MF, in 2001 GA[12] decided to directly oversee activities in Paris and Lyon. MF now managed operations on a daily basis (QN4, 3: 56–57) and referred back to GA for instructions.

The organizational structure of the Secondigliano counterfeit company in France was a loose network composed of local managers and their close associates (often relatives). The personnel changed locations and roles frequently, so it did not even resemble an unorganized Camorra clan because it was so fluid, adaptable, and permeable. This was a star-shaped network, with Naples at the center of all structures and activities. The company's power, leadership, and organization linked back to its headquarters in Naples, as did its operations in Germany, Spain, and the United States. The company did not employ new personnel, but instead recruited Neapolitans already familiar with France and its counterfeit sector. For example, the French local manager, MF, had been close to the Zaza clan during the 1980s and Zaza was a sworn enemy of the Secondigliano alliance; his nephews have been its archrivals ever since. This free and easy recruitment is a sign of flexibility and openness. It may also be an indication of the presence of the Camorra in the *magliari* network work in France as early as the 1970–1980s, as suggested by the French police (BRIF).

The local area managers imposed and supplied Camorra-sponsored products to the *magliari* network in France and looked after them. They were rapid and prompt in their operations, as was the case when some Secondigliano managers started to threaten the *magliari* protected by the Di Lauro clan: "minutes after being threatened by GA the *magliari* contacted ST [the Di Lauro local manager], who looked for GA to confront him. But did not find him" (QN4, 1: 74). The issue was not resolved locally, but in Naples, after a meeting between the leaders the message returned to France was clear: "[you] must not fight, [you] must try and get on" (ibid).The leaders resolved the problem and reintroduced peace among the different players. However, unrest quickly reappeared when one of the young hotheads of the Secondigliano alliance threatened the Di Lauro representatives, requesting that they close down their shops (QN4, 1: 75–76). The resolution agreement was not a general one, but reached through compromises in Naples for the long-term benefit of all. Locally things could become violent if Naples did not intervene with its market rationale.

This form of Camorra did not impose its internal value system on French citizens nor did it set up a salary system. To the French, the clan sold its fake goods through its network of door-to-door sellers. Violence and threats were never directed to possible customers, but solely against Neapolitan *magliari* who understood the underlying criminal code. On rare occasions, the local area managers were undermined by the *magliari*, who did what they wanted: for example, they took the goods they wanted, cameras instead of drills (see QN4, 3: 61). This produced tensions. No central salary system was ever introduced in France because all profits were transported back to Naples either by *magliari*, members of the board of directors, or through bank transfers to fill the common fund and pay local producers. This was neither investment nor physical control.

In France, the Secondigliano company managed its enterprise network of sellers through its trusted area managers. France was clearly used solely as a marketplace for counterfeit goods. The company was present not as a criminal association (see TN15), but as an invisible economic structure. This was neither the transplantation of a Camorra clan undertaking its traditional Camorra activities, financial investments, nor physical control over the territory, but instead the management of an already established network of *magliari* selling Camorra fake goods using mafia methods.

## The Counterfeit Market and City Clans, *Les Outilleurs Napolitains* (2004–2013)

France discovered another Camorra outfit specializing in counterfeit goods in 2008 when a bank notified French police in Toulouse of some suspicious transactions, in particular, the exchange of checks for cash by individuals staying in hotels and not permanently resident there (BRIF). These patterns of behavior replicated themselves across France, as did the modalities used to sell the counterfeit electronic goods. Unlike the Secondigliano alliance, these groups were no longer dealing in counterfeit clothes, but in fake motors, hedge cutters, and other agricultural electronic goods.

At Eurojust's request and with the backing of the Neapolitan DDA and the French desk at Eurojust, a European-wide investigation was opened to test the hypothesis that "there exists an international organization connected to the Camorra, with its headquarters in Naples, dedicated to the importation from China of various counterfeit goods that are sold in a number of European states" (PN13: 2). This inquiry involved five states (France, Belgium, Germany, Spain, and Australia); some were more willing to cooperate than others, and they all tackled the investigation differently, which may explain why some scams are still ongoing. Investigators uncovered the extent, reach, and flexibility of this Camorra, and particularly its disengagement from the host territory as teams of *magliari* systematically moved around selling different types of fake products. This Camorra, a mixture of different clans with no common project, controlled the whole counterfeit process from production to commercialization with representatives located at crucial points where teams organized and managed the various phases of the operations (see PN14).

The importation of fake goods into Europe was via Naples, Málaga, Nice, or Barcelona, using local import-export companies. In these cities, companies and associates close to the Camorra oversaw the transition of goods to the point of sale. Local regional managers gave the goods to the *magliari*, but individuals with connections to the clan would collect the money. The money was always sent back to Naples. But what was the specific connection to the Camorra? One investigation suggested that the only visible connection to the Camorra was perhaps that the local managers used the same lawyers as Camorra clans (BRIF).

Whereas the Secondigliano company initially adopted a hierarchical and hands-on economic structure, this Camorra was different. It was more indirect, remote, and distant, controlling from Italy, through brokers and mediators, the producers, importers, and key managers in these new settings by imposing taxes and payments rather than directly managing operations. Here "business-inspired rules of action and business-shaped criteria of rationality" ruled (Bauman, 2000: 4).

How did this relationship begin? In the 1980s, Camorra clans had invested in the counterfeit industry and, specifically, in the businessmen who owned import-export and production companies. The term "businessmen" needs to be qualified: these were not fully law-abiding businessmen, but shady entrepreneurs who lived at the border of legality and illegality. These classic Camorra businessmen used their close relationships with criminals to maximize their own activities, whether legal or illegal. They used the *camorristi* as much as the *camorristi* used them.

These businessmen were keen to negotiate sponsorship from any Camorra clan rather than become fixed Camorra partners. They too were fluid—ready to dismantle and remount their activities anywhere. One such example is KL. He "was a businessman from Forcella and always close to our clan. He dealt with the importation and sale of electronic goods from Thailand, Hong Kong, and China. Another sector he worked in, which was just as profitable as it was important, and which we paid for, was then inherited by the Mazzarella and Misso cartel and then by the Secondigliano alliance, was the importation and selling of drills" (SGv, 3/4/2008, in PN13: 3–4). They provided clans with imitation goods, and the clans controlled the distribution and sale process by employing *magliari*, who may be very difficult to identify as being close to the clans. This shifting from group to group meant that, in the long term, these businessmen gained more and more self-confidence.

In France, similar modalities were adopted in terms of selling goods, managing the traveling network of *magliari*, and returning the money to Naples. Once one region had been targeted and done over, the *magliari* moved on to a new region, and the majority of regions in France, from Brittany to Toulouse to Lyon, have all been visited.[13] A similar commercial strategy to that of the Secondigliano company was uncovered, but this time it appeared to be individuals close to the Mazzarella clan who were involved and who targeted a variety of countries. In France local managers and *magliari* would travel around the different regions. The *magliari* network was vast and made regular trips to Naples. The local area managers—families permanently living in France, but with Camorra contacts—usually had companies and shops in strategic cities such as Nice. These families would manage the importation and distribution of the counterfeit goods and the *magliari* network. They also enabled Camorra families and fugitives to take holidays in France (see PN17). These families were not specifically sent out by the Camorra in an expansionist strategy, but were mobilized by the Camorra in their criminal project, as they lived there and were familiar with the sector. They can be seen as an invisible support system (see CAAP5 and PN17).

One account explains that in the region of Toulouse, there were about twenty *magliari*, for the most part from the Naples area, who rented flats for about two months and no longer. Merchandise (electrical goods made in China and of very poor quality) was delivered to and held in storage facilities, and they would then go around the Toulouse countryside selling their agricultural goods to unsuspecting farmers. *Magliari* would try to sell merchandise for 1,000 euros, adding more items to the deal if necessary to conclude the sale, going as low as 200 euros (BRIF).

In particular, they targeted isolated farms in the countryside where they could negotiate with their customers undisturbed. They would always use the same kind of scam: "They were returning from an agricultural show, and as they must take a plane and could not take these goods with them, they were prepared to sell the remaining merchandise at a low price. Sometimes they managed to convince farmers that they would one day need an electric generator because there might be a power cut in electricity during thunderstorms. The problem is that the majority of these goods were dangerous and did not follow any European security standards" (BRIF). It is estimated that the group based in the Toulouse area made around 1 million euros in a year. Indeed, when the leader was arrested he had more than 60,000 euros on him in cash and was with a woman who had opened a bank account in her name. It was the suspicious activity on this bank account that triggered the investigation.

Another related case was finally judged in Marseille in April 2014. Five members of the operating group—local area managers—were sentenced from six months (suspended sentence) to two years in prison and fined 8,000 to 40,000 euros (Trib info, 2014). In the official sentence, not one reference was made to the Neapolitan Camorra, and yet it would appear the group used the same modalities as the Mazzarella clan even though they were close to the Secondigliano company and the Contini clan.

The Camorra's presence in the counterfeit sector in France demonstrates its adaptability. The change was not a question of criminal identity but one of economic strategy. The rationality of money ruled its structures and actions, where there was no longer a sense of collectivity but rather of individualism. Counterfeiting activity underlines how the Camorra exploited business opportunities in different markets and how it works in loose teams that can assemble and dismantle in seconds. For example, some operations were immediately changed when law-enforcement agencies understood the modalities employed and the routes used.

## Contraband Cigarettes and International Drug Trafficking

Between 2009 and 2014 contraband and counterfeit cigarettes in France were stable at 14 percent of the total market (KPMG: 86). Whereas in the recent past contraband cigarettes were controlled by Chinese crime gangs who produced and imported them into France and Europe (CD), in 2015 they come in from France's closer neighbors. Not one Neapolitan clan was identified as directly involved in the French contraband market, although Camorra clans sponsor and allow Neapolitan businessmen to import contraband cigarettes into Europe for various markets (including the British) via the Balkans or Greece, as long as they pay a tax.[14]

As already mentioned, during the early 2000s many Camorra clans specialized in drug importation, turning their back on contraband cigarettes. In 2010, some Camorra associates renewed interest in contraband cigarettes. Although it is no longer perceived as a major economic activity, clearly they still keep an eye on this sector. The Camorra's exact involvement in drug trafficking into and out of France is difficult to prove and quantify. Its presence appears temporary, brisk, and more detached because, compared with Spain and the Netherlands, France is neither a wholesale country nor a market with which the Neapolitans are familiar.

Three different forms of Neapolitan involvement in drug trafficking have been identified. First, there is the direct involvement of *camorristi* who pick up drugs in France and sell them in Europe. In 2009 four Camorra members were arrested in Mulhouse, close to the Swiss-German border, as they were taking possession of 18 kilograms of cocaine, but this kind of direct involvement by Camorra members (traveling to France themselves rather than using brokers) appears to be rare. 'Ndrangheta clans, by contrast, have members living permanently in France: Calabrian immigrants who traffic directly in drugs, as was the case of FG and DG, who lived in the south of France[15] and were convicted in 2010 in Marseille.[16]

Some accounts suggest that during the 1980s, *camorristi* imported drugs through Paris to sell in the Netherlands and Germany. This no longer seems to be the case because of the necessity of familiarity with a particular market.

The market in France is already dominated by the Corsicans and the emerging Maghrebin groups (DC and NB). Thus there is no space for Neapolitans.

Second, since the mid-1990s, clans have used France as the main transit country between Spain and their home market. Its geographical location, like Germany's, makes it an essential transit country in getting goods into Italy. The PACA region in particular is the corridor from Spain to Italy within the Schengen space. The potential for couriers to be stopped in France is an "unavoidable" problem, as one courier explained: "If they stop us in France . . . the stuff from Spain, the stuff I bought I will need to throw away. . . . They check inside and out" (TN14: 177). Although the numbers are unclear, the arrests of Neapolitans between Spain and France highlight the availability of people to act as couriers, in particular, those who were indebted to the clan. For example, MBL and PR, both Neapolitans, aged fifty-eight and forty-seven, respectively, were arrested in 2004 at the Perpignan border returning from Barcelona, Spain, with 89.846 kilos of cocaine hidden in a "double panel" in their car. MBL explained that "in [financial] debt [to the clan], he had accepted this work, and for this purpose he had bought an impounded car and fixed the hidden panel himself. . . . His role was limited to driving the car to Italy, [where he would] leave it open and the keys placed on the windscreen in the parking lot of the AGIP petrol station immediately after the border" (CAAP1: 2). "An unknown individual had given him a suitcase not full of tobacco, but cocaine. Out of fear, he did not dare refuse to take the drugs that he himself placed in the car (double panel)" (CAAP1: 2). Clans employ all kinds of methods, an observation reinforced by 2006 figures for foreigners arrested for "trafficking cocaine into or within" France: after the Nigerians (16 percent) and the Dutch (12 percent), Italian nationals (7 percent) represent the third-highest proportion of foreigners (UNODC1, fig. 56: 94).

Third, drugs are collected in France by so-called brokers. Brokers are not formal members of the Camorra, but associates who act on behalf of Neapolitan clans and buy from transnational drug-trafficking rings in France. The use of brokers is an illustration of the Camorra's flexibility and adaptation to new situations: goods are picked up in France and transported to markets in Italy. Camorra clans buy drugs from brokers in France as well as Spain. The geographical location of France, a natural marketplace, means that it plays a special role at the center of transnational organizations' activities.

These cases show that there does not need to be new markets for clans to expand into, and that the location, the conditions of the natural market, and the type of clan may explain why and where they are active. In 1988, the Neapolitan Michele Zaza, a recognized international smuggler, "transferred his illicit interests out of Naples, between Rome and the Côte d'Azur" (TN9: 6), from where he managed his contraband activities. Although evidence is limited, his story suggests that he was ahead of his time because of his investments in the legal economy. He almost completely recycled himself, like many mafia bosses, into a business manager.

## Contraband Cigarettes and the Zaza Clan

Michele Zaza was not a typical *camorrista* because he had been co-opted into the Sicilian Mafia, together with Antonio Bardellino and the Nuvoletta brothers, which gave him an edge and made him a serious threat. In addition, he specialized in one main criminal activity: the smuggling of contraband cigarettes. Unlike other bosses, he was not extensively involved in traditional Camorra activities, such as extortion, loan-sharking, or illegal betting (RM), nor was he particularly interested in the territorial sovereignty of his districts, Il Pallonetto di Santa Lucia, San Giovanni a Teduccio, and Portici. Nevertheless, according to Judge Paolo Mancuso, "he had an extraordinary role in Naples. In the 1970s, he was the most important criminal figure in the city" (PM).

Indeed, Michele Zaza plays a decisive role in the history of the Camorra abroad because he was one of the first *camorristi* to travel extensively and target new territories for their criminal and money-laundering potential. In the early 1980s, he developed business ventures in Los Angeles with other criminal networks; in the mid-1980s, he developed them in Paris and the south of France. He was everywhere. He left Naples in 1983 to settle in Rome, but in 1988 moved permanently with his family to a small town, Villeneuve-Loubet, near Nice in France, where he became involved in the smuggling of contraband cigarettes and money-laundering operations.

Until 2014, a Zaza clan as such did not exist in Naples, although Michele Zaza's criminal power and patrimony were visible through his nephews in the Mazzarella-Zazo clans: "at the death of Michele Zaza [1994], it was Ciro Mazzarella who clearly inherited his legacy in the business-criminal world" (LGv, 18/10/2002: 5). In February 2014, new alleged activities of his relatives and nephews in Rome were identified when twenty-nine members of the Zaza clan were arrested in the capital and Italy.[17]

### THE ZAZA CLAN: ITS MEMBERS AND TERRITORIES

Michele Zaza was born on the island of Procida in the bay of Naples in 1945 and became the leader of the Zaza clan in the 1970s until his death in Rome in 1994. He was a dynamic and enterprising cigarette smuggler[18] who was said to be "a very socially dangerous *camorrista*" and "the leader of an important clan in Campania with links abroad and involved in illegal trafficking (contraband cigarettes and drugs)" (CApN: 3–4). His local power and reputation stemmed from his membership in the Sicilian Cosa Nostra and the fact that he was part of the NF leadership that countered Cutolo's NCO expansionist project during the 1980s. National Antimafia Prosecutor Franco Roberti has suggested that Zaza was "more *mafioso* than *camorrista*, already then he behaved as a *mafioso*" (FR). This may explain why he was ahead of his time in terms of Camorra mobility.

During the late 1970s and early 1980s, the Zaza clan was considered an important player in the Neapolitan underworld. It was never clear to the authorities whether it was Michele or his elder brother, Salvatore, who was the true leader. A police report in 1983 credited Michele: "Salvatore Zaza is the head of the family, which is continually led by his younger brother, Michele. Michele Zaza is in fact the brain" (QR1: 429). Indeed, the prosecutor Paolo Mancuso argues that Salvatore "had a secondary role" (PM). When Michele left for France, Salvatore did not move with him but remained in Rome.

Michele Zara was a crafty leader: "He was a magnetic person. He was a person who certainly had charisma, was incredibly lively and had great communication skills. . . . He was something else, he was a [real] firework" (PM). He used his "*furbizia*," his cunningness, to get himself out of difficult situations. An old trick he used was to pretend to be ill to reduce possible judicial punishment, and he used his heart condition as a "winning strategy" (CAAP1: 109). Or he would use money to buy himself out of trouble by corrupting police officers when necessary (see LGv, 9/10/2002). In November 1982 when he was in isolated confinement at Regina Coeli prison in Rome, he even managed to send a telegram to his father-in-law (QR1: 445). The journalist Calvi (1993: 139) believes that similar manipulations also frequently took place in his dealings with the French judicial system. Judge Solange Marouchini argues that he tried to intimidate her while she was investigating his activities in Marseille, but that she was having none of it (SM).

He was respected, authoritative, determined, and organized, as the *pentito* Fiore D'Avino explained: "Michele Zaza was a man of honor, but he was also the true leader of the family because of his charisma, because of his capacity to organize the traffic of cigarettes according to the Sicilian rota system,[19] . . . and lastly, for his forthrightness in deciding the elimination of his enemies" (FdAv, 28/1/95, in TN8: 17). In addition, he was well respected by his business partners, which meant that they conducted their activities as equals. Various judicial and police documents reveal the nature of his social capital. Perhaps his extensive national and international criminal and business contacts (see QR1) highlights this social capital, or his possible links with politicians and law-enforcement agents. Plentiful social capital may explain two things: first, why and how he was able to move abroad successfully; and second, how he developed thriving contacts in France.

Michele Zaza was born into a large family. His father, Pasquale, a fisherman, and his mother, Luisa Montagna, had six children. Michele was the baby of the family; there was a seventeen-year age gap with one brother and a twenty-year gap with a sister. His family played a pivotal role in his criminal career: they made up the inner core of his organization and provided constant support. One judicial document noted that "many relatives provided him with 'alibis' as front names of properties or as administrators of companies" (QR1: 2). They even provided fictitious front names and numerous bank accounts that he could use to recycle and reinvest his illegal profits. One maternal uncle acted as an administrator for one of his companies and explained: "The company '4 novembre 98' belonged to Michele Zaza and I only pretended.... I was in fact only a front man" (TN1: 13). Another close relative fully involved in Zaza's business ventures was also believed to be close to the Sicilian Mafia (Calvi, 1993: 72–73, 85, 140), so he was a well connected and useful ally.

In the 1980s, these relatives became functional tools for Zaza's criminal projects. Between 1980 and 1983, when he ventured to Los Angeles, it was on family contacts resident there that he relied: extended family members living in Los Angeles and members of the Italian business immigrant community gave continuous help and advice (QR1: 388). The support of his tight-knit family has often been ignored in other accounts, and yet was an essential part of his criminal power both in Naples and abroad.

The second layer of Zaza's organization was made up of his faithful foot soldiers and business associates. His foot soldiers were often steadfast friends as well as an army of young dutiful men who admired him, but none of them moved to France. They executed his orders obediently and did his leg work: in the summer of 1981, two young criminals "went to Bulgaria to upload contraband cigarettes, embarking heroin at the Dardanelles Straits to ship to Italy for the Zaza clan" (QR1: 467). His business associates, so key to Zaza's organization, were less visible and more mobile. More than mere accomplices, they were his economic advisers and proactive partners who provided advice, support, resources, and contacts for all his activities. On the surface, they were legitimate businessmen, but in reality they were involved in activities in which the illegal mixed easily with the legal. In this way, he surrounded himself with loyal, helpful, and intelligent associates who regularly assisted him. They had a symbiotic relationship.

Individuals such as NB and NG were such businessmen (QR1). These self-confident individuals often crossed the line of legality, especially when they used intimidation. Violence was always in the background and they felt they could use it easily because of their close relationship with the boss, Zaza. A good example was when "a branch of the Santo Spirito Bank, in Naples," gave one of NB's relatives "a 70 million lira loan without guarantees . . . and there was no urgency to pay it back. [. . .] The bank director then did all he could to get the money back, without avail" (QR1: 340). NB behaved in true Camorra fashion, knowing that the victim could do nothing about it (QR1: 341).

It is difficult to get a true sense of the numbers in the Zaza clan in Naples because of the unreliability of the data. What the figures do show is that it was a large clan. *Carabineri* reports identified 216 Zaza clan members in 1988 (Allum, 2000: 383) 144 members in 1993, 179 in 1994 (Allum, 2000: 409), and 28 in 1995. They recorded that it was a predominantly male clan: in 1988, 212 members were male and 4 were women (Allum, 2000: 383). These figures are questionable, but they do give an indication of size. Zaza also influenced future generations of Camorra leaders who grew up in his clan, such as Ciro Mazzarella, Fiore D'Avino, and Mario Fabbrocino.

The third layer of Zaza's clan was his international associates. His defeat of the Marseillais over drugs in Naples during the early 1970s gained him local respect, international prestige, and fast-track entrance into the Cosa Nostra. In 1974, his membership in the Sicilian Mafia and the Bontade family brought him a multitude of contacts, networks, opportunities, associates, and expertises (TN1). Thanks to them he became involved in "the biggest market of international drugs trafficking" (QR1: 447): "a real and true 'international holding' of crime, with a strong international drugs-trafficking business between Italy and North and South America" (QR1: 318). This transformed him into a Neapolitan international player who fraternized with members from the Sicilian, South American, Corsican, and North American mafias (TP1).

In the early 1980s, the Zaza clan had both solid local roots and global criminal networks. When Zaza moved to Rome, and then France in 1988, he left his loyal foot soldiers, his headquarters, his heirs, his fortune, and a tense interclan situation behind him in Naples.[20] His criminal base did not relocate to France but remained firmly rooted in Italy; members either joined the Mazzarella nephews or chose to go it alone, such as JK. He was "45 years of age, [his nick name] for the Camorra, [was] 'Brill Cream.'" According to investigators, he "is *a pezzo da novanta* [a big shot] of the Zaza clan, according to some *pentiti*, his deputy and his loyal right-hand man."[21] However, Zaza's intimate business associates did follow him to the south of France, at various moments and in different guises, where it would appear they carried on with their shady economic deals. Their presence was noted at a hotel in the south of France after Zaza's move. Zaza suggested that this was mere coincidence: "He admitted knowing them, but claimed he did not know their motives for coming to Nice" (TGIM1: 115). It even appears that one business associate settled near the French-Italian border to be close to Zaza.

In France, Michele Zaza was now a loner, a solitary *camorrista*, but also a well-connected criminal manager involved in fluid international networks and financial projects. In terms of the clan in France, there was no French mass membership or members from the immigrant Neapolitan community. French police did not discover a Neapolitan settlement in Nice but an international manager at the center of several webs and networks of contraband and illegal activities. No direct decisions about criminal activities in Naples were made in France, only decisions about local activities (which were also linked to Italy). The Zaza organizational structure in France appears completely different from what had existed in Italy. Zaza was now involved in crime management, not in crime itself, and did not seek to recruit new French foot soldiers. Rather, he put together a loose network of qualified associates that would function with other criminal international networks.

From a French judicial document (TGIM1), an outline of Zaza's contraband network in France in 1988 can be drawn (see figure 4.2). It did not resemble the structure of a Cosa Nostra family or even a Neapolitan clan. This international organization of fifty-two individuals, like the De Falco network, was a flat, fluid network across different territories. It was not hierarchical, though members knew who the organizers were, and it is clear that Zaza's right-hand man (node 46) was the person who carried out activities on his behalf (node 31). The relationships between nodes were mostly transnational (more than three countries), the origin of each actor was multiethnic (more than two nationalities involved), and the organization's agenda was versatile, with no obvious relationship with Naples. The average age of the actors was forty-three with a few women (nodes 29, 30) offering support but not involved in the crimes themselves (TGIM1).

Women were important, however, and Zaza benefitted from their support both in Naples and in France. A 1983 Questura di Roma document noted the difference between Neapolitan and Sicilian women when it came to involvement: it "confirmed the thesis in relation to the role of women . . . , wives and daughters of important Camorra bosses have been accused because this investigation has demonstrated their direct participation in their husband's activities. The Sicilian women did not appear during telephone intercepts other than in their normal presence at home" (QR1: 491).

Zaza's wife was found "not guilty of Mafia association" (TN1: 9) and was a loyal wife (QR1: 327). The only accusation against her was the fact that "she appears to have owned a villa and flat located in Naples in via Petrarca, in her name . . . which was effectively available to her husband" (TN1: 9). In France, she was always very discreet and denied any involvement in her husband's criminal activities: "She affirmed that her husband had never told her about his activities," although the French court found that she "respected all the rules of her husband's life" (TGIM1: 116).

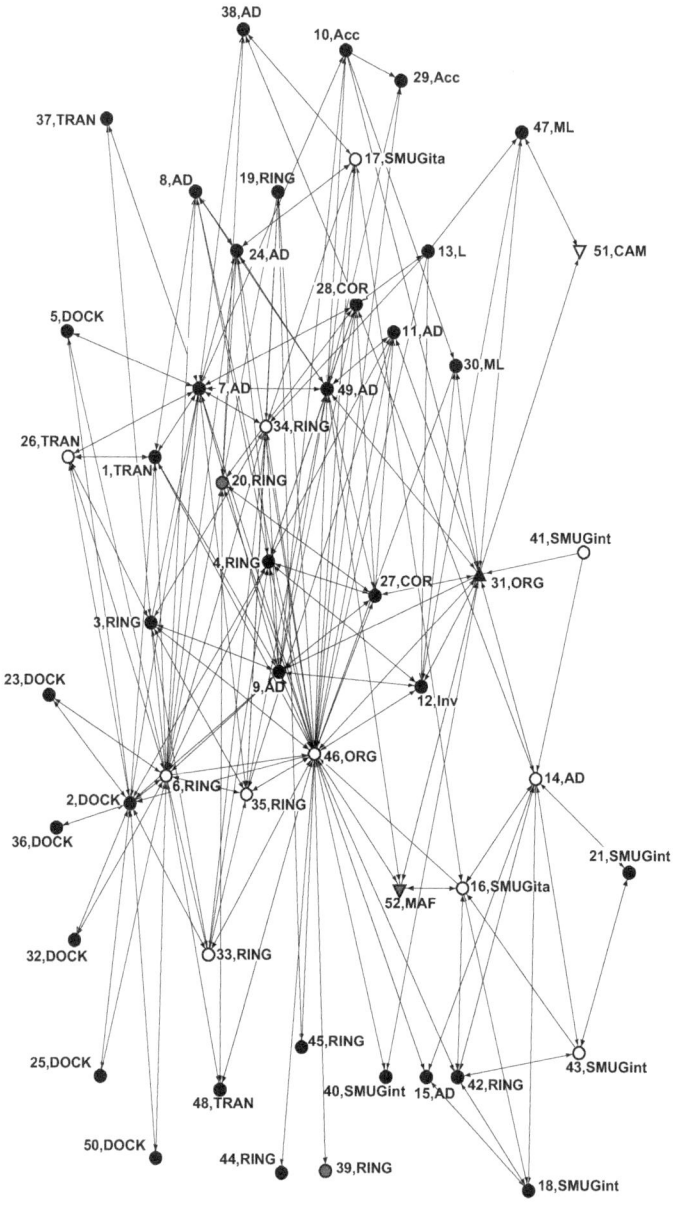

**Key**

Colors: grey (Italy), black (abroad), white (travels)

Shapes: △ = clan member  ○ = non-clan member  ▽ = other clan

Roles: transporter (TRAN), docker (DOCK), contraband ring (RING), organizer (ORG), corrupted administrator (AD), investor (Inv), money laundering (ML), accomplice (Acc), international cigarette smuggler (SMUGint), Italian cigarette smuggler (SMUGita), corrupt officer (COR), Camorra clan (CAM), mafia clan (MAF)

**FIGURE 4.2** The Zaza contraband cigarette network in France (1988)

Territorial control in Naples was less important than for other clans, but nevertheless this group still retained a distinct internal value system, predominately based on respect, trust, family, *omertà*, and survival. These values were embedded in Naples, but rarely used in France. In France Zaza appeared outwardly to lead "the life of a quiet father,"[22] which is probably what he wanted. In this way, there was a certain manipulation of the lack of awareness of Italian mafias in the new setting.

Violence was extensively used by the clan in Naples. Judicial documents point out that Zaza was "not only dangerous" but also used violence, psychological intimidation, and *omertà* that deviated from his association (see TN1 and GF1). Luigi Giuliano stressed: "Zaza had made disappear, or strangled, a certain number of smugglers from (his) district, Santa Lucia" (LGv, 18/10/2002: 3). To impose his supremacy, he consistently used violence. In France, verbal threats were occasionally used, but the prosecuting judge clearly stated that "there was no evidence of violence in Marseille" (SM).

Although documents offer only a limited picture of Zaza's organization across territories, it seems a very modern organization, with structures that were less territorial and visible in order to secure maximum profits. He did not undertake functional mobility as we define the term. He became light and liquid, as he had no roots and sought a more peaceful situation than had existed in Naples, but still, his original power base seems to have provided him with all the resources, members, and money he needed. As such, he did not establish a Camorra settlement but continued to be a player in the international contraband sector.

## ZAZA CLAN ACTIVITIES

Drawing a coherent overview of Zaza's criminal activities has been complicated. Whereas some activities are well documented in judicial decisions, for others there is less concrete evidence. In terms of documented activities, Michele Zaza was convicted of cigarette smuggling in Naples and France. He was also suspected of involvement in drug trafficking, money-laundering activities, and an attempt to buy the casino in Menton, which his accomplices sought to use to launder money made from drug trafficking (Calvi, 1993: 144–155). The documented examples, considered together with other pieces of information, help us to piece together a panorama of Zaza's activities.

Before Zaza moved permanently to the south of France in 1988, he was already heavily involved in various forms of local and international trafficking centered around the smuggling of contraband cigarettes. When he moved to France he did not diversify his activities, but rather applied his expertise in a new location, consolidating his position in the international market. During the 1970s and 1980s, the Zaza clan had been involved in two main activities. On the one hand was the smuggling and sale of cigarettes locally in Naples, initially by Zaza alone and then as part of the Sicilian import rota system (see Behan, 1996). This provided jobs for the local community and Zaza was often compared to Fiat and Agnelli as a job provider. The clan's defining feature was that "essentially, Zaza minded his own business with smuggling activities. He did not undertake extortions that we are aware of" (RM). Since his main activity was less territorial, Zaza was less interested in imposing his power locally and became fully immersed in international trafficking networks. The money made from smuggled cigarettes was also laundered in Naples with the help of accomplices. The preferred investments were real estate and legitimate companies (see GF1). On the other hand, the DEA, the American Drug Enforcement Administration, suggested that as a member of Cosa Nostra,[23] Zaza played a significant role in international drug trafficking, organizing together with the American mafias (especially the Gambino family) part of the Pizza Connection (1975–1984). Indeed, as these groups were heavily targeted by law-enforcement agencies, they turned to the Neapolitans, and Michele Zaza in particular, for help. The Sicilians gave Zaza and the NF Camorra "the task of heroin trafficking from the Middle East to the Mediterranean to North America" (QR1: 432), and he "trafficked cocaine from Caracas to Florida to Italy" (QR1: 429). It was suggested that he opened a factory in Rouen, France, to help with these activities.

Closely connected with contraband cigarettes and drug trafficking were Zaza's money-laundering activities: "as previously reported, the money made from traffics of this organization passes to Los Angeles through the Zaza family" (QR1: 430). Zaza also sought to recycle his money in Paris and Rome through front names and companies. On a global level, the financial implications of this international crime network were important, whether we consider the Cuntrera family in South America, the Sicilian Mafia families in Venezuela and North America, the Zaza family in Los Angeles, or the Caruana family in Montreal: "This patrimonial aspect of the criminal organization . . . is the most important dimension, demonstrating how it has created a system that has managed to control an important slice of [international] drug trafficking and convert it into goods, the fruits of their labor" (QR1: 486).

Zaza's arrest in Paris in 1982, and increasing Camorra unrest in Naples, "put into crisis the organization's system of illegal activities that he had established in Los Angeles" (QR1: 430). By 1984, Zaza was under increasing pressure. He had been arrested on numerous occasions and his smuggling business in Naples was under attack from other Camorra groups, who wanted to force him to pay them. "To force him to do this, we blocked his motorboats and killed his men" (LGv, 18/9/2002: 3). These events forced Zaza to make a life changing decision: he first looked to Rome, and in 1988 abroad, for his future. In Nice, he appeared to live the good life, but investigations soon indicated that he was indeed the "king of the Côte d'Azur"[24] because of his supposed involvement in an international cigarette smuggling ring, in drug trafficking, and in money-laundering activities such as buying casinos (FR).

In concrete terms, French prosecutors believe that between March and October 1988, seventy-one containers containing 62,300 cartons of cigarettes from Switzerland, Belgium, and New York had traveled through Marseille, destined for Saint Martin in the Dutch Caribbean. They never reached their destination. They were diverted at Marseille and sent via lorries with false documentation and the collusion of customs and excise officers to France, Italy, or Spain. This was an intricate scam that involved a variety of teams (French, Spanish, and Italian) and at least thirty companies that all contributed to the logistics of getting the smuggled cigarettes to their new destination (TGIM1: 46–47; see also AN1).

Michele Zaza, with his associates, managed this contraband operation. He was the manager and the expert who made the vital decisions and put into place a smooth and efficient smuggling system, with key people in the right jobs and the necessary people paid off. To assist him, he recruited a loyal right-hand man, an Italian named Dario Sacca. But when Zaza felt that Sacca was getting more credit than was due, he burst out during the trial, "I am much more important than Sacca, I have always had a much more important role than him. He is only a minor player, who undertakes small jobs. I am an international player in the traffic of cigarettes (Italy, Spain, United States, Greece, Belgium, Malta, France, etc.). I have always been involved in cigarette trafficking" (TGIM1: 112). French investigators, who were not used to these techniques and methods, had difficulty seeing exactly what he and Sacca were up to. Michele Zaza was sentenced on 19 July 1991 by the Court in Aix-en-Provence to four years in prison, but having already served half of his sentence he was released in November 1991.

There are also traces of other, more sophisticated, criminal activities. For example, it is believed that Zaza was involved with different criminal groups, among them the Corsicans, to buy the Ruhl casino in Nice. Also attempts were made to launder money made from drug trafficking using different scams (including the use of checks and false invoices), frauds, and front companies in French casinos in the south of France. It is even suggested that some politicians were co-opted by Zaza's group to try to convince the state that theirs was the best offer to buy the Menton casino, but it was blocked (Calvi, 1993: 144–149; MI3).

During Operation Green Sea the police "dismantled a Cosa Nostra-Camorra ring of thirty-nine people involved in cocaine trafficking and money laundering in Italy, France, and Germany." In particular, an elaborate network, probably based on drug-trafficking money and including employees of the casinos and directors of dubious companies, worked together with the traffickers. One of the key go-betweens in this network had also been involved in Zaza's contraband activities: "he put together a solid network of business activities and real estate investments in order to recycle illegally made profits."[25] Other criminal activities (such as diamond, check, and art trafficking) were also suspected, though Zaza's role was never fully proved. We can, however, say that Zaza saw the future of the Camorra in terms of a financial presence abroad without a set territory. Maybe this is one of the differences between mafias and camorras: mafias can become independent, rootless entities, whereas camorras still rely heavily on their local territory.

Zaza remains emblematic of the Italian Mafia's infiltration across borders. Zaza is not an isolated case even if often "fugitives in France do not commit any crime for [their] legal system, [...] they do not hesitate to open shops in France, with a particular interest in pizzerias or leather shops or to establish a multitude of real estate companies" (Calvi, 1993: 154). Many of Zaza's activities are difficult to prove, and what this former *camorrista* and now retired businessman may have been doing on the Côte d'Azur may never be fully known.

### ZAZA CLAN ACCOMPLICES

Michele Zaza's social capital, his charisma, and his role within international crime networks gave him such power and prestige that he could count on many different types of accomplices, from intimidated subordinates to full-blown equal partners. There is evidence of subordinate entrepreneurs who, after having been intimidated by him, did as he wanted—after all, he was a convincing *mafioso*. More interesting were the "compenetrative" accomplices who surrounded him, those close associates whose external façades suggested they were respectable and legitimate businessmen, but whose real role was to support Zaza in his criminal activities and exchange skills with him.

Zaza could count on two of these: one was a close relative, SL, who owned retail companies in Rome and Paris, the other was an adviser-accomplice, NB, who also had financial interests in these cities. Both associates moved to France with him, and without these skillful and knowledgeable businessmen Zaza may have been less successful. SL was a supposedly legitimate businessman who put his commercial interests at Zaza's disposal so he could use them to launder his money (QR1: 429). He was openly complicit because he had interests in Zaza's criminal projects and always helped out. NB was originally a businessman based in Rome and one of Zaza's key advisers, who once said, "I would do anything for Michele" (QR1: 322) NB's complicity came in a variety of forms: First, he constantly assisted Zaza, even when ill, helped him with travel arrangements (for example, providing his brother's passport to Zaza for travel), and offered financial advice. Second, he was extremely well networked: he had contacts with the Sicilian, South American, and New York mafias and acted as mediator between Zaza and other criminal communities. Third, he made his companies available to different mafias for money transfers and recycling of money. Lastly, together with Zaza and others, he bought a factory in Rouen, France, which was believed to be more than a factory (see QR1). He was no passive, subordinate entrepreneur, but rather a full participant in Zaza's activities, which may explain why he moved to the south of France.

Zaza also had accomplices in France. In his French contraband scam he bribed the key players. These were the managers of the docks of Marseille's harbor, who turned a blind eye to his activities, and customs and excise officers. They were complicit accomplices who had meetings with the boss and were necessary to guarantee a successful operation. As the French prosecutor underlined, "a criminal organization can only work if it corrupts those around it in order to impose its mafia system" (SM). Zaza's success was due to accomplices in different locations. Typically the accomplices we have encountered have been Neapolitans and Italians who traveled when necessary, but Zaza also co-opted many French and foreign accomplices who helped him in various ways, whether as complicit accomplices or partners in joint ventures.

On 27 March 1994, Zaza was extradited back to Italy because he was wanted for mafia association, and died later that year of a heart attack at the age of forty-nine. Perhaps he was ahead of his time and judicial systems were always playing catch-up to understand what he was doing. But it is difficult to describe Zaza's behavior as functional mobility, as we have defined the term, because a link back to Naples was hard to trace. His associates were clearly involved in various criminal activities in Italy and his smuggling operation was an international network involving diverse nationalities and different investors, individuals, territories, modes of transports, markets, and alliances. He exploited his host country, and without solid roots in Naples, he became a more difficult criminal quantity to identify—an invisible presence.

## International Network of Drug Brokers (Tiro Grosso) (2002–2006)

The geography of France and its proximity to Italy has determined the nature of clans' involvement in the French drugs market. A growing class of brokers has developed who represent Camorra clans in international drug-trafficking rings. In 2006, a "European brokerage system" was identified (TN14: 30) that functioned across Western Europe but was located in France because of its geographical centrality and because some of its key members belonged to the French criminal underworld: "The Neapolitans established a new organizational model with groups of 'brokers' who acted as mediators between the international groups who look after the selling and the local clans that deal with the distribution across a specific territory" (TN14: 28). The brokers acted on behalf of individual Camorra clans to negotiate and buy drugs from international drug networks and cartels. They traveled to and from France to organize drug deals for their clients.

This system reduced the direct involvement of clans with foreign drug importers. They no longer had to deal with issues such as organization or transportation. Instead, the brokers looked after all the messy organizational aspects of the trafficking from Spain, France, and the Netherlands into Italy and Naples. Camorra clans were less directly implicated, had less of the hard work and hassle, and became less visible because someone else was doing all the work (such as contacting the wholesaler, undertaking negotiations, and organizing transport). This system cannot be described as the "implantation" of Camorra clans in France, but rather business transactions made on behalf of interested *camorristi*. Some Camorra clans, however, still prefer to import directly, among them the La Torre clan, the Nuvoletta clan, and the D'Alessandro clan.

After four years of investigation,[26] the Italian and French judicial and police authorities in 2006 discovered an extensive transnational drugs network providing hashish, heroin, and cocaine to brokers who represented Neapolitan Camorra clans. This international multiethnic network (including French, Spanish, Dutch, Iraqi, Bulgarian, Peruvian, Dominican, Filipino, Venezuelan, and other South American citizens) connected South America to Europe, utilizing many different routes and dealing in various types of drugs that were sold across Europe (see TN14).

This international ring had three different organizational and geographical levels: (1) The top level was Colombians, who were the importers and sellers, often based in Europe. (2) French and Italian brokers, who were the managers of the distribution of the drugs and oversaw the different phases of the operations. (3) The buyers—the Camorra clans in their local territory in Italy. These brokers regularly traveled and engaged with international drug-trafficking networks for the clans based in Naples.

South Americans living in Spain and Italy arranged the importation of drugs from Colombia and then sold them to various groups of European brokers who distributed them to the different national markets. Two brokers in this European system were violent members of the Marseillais milieu. From Marseille, they sold to Camorra clans, but took all the risks and assumed full responsibility and the financial burden if there was a loss. They had easy access to labor, arms, and contacts, which made them efficient in their role and ideally located to import drugs into Spain and facilitate trafficking into Italy. Often they would travel to pick up their supplies in Spain or the Netherlands and deliver them directly to Italy, although there were also Italian brokers who would travel to Spain, the Netherlands, and Marseille for meetings.

These brokers maintained contact with clan representatives on an ad hoc basis. They invested financially in the transactions as well as coordinating them; they would "personally finance the importation of the drugs from abroad and then sell them to various local clients, who in turn would 'retail' them across the territory" (TN14: 625). These brokers sold to markets in the north and the south, where their local clients were individuals, often Camorra members, who were even used as couriers, for example, for trips to Croatia or Montenegro to collect cocaine from the Balkan route. Some Camorra members also invested in the importation and sale of drugs, although in a very indirect way, through associates who set up false companies to transfer money to brokers. The establishment of this brokerage system in the international drugs market was "exclusively introduced with the aim of improving the management of the distribution of drugs to the different Camorra clans operating in Campania" (TN14: 40).

Varied forms of transportation into Europe were used by the international drug networks: the shipment of cocaine from Venezuela was by containers (supposedly carrying mangos, but in reality carrying 250–400 kilos of cocaine) to France (Fos-sur-Mer), or by car from Barcelona to Naples (TN14). Between 2002 and 2003, more than twenty journeys were undertaken by French couriers, who transported 10–30 kilos of cocaine per journey. Moreover, in order to avoid detection, a relay convoy system was used, as well as different cars to cross the Spanish and then the Italian borders. The goods would be hidden in concealed car trunks and the smugglers would use complex coded language (CAAP2) to avoid detection.

It could be argued that this network structure was temporary and more adaptable than the divisions organized internally by the clans themselves: it changed forms of transport and routes whenever necessary, there was a continuous flow of money via Western Union into different companies' bank accounts, and the contacts used were not necessary the same from transaction to transaction. But the changing values on which this brokerage system was established are evident. It was no longer based on traditional values of trust and loyalty, but instead on money and avarice. When members were considered untrustworthy, they would be bypassed. On one occasion, for example, when the usual system of using the Marseillais brokers did not work, the Italians negotiated directly with the Colombians, and on another, when French brokers had their money stolen in Naples, they believed that "it was their client [the Neapolitans] who had ordered the armed theft of the money they had just been given after a delivery" (CAAP2: 21). There existed very little trust among the different actors.

This European brokerage system was thus based on the notion of continuous supplies: it relied on local demand, financial power, and the use of firearms. The brokers were not the drug traffickers themselves, but only the mediators, the go-betweens, the middle men, who bought directly from the native suppliers (the South Americans and Spanish who were present in Europe) or used suppliers based in the Netherlands, Croatia, or Montenegro to sell to clans. These cases illustrate the sophisticated nature of international criminal networks.

## Individual Brokers (2008)

UB, a former lieutenant of Michele Zaza during the 1980s, already had international contacts, traveled around Europe, and was connected to high-ranking *camorristi*. He is a good example of an independent broker. He was considered by the French authorities to be "close to the Camorra." The "Neapolitan police confirmed that UB was an individual 'with great criminal prestige,' having a criminal record in France; he was a member of the clan led by Umberto Ammaturo, who was an important member of the NF and an international drug trafficker" (CAAP3: 59).

Between 2007 and 2008, UB was arrested for his role in various drug networks. In 2007, he was believed to be an independent broker in an international drug ring that imported cocaine from Peru into Rotterdam, through to Paris and Marseille, and then either to Spain or Italy. He used his contacts to put the top Dutch manager of the international drugs network in touch with the Colombian wholesalers, one of which was his cousin, a Neapolitan resident in Venezuela (CAAP3: 15–18). Once the goods were in France, he would seek to sell them to clans in Naples.

This international network was made up of many different nationalities (from France, Holland, Congo, Algeria, Bulgaria, Belgium, and Venezuela), with the two main managers based in Europe. They "organized importations of cocaine originating from different South American countries and destined for France and Italy via the port of Antwerp. The goods were usually presented as legal freight. They used the names of existing legal French import companies . . . and established false Belgium offices or branches'" (CAAP3: 9). The leader of this drugs network was based in Paris and his main interests were in France (CAAP3), whereas UB's role, as a broker, was to sell drugs to clans in Naples. In 2010, UB was sentenced to six years in prison by a Marseille court for his role in this international drugs network.

In 2011, he was sentenced to ten years by a court in Paris for the "importation and possession of drugs." He was accused of having swapped a suitcase with a member of a drugs network, and 191 kilos of cocaine had been found when a number of members were arrested. His lawyers defended their client by arguing that he had never been convicted for "Camorra association" in Italy.[27] And this is precisely the point: He formed part of a mobile international drugs network that imported drugs into Europe. He would buy those drugs and transport them to Italy for the clans in Naples. He was not a member of a clan with a territory to defend, but an independent broker who mediated with international drug networks and provided services and goods. He negotiated competitive prices and transported the goods to Italy. The relationship between the Camorra and these brokers is difficult to detect. Here the Camorra is in its most flexible form, taking advantage of every available economic opportunity through autonomous brokers. It becomes invisible.

In this chapter, we have seen how Camorra groups and individuals in France move about, shift tactics, and adapt in order to respond to the economic opportunities and exploit the country's lack of understanding of the international drugs-trafficking phenomenon. But they also manipulate the natural friendship and sympathy of the emigrant communities that exist there.

# 5

# CAMORRA CLANS IN SPAIN
## Granada, Tarragona, and Tenerife

Since its transition to democracy in the late 1970s and its entrance into the European Union in 1986, Spain has been considered by many *camorristi* as an El Dorado, an accessible paradise in which to conduct criminal activities undisturbed and strike gold. This may explain why, over the last thirty years, many *camorristi* have made it their second home. But there is another reason: its place in the European drugs market. From the existing evidence, it could be suggested that of the Camorra clans with links to Europe, around seventy percent have connections to Spain, where they seek to profit from its structural conditions, in particular, from Spanish institutions, its legal system, and economic opportunities, especially its wholesale drugs market.

Of the five countries studied, Spain is the *camorristi's* preferred destination. In 2009, it was estimated by the Italian police and judiciary that 70 percent of *mafiosi* (249) on the run were hiding in Spain.[1] Indeed, according to Raffaele Cionti, the Italian police liaison officer based in Madrid in 2012, between 2005 and 2010, 62 leading *camorristi* were arrested in Spain, that is, about 12 a year. He argues that "*camorristi* adopt behavior that is completely different from that used in their homeland. . . . They do not use threats. Indeed, they seek to . . . make themselves as invisible as possible" (RC). The *pentito* Gennaro Panzuto explains: "If they [*camorristi*] have connections with Spanish people, it's a commercial relationship with the aim of opening shops, restaurants, and so on" (GP). As a consequence, there may be a possible increase in collaboration between Spanish and foreign groups: in 2005, it was estimated that of 471 criminal groups investigated, only 120 (25.5 percent) were entirely foreign in composition (Sands, 2007: 213), whereas in 2010, of the groups investigated, only 17 percent did not include Spanish citizens (S1: 3).

**TABLE 5.1** Case studies for Spain (1980–2015)

| CLAN | DATES | LOCATION/ITALY | LOCATION/ABROAD | CRIME |
|---|---|---|---|---|
| Misso clan/ De Tommaso team | 2000–2006 | Sanità, Naples city | Madrid and other regions | Acquisitive crime |
| Secondigliano alliance | 1990–2000 | Secondigliano, Naples city | Madrid | CF |
| Other Camorra city clans | 2008– | Naples city | Malaga, Madrid, Barcelona, Valencia, Seville | CF |
| De Falco clan | 1986–1994 | Casal di Principe, Caserta | Granada | Drugs/ML |
| Amato-Pagano clan* | 2000–2006 | Melito, Naples city | Madrid, Barcelona | Drugs/ML |
| Polverino clan | 1994– | Quarto, Marano, Naples | Barcelona, Malaga, Alicante, Ceuta, Caetellon, Cadice | Drugs/ML |
| Nuvoletta clan | 1995–2008 | Marano, Naples | Tenerife | ML |

*The Amato-Pagano case study is not elaborated fully here, but its most salient points are referred to where necessary in the different chapters.

Six cases have been chosen to reflect the variety of Camorra individuals and clans that have been active in Spain between the 1980s and 2015, illustrating different aspects of their mobility. Although Italian journalists have reported Spanish police investigations into the involvement of Camorra associates in illegal waste dumping in 2012,[2] clans were predominately present in our four main identified sectors (see table 5.1).[3]

## Acquisitive Crime

During the summer months Spain becomes particularly attractive to criminals because it is the destination for around sixty-one million foreign tourists a year.[4] In a form of "mobile banditism" (DP1: 141) by traveling criminals or criminal tourists, bank robberies and ad hoc snatch thefts of Rolex watches now take place regularly in mainland Europe. Although the numbers are believed to "remain low," Gómez-Céspedes has pointed out that "it is very difficult to know the scale or cost of organised robberies in Spain" (2012: 177).

However, the Spanish Association of Jewelers, Silversmiths, and Watchmakers has slowly started to acknowledge this form of modern banditism as a problem for the Spanish economy: "back in the year 2002, the then president of this Association stated before the Senate that robberies had cost the sector 17 million euros in 2000 and 32 million euros the following year" (Gómez-Céspedes, 2012: 177). For example, in 2008 it was reported that "a lengthy Civil Guard investigation has broken up a major gang of bank robbers, said to be the largest in Spain, which is believed to have carried out 34 armed robberies in seven Spanish provinces: Granada, Málaga, Murcia, Cuenca, Madrid, Burgos, and Alicante. Their total haul between April 2006 and March last year was 750,000 €." This gang was made up of Italians, a Belgian, and a Spaniard, and "its main base was in Marbella, in Málaga province, and they were closely linked to another gang in Marbella from the Mazzarella clan of the Neapolitan Camorra—the Naples Mafia."[5]

Many Neapolitan petty criminals, before entering the Camorra, specialize in different forms of acquisitive crime, from bank robberies (organized or unorganized, violent or nonviolent) to ad hoc bag snatching and theft of Rolex watches and jewelry,[6] to mention a few. This may be explained by the fact that some Camorra associates control the stolen Rolex market in Naples and have involved Camorra leaders in their scam. Here they are not exporting their Camorra activities, but extending their basic criminal skills as they target specific countries for their resources. Some associates of the Misso clan were involved in such activities.

## Acquisitive Crime and the Misso Clan

For a long time, the smaller Misso clan, from the Sanità district and allies of the Mazzarella clan, controlled robberies in the city—"not one robbery can take place if the Misso clan is not in agreement or provides support" (SGv, 14/12/2004). The clan also had associates under its protection who were involved in general illegal markets and scams; in particular, the De Tommaso brothers based in Forcella, who had previously been sponsored by the Giuliano clan. These brothers, two old-time cigarette smugglers, controlled the stolen Rolex market and rigged auction houses in Naples with the complicity of the Misso clan. As part of this activity, it would seem that they controlled the market of stolen goods, specifically Rolexes, imported from Europe by Neapolitan thieves who had snatched them (see PN12 and GF2).

From 2000 onward, thieves and burglars were "forced to give them, or sell them their stolen goods from abroad" (GMv, in PN12: 186), and, as one of the De Tommaso brothers suggested, violence was always a possibility (PN12: 45). Although these individuals were on the fringes of the clan, they were the brains behind the operation and sought Camorra approval. According to police investigations, a team of "roaming and traveling petty criminals" close to the brothers left Salerno in July 2004 by ferry with their motorbikes and went to Marbella to steal goods. They then returned with their stolen goods to have them either sold or melted down, and the clan would take a cut (see GF2). This scam was purely a Neapolitan affair with no money leaving Naples or being invested abroad, but rather into the clan.

Figure 5.1 represents the brothers' fluid network of Rolex thieves and rigged auction scams and their links with *camorristi* (GF2). Slowly, these brothers

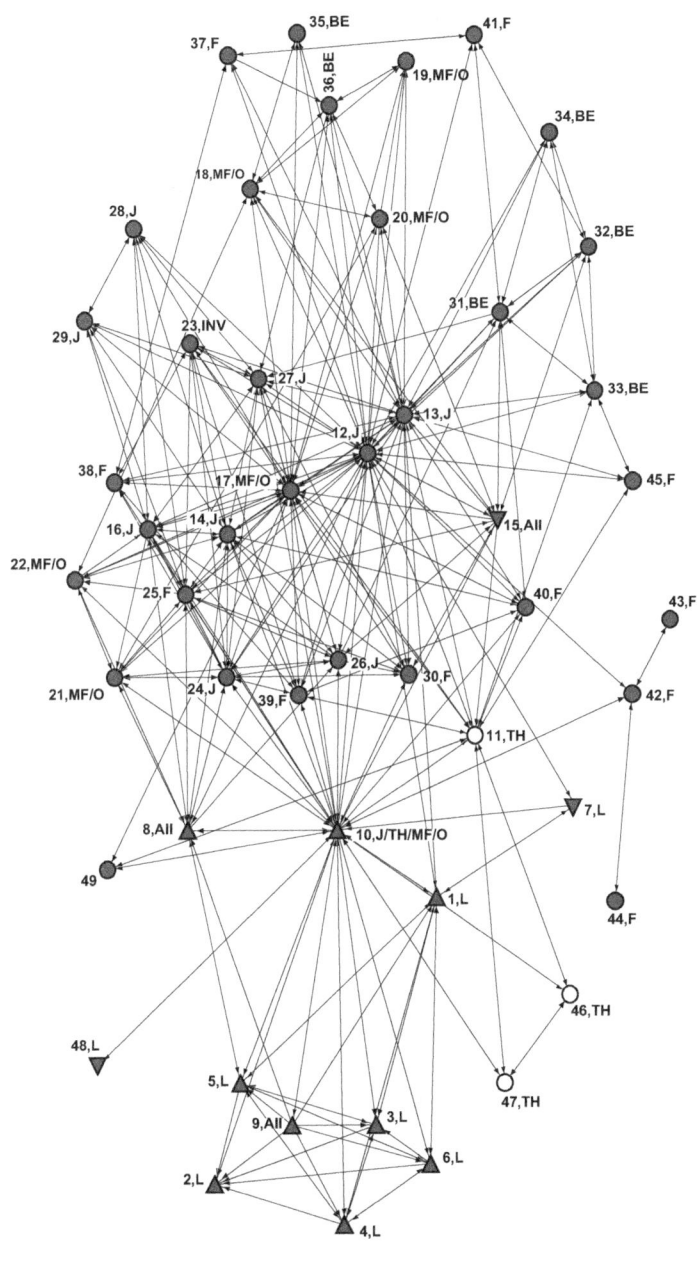

**Key**

Colors: grey (Naples/Italy), black (abroad), white (travels)

Shapes: △ = clan member   ◯ = non-clan member   ▽ = other clan

Roles: leader (L), front name (F), bank employee (BE), manager of rigged auction fraud (MF), organizer (O), jeweler (J), thief (TH), all Camorra activities (All), investor (Inv)

**FIGURE 5.1** The De Tommaso brothers and their acquisitive crime networks (2000–2006)

increased their involvement in core Camorra activities and took on more important executive roles as clan members were arrested. One De Tommaso brother, the main scam organizer (10), is the node between the clan (1–8) and the other criminal activities (12–49); there is a blurring of lines. For the Rolex scam, members were Neapolitan, there was no involvement with foreign criminal gangs or context, just a team composed of three players (11, 47, 46) who foraged around Europe, snatching where they could and what they could, Rolex if possible, to be sold in Naples or abroad,[7] which the clan supported and profited from.

This case represents neither the traditional Camorra nor its modern business face, but is a return to basic criminal skills. These Camorra associates were not diversifying, but purely exploiting the opportunities and resources available in Spain, and made sure the clan benefitted from them so that all were happy.

## The Counterfeit Market

The nature and extent of counterfeit activities in Spain is nebulous. In 2009, the Spanish Ministry of the Interior did not deem this criminal activity to be a particularly vibrant one (S2).[8] In 2015, it became a priority. For Camorra clans, however, Spain has always represented a healthy market and destination for their counterfeit goods. Figures of articles intercepted in Spain in 2010 show that between 2009 and 2010 there was a 184 percent increase, with clothing and accessories usually the main items sold (EC3: 22). Identifying single clans involved in these activities has been difficult because of limited open access information, but it has been possible to ascertain that Spain has witnessed two waves of Camorra counterfeit involvement (see table 5.2): the first was brought about by the Secondigliano counterfeit company (see ch. 3) and the second by the Mazzarella and other city clans, as in France. Both are analyzed here.

**TABLE 5.2** Waves of Camorra involvement in counterfeit goods (1990s–2000s)

| DATES | CLANS | CAMORRA INVOLVEMENT |
| --- | --- | --- |
| First wave: 1990s–2000s | Alliance of Secondigliano (AS) | Direct investment + management |
| Second wave: 2000s– | Mazzarella clan, AS, Contini clan, Stolder clan, others. | Direct investment + businessmen-associates manage the operations |

## The Counterfeit Market and the Secondigliano Alliance (1990–2000s)

Evidence suggests that the Secondigliano counterfeit company was active in Madrid and Portugal during the 1990s, where it sold cutlery in particular, but also tableware, leather jackets, and fake Olympus cameras. Its Spanish operations followed a similar pattern to elsewhere in Europe, but with many importation activities running concurrently. No fixed Camorra settlement based in Spain was identified, but a member of its board of directors, SB, was. In the 1990s, he became the local area manager, regularly traveling to monitor activities, sort out deals with producers and local sellers, and take instructions (QN4, 3: 110–123). In particular, he imported fake goods and organized their distribution via the main warehouse in Madrid, to which the Spanish *magliari* referred to for goods. This warehouse was the company's operating base in Spain, which was a node in its larger international fake-business network. He oversaw these operations because thanks to previous investments in real estate, he was familiar with the country (QN4, 1: 61). By early 2000, another member close to the Licciardi clan installed himself, coordinating activities in situ and traveling often. It is not clear whether violence was ever used toward the *magliari*, but that is not to be excluded.

Import techniques developed to avoid customs inspections: either by direct importation from China to Madrid, bypassing Naples, or through Naples using legal import-export companies in Italy and Spain. The use of legal companies became essential, as in 2000 when goods were exported from Naples to a legal company in Barcelona owned by a Neapolitan with an Italian criminal record (QN4, 3: 122). Using legitimate companies, often co-owned by *camorristi*, guaranteed peace of mind and success, as no one suspected these companies of being involved in counterfeit scams, tax evasion, or money transfers. In this way the Secondigliano counterfeit company, together with its businessmen-accomplices, was able to manipulate economic rules and regulations to pass off its counterfeit activities as quasi-legal. Here the Camorra no longer manifested itself as a heavy criminal association but as a bodiless economic strategy, slowly infiltrating the Spanish legal economy via the counterfeit market.

## The Counterfeit Market and City Camorra Clans (2008–)

In 2010, the Spanish authorities discovered a counterfeit organization with a structure similar to the ones identified in France and Germany in 2008. This organization appeared to be another part of the Camorra city clans counterfeit operations. Like a snake that has shed its skin, this new counterfeit organization, compared with the Secondigliano company, had evolved and adapted to its new settings, markets, opportunities, and obstacles. Its new organizational structure, promoted by the Mazzarella clan, was more open and flexible. The involvement of *camorristi* in the day-to-day management of these counterfeit activities was less direct in contrast to Pietro Licciardi's management style. Now, through their so-called legitimate business associates, often relatives, they remotely and indirectly controlled the whole process: the investment, production, importation, transportation, and sale of fake goods.

The main actors were businessmen who lived on the edge of legality and who had historic links with *camorristi*. For example, the Sista brothers, historically connected to the Mazzarella clan, set up an import company in Málaga with an established business partner in Spain in order to receive their electronic goods (chainsaws) directly from China. The labels of the brands (Husqvarna, Stihl, Bosch, Honda, Hitachi) were sent separately. This operation allowed goods to arrive legally, directly or indirectly (via Naples), at a destination using Spanish bank accounts for money transfers, probably with the help of local area managers. The only visible link that could be made with the Camorra was the origin of the different players: the *magliari*, the local area managers, and the warehouse owners were all Neapolitan.

The connection with the Camorra was intangible once the Mazzarella clan had invested its money. No longer a criminal clan, it became a loose multiethnic network with key players in China, Naples, and abroad who managed operations and the distribution of goods via the *magliari* network. In 2011, the Spanish authorities discovered a network composed of sixty-two Italians, one Spaniard, and one Brazilian.[9] Profits were easy—an Italian Ministry document estimated that "the cost of an electric generator from China would be about 35 euros and it was sold to the customer for 400 euros" (MSE1: 151). As a result, it was calculated that a group of two *magliari* could make about 250,000 euros in two to three months (MSE1: 152).

This new version of Camorra counterfeit operation had five stages. In the first phase, Neapolitan businessmen sent original articles, usually clothes, machinery, or tools, to China to be reproduced. In the second phase, associate Chinese producers fabricated imitation copies. In China, twenty-five producers were identified, but they had not technically broken the law. In the third phase, the counterfeit goods were shipped to Europe (Valencia, Málaga, and Seville, since Naples had become too risky) via containers and delivered to import companies (twenty companies were identified) in ports where Camorra associates had trusted contacts. Once the goods arrived in Europe, in the fourth phase, they were stocked in warehouses and depots, where the local area managers added the "made in Italy" labels and distributed the goods to the *magliari*. The last phase was the selling of the products by *magliari* across Spain: each region had a local area manager (with a warehouse) who managed and looked after the *magliari*, dictating the prices and selecting the products.[10]

Profits made here were vital for these clans because they were not automatically reinvested into new activities, but were carefully returned to the Neapolitan headquarters to subsidize the common fund. The Camorra's presence was quasi-invisible: although it had no direct physical presence, it made a financial investment that connected Naples to other territories.

## International Drug Trafficking

Since the late 1980s, Spain and the Netherlands have become the centers of the European cocaine and hashish markets because they are the two *main* entry points for these commodities (Gounev and Bezlov, 2010). Spain's geographical proximity to South America (for cocaine importation), North Africa (only 14 kilometers away, for hashish importation), and Italy (for transportation) means that it has become a necessary wholesale market for Italian drug traffickers. It is not only a destination and transit country, but since the 1990s it has also become an indispensable European drugs distribution center, one of the most important wholesale markets, predominately for cocaine, hashish, and cannabis, where many criminals conglomerate to buy their goods.

Geography is decisive and determines Spain's strategic position at the heart of the European drugs trade, as the three main techniques systematically used for the importation of cocaine show. First, bags full of cocaine are dropped into the Atlantic and then collected by Galician groups and distributed in Europe by sea and road routes. Second, drugs arrive in containers via the port of Barcelona (cocaine) or the Gibraltar straits (hashish) and are then circulated via road or sea to Italy. Third, drugs are brought in via airports (such as Barajas airport near Madrid), using couriers with the drugs in suitcases or hidden on individuals (see QC1).

In addition, the absence of efficient, homegrown organized crime groups as potential rivals, the presence of South Americans living in Spain (Savona, 1999: 107) and its relatively weak antimafia legislation all explain why that country has become an attractive destination not only for *camorristi* but for other criminal communities as well, such as the British or Russians. However, after the terrorist attacks in 2004, the Spanish government clamped down on criminal-terrorist activities, and this had the indirect effect of pushing drug trafficking toward the Netherlands as possibly an easier entry point. This clampdown did not last long, as Spain returned to being one of the most accessible gateways into Europe for drugs, for both for cocaine from South America and hashish from North Africa.

In 1996, the DEA, estimated "that 80% of all cocaine destined for Europe transits through Spain" (Savona, 1999: 107). In 2007, Europol reported that "the Spanish authorities seized almost 38 tonnes of cocaine, much of it at sea, representing about 50 percent of the estimated total quantity intercepted in Europe" (EMCDDA1: 25). During the 2000s, Spain remained a predominant European marketplace. Average cocaine seizures between 2006 and 2009 reflect this: 35 percent compared with 12.3 percent for Portugal, 7.55 percent for France, 8.2 percent for the Netherlands, and 4.1 percent for Italy (although reportedly these seizures are declining in Italy, PCM). These figures, however unreliable, still indicate a flourishing marketplace (see table 8 in UNODC3: 18). But our understanding of the true extent of the phenomenon remains limited because, as Franco Roberti pointed out, "we can recall how in one year (2006) alone in Naples and its provinces, more than 1 ton of pure cocaine and nearly 6 tons of hashish were seized, but such enormous quantities, according to the DCSA (Direzione Centrale per i Servizi Antidroga), are not even the equivalent of 10% of the drugs trafficked into our country" (2012: 241).

Cocaine and hashish are the main drugs imported into Spain and of interest to the Camorra. Many Camorra clans have identified the continuous relationship between the demand for cocaine in Italy and the supply in South America. They saw the significant amounts of money that could be made from this activity (MV). The profits made are so substantial that, in spite of the risk, it is considered a worthwhile enterprise. In 2010, 10,898 kilograms of cocaine, 95,413 kilograms of hashish, 110 kilograms of heroin, and 190,947 ecstasy pills were seized in Spain (S1: 5). It was estimated that "the international drugs trade makes 75 billion pesetas (more than 450 million euros) each year, which is more than double the Spanish state budget (Gomez and Gurrieri, 2001: 35). Hashish, on the other hand, is smuggled into Spain from Morocco via Gibraltar, and it has been estimated that almost all of it originates in Morocco (UNODC5: 81); it represents 50 percent of hashish seized in the world; and 70 percent of hashish seized in Europe is seized in Spain (Sands, 2007: 213). The traditional routes were Capo Spartel to Huelva to Galicia or Portugal, Tangeri or Ceuta to Algeciras or Gibraltar, and Cabo Negro to Bahia Alhucemas to Almeria or Barcelona (see Savona, 1999: 108). In 2006–2013, the Polverino clan used similar routes from Gibraltar into Spain for hashish.

As a consequence, many Camorra clans have reinvented themselves as drug-trafficking clans from their previous contraband incarnation. The Gionta clan from Torre Annunziata, for example, was once known as "*i contrabbandieri*" ("the smugglers"). The larger the clan, the more resources, opportunities, and personnel it has at its disposal to establish itself in the host country. Its deep local roots produce stability, which in turn allows it to place people abroad, making it an efficient drug-enterprise network. Smaller groups are more ad hoc, temporary, and less systematic in their drug-trafficking organization and strategies.

As not all Camorra clans can import directly, many have resorted to brokers to mediate between them and their suppliers. Thus an additional layer of extraterritorial and disengaged networks exists. For example, city clans such as the Mazzarella clan used the services of brokers such as LPC, who ran a drug-importation network that included Neapolitans, Romans, French, Americans, Bulgarians, and Spaniards, and supplied them with hashish (see GF3). And there are many more international brokers like him.

Official UN statistics on drug trafficking in Spain do not reveal the presence of Neapolitans: in the 2008 figures, Italians were not listed as a nationality of persons arrested in Spain for cocaine trafficking (UNODC1: 89, fig. 53). This may be because they were arrested for mafia association at the request of the Italian authorities. And yet, using a Neapolitan lens, it becomes possible to see how the majority of Camorra clans involved in drug trafficking *do* travel to Spain as part of their activities. For example, between 2009 and 2011 drug traffickers from the Contini, Mazzarella, and Giuliano clans were all arrested in Spain for cocaine trafficking. They combined being on the run with directly managing the drug-importation division of their clan.

## Camorra Clans and Drug Trafficking

By 2005, drug trafficking had become big business for Neapolitan clans because the returns outweighed the significant risks. It was *the* business to be in. Many clans are involved in the local drug distribution of cocaine and hashish, but importation from Spain requires international contacts, fluid organizational structures, methodical coordination, and wise leadership. Whereas all types and sizes of clans attempt to import drugs into Italy to sell in their home territory, it is only the larger clans that can effectively establish a dominant position in the local and national markets with firm contacts abroad. It was estimated in 2005 that the Camorra made 16 billion euros a year from drug trafficking.[11]

The two clans analyzed here are the De Falco clan from Casal di Principe (1986–1999) and the Polverino clan from Quarto (1999–2014). The Polverino clan has been described as one of the main criminal players in the international trafficking of hashish (see PN15, PN16, and TN23) and a "near perfect" drug importation organization (MdG). It managed to combine deep local roots in

Quarto and Marano with a flexible international economic approach, making for a light business network that was "shaped and reshaped by its twists and turns" (Bauman, 2000: 7), rendering it a profitable and cooperative network. It is a good example of how the local territory provides the power to maintain a presence abroad. These two cases also show how clans have evolved in this market over the last three decades, always updating their organizational structures and methods of operation. They highlight flexibility, adaptability, and versatility, but also a strong link between the local territory and global markets.

## Drug Trafficking and the De Falco Clan

Those *camorristi* who were influenced by the Sicilian Mafia discovered Europe before the 1990s. Antonio Bardellino was one of the first to understand the importance of host countries for his economic activities, especially after the introduction of the Rognoni-La Torre law in 1982. He encouraged members of his criminal confederation who had problems with the law to move abroad for good (to countries such as France, Spain, Portugal, Brazil, and San Domingo) and further their long-term business activities.

Nunzio De Falco, of the De Falco clan, a member of the larger Bardellino-Iovine confederation, was one such representative, as was the boss, Mario Iovine, "who, on the run at the time, used to spend long periods abroad, and in particular in France and Brazil, [where] he had opened an import-export company of fish paste that served as a cover for the activities of cocaine trafficking" (TN4: 10). Although Nunzio De Falco is predominately remembered for ordering the murder of Don Peppe Diana, the priest from Casal di Principe, in 1992 (see CASMCV3 and CASMCV4), his presence in Spain from 1986 onward makes him an interesting case. He was one of the first *camorristi* to be identified abroad and one of the few whose activities can, more or less, be traced. He demonstrates the importance of the local territory for Camorra clans.

### THE DE FALCO CLAN: ITS MEMBERS AND TERRITORIES

Before 1988, Vincenzo De Falco's clan structure was that of a blood family within the larger hierarchical Bardellino-Iovine confederation. The confederation had a pyramid structure: the Bardellino family at the top, then a deputy (Mario Iovine), subordinate lieutenants (Francesco Schiavone, Francesco Bidognetti, Vincenzo De Falco, Vincenzo Zagaria), and at the bottom foot soldiers and allies, with power flowing down from Antonio Bardellino. He was the ultimate leader with his own criminal family and a solid power base in San

Cipriano d'Aversa, but was assisted by his deputy and his four eager lieutenants, who surrounded themselves with their reliable families and foot soldiers. Each clan assumed a "generational family" structure (Gribaudi, 1999: 92) and was, as a result, very efficient. Vincenzo De Falco ('O Fuggiasco), was an emerging lieutenant in the Bardellino-Iovine confederation. His older brother, Nunzio De Falco ('O Lupo), was one of the confederation's first representatives to move permanently to the north of Italy and later to Spain, where he worked for them. However, in 1991 all this fundamentally changed when Nunzio no longer had a set territory, market, or Camorra clan to count on.

Vincenzo De Falco managed his family, but took direct instructions from Bardellino. De Falco was responsible for the north of Caserta. Across the Casertano territory there were twenty-two loyal territorial groups that referred back to Bardellino (DIA1: 51–52). In the 1980s, the Bardellino-Iovine confederation was estimated to have 484 members, but by 1994 the membership had declined to 179 whereas the new Schiavone-Bidognetti confederation had 219 members (Allum, 2000: 373, 406; 412).[12] This decline may have coincided with Bardellino's prolonged stays abroad during the early 1980s when he started to lose interest in his home territory, leaving his lieutenants to squabble over it.

De Falco's brothers all chipped in to make the criminal family functional: Giuseppe helped in the day-to-day running of the clan and Mario and Antonio had important supporting roles: Mario became a traffic warden thanks to a fixed exam,[13] and Antonio, the older brother, already in 1982 was helping the confederation logistically by building shelters, hideaways, and double doors to allow fugitives to hide in their families' houses, for example, one was installed in Vincenzo's bathroom (CSv, 25/10/93). Nunzio worked for the clan abroad.

The inner core of the clan was made up of Vincenzo De Falco's five siblings and their extensive family units. Kinship dominated all aspects of clan behavior, as tight blood ties remained the strongest rule and dictated terms; they were the root of the clan's organization and operations. The outer core was Vincenzo's army of obedient associates who took orders, assumed various roles, and were responsible for different tasks in the clan, while at the same time retaining a certain autonomy in their own territories.

In particular, Vincenzo had four close lieutenants, emerging bosses in their own right, who assisted him greatly and through whom he controlled an extensive territory (from San Tammaro, Villa Literno, to the high Matese region). He had two other important allies who were completely independent: the Esposito clan from Sessa Aurunca and the La Torre clan from Mondragone (see chapter 6). They provided logistical and criminal support when necessary.

In 1981, Nunzio lived in Como, where as a representative of the confederation, he became its "reference point in the north of Italy" (CSv, 25/10/1993: 3) and became a crucial player strategically, coordinating its commercial activities: "He managed the introduction of explosives and arms into Italy from Switzerland, Germany, and Austria," the "drug trafficking that was given to him by BAX (for Antonio Bardellino)," and the "illegal gambling halls in the province of Como and Milan" (ibid.). Nunzio also continued other criminal activities on the side. On a number of occasions, he was arrested for mafia association, kidnapping, drug trafficking, drug distribution, and even attempted extortion with the use of violence and intimidation (see DIA1). So although he was permanently living in Como, he remained a member of the larger Bardellino-Iovine confederation and his brother's clan, both located in the Casertano region. He had no need or desire to set up a new independent clan.

Forced to move, Nunzio did not return to settle in Casal di Principe but went to Spain, near some Calabrian friends (PZ), where between 1986 and 1990 he continued working for his brother and the general confederation (ADTv, 19/12/95). He managed the importation of drugs and arms into Italy and recycled money in the legitimate economy. A judicial document noted: "Vincenzo De Falco operated, through his brother Nunzio and his cousin . . . the De Falco clan and in particular, Nunzio managed imports of cocaine into Italy. With the profits from drugs and extortion, they bought in Málaga, in Barcelona and Seville, pizzerias, restaurants, hotels, and factories. Nunzio De Falco managed these businesses" (CSv, 15/7/1993 in TN3). The seat of the clan's power remained firmly fixed in Casal di Principe, whereas it had an operating base in Granada (SG).

Bardellino was a greatly respected and authoritative leader. He reigned supreme because he was charismatic and shrewd, but also because of his close Sicilian connections. These qualities helped him develop both a long-term criminal vision and extensive social capital in the form of national and international criminal and business contacts. However, it was Vincenzo who managed the operating base in Spain on a daily basis, visiting regularly when he was on the run. One associate explained that Nunzio "talked about the activities that he started there, a pizzeria; these activities were started with the money that Vincenzo De Falco and Giuseppe De Falco gave him" (GQv, 20/6/01).

Both in Como and Granada, Nunzio was under the protection of the Bardellino-Iovine confederation until Bardellino was murdered in 1988. And then under the protection of his brother until Vincenzo's murder in February 1991. Until his brother's murder, Nunzio was a one-man operating cell based in Granada, functioning as a drugs network for the confederation with extensive Italian criminal and business contacts in Spain and France. Nunzio was, in a way, an "ambassador" posted abroad representing the confederation's interests and relying on it for instructions and funding. This gave him security, power, and self-confidence.

After Bardellino's murder, the De Falco clan continued as part of the successive umbrella confederation led by Vincenzo De Falco, Francesco Schiavione,[14] Francesco Bidognetti, Mario Iovine, and others—what would become known as the Casalesi clan. They preserved a confederation model wherein each leader had a clan with devoted foot soldiers, but they coordinated collective decisions and strategies together. In a continuous flow, orders, instructions, and money came from Italy to be invested in Spain, while firearms and drugs were sent back to Italy to be sold on the local market. The Granada cell was in constant contact with Casal di Principe and existed thanks to it.

When in 1988 Vincenzo De Falco became one of the main leaders of the confederation, he was greatly regarded. One of his members recalls: he "was Francesco Schiavione's [the main emerging boss] equal. . . . Vincenzo De Falco had enormous charisma, his decisions would predominate, not those of Schiavione" (GQv, 28/5/01). Moreover, Vincenzo had a lot of social capital, which may explain why he was considered "the most dangerous of the group" (DIA1: 95). He had "good relations with the political world in the Casertano" (ibid.) and was well connected with lawyers (CSv, 27/10/1993). This aspect probably bothered the other emerging leaders, especially Schiavone and Bidognetti, the most. But in Spain none of this social capital was exported. There is no concrete evidence of Nunzio trying to corrupt local customs officers, policemen, or politicians, as the clan did in Italy or as other clans would try to do in the future, but we just do not know.

In 1990, the situation radically changed for Nunzio. War was declared against Vincenzo because of internal rivalries,[15] and culminated in his murder in February 1991, and Giuseppe's a year later in March 1992. Nunzio fought back. He tried to govern two territories simultaneously, but it became to some degree impossible, as the Schiavone-Bidognetti clans adopted a violent termination policy across the local territory (SG). He naturally took command of the few remaining loyal followers in Italy as revenge was sought. However, this proved extremely complicated, as he "stayed for [only] a brief time in Italy putting together a group to counter the dominant Casalesi clan, then he moved back to Spain, where he continued to coordinate the activities of his members" (CASMCV3: 65). Nunzio no longer had a specific home territory, only a "prolonged absence" (CASMCV3: 65–66) from home, and Spain became more a place of refuge than a source of opportunities for the clan.

The elimination of Nunzio's clan headquarters transformed his situation dramatically in Spain, as he was expelled from the confederation. In 1992, this Camorra operating cell lost its local power base and Nunzio became totally isolated. No longer part of an organized confederation structure, he received no instructions or orders from Casal di Principe to provide goods for the home markets. If anything, confederation members demanded that he hand over the assets he had been managing in Spain. As an aspiring leader, Nunzio had tried to organize a Camorra clan from Spain and be in two places at once. But without his brother's charisma or respect, and more importantly, without a physical presence and visibility in the Caserta region, he ultimately failed and was unable to cultivate what remained of the clan's local roots.

As a result, Nunzio recycled himself into a broker, an independent player in the international drug-trafficking community, with many contacts in Spain and Europe: "Nunzio De Falco had established a criminal group dedicated to different crimes that were undertaken in southeast Spain" (QC1: 28). He predominately imported drugs into Italy and, now more than ever, relied on his family ties to provide markets and buyers. His cousins from both sides of the family, based in Italy, became essential in his different drug networks.

Prior to 1992, the composition of the De Falco clan was mostly family members with extensive loyal soldiers. Based on the analysis of judicial documents of the Casalesi clan (including the De Falco clan) in Italy pre-1995–1996 (TN3 and TN4),[16] the average age of members varied from thirty-nine to forty-six and the membership was predominantly male.[17] Police files probably only provide half the picture in terms of numbers of members, but this confederation was generally considered to have a large membership, a minimum of one hundred members with a wide range of jobs.

Some of Nunzio's drug-enterprise networks were identified during the early 1990s as he lost control in Italy. Figure 5.2 represents three of these overlapping drugs network (see QC1 and TN3). They reflect fluctuating, looser, and more open networks in contact with foreign criminal representatives. Nunzio in Spain and his cousin in France were the only Italian members abroad; the rest of family members were still heavily involved from Italy but they were petty criminals rather than *camorristi*.

One level of analysis shows how ethnic based these networks still were: the majority involved were Italian, apart from the drug importers (Argentineans, Brazilians) and couriers (Spaniards) (QC1). Of the 92 members involved in the different networks, about 10 were women. In another drugs network, only Nunzio was based in Granada: the others were based in Spain (node 85 in the figure) and Italy. The average age of members was about 37 (see QC1). Figure 5.2 shows that Nunzio was no longer a Camorra operating cell based in Spain with links to an Italian territory. As opposed to the hierarchically structured Casalesi clan, he was now a broker working in the international drug-trafficking community, but also managed other knock-on activities such as car trafficking and counterfeiting.

Few active women were identified, but this is perhaps because the material analyzed was produced during a period when women were generally less

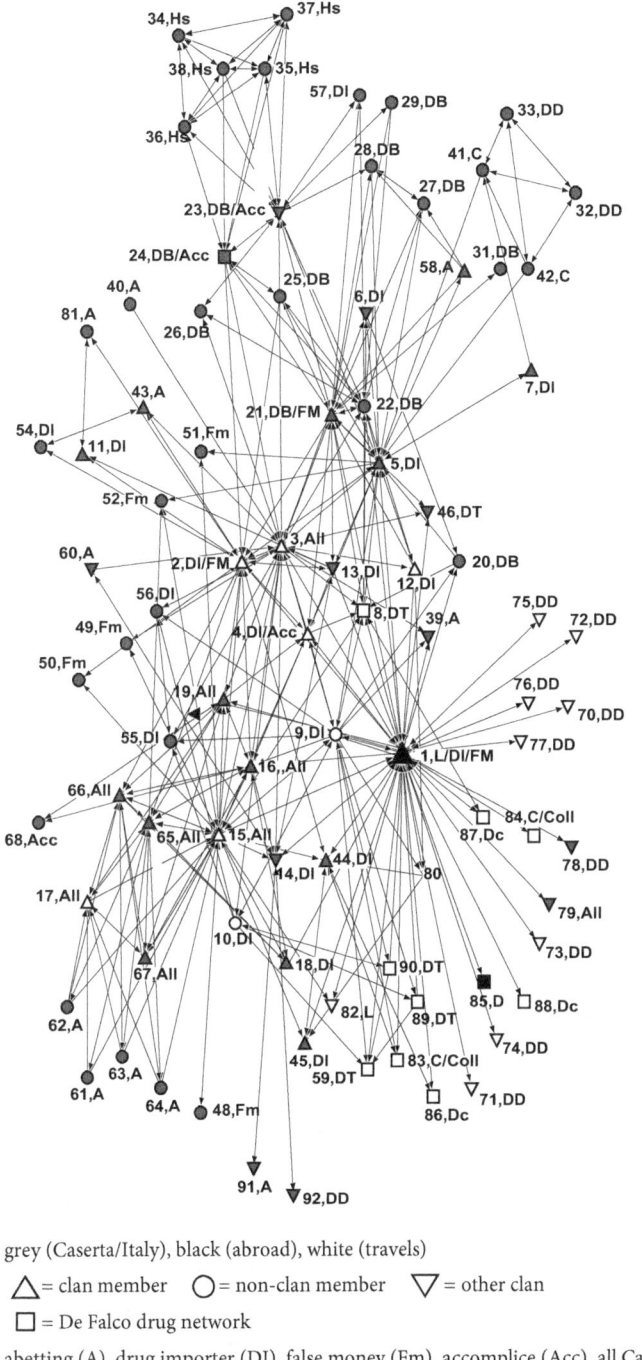

**FIGURE 5.2** Nunzio De Falco's drug networks (1992–1995)

taken into consideration by judges. The partner of one of the leaders argues that women were present in the confederation and acted as a solid foundation: they were involved in their men's activities. One simple example is when the wives of certain bosses sought to convince the wives of arrested members who were potentially thinking about becoming state witnesses not to collaborate with the state (see CASMCV1; QC1). The De Falco men also had lovers[18] who were fully participant in their activities. In Spain, no Italian women members appear, although one Spanish woman was identified as part of the expedition team in the murder of Mario Iovine in Portugal (QC1).

According to Michele Siciliano, "the De Falco family recruited many people in Spain," but did Nunzio really recruit new full-time Spanish members, even into his network, after 1992? Locally in Casal di Principe, recruitment was similar to that of other clans. Blood ties, shared prison experiences, and common criminal skills were all qualifying criteria. There was no transparent recruitment process as exists in a legitimate business. Vincenzo was particularly good at enrolling unrelated outsiders and sympathizers to his clan. He recruited individuals from all walks of life, from lawyers to doctors to police officers (CASMCV1), and he also managed to co-opt individuals who would favor his clan's economic activities, hide their firearms, and make houses and rooms available for meetings.

In Spain, it transpires that Nunzio sought assistance from the local petty-crime community. He engaged with them constantly but did not recruit them. For example, when he was commissioned to murder Mario Iovine in Portugal in 1989, he recruited two young Spanish people to do the job, not Neapolitans. Local Spanish police also noted that his villa-bunker on the periphery of Granada was guarded by Italian and Spanish guards who were probably armed (QC1). The dynamics of Nunzio's entourage after 1992 changed, as he could no longer count on the local community in Italy. Now his pool of support was much more limited, and therefore he probably turned to other criminal communities more frequently and intensely: close relatives in Italy, the local petty criminals in Granada, his international drugs networks, in particular South Americans, and his Italian businessmen expat contacts (see QC1: 20).

The internal values of the De Falco clan were strongly embedded in Casal di Principe, but there is no systematic trace of this entrenchment in Spain. In Casal di Principe, clear rules were respected. The clans imposed their power on members and social consensus on ordinary citizens, either through enforced recognition or violence. The rules of *omertà*, respect, violence, and tradition were all values manipulated by the clan to dictate behavior and inform decisions, and if violated, resulted in ruthless punishments. There was a lack of discussion, negotiation, and peaceful conflict resolution. For example, the boss Mario Iovine killed his mother's lover to maintain the "honor of his family," and one member wanted to kill DS because he "had taken advantage of a girl in her home"—the girl's house was used by the clan as "a place for refuge, for meetings" (GQv, 28/5/01).

In Spain, this Camorra value system was not replicated by Nunzio. However, some features of the system did come to light from time to time. For example, the clan's use of violence abroad. Although the confederation had a reputation for being particularly violent, cruel and "bloody" (MS), up until 2010 there had been a general reluctance among *camorristi* to use violence to impose their rules and values abroad, as this would have drawn attention to their presence and activities. There was no evidence that Nunzio used frequent violence in his local Spanish community or imported it for his business activities, but he did still use some for the resolution of Camorra problems. He *did* order violent acts from Spain: the murder of Mario Iovine in 1989 was organized in Spain and the murder of the local priest Don Peppe Diana in 1992 was ordered from Granada to implicate his rivals. This reminds us that Nunzio remained fundamentally a *camorrista* at heart, as he still used violence, but in a measured way and only for certain specific purposes. A clear strategy in Spain had been adopted to avoid detection and the use of violence whenever possible.

Like all Camorra clans, the fundamental glue holding the social cohesion of the De Falco clan together was its common fund, *cassa*—its central bank. Money made from basic criminal activities (such as extortion rackets) went into the common fund and was also reinvested. The Casalesi clan always had money: for example, during the 2000s, wives were paid 10,000 euros a month (ACa). The *cassa* continues to be a vital feature of the group (ACb) and, of course, the richer the clan the more it could provide for its members.

Before 1992, the De Falco clan had a common fund in Italy. In Spain, the operating cell had none. It was not moved there nor was a new one established, as there were no members to look after. So as the De Falco clan's power declined, its operating cell in Spain lost capacity and it became problematic for the leadership to keep replenishing its common account. With insufficient money coming in, the clan had difficulties sustaining a common fund in Italy, although one member maintains that salaries were still distributed (GQv, 6/6/2001). As a consequence, it could be argued that Nunzio as an operating cell was no longer the representative of a Camorra clan but became a lone drugs broker in an international context. Thus, without a common fund, a group has less cohesion, less sense of direction, and a weaker identity. The history of the De Falco clan shows how fundamental territory remains for a Camorra presence abroad.

### DE FALCO CLAN ACTIVITIES

Although there were clearly differences in the internal values and modi operandi in Italy and Spain, in terms of activities before 1992, the De Falco cell connected both territories in a continuous flow of people, goods, money, and information. In Italy, the confederation undertook core territorial activities such as extortion, firearms trafficking, selling drugs, and securing public subcontracts. In Spain, the activities of the operating cell were extraterritorial: mainly drug trafficking (also producing and distributing counterfeiting money) and money laundering (QC1), both of which linked back to Naples.

The Bardellino-Iovine confederation and, later, the Casalesi clan have, compared with other Camorra clans, been at the vanguard of economic activities. This is why they are considered to be "more of a Mafia than a Camorra" (FR). Bardellino's direct contact with the Sicilians no doubt made him understand in the 1980s the importance of merging illegally made profits into the legal economy and of avoiding tough legislation. He adopted the so-called Sicilian business model, based on infiltration into the legal economy to recycle illegal profits. This was mainly done by penetrating companies "close to the clan" in order to win subcontracts through them (DIA1: 53) or by setting up new companies with front names. Bardellino specialized in the cement sector, and once he set this system in motion, his heirs and other clans would follow.

By 1988, the internal organization of the confederation was more efficient and activities were organized into rational departments. They were managed by the leader, who oversaw everything and was involved in two main types of activities: (1) the illegal department, made up of traditional core criminal activities and (2) the legal department, organized around legitimate activities through which companies gained public subcontracts for the clan. Extortion rackets were a regular and fundamental illegal activity, as it allowed clans to physically control the territory. There were not only small extortions against local shops but also larger ones against national companies that won public contracts in the region. One of the members of a satellite clan explains: "What do I do? . . . I lived off extortions . . . I undertook extortions in all regions of the Casertano, in Casale, in San Cipriano, in Sant'Antimo, in all the areas of the Casertano, like they did" (GQv, 20/6/01). There are some suggestions, but it is not clear whether Nunzio undertook extortions in Granada, and if he did, it still does not appear to have been systematic, although there were traces in Como.

For the confederation, Spain represented an important wholesale market for drugs and investment opportunities. Nunzio's initial presence in Spain was linked to drug importation activities into Campania. He was strategically located there as part of a wider drug-importing network and was not an isolated Italian businessman. He was a self-confident manager, a key node between the clan's drugs activities in Italy, Spain, and Europe. It would appear that from Granada he managed one specific route, as he had done from Como during the 1980s.

Between 1986 and 1991, in other words, between the death of Antonio Bardellino and the murder of Vincenzo De Falco, drugs and arms were bought and trafficked into Spain and exported from Granada for the market in Casal di Principe (see QC1). The De Falco clan did not trade or sell to others in Spain, but bought solely to sell in Campania and Italy. As a police document explained, "the international drug trafficking of this organization . . . we can assume most certainly uses Spain as the transit territory for an important amount of drugs . . . coming from South America (especially Brazil), then sent to Italy and other confining countries to be distributed by local criminal organizations. This is the case for the De Falco clan" (QC1: 245).

There appears to have been a link between the money made from illegal activities in the Casertano and its investment in drug trafficking and business opportunities abroad. Vincenzo De Falco followed Bardellino's business logic closely and Nunzio applied his efficient recycling model that had been so successfully used in Italy. But as Vincenzo had good political contacts, he did not necessarily need to infiltrate companies (using violence or lending money), but rather directly influenced the allocation of public subcontracts to companies close to him. This Camorra is a very modern, money-orientated one, always seeking out new business opportunities. For example, it is believed that the Bidognetti clan was already interested in the illegal transport and disposal of rubbish in the early 1990s (AdTv, 19/12/1995).

It is suggested that Nunzio De Falco laundered money in various legitimate business ventures in Spain. The Spanish police noted the successful investments and commercial activities he was involved in: he managed an Italian pizzeria, was the administrator of another (QC1), and bought real estate. It is for this reason that the police considered De Falco to be "the operating arm in the management of drug trafficking, counterfeit money, extortion, as well as money laundering" (QC1: 17).

Both the war against the Casalesi clan and the loss of his local territory transformed Nunzio's activities. In Italy, he attempted to continue his core Camorra activities, especially extortions and drug trafficking, but this created tensions, as his rivals blocked all his local transactions, giving him a very limited margin of maneuver. For example, his clan members continued to impose extortions, which forced some businesses to pay twice: "I undertook an extortion against a guy that worked in the Teverola region. They were building an important shopping center. . . . I received the sum of 30 million lire. The relative of S told me that the building site already gave a kickback to the Casalesi clan" (AdTv, 19/12/1996).

Once defeated and no longer tied to a set territory, Nunzio's markets and support systems necessarily shifted as he adapted his behavior, priorities, and strategies. His main activity remained drug trafficking, perhaps because of his previous knowledge and contacts, but he could no longer rely solely on Casal di Principe; the whole of Italy now became his market: "Part of the drugs had to go to the group from Mondragone and another part to the group of Carinaro so that, thanks to the drug trafficking, we could finance our war with the Casalesi" (AdTv, 16/7/1996).

Nunzio went from being a self-assured Camorra representative to an independent drug broker managing the importation and exportation of drugs across Europe into Italy. He imported the goods from South America, distributed them locally in Granada, and sold them to other criminal groups while also importing cocaine into Italy. He therefore went from concentrating solely on the Italian Neapolitan markets to selling wherever he could. For example, it is believed that he controlled the distribution of drugs in Granada through a group of gypsies and sold drugs to contacts in the United Kingdom, France, and Switzerland (QC1).

He also became involved in other criminal activities that would make him more visible, such as stolen car scams; after all, he remained a criminal involved in drug and arms trafficking, bank robbery, and extortions, and he had close contacts with Neapolitans and Casertans. Casal di Principe was no longer his center of operations, and with no set territory or structured organization, he became a free agent and involved in different criminal activities.

### DE FALCO CLAN ACCOMPLICES

In Italy, we must not forget that the De Falco clan, as part of the Bardellino-Iovine confederation, benefitted from the support of many accomplices. They legitimized and normalized the clan's presence across the territory. Vincenzo De Falco was charming and had great social capital, which attracted many white-collar professionals such as businessmen, politicians, and lawyers, whose behavior ranged from "complicit" to "compenetrative" (Sciarrone, 2011b). At times it becomes difficult to distinguish between them and hard-core *camorristi*, as the symbiosis was so good.

After Vincenzo's murder in 1991, Nunzio still enjoyed this support in Italy. A former associate explained that one supportive accomplice "was a member, but he did not commit crimes. He was a member in the sense that . . . he was a front man, he looked after the economic aspect of the organization. He was given some contracts, such as that of Regni Lagni, the third lane of the motorway, other important construction jobs; he then channeled these profits into other activities. . . . He looked after these aspects, but he would also put at our disposal his house if we needed to commit some crimes" (GQv, 13/6/01).

Gradually, however, Nunzio's rivals, the Schiavone-Bidognetti clans, isolated his possible accomplices, and this weakened his clan to such a degree that his few remaining members could no longer count on local or regional support. People were afraid to deal with them because of the possible repercussions. After the murder of Giuseppe De Falco in 1992, Nunzio was totally abandoned and isolated. The picture in Spain is much less clear. To establish a base in Spain, it can be assumed that Nunzio must have had some help among professionals circles, and there are some indications that he benefitted from the help of Spanish, Italian, and Neapolitan criminal and business communities there. But there is little systematic evidence for us to draw conclusions.

Nunzio De Falco was arrested and extradited back to Italy in 1995, where he is now serving a life sentence (see CASMCV3 and CASMCV4). His experience shows what happens to a Camorra representative without a fixed territory or the internal cohesion of traditional values in an intimate group. He simply became an independent broker, an organized criminal in the international drugs-trafficking community, perhaps more liquid, dangerous, and less predictable than before.

## Drug Trafficking and the Polverino Clan

Compared with the De Falco operating cell in Spain, the Polverino clan approximately fifteen years later was a much more efficient machine. The boss, Giuseppe Polverino managed to establish an effective drugs importation business operating in two Western European countries simultaneously: Italy and Spain.[19] In 2012, Italian and Spanish police finally arrested him, "Mr. Hashish," in Jerez de la Frontera at the tip of southern Spain. Two years earlier, he had been identified as the market leader, for twenty years, of the Italian hashish market, importing from Morocco via Spain into Italy (to Campania, Lazio, Puglia, and Sicily) (TN23) while based in Come Ruga (Tarragona, near Barcelona). A former associate, Domenico Verde, explained that in Spain there had been "a real expansion of the clan" (DVv, in PN15: 46).

The Polverino clan's operations highlight once again how interlinked Spain and Italy were, but also how interconnected drug trafficking and money laundering are. This clan is emblematic of the sophisticated face of the modern Camorra, especially the drug-trafficking clans. Our analysis illustrates the clan's ability to control its local territory through the use of violence, selling of drugs, and winning of local public contracts, and the clan's ability to exploit the global opportunities available in Quarto and Spain through its drug-importation business and its money-laundering operations.

For many years this clan appeared "dormant," "silent," and "inactive" because it had not undertaken any violent or eye-catching criminal acts locally in Italy.[20] But this was merely an illusion. Evidence now suggests that for six years (2006–2013) the clan was very active in the European drugs market, becoming a truly "glocal" (Hobbs, 1998) presence in Naples and abroad.

## THE POLVERINO CLAN: ITS MEMBERS AND TERRITORIES

The Polverino clan, also known as "the clan from the mountain top" (PN15: 4), has since the late 1980s controlled the territory of Quarto, the Giugliano districts, and towns north of Naples. It was led by Giuseppe Polverino (Peppe 'O Barone), who started his criminal career in the powerful Nuvoletta clan from Marano (see PN3), his "mother clan" (TN23: 42): "the dirty work undertaken by Polverino for the Nuvoletta clan was, among other things, international drug trafficking (in particular, the importation of hashish from Spain). . . . That dirty work has, however, allowed the same Polverino group to take off, first, from an economic-financial point of view, and then in terms of political-criminal leadership" (TN23: 40). Giuseppe learned his criminal and business skills from a leading member of the Nuvoletta clan, and then graduated to taking instructions directly from the boss, the infamous Don Lorenzo Nuvoletta, his main criminal sponsor.

It is believed that Giuseppe Polverino had been a clan member since 1986 (or earlier) and was promoted to leading his own team when an older lieutenant was murdered. At that time, he predominantly used his skills in the illegal building sector (PN3: 21) while also becoming "the leader of the Nuvoletta's military group" (TN23: 40); in other words, the head of the clan's security service. So he combined violence with good business acumen. But he was no ordinary *camorrista* and his activities must be put into context to understand his strong local roots. He was not born and bought up in a poor family, but one that owned many different companies and businesses. It has been suggested that during the 1980s his relatives' meat and bread businesses (various butchers and bakeries) were able to flourish in parallel and thanks to his increasing criminal power (PN3: 25–26). His initial investment, however, needed to come from somewhere, perhaps his core illegal activities, such as extortion rackets and drug trafficking. It is not clear if violence, threats, and the power of the criminal association were used to impose products on companies or to win subcontracts, allowing his family's businesses to gain a quasi-monopoly position in these markets.

Polverino was a bright criminal who followed the Nuvoletta's strategy and saw the economic potential in the building industry. Applying the successful Sicilian business model used by Cosa Nostra, he used clean front names to head up companies that were set up with illegal profits, and he used mafia methods to impose their products on various buyers. He thus recycled illegal money into cement companies and eventually reinvested in other legitimate businesses, such as farms, livestock, and properties in regions as far away as Umbria, Veneto, Emilia, le Marche, and Lazio even before he started to manage his international drug-trafficking network (PN3: 26). Thus, although present in the legitimate economy, he cannot be described as a businessman turned *camorrista* already active in the legal economy. He was a *camorrista* fortunate to have access to legitimate companies that used mafia methods to conduct business. To say that he was present in the legitimate economy is to underplay his criminal origins, agenda, and methods.

During the late 1990s, Polverino "supplanted" the Nuvolettas (PN15: 4) in power, activities, and vision because he had more members outside of prison and he proved to be more organized, resistant, and financially successful in his criminal and legal business activities. Although connected by their past, these two clans were not partners, even though they sometimes did business. Polverino's deep roots in the local community and the complicity of many politicians, businessmen, and professionals enabled him to control many illegal and legal activities.

The story recounted here begins in 2006 when the clan's relationship with Spain was once again reignited. A fugitive since 1992 (PN3: 42), Giuseppe Polverino was arrested in 1997 and again in 2001 for his involvement in drug trafficking. He spent time in prison until 2006 when he decided to violate his parole conditions[21] in the Province of Pisa and move to Spain because he feared the police were monitoring his activities (PN15: 75). On the run, he contacted a previous associate (a former butcher turned fugitive drug trafficker) who had moved permanently to Spain for help and business contacts. From Spain, he set about restructuring his various drug-importing teams and reorganizing his clan's illegal and legal activities in Quarto.

By 2001, Polverino had put into place an efficient drug-importation structure in Spain. A former member explained: "I use the term 'branch' because Polverino established in that part of Spain from 2001 onward a branch that looked after his business and real estate interests in addition to the drug trafficking he undertook through different members of the organization and front men who were permanently based in Spain" (SIv, 16/12/2004, in TN23: 155). By using the term "branch," he misses the fundamental relationship between the two territories and the subtle connection between them. Without the initial extortion money made in Quarto, there would be no drug-trafficking activities in Spain, and with no drug-trafficking activities in Spain there would be no money-laundering activities in Italy or Spain. The clan thus developed an interconnected criminal structure between Italy and Spain: money, goods, and men constantly flowed back and forth between territories (see TN23 and TN24), with Quarto, the home territory, at the center of all operations, even with an absent boss.

In 2006 and while based in Spain, Polverino managed his clan like an international company. It was a business with many small operational bases (in Quarto, Tarragona, Alicante, and Málaga) and its official headquarters in Quarto. From Spain, he undertook the difficult task of managing different localities. Whereas Nunzio De Falco had failed to retain power from abroad, Polverino succeeded, as "nothing is left to chance." He controlled the local territory, members, and criminal activities: "nothing moves in Marano and the surrounding towns, in terms of legal and illegal activities, if there is not the agreement of the boss, GP" (TN23: 58). He was its "*dominus ex machina*" (TN23: 57).

The leader's power was thus extraterritorial with many decisions being made abroad, even ordering a murder.[22] The location of the clan's power, however, remained fixed in Campania. To many members, the boss was like "a ghost," but he did everything he could to be present in Quarto to avoid his absence having a negative impact on business. He was "omnipresent" (TN23: 37) in his daily contact with his lieutenants. He sought to manage their activities, and his fugitive status did not change this in any way. He probably did return to his home territory as often as he could, but this went undetected by the police, probably because he moved around in butchers' vans (DVv, 11/1/2010: 467).

Indeed, Polverino was extremely careful to avoid detection. Some recount that he would discuss business with his uncle in the middle of a field to avoid being overheard.[23] At one time, a "red telephone" (TN23: 187)—an exclusive mobile hotline between Spain and Quarto-Marano—was used for direct communication with the boss.[24] This mobile phone was in the hands of one member only, who jealously guarded it, and others had to pass him messages for the boss. There was also an extensive use of text messages (short message service) to keep him up to date with local developments. More recently, police have insisted that he used only *pizzini*, small written letters with instructions, for fear of being detected. Some members would even drive to Spain specifically to deliver him these notes.

For more important decisions, members traveled to Spain to talk over clan-related matters directly with the leader. In particular, he held meetings to review the financial situation of the clan: "such meetings . . . were held to discuss the workings of the common fund; . . . with GP present" (DVv, in TN23: 311). In this respect, decisions were made extraterritorially, like the Amato-Pagano clan, and Polverino's personal power traveled with him. But he dealt mainly with members who recognized his power and not new Spanish recruits. He focused much of his attention on the clan's stable territory in Quarto, where the clan's foundation lay, as well as his drug-importation business. His power did not decline as a consequence of his absence from the home territory because he clearly realized the potential dangers and constantly engaged with his local territory, either through his physical or delegated presence, or via telephone calls or regular meetings with members in Spain.

The location of the clan's power was entrenched and the nature of Polverino's leadership remained solid and traditional. He had "the uncontested role of leader" (TN23: 876) and all the necessary experience, skills, and aura to lead a complex transnational organization: "he immediately presented himself as the leader, with authority and charisma, and made it clear that all the others were his subordinates" (DVv, 22/1/10: 471–472). Respected, admired, and feared by his clan members, he behaved like a feudal lord in front of his soldiers, who were utterly devoted to him. One member even described him as "the crown on my head" (TN23: 817). The fact that no one sought to challenge him suggests that he had total respect from his men. They probably slightly feared him, with his great authoritarianism and modern criminal intelligence, which may explain why he was so successful.

Polverino also understood the need for a rigid hierarchical leadership, one person in control: "all decisions relating to the criminal life of the organization, and in particular the more delicate ones, need to be taken solely by the *capo clan*" (TN23: 116). Unlike other clan bosses, he did not share his leadership with his uncles or brothers-in-law, although he did respect and listen to his uncle Antonio. He was in sole control of the clan at all times, while acknowledging the need for flexibility to manage his international drug-trafficking operations more efficiently, which also reflects his criminal insight. He was an esteemed figure with a good amount of social capital in the Neapolitan and national criminal worlds, as well as in economic and political spheres, enjoying extensive contacts with white-collar professionals and a good relationship with local politicians in Quarto, all which reinforced his local power.

The clan in Quarto was a tight-knit family unit with a vertical hierarchical structure around one dominant leader. This was the traditional Sicilian pyramid model (see Falcone and Padovani, 1993), different from the new Camorra generational model. The leader was at the top and his blood family at the base, surrounded by lieutenants, with accomplices as the looser periphery further down. Polverino was actively helped by his many relatives who were involved in different aspects of his business empire, often in legitimate shops, companies, and properties. One brother-in-law was the owner of a company that was in fact managed by Polverino, and female relatives were systematically used as front names for properties and legitimate businesses, thus participating in the diversification of the clan's illegal funds into local real estate and the economy in Marano (PN16). Blood ties provided privileged status. At times some of his relatives lost his trust, as in the La Torre clan, and important criminal positions were then filled by criminal veterans from the Nuvoletta clan who had the experience and know-how.

By the late 1990s, there were clearly defined roles and departments in the clan to optimize individuals' skills: (1) a legal department and (2) an illegal department (including an extortion division and a drug-trafficking division, its main moneymaking activity). Each department had a manager, a *capo zona*. The extortion division was based solely in Quarto, whereas the drug-trafficking division, made up of various operating teams and levels, was based both in Quarto and across Spain.[25] The extortion division was characterized by the use of violence and existed solely in Italy. It remained firmly based in Quarto, whereas the other two departments were mobile and transnational. Polverino was the managing director of these different departments but was assisted by capable advisers. The same pattern appears for the legal department and its money-laundering division, which specialized in public subcontracts and investments; this team was based both in Quarto and Spain. The blood relations were allocated respectable jobs in this department locally: for example, a vineyard near Naples was managed by a relative, and many other relations acted as shell companies and front names. The legal department had not only front companies and properties but also trading companies—bakeries, butcher shops, farms, livestock, and properties.

Local *capi zona* organized their members according to the instructions given by the leader from Spain. Members had specific roles, making the clan efficient. However, when members were considered inadequate, they were quickly replaced, as in 2008 when an experienced *camorrista* and *capo zona* came out of prison and was effectively demoted. Previously, he had managed activities in Quarto. After prison, the boss transferred him to less risky tasks. His role was given to a younger, more cunning *camorrista* who had proven himself to be particularly able and had gotten on the right side of the boss (see TN23).

This family crime enterprise, with its headquarters in Quarto, extended into Spain, where it became a complex drugs network made up of three to four teams. These teams, *paranze*, were led by drug brokers scattered across Spain, they were organized as operating bases, with five or ten Neapolitans living there in total. No other Polverino relatives or clan members were based in Spain permanently, apart from Giuseppe.[26] He was at the heart of all operations and oversaw the different drug teams who constantly referred back to him. But it was a loose network that relied heavily on team leaders, who were all Polverino's close associates and clan members. Each team was made up of three to four Neapolitans who traveled to Spain to meet with their broker.

The broker and team leader Domenico Verde explains the organization of his *parenza:* "I was the leader of a team who managed the international trafficking of hashish. My loyal associates were SN and GH, they specifically dealt with placing the hashish (which I bought in Spain, importing it from Morocco) on the market in the various Italian regions. They had an established and extensive national distribution network" (TN23: 552). Although these brokers had a certain amount of autonomy to manage their own team members, activities, and routes, they were nevertheless totally subordinate to Polverino, who would invest in their drug deals and needed to give approval. They in return showed respect and payed him a cut, which would go into the clan's common fund.

This drugs network showed a fluid organizational structure, with many different alliances, members, and agreements that continuously needed renegotiating; nothing could be taken for granted. Between brokers, internal bickering and rivalries often appeared that created tensions and possible complications that Polverino, as the top manager, had to keep under control in order to keep his drug-importation business afloat. His management style of preferential treatment was impossible in Spain, as it might have produced even more problems with his team leaders, who might have abandoned him. What emerges is a Camorra that transforms itself into a loose network once it crosses borders,[27] introducing less rigid dynamics, greater freedom, and more flexible business teams and deals; one and the same organization, but with different features and behavior.

Figure 5.3 represents the Polverino clan as captured in three judicial documents (PN15, TN23, TN24). It shows how the territory abroad is now an integrated feature of the Neapolitan clan. The leader (node 73) had permanent operating bases in Spain that managed the drugs importation network (e.g., nodes 2, 9, 10, 14, 15, 24, 29, 30, 31, 34, 35, 37, 51, 52, 53, 58, 64, 70, 76, 78, 90, 91, 92), and the business sector in Italy (e.g., nodes 1, 4, 5, 7, 16, 8, 25, 39, 32, 17, 50, 40, 41, 42, 44, 45, 47, 81, 82, 84, 85). He connected the criminal activities and was mobile and could travel (white). This drugs network reflects a fluid and interconnected organizational structure: a few important nodes (the central part of the network) are significantly interrelated across Italy and abroad. These few nodes are connected to many functional nodes in Naples and have a hierarchical relationship with those nodes based abroad or that travel.

The composition of the clan shows a wide variety of members. Judicial investigations document how petty criminals, international drug traffickers, businessmen, and politicians with different backgrounds and professions (PN16) all worked for the clan's interests. In Quarto, clan members were Neapolitan, but in the drugs network, nationality was no longer a factor. Polverino's network bought drugs from many different foreign groups and also employed a Polish network to import supplies when other members were arrested in 2013 (TN24). Until 2011, no Spaniards or Moroccans appear to have been recruited into the clan, but there was close collaboration with local Moroccan suppliers and available couriers to conclude their drug deals.

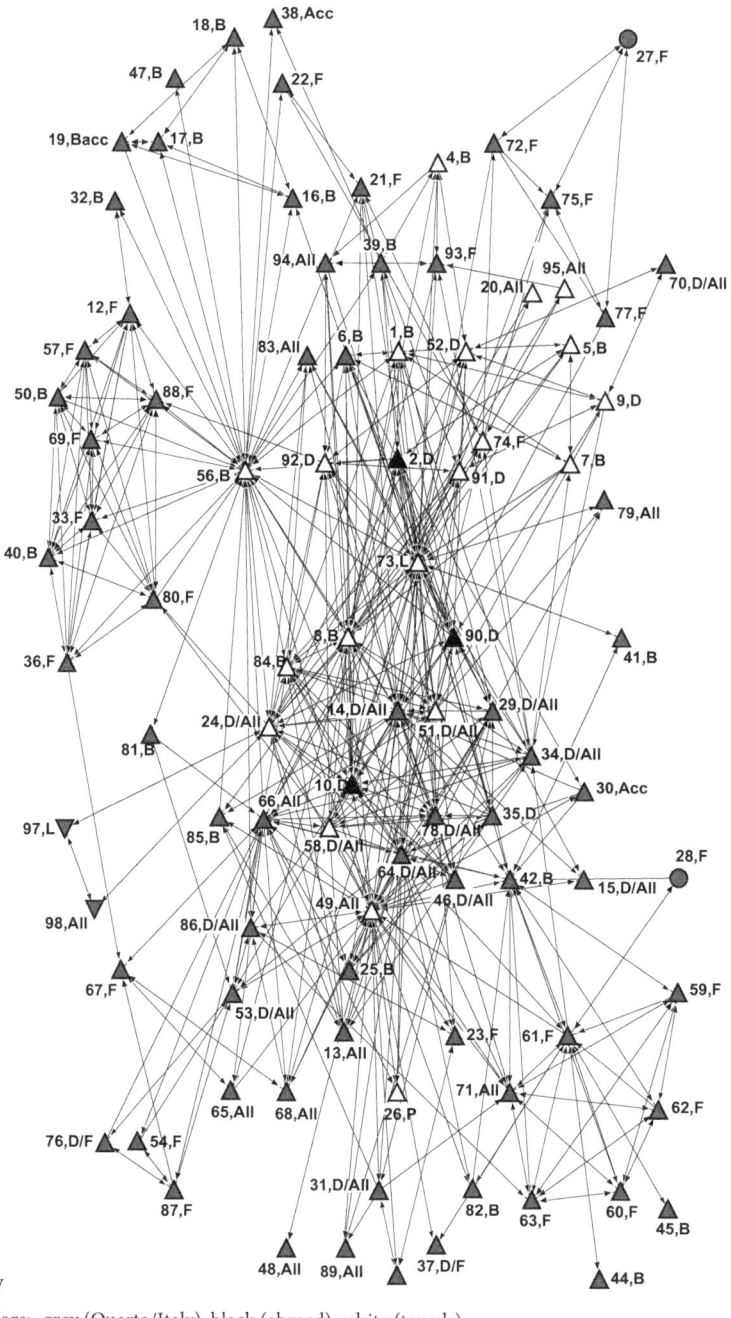

Key

Colors: grey (Quarto/Italy), black (abroad), white (travels)

Shapes: △ = clan member   ○ = non-clan member   ▽ = other clan

Roles: businessman (B), front name (F), politician (P), drug business (D), all Camorra activities (All), accomplice (Accom), leader (L)

**FIGURE 5.3**  The Polverino clan and its drug network in Spain (2009–2011)

After 2011 and important arrests, Spanish members may well have been recruited, as technical advice was needed after the arrest of the traveling Neapolitan adviser.[28] It has also been suggested that some members frequented a terrorist cell,[29] but this remains unproven. Members of the drugs division worked, communicated, and traveled between two national contexts and territories. In Marano, members covered different tasks and districts. Some engaged in loan sharking, drug dealing, and extortion rackets. All remained territorially based and rarely traveled to ask for advice; foot soldiers and killers in particular did not appear to travel.

Within the clan, there were three categories of members involved in the international drug-trafficking network: (1) permanent residents who lived in Spain and Marano but did not and could not travel, (2) occasional travelers who visited both territories to make sure that all was in order, and (3) commuters who continuously traveled to and from, transporting information, goods, or money. It has been estimated that some business advisers even traveled to Spain more than twenty times a month (PN15: 9).

Women were fully integrated into the organization but seldom visible. In particular, female relatives played a vital role in the legal department as front names and company administrators to expand Polverino's financial, property, and business portfolio and hide the true origins of his money. As a consequence, these assets often went unnoticed by the authorities and the women continued to enjoy them while the men were in prison. In addition, it is noticeable how some women, feeling self-confident because of their men's power, became arrogant and violent; one even used intimidation to sell her products to clients.[30] There were a few women in the drugs network: In Spain, the boss had Brazilian women relatives who supported his activities. A woman was part of a drug-courier team who also threatened the partner of a *pentito* in Spain (see TN23). When emergencies forced urgent measures, and when the clan experienced judicial difficulties, women became more visibly active: they took messages to the boss in prison and some, even the boss's daughter, moved to Spain to take over the drugs network.[31] Some clan members even employed a woman to manage the drugs network from Spain when many of its members were in prison (see TN24).

The clan's value system was deeply embedded in Quarto but was never replicated in Spain. The clan developed a precise internal code and imposed external rules. One of the code's defining features was the free use of violence, which remained for the clan a solid root, its force and its power. Violence was never used in an ad hoc or irrational manner, but was part of an acknowledged strategy to control its territory and its citizens' daily lives. There existed a "capillary control exercised by the clan over its territory of origin" (TN23: 572). Members walked around with firearms, threatening citizens if they did not do what they wanted: "with an arrogant and pleased tone, LI recounts the period during which he walked around the streets of Quarto armed, without fear of being arrested" (TN23: 444). The clan also murdered its own members if they were thought to have violated the internal code. For example, in December 2012, a member involved in drug trafficking was murdered in broad daylight because of an internal disagreement.[32]

In order to control the economic activities across its local territory, the clan employed violence, especially to collect kickbacks. The clan regularly threatened supermarkets, petrol stations, local companies, and even street-sellers selling fireworks to obtain their regular kickback (see TN23: 526). Mafia methods and violence were also used to take over legitimate companies. For example, a bakery was bought by one RT in 1995: "the said business was owned by a certain FI who had turned to RT for a loan. Not being able to pay back his debts, he was forced, after a violent aggression . . . , to hand over his business" to the clan, "who from that moment became the owner" (see DVv, 25/11/2001).

No evidence of such social and economic control was identified in Spain. It could, however, be suggested that the clan did not seek to control Spanish citizens and the business activities that took place in Tarragona and other localities because this was not in the nature of its presence. As Bauman might have, pointed out, the control of the territory by the Polverino clan would have been "capital intensive" (2000: 188), requiring a more rigid organization that the clan was just not interested in implementing. The Polverino clan wanted to exploit economic resources and goods in Spain, not colonize it, considering all the complications that this process would have involved. It merely wanted to infiltrate the drugs and real-estate sectors. However, clan members did not hesitate to use threats against fellow Neapolitans and clan members in Spain when the clan felt under pressure. For example, when Domenico Verde decided to collaborate with the state in 2010, his companion and child, who were still living in Spain, were threatened by clan members, who organized a special expedition to warn them of what could happen to them if they did not seek to block Verde's collaboration with the state (see TN23: 924).

The stability of the clan was due to its continuously operating common fund based in Quarto. The fund was managed locally, though the boss oversaw operations from Spain. SC kept the books, "which allowed him to keep the whole management aspect under control" (TN23: 345), and which he communicated to the boss. This common fund was constantly replenished with money from the drug network in Spain and was fundamental for paying members, providing legal assistance, and supporting those in prison. Profit from Spain became essential revenue for the common fund based in Naples, as it paid members in Quarto and kept the clan afloat (TN23: 5).

## POLVERINO CLAN ACTIVITIES

By 2000, the Polverino clan had a strong presence in the legitimate economy in legal companies such as bakeries, butcher shops, and farms. By 2006, Polverino, operating from Spain, had fingers in many pies and was the manager of a significant illegal and legal business empire: he had an extensive food empire in Naples, Quarto, and Marano, he controlled many extortion rackets, he managed an international drug-trafficking empire, and made financial investments in Quarto and abroad. This explains why, compared with the De Falco and Amato-Pagano clans, he was in a better position to develop illegal networks abroad and to understand the different opportunities the Spanish economy had to offer.

The extortion division was based on the idea that wherever possible, members would impose a tax on existing or new businesses. This division was composed of both *camorristi* and complicit businessmen who targeted, in particular, construction companies and their new building sites. Businesses in the local districts were all expected to pay the clan a tax in order to be allowed to open and undertake their activities undisturbed. The clan was particularly efficient in seeking out businesses that were not paying their tax and making sure they understood that they would all have to put themselves in order—in other words, pay up. Teams of men would closely monitor and control the territory to see who was up to what. Local businessmen in particular, acted as lookouts for the clan; they would spot businesses that were not paying up or new businesses that were about to open and would tip-off the clan. As did SD'A, a builder who kept the clan constantly informed.

But the clan also undertook more subtle forms of extortion in which they forced their products on companies. For example, the manager of a cement company and his colleague would go around all the building sites of their districts to impose the clan's products on builders. "In a threatening way," they would "invite" various building site managers that had been "visited" to buy their goods from the clan's company: "Why [not]? Do you not like our cement? Do not worry, we will deliver it" (TN23: 16).

The same methods applied for the installation of elevators. The brother of a *camorrista* installed elevators for a living and he would ensure that if one was necessary in the region or building, it would be ordered from his brother. Another subgroup was allowed to undertake loan-shark activities in Quarto, and this became a lucrative business: at times they offered a 5 percent monthly interest rate—or a 60 percent annual interest rate (TN23: 564)—which was impossible to pay back and thus left the client indebted to the clan. The clan made an enormous amount of money from loan-sharking, which it could then reinvest in its drugs division. This meant that the clan had an army of people indebted to them, whom they could use as they wish.

In 2006, Giuseppe Polverino reinstalled his drugs empire in Spain. Between 2006 and 2013, it is believed that his clan was the main criminal organization importing hashish into the Campania region and Italy, selling hashish at between 1,600–2,000 euros a kilo.[33] For him it was like returning to the office to take up his job as executive manager after a leave, but based in Spain instead of Italy. The change of location did not alter things. When he arrived in Spain he had a clear criminal strategy in mind and no intention of abandoning his local territory. He used his know-how developed in Italy to exploit the opportunities available in Spain for the clan in Quarto: money was taken to Spain to buy drugs that were then exported to be sold in Italy and the profits made from selling of these drugs was invested in Spain.

The Spanish drug-trafficking division of the Polverino clan was a flexible transnational network made up of importing teams, each managed by a broker, under the supervision of the Camorra boss. The brokers lived permanently in Spain (Málaga, Alicante, Tarragona), coordinated the negotiations, deals, transport, and delivery of drugs, and maintained direct contacts with the Moroccan suppliers, who would import hashish from Morocco. Being present in Spain was key to the success of this business activity. Each team, *paranza*, large or small, had the same objective but adopted different operational modalities according to its knowledge and contacts.

Domenico Verde, for example, worked solely with three associates, who carried out all vital tasks. They transported money, *puntate*, from Italy to pay for the supplies and exported the drugs overland back to Italy, which they put in local depots on arrival and then sold them in their drug piazzas and distributed them to representatives from other clans. Finally, once the profits amassed, they exported the money back to Spain to be invested in various lucrative projects. This team was highly efficient but also had special permission by the boss to have its own small deals on the side. For example, it had a Brescia connection and also supplied the Sicilian Mafia and Calabrian 'Ndrangheta networks (PN15: 4).

Another broker had a more complex form of organization at his disposal and more members. He used vans instead of cars and employed a separate distribution team in Marano. In this case, the money was bought to Spain by a member of his *paranza* in a Spanish van from Marano. Once in Spain, the money was handed over or deposited in a safe place, from which it was collected by the Moroccan team (*el cambista*). Another person delivered the drugs to the couriers. The broker made sure that the transport team was ready and paid (for petrol, tickets, etc.). Goods were then transported in fruit and vegetables vans in order to go unidentified.

These vans went by ferry from Barcelona to Civitavecchia,[34] where they continued down to Marano (PN15: 106–107), and there a separate distribution team took over. It coordinated the arrival of the drugs and their distribution locally, as well as the collection of funds, *puntate*, and their transportation to Spain (see PN15 and TN23). Polverino imposed rigid rules but was versatile enough to employ different nationalities when necessary and do business with other ethnic groups.

Once this network was dismantled in 2010, it rapidly regrouped, employing a new squad of couriers. With many of its trusted soldiers in prison, it sought out different options and ad hoc temporary arrangements in order to adapt to an emergency situation. The latest importing team was made up of Poles (see TN24) and the operating base in Spain involved a mixture of nationalities predominately Neapolitans but also Spanish and Moroccans, whereas activities in Naples were still undertaken by Neapolitans.

The legal department was predominately located in Quarto, where the majority of the legitimate business concerns were based. These commercial activities were often used for money laundering. Companies considered to be above suspicion, in the food sector (meat and bakery companies) and in the cement and building industry, were often used to cleanse money gained through local criminal activities. These activities formed part of the clan's money-laundering cycle: money made in Quarto from illegal activities was systematically invested in these legitimate business ventures but also in other investments such as apartments, cars, and boats all owned by front names.

There are ample examples, including bars in Villaricca and in the shopping center Quarto Nuovo, that were officially managed by third parties but are believed to be linked to the clan (TN23: 12). These were friendly agreements, but some businesses in Italy were also acquired through the use of illegal mafia methods. The clan accumulated companies fairly easily. Some company directors turned to the clan for financial assistance when they could no longer pay their debt, and surrendered their company to the clan while remaining the official owners *only* on paper. Others were forced into giving their companies to clan members.

In Spain, businesses were also bought to cleanse money, but without visible mafia methods being employed—no violent or threatening behavior, but rather financial methods. One example, a building company in Tarragona that was formally owned by a relative of an Italian businessman who was an acquaintance of Polverino, was seemingly under that relative's control. Thanks to this company, the clan bought land to build twenty-five villas that were sold for around 250,000 euros each (PN15: 181, 325). In this way, the clan was able to undertake an official transaction using a legitimate company based in Spain. Violence would have defeated the purpose of the exercise: silent financial takeover and control.

The chosen sectors in Spain were real estate and the construction business. The modalities for laundering money were fairly simple: local Spanish bank accounts were used; some associates had access to them and others transported the cash directly into Spain. Polverino proved to be an intelligent international manager of a crime and business empire in different locations.

## POLVERINO CLAN ACCOMPLICES

This clan was successful in its infiltration of the legal economy and politics in Quarto and Spain because of the support of its accomplices. Polverino's social capital was widespread and he benefitted from good relations with the local criminal, business, and political communities. One local politician even traveled to Spain to ask for Polverino's advice. Why did these relationships develop? First, because the boss did not resort to violence in his dealings with his accomplices, and, second, because they gained something from their relationship with a Camorra boss: recognition, legitimacy, power, or money.

Like any intelligent executive director, Polverino sought good advice. He used the techniques, organizational structures, and operating methods of able businessmen and he surrounded himself with businessmen because they were effective. As one associate explained: "these individuals are to all effects 'members'—even though they are not part of the military set up. Indeed, they were given the exclusive task of exploiting their business skills to invest money for the clan" (PN15: 43).

In Quarto, Polverino managed to co-opt a significant number of white-collar professionals such as businessmen. These professionals facilitated the clan's presence in the legal economy. They acted as intermediaries between illegal and legal sectors, using their bank accounts or companies for clan activities. This was a functional exchange of skills, knowledge, and money. For example, in order to escape Italian judicial requisitions, criminals could not appear as the official owners of companies, which would be seized, so the clan used the names of professionals as substitutes. No doubt they received something in return. The authorities believed that one top clan member was involved with about fifteen companies, and the fact that his name appeared on none of the paperwork was thanks to his regular use of front names as for the official owners. In Campania, there were some important companies that were almost entirely financed by the boss but managed supposedly by legitimate businessmen (see PN15 and PN16).

The money-laundering modalities used in Italy were replicated in Spain and the same personnel were employed: Neapolitan businessmen who had helped Polverino put down economic roots and extend his financial power in Italy. Now they were transposed into the Spanish context. Legal structures, companies, and procedures were established by them, as in the case of the La Torre clan, so that when the moment came to transfer money, or to make an acquisition, it was not seen as an unusual or exceptional act, but as something very normal. It appears that no Spanish businessmen were approached in Spain before 2011,[35] but after mass arrests of Polverino's Neapolitan associates and advisers, perhaps they were.

There were different types of connivance by businessmen. One family, for example, a father and three sons, were complicit accomplices to the Polverino clan because they put their names at the disposal of the clan without seeking to be involved in or profit from its activities. They were independent businessmen who acted purely as front names. On paper, they appeared as the official owners of two local restaurants when, in reality, it was one of the boss's relatives who was the true owner. Polverino managed, decided, and profited from the business. In this way, the GLT family favored the activities of the clan without seeking to profit from them.

Other businessmen participated more directly. MN and DF are two good examples of "compenetrative" accomplices. Both businessmen, active in the construction industry in Quarto, were part of Polverino's local inner circle of economic advisers (PN15 and PN16). MN remained local in Marano and used his political influence in the clan's favor. He was a close friend and knew the boss's family and other members of the clan well. He owned, managed, and was an associate of various companies, all of which were involved in either the building sector or supplying goods and services to hotels and restaurants. It is believed that, thanks to his contacts with the clan, he became an important and well-respected local constructor able to win substantial public contracts. His legitimate companies were used to recycle the clan's profits, but he also personally benefitted from the situation, increasing his own fortune and reputation.

DF was actively involved in the clan's commercial activities both in Italy and Spain. Described as Polverino's "*éminence grise*" (PN15: 74), his brain, DF gave the boss useful business advice. Although DF was on intimate terms with the boss's family, he always sought to maintain his reputation as a law-abiding and honest businessman (PN15: 161). But he was fully devoted to the boss. This devotion took various forms: He accompanied Polverino to Spain when he left Pisa in 2006, he frequently traveled to Spain to discuss business and give advice on deals and investments, he was the front name of a villa with a swimming pool in Spain (PN15: 9), and he used his knowledge and resources in Spain to help the clan. In particular, although never permanently based in Spain, he put his residency status in Tenerife, his financial resources, his bank accounts, his properties, his businesses, and even his Spanish identification number at the boss's disposal for the clan and its money-laundering activities (see PN15 and PN16). He was considered "the economic brain behind the criminal outfit" because he was "the factotum" of the boss with regard to real estate and many other business activities" (PN15: 9). In short, he was officially a businessman who befriended the local boss and became a compenetrative entrepreneur and full-time member of the clan.

This clan had a truly dual international identity, operating in at least two national contexts[36] and engaging in mobility for the benefit of the home territory. Spain can be defined as having a dual commercial function for the clan: it provided goods and investment opportunities thanks to an intricate link between Italy and Spain, whereby constant flows of goods, people, and money traveled in both directions. It also provided a place to hide. The Polverino clan implemented a mafia economic strategy in its invisible drugs network in Spain rather than being a visible criminal association.

## Money Laundering

Until the global financial crisis of 2008, Spain was a young democracy with an expanding economy, a developing infrastructure, and evolving political institutions. This made it a vulnerable setting and a particularly attractive one for money-laundering operations: its lack of systematic bank checks on economic transactions, its perceived weak law enforcement, as well as the investment potential of many speculative building projects along the Spanish coast and the booming tourism industry that accompanied it. As one *pentito* explained: "Spain was the preferred destination for reinvesting money made from drug trafficking because there were very few controls, the antirecycling law was less strict, and the law against drug trafficking was less severe" (SIv, 3/11/2011, in PN16: 94).

Spain's banking system was in particular considered conducive to money laundering by foreign drug traffickers: "Personal accounts and wire transfers being the principal method, and money orders the first instrument. Other popular methods are represented by buying and selling real estate, currency conversions in exchange houses and depositing funds in gambling casinos" (Savona, 1999: 108). There has existed since 1993 a Spanish financial intelligence unit (SEPBLAC) set up to gather intelligence and investigate money-laundering activities in Spain, but its "lack of resources for its AML/CFT [anti-money laundering/counter financing of terrorism] regulatory function may negatively impact on its overall effectiveness" (IMF2: 5). This may explain why *camorristi* continue to target the Spanish economy, using different money-laundering techniques.

The case that follows suggests some possible money-laundering activities in Spain, although the evidence is scant. The Nuvoletta clan is an example of how mafias functionally target a host country over decades in order to launder their profits and make investments, whatever the state of the clan in the home territory.

## Money Laundering and the Nuvoletta Clan

The Nuvoletta clan from Marano, a town on the outskirts of Naples, was one of the most powerful clans between the 1970s and 1980s (see PN3). In 2012, its status was less pronounced, as the Polverino clan from Quarto had come to dominate the area (DNA3: 81). Together with Antonio Bardellino and Michele Zaza, it led the way in transforming the rural Camorra into a business Camorra, which it did with the sponsorship of Cosa Nostra during the 1980s (Sales, 1988).

The clan's presence in Marano is less visible as of this writing than in the past. Since 2001, it has been considerably weakened although it was very active during the 1980s–1990s, both in the drug-importation sector (see chapter 4) and in money-laundering activities. In 2014, the clan still persisted, as some of its members continued to traffic drugs into the region, but there was no clear local clan structure or leadership.

Since the early 1990s, members of the Nuvoletta clan have regularly turned up in Spain, both for drug trafficking (cocaine, hashish, marijuana) and, more importantly, the evidence suggests, for money-laundering activities. Some of its members were identified in Tarragona, the Costa del Sol, and, more specifically, the Canary Islands (in particular, Tenerife, Adeje, and Arona).

### THE NUVOLETTA CLAN: ITS MEMBERS AND TERRITORIES

At the height of its power in the 1980s, the Nuvoletta clan controlled the small town of Marano to the north of Naples. Active since the 1970s, the clan ran an efficient family crime enterprise with clear traditional values and rules: it controlled the territory, determined economic activities, and greatly influenced local politics and the distribution of public subcontracts (Allum, 2006). Since 2002 it has been less visible, the Polverino clan being the dominant force in Quatro, Marano, and in northern Naples. These two clans share the same territory and have a strange relationship, being both rivals and partners at the same time; they cohabit with different equilibriums, tensions, and projects. And although the Polverino clan has been more criminally active between 2000 and 2010, it should be noted that in June 2015 investigators in Milan arrested ten members of the Nuvoletta clan who had supposedly transferred their activities to Baranzate (Lombardy) and were involved in restaurants and the selling of dairy products.[37]

Here we recount a moment of disjuncture between the clan's weaker local Neapolitan presence and activities abroad where there existed a stable and flourishing operating base that was identified in Spain between 1995 and 2008. The clan appeared as an active economic presence without necessarily having a local home territory. Historically, the Nuvoletta clan has always been centered in a large and tight family unit inhabiting a specific contained geographical location, the Poggio Vallesana hilltop estate in Marano, the family's residence, district, and seat of power. The power of the clan lay in its extensive kinship-based membership, its strategic geographic allies, its economic prowess, its range of associates, and its territorial control. Blood ties were paramount: "Family relations and leadership roles have structures that in some way superimpose themselves and are the same . . . everyone is in some way related to the Nuvolettas" (TN13: 12).

However, since the arrest of the last Nuvoletta brother, the boss Angelo Nuvoletta, in 2001,[38] and the death of one of the Nuvoletta cousins in 2002, this clan has been rather quiet; the Polverino clan controls its districts, even though a young generation is still around. Until 2001, there was a clear attempt to keep the clan under family control and pass the leadership to the younger generation of Nuvoletta men. But this did not work out. Some members explicitly complained about the "power crisis" and Angelo Nuvoletta's determination to "keep power in Poggio Vallesana and not delegate power" to another family (TN13: 24). The boss chose a close relative "to replace him and keep the leadership of the clan in the [Nuvoletta] family." As a consequence, "the reputation of the clan is in crisis" and "many members have complained and have nostalgia for a recent past when the leaders of the organization . . . had power and were respected in the area" (TN13: 20). There was a perceived lack of leadership, identity, territory, power, and this was reflected in the clan's disjointed activities both in Marano and in Spain.

It has been suggested by journalists that different organizational structures were tried to salvage the clan. For example, that three closely interrelated families would share their benefits in equal parts: the Nuvoletta family, the Simeoli family, and the Polverino family.[39] These solutions were tried and failed. This crisis, and the subsequent decline of the Nuvoletta clan, reflects the importance *camorristi* attach to the solid blood family unit as the determining quality of leadership. It highlights how leaders believe that blood ties guarantee survival and success, regardless of skill, contacts, or intelligence. Angelo Nuvoletta's insistence on having a blood relative as a leader significantly weakened the clan and its solid power base in Marano, and ultimately ceded power to the formerly subordinate Polverino clan. The formerly hierarchical Nuvoletta clan structure gave way to a more diluted group made up of four or five members who had their own little clans but responded to Polverino as an overall reference point. These smaller clans within the group included some foot soldiers and business accomplices as well as the older generation of wise leaders and advisers who had been close to the Nuvoletta brothers. While retaining their respect and status, this older generation did not set up its own clan or relaunch the Nuvoletta clan, but adapted to the new Polverino sphere of influence, helping and giving advice. They were left alone and always took their cut of the deals, but they were not leaders in their own right, which left potential for the Nuvoletta clan to eventually reorganize once again in the future.

But there still existed some residual local territorial Camorra elements in Marano. Nuvoletta Members resisted complete disappearance and maintained a common fund. The fund worked as "a form of efficiency" and "self-protection" with the "the payment of salaries to the wives of prisoners" (TN13: 14). These very basic tools of operation were important because they maintained some collective identity of the Camorra group. Members in Marano continued to regularly use violence to try and maintain order and gain the respect that was their due, although there was no clear leadership or structure; it was an evaporating and fragmented clan. In Spain, however, the clan was present only in the form of financial representatives: "there was no Camorra-like behavior based on violence, threats, and oppression" (GB); they were foreign businessmen investing in the Spanish economy.

Between 2003 and 2008, a succession of members of the Nuvoletta clan appeared in Tenerife; some of them were on the run from the Italian police, others were not. There was no clear organizational structure comparable to a clan, no criminal family settled in Spain with twenty to forty members: "In Tenerife, there was only the clan's economic structure ... there was a complete absence of violent foot soldiers" (GB). It is believed that members of the clan had been there for three decades. Members sought to place the clan's money in profitable business opportunities and set up legitimate commercial activities (real estate, tourist industry, etc.). They wanted to integrate into the local economy without being detected. But the fact that many were on the run meant that sooner or later their behavior would be noted. This was not a clan but a loose network of business representatives or a "corporate network"[40] that had identified possible investment opportunities and perhaps had support from an already existing infrastructure or the Italian community. Indeed, some inhabitants from Marano have moved permanently to Tenerife.

Figure 5.4 represents the different relationships between the various actors and highlights how the Camorra leaders (nodes 5, 9, 6, 4, 2) were just as important as the other players. It shows how the clan structure produced a loose network that had members in both locations and how money launderers were fully integrated into the structure. Thus, although in Marano there was practically no criminal clan or concrete leadership controlling the territory, money-laundering activities took place in Spain. The leadership and the locus of power were evaporating, but money was still being laundered abroad.

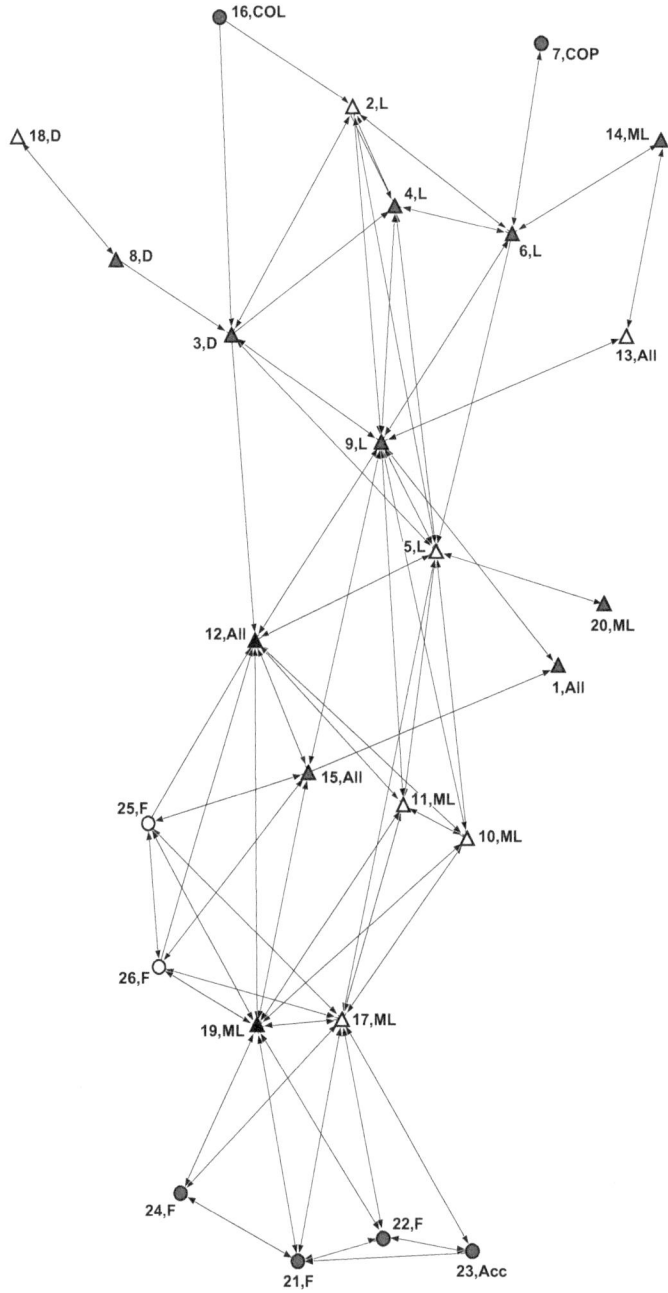

**FIGURE 5.4** The Nuvoletta clan and its money-laundering network in Tenerife (1995–2008)

As the Nuvoletta clan had been a large clan, it was able to employ a vast range of members in its criminal activities at home. There was a rationalization of roles and jobs, from killers to drug-pushers to white-collar professionals to politicians. For the clan's money-laundering activities in Tenerife, this was also the case. These activities were not undertaken by random individuals but by trusted and experienced members who were close relatives of the boss. They were systematically present in Tenerife. Family was again prioritized, even if some members were unreliable. When in 2006 two cousins were considered below par, they were soon replaced by other members who were considered more able.

On the run, the clan's business representatives moved to Spain to develop money-laundering business activities. They became the clan's economic advisers and investors abroad. They were not interested in territorial power and were thus less attached to a set territory. They did not present themselves as criminals but as law-abiding businessmen and respectable members of the community, investing in local Spanish economic activities.[41] They often surrounded themselves with Italian associates. It is believed that one member had six advisers based with him in Spain, and in 2011 thirteen people in the network (clan members and associates) were arrested for Camorra money-laundering activities in Tenerife (Adeje and Arona). These Neapolitans were no longer exclusively working with fellow Neapolitans but in a multiethnic network of associates, which included a British and a Moroccan national.[42]

### NUVOLETTA CLAN ACTIVITIES

At the height of its power during the 1980s, the Nuvoletta clan was very present across its local territory: in extortion rackets, drug trafficking, defrauding the EU Common Agricultural Policy policy, and winning public subcontracts through its political contacts (Behan, 1996). The clan did not yet have a corporate internal structure. Members multitasked, undertaking illegal and legal activities and using violence when necessary. But since 2000s, it is believed that the Nuvoletta clan moved away from its main Camorra activities and concentrated on investing its illegal profits in the legal economy. It diversified its investments in discos, bars, tobacconists, shops, a milk distributor, and a horse rearing and selling company to hide the origin of its illegal money. A judicial document noted that it differed from the Polverino clan in that "the Nuvolettas dedicated themselves to the building sector in particular, and the Polverino clan controlled the criminal activities" (TN13: 14). Indeed, construction was its main investment sector, so much so that it often had to pay a tax to other Camorra groups in order to undertake its building activities across other territories.

Although the true extent of the clan's money-laundering activities in Spain has been difficult to analyze because of its covert nature and a lack of Spanish police or judicial evidence, a very general overview is developed here to suggest a possible pattern of Camorra behavior in these financial sectors abroad. Money-laundering was not new for the Nuvoletta clan, as it had specialized in these activities in Marano and in Italy. There are many examples, but the modalities of what the clan did abroad may have differed; it was clearly seeking to be less violent.

In Marano, the clan employed both the force of intimidation and its political contacts to win public contracts in the construction industry. For example, the development of apartment buildings in Marano in the early 1990s was taken over using mafia methods. These construction projects involved one businessman who acted as a front name and used violence in order to coerce others into selling him their property. Front names were always used to cover the clan's activities, which were remotely controlled by the clan so that it could invest money in building projects. Clan business representatives appear to have used the possible legal and financial loopholes to disguise the true origin of the money invested in construction projects.

The continuous trips of clan members to Tenerife and Gran Canaria might suggest that their economic activities in these locations were worthwhile. A local Spanish newspaper noted their presence in 2004–2005, 2005, 2009, and 2010. Already in 1997, through a relative of the Nuvoletta brothers, the clan appears to have invested in Tenerife (see TN13) using a Camorra holding company with subsidiary companies that were involved in real estate activity, hotels, restaurants, luxury boats, and vehicles.[43]

One particular project is worthy of note: the construction of a holiday complex in 1999 in Tenerife. Businessmen close to the clan were all present during the initial phase of construction of this tourist village and were the real driving force behind the project. And when they were wanted by the Italian authorities, they moved permanently to Spain to oversee the project. They registered their companies locally, opened Spanish bank accounts, included fellow businessmen from Marano in these projects, and got building permits. Some businessmen even paid taxes in order to guarantee getting a permit to allow the development of the tourist village in Tenerife (TN13), which is now a flourishing holiday complex. They presented themselves as legitimate businessmen: one was the owner of a travel agency and the other a successful investor.

These pieces of the puzzle regarding money laundering abroad do not explain the elaborate process by which money made from extortion rackets and drug trafficking in Marano was invested in Tenerife. We can only suggest that the constant presence of businessmen close to the clan may indicate that they found a way to recycle the clan's money through legitimate Spanish companies. In this activity, there was no need to engage with foreign criminal groups; the businessmen had only to find the appropriate financial interlocutors in situ.

### NUVOLETTA CLAN ACCOMPLICES

The Nuvoletta clan in Naples had all sorts of accomplices in civil society, the business community, and the political world, which made it a powerful clan. For example, when a clan member started to collaborate with the state, the clan sought to block this initiative using all the accomplices at its disposal to do so: "they sought a lawyer to contact him and mobilized a doctor inside Poggioreale prison to dissuade him from continuing in his collaboration and reassure him about his future" (TN13: 14). These were complicit accomplices who were bribed and paid off. Subordinate and collusive entrepreneurs were also available: in one case a businessman was threatened into doing what the clan wanted, and in another, a long-established criminal became a compenetrative businessman who worked in the interests of the clan.

The exact nature of the accomplices in Spain is unclear owing to a lack of investigations, but they are there in different forms. One interesting accomplice did appear publicly—a lawyer. He was from Marano but was often present in Tenerife and accompanied his clients to business meetings, even to Madrid. He was also photographed with the local European People's party candidates as he stood for election in Adejde and Tenerife.[44] Although he withdrew his candidacy, this may be an indication of clans perhaps targeting local politics in Spain and their interest and willingness to do so. This example illustrates that accomplices are becoming more and more transnational and mobile, traveling across borders with ease to assist their clients.

In Spain, *camorristi* are very active. If they have to move from Campania, they prefer to go to Spain. This is because Spain is an important drugs wholesale market and has numerous financial opportunities in classic money-laundering sectors such as real estate and tourism. Spain, like Eastern Europe, is still a relatively new democracy with disjunctures in the institutional and market systems and rules and values that can be easily manipulated.

# 6

# CAMORRA CLANS IN THE UNITED KINGDOM

Preston, London, and Aberdeen

The United Kingdom is the last country on our journey. And perhaps the least prepared for Italian mafias. It is an island with a long history, strong state institutions, a vibrant economic center, a multicultural society, and relatively poor weather. Although very different from Italy, it still attracts *camorristi* because of its culture, legal system, and economic opportunities. In 2012, the prosecutor Michele del Prete argued that the Camorra functionally chose the United Kingdom "for business, to develop its money-laundering activities and hide fugitives" (MdP). *Camorristi* are not interested in controlling a physical location but in subtly colonizing the legitimate economy, since there were already, in 2013, seven thousand organized crime groups with thirty thousand individuals active in the United Kingdom (HO2: 4).

Mafia, 'Ndrangheta, and Camorra members and their associates have been present and active in the United Kingdom for some time. For example, "in 1968, ten members of the [Caruana] clan had been convicted of drug trafficking in England and Canada" (Robinson, 2000: 244).[1] However, their specific organizational structures, activities, and accomplices remain unknown. This is often because British police have not investigated mafia members, since they have not officially broken English or Scottish law, and thus the police profile is minimal.

Clan members may be involved in illegal activities, but they remain below the radar of local police. For example, in 2013, a local police force identified six criminal groups made up of Italian nationals engaging in money laundering, economic and web-based fraud, violent criminal activity, organized theft, and drug-related activities, but only one was identified as having possible links

**TABLE 6.1** Camorra case studies in the United Kingdom (1984–2014)

| CLAN | DATES | LOCATION/ITALY | LOCATION/ABROAD | CRIME |
| --- | --- | --- | --- | --- |
| Piccirillo clan | 2006–2007 | La Torretta, Naples | Preston, Lancashire | Acquisitive crime |
| Caldarelli clan | 2004–2014 | Il Mercato, Naples | London | CF |
| Secondigliano alliance | 1990–2000 | Secondigliano, Naples | London | CF |
| La Torre clan | 1984–2005 | Mondragone, Caserta | Aberdeen, Scotland | ML |

to an Italian mafia group, whereas the others were not systematically investigated. As a high-ranking police officer pointed out in 2012, "at the moment we only have half the picture in the United Kingdom, what we need is to get the complete picture with the other half, and this might take some time, but it's a goal that is worth aspiring to" (BPO). Lack of precise knowledge of these groups and their activities has far-reaching implications in developing coherent local and European cooperation in the fight against Italian and European mafias.

The Camorra described in this chapter is rational, somewhat commercial, and invisible. Three out of the four general Camorra activities that *camorristi* undertake in Europe are identified (see table 6.1). The one activity in which it did not appear to be directly involved was the importation of drugs for the British market; perhaps drug trafficking was not worth its while. However, the smuggling of cigarettes by Camorra associates did start up again in 2010. Money-laundering activities are particularly difficult to detect because British police lack evidence, but unofficial evidence suggests that the United Kingdom is becoming an increasingly attractive destination for these kinds of activities. In this chapter, the activities of four groups of *camorristi* are analyzed; two former *camorristi*, who spent time in the United Kingdom, provide a good insider's view of the clans' operations. These cases illustrate how Camorra groups come to the United Kingdom and undertake their activities undetected.

## Acquisitive Crime

The detection of acquisitive crime undertaken by members of organized crime groups is not prioritized by the UK authorities. As a result, it is difficult to identify general tendencies. Whereas the Dutch and Spanish authorities are aware of the phenomenon, British law-enforcement agencies have tended to consider acquisitive crimes as a local level-1 crime[2] rather than evidence of possible activities of international organized crime groups. Thus there exists hardly any material about this type of crime in the United Kingdom and very little about the culprits compared with the data provided by the German BKA (see BKAa). However, it has been possible to reconstruct one such case that is a good example of the potential relationship between acquisitive crime and *camorristi* and the potential dangers for a host country unfamiliar with *mafiosi* who might have long-term projects.

## Acquisitive Crime and the Piccirillo Clan

Gennaro Panzuto of the Piccirillo clan from the central districts of Naples was discovered in Lancashire in 2007 thanks to collaboration between British and Italian police. He was wanted by the Italian authorities to stand trial for extortion. According to local police, he was not involved in any traditional Camorra activities in Preston. He himself explained that he cooperated with some questionable white-collar professionals who introduced him to crime in the United Kingdom and was arrested before he could develop a serious economic presence, which, he argues, was his long-term intention. This is also the only case in which violence was employed as a method against natives, albeit criminal natives, and unlike in Naples, it was not used to enforce Panzuto's own Camorra power but rather that of his local hosts.

### THE PICCIRILLO CLAN: ITS MEMBERS AND TERRITORIES

Gennaro Panzuto ("Genny"), was a bright man born in the wrong place. He started visiting the United Kingdom on and off in 2005 and then spent a year and a half living the quiet life in Preston with his girlfriend, kids, and a few associates. All this below the radar of Lancashire police, although on the run from the Italian authorities. In May 2007, he was arrested by Interpol at the request of the Italians. Locals were shocked by his arrest. He had followed the traditional pattern of a fugitive who keeps a low profile; according to one police officer working on the case, he did not behave "in a particularly eye-catching way." Instead, he "conducted a very reserved life" and sought not to "attract any attention" (IPO). After extradition in late 2007, he became a state witness.

Gennaro was a leading member of the fragile Piccirillo clan from the Torretta district—a district the clan shared equally with the Frizzero family. La Torretta is a small and strategically placed central district next to the elegant districts of Chiara, Mergellina, and Posillipo on the waterfront. The leaders were Panzuto's uncles, Rosario and Ciro, two smugglers and drug dealers who had taken a clear stand in the war against Raffaele Cutolo and the NCO during the 1980s. Although young, this gave them a criminal reputation, hard-earned respect, and power. Rosario Piccirillo (Rosario 'O Biondo), was the acknowledged leader and, as such, never moved from la Torretta, where his strong territorial presence countered possible rivals. But in reality, power and criminal control moved from one family to the other like a pendulum, depending on which clan was being investigated by the judiciary. As a result, power was determined by the clan that had the most leaders and members out of prison.

Between 2005 and 2007 the clan's leadership became extraterritorial, as Panzuto became the de facto leader while his uncles were in prison. From Preston, he tried to organize the clan's warring strategy against the Frizzero clan and manage its criminal activities from afar. However, the clan's seat of power remained fixed and territorial. His absence did make local decision making problematic, but he was in regular contact with his district: "I was in England at the time... and I gave orders to LS and GZ" (QN11: 5). He did not delegate power to one person, probably because of the lack of competent replacements. In fact, he believed he could lead the clan even from the United Kingdom: "I managed my absence, the business, and the war in Naples... it is not something that everyone can do" (GP). He did this by communicating orders to his men and traveling back and forth when he could. Indeed, when he was arrested he was on his way back to Naples to deal with a rival. He tried to be in two places at once while his orders dashed across Europe, but his territorial power base remained firmly established in Naples, a vital territory that earned him respect and produced revenue.

In the United Kingdom Panzuto was not the leader of a clan, but became involved with some British "friends." These were dubious local professionals from Preston to whom he was introduced by Neapolitan associates. He became their bodyguard and general associate who subordinately obeyed their orders. In particular, he threatened individuals. His British contacts wanted to help him out, but above all they were interested in pursuing their own criminal activities. Although virtually present simultaneously in Naples and Preston, he did not have his own independent British clan and set territory, but developed a functional relationship with his English associates. This was stopped in its tracks when he was arrested. But the exact extent of the roots he could have put down, if any, or whether he would have fully integrated into the British criminal world, is unclear. As he explained, "my ambition was to open several big shops selling shoes, household goods, furnishing for bathrooms, paintings" (GP).

In 1997, it was estimated that the Piccirillo clan had twelve members (Scribani, 1997: 23[3]), and by 2013 it had twenty-three (QN14: 1). In the early 2000s, it was generally considered a medium-size clan and not particularly menacing. It was not a generational family but a tight-knit intergenerational one based on a nephew (Panzuto) and two uncles. An aunt of Panzuto's had married one these former smuggler-cum-clan leaders. As Panzuto explained, "he is an in-law, but for me he is like blood," and he flanked his uncles in the day-to-day running of the clan. The Piccirillo clan had a limited membership and a very basic internal structure based on economic survival strategies and a hierarchical leadership. The nephew and two uncles were at once the leadership, the power axis, and the nucleus of the clan, with other relatives and loyal friends providing the periphery. Together, they made the executive decisions about the clan's affairs, each being surrounded by a small cluster of trusted foot soldiers who implemented their orders.

The Piccirillo clan's structure did not replicate itself in the United Kingdom. Instead, it was the extension of a small Camorra family and became a flexible but dependent structure rather than a separate or semiautonomous group. When Panzuto moved to the United Kingdom permanently, he took two or three loyal soldiers with him who needed to be away from Naples, as they could eventually help him in his new host environment. He explains his interest in the United Kingdom: "I took this opportunity to go to England for two reasons. The first reason was to take some time out and fresh air, because after six years in jail, you come out a little bewildered. Thus, to collect my thoughts and understand who I could trust and who I could not. At the same time, I was going to see, to verify, what my friend had told me [about the economic possibilities]" (GP). Thus in the United Kingdom there was no Camorra clan but only a tiny handful of members in a very loose ad hoc structure working for some British contacts. It is difficult even to suggest the concept "clan" to describe one leader with two associates. Size may also explain the lack of resources and social capital to sustain more sophisticated extraterritorial activities.

Panzuto's group in Naples was considered strategic by the larger clans because they could co-opt it into their alliance as they sought criminal hegemony over the whole city. Allegiances were indispensable for survival in the Camorra underworld, especially for these clans. The Piccirillo clan was regularly courted to become a satellite clan for these larger groups. In the 1980s, the clan joined the NF and then became a close ally of Gennaro Licciardi of the Secondigliano alliance. Eventually, it chose this alliance because it provided greater benefits for both partners: the smaller Piccirillo clan gained support and protection while the larger Secondigliano alliance acquired more territorial sovereignty in its long-term conflict with rivals, the Misso-Mazzarella cartel. Long-term criminal alliances and loyalty were soon replaced with fickle and temporary agreements.

In this context, Panzuto sought to survive. Often his behavior was considered inconsistent and "double dealing." He was concurrently a member of his own clan, of the more important Torino clan, and of its sponsors, the Secondigliano alliance. He had different jobs, roles, and responsibilities for each level: for example, he was a charismatic leader for his clan, and a killer, trusted associate, and subordinate ally for the more powerful Licciardi family and had special access to its leadership. His membership was multileveled, flexible, and mutable as he traveled and moved rapidly and sought to be in many places at once.

Women in the Piccirillo clan do not appear as direct protagonists. But they were there, providing constant assistance to ensure the continued existence of the clan and allow the men to pursue their criminal activities undisturbed. Generally limited to traditional supporting roles—passing messages, hiding fugitives and firearms—they also appreciated new economic possibilities when opportunities appeared. They were anything but ignorant. For example, they were able to appreciate the United Kingdom as a land of economic opportunities that had a lax judicial system.

The Piccirillo clan's internal value system had deep roots in Naples and was not reproduced in the United Kingdom, as there was no need. Based on established values such as respect, *omertà*, honor, law and order, prestige, obedience, conformity, and territory, clan behavior was limited to Neapolitan but not British civil society. For example, the clan sought to explain the homosexuality of one of its members to their allies because this fact had created problems of reputation that needed to be ironed out. In the United Kingdom, this private identity or act did not concern anyone beyond the few members in situ because it was not considered a problem by local citizens. Clan members were more interested in adapting to the host country's values in order to exploit the invisibility that this provided. For example, Panzuto explains that he had to fit in and what he did to blend in: "I never drank beer. I didn't used to drink. Starting to drink beer was beyond my control. I started in England because, you can tell me, when you are invited to drink, if you hesitate, people somehow get offended. So although I am a street kid, polite manners are very important to me, do you understand" (GP)?

Territorial control in Naples was crucial to the Piccirillo clan's existence and resilience. It achieved this through the systematic imposition of extortion rackets and the regular use of violence. Threats and violence were perpetually used against other clans but also toward its own members and citizens when they did not show the clan the required respect (QN11: 3). This use of fear and violence imposed a persistent blanket of *omertà* to terrorize and control members and citizens in order to show the clan's supremacy over everyone. In Naples, it was vital to be visible and control the local territory, abroad it was more important to disappear into the background. As Panzuto explained: "It might sound strange, but here [in Naples] we stand out unconsciously, whereas abroad it is natural for us not to stand out. We blend in."

But Panzuto *did* exercise violence in the United Kingdom. He was asked by his hosts to use violence to get their clients to pay back debts. In effect, having identified his status as a *mafioso*, they used him for his Camorra reputation to enforce their power within their criminal community. He was hired as a bodyguard and money collector for his easy use of violence, but his acts of violence were not to establish his criminal hegemony in Preston. He did it as a favor to his hosts and not to colonize a set territory or impose his Camorra power. He was a hard man, but he did not engage in violent acts in the United Kingdom on his own initiative, as this would no doubt have blown his cover.

It may be exceptional that this small clan also had a common fund and a salary system from which it paid its members and their expenses in La Torretta. Thanks in part to money received from its alliances with larger groups, the common fund kept the clan going, but it was unnecessary to transfer it to the United Kingdom, as funds were not needed there.

### PICCIRILLO CLAN ACTIVITIES

The Piccirillo clan's criminal activities were limited because of their reduced personnel, resources, and territory, which meant that in turn, it did not have a clearly organized and efficient internal structure. The very basic organizational structure meant that members often multitasked. The clan's traditional activities were extortion, loan-sharking, and selling drugs.

Extortion was key. Members regularly extorted from local shops (garages, bingo halls, butchers) using threats and violence. On one occasion, when the owners of a betting shop did not respond to their demands, they threatened "to close the shop and shortly afterward extortion money was demanded. This act of intimidation was undertaken to clearly show that the territory was *now* dominated by the new Camorra clan, the Piccirillo clan" (QN11: 1–2). Builders working in their district would have to pay 5 percent of their contract to the clan. These were typical Camorra activities, even if undertaken by a minor clan who often had to agree to pay 50 percent of their profits to the bigger clans (see QN11: 9). The Piccirillo clan did not import drugs directly but brought them locally from its sponsors, the Secondigliano alliance. Distribution represented a significant slice of the clan's daily business, especially selling to middle-class professionals in the nearby upmarket districts. Gennaro Panzuto also maintained that his clan had political contacts through professionals who put themselves "at the clan's disposal."[4]

In the United Kingdom, these Camorra activities were never replicated, as Panzuto predominantly followed the instructions of his British criminal associates while taking time to see what he could develop. Thanks to his contacts, he engaged with local criminal underworlds, such as those in Preston and Liverpool, and was involved in various makeshift, small-time organized crime scams: credit card and car fraud as well as cigarette smuggling. Panzuto's explanation gives a sense of the ad hoc nature of the activities: "I have to tell you that the cars they supplied me, I then, smartly, I would keep some of the cars. In fact I set up a real business. I would resell the cars that they gave me.... No, no, they would do it. I didn't do anything. I would tell my friends: 'Look, I need a Bentley Continental. How long would it take you to get me one?' [They would answer,] 'Listen, Gennaro, I am now setting up a new company, I'll get it for you with the new company, because with the old one we already got three cars'" (GP). He did not initiate any of his own Camorra activities.

The danger here was Panzuto's developing collaboration with his British associates and the potential for undertaking money-laundering activities together, although "the concrete future projects were always of a commercial nature—opening up pub chains, restaurants, and especially shoe shops . . ." (GP). Panzuto did suggest that one possible common project could have been to open shops in Naples and the United Kingdom with the goods provided by his British contacts and front names.

For various reasons, these activities in the United Kingdom were never fully investigated by British police after Panzuto was arrested. He had not yet developed his traditional activities, as they were shaped and reshaped by people and events. So his activities were more organized crime than sophisticated mafia association but the potential was there for him to develop both.

### PICCIRILLO CLAN ACCOMPLICES

Panzuto could not have gone to the United Kingdom so easily without the help of informed accomplices. Before moving to Preston permanently in 2005, he had already visited the United Kingdom on various occasions and, thanks to one of his associates in Naples, had developed some stable British contacts. They became an already established, friendly infrastructure in loco. Accomplices have tended to be from the local Italian immigrant community, but this case is different, and highlights how ethnicity is gradually becoming less vital.

Panzuto's support system was not the local Italian immigrant community but a group of well-informed British white-collar professionals from Preston. They were solicitors, lawyers, and accountants who were "above suspicion," to use a *camorristi's* term. These apparently law-abiding citizens undertook fraudulent criminal acts such as insurance scams, credit card fraud, and cigarette smuggling. According to Panzuto: "If we want to talk in English terms, they were the ultimate criminals. And I will explain [that] it [is] for a simple reason: they would take a sheet of paper, pass it through here, and would take one million pounds through VAT alone, through VAT expenses deducted in three countries (GP)." This example stresses once again the importance of complicity between *camorristi* and white-collar criminals, but also the importance of local knowledge and that both partners have something to gain from the relationship and exchange knowledge, skills, and techniques.

There were many different types of accomplices. The British business accomplices were complicit but were not interested in Panzuto's Camorra agenda, only in their own. Initially it was the British who had the upper hand in this "friendship" and he was a subordinate. They used him for his criminal reputation, his willingness to please, his interest in forging links, and his free-and-easy use of violence to threaten individuals. But he also used them: he sought to hide in the United Kingdom and wanted to exploit them for his long-term criminal projects. As he explained: "In my imagination, once I'd gained a very strong economic position there, opening shops, big stores, then my uncle would have come out.... If my uncle wanted to stay in La Torretta, he could have remained. In case of a serious problem, as I have always done, I would go back [to La Torretta] and solve it, but then I would go back immediately to England." He goes on: "My ambition was, as they [his British business accomplices] had several companies, for example, if I wanted to open a shoe shop in Naples, automatically I would go to them and say: 'Please open a shoe company.' I would have them buy lorries full of shoes that they would drive to Naples. The profit, which could amount to £500,000, would be shared between them and me. Where should my ambition have stopped?" (GP). For the time it lasted, Panzuto's relationships with his British accomplices were instrumental; it was a functional partnership that suited the criminal agenda of both partners. This relationship might have changed in time, becoming more permanent and controlled by Panzuto.

Gennaro Panzuto's experience highlights various points. It demonstrates the ad hoc, unstructured, and disengaged nature of smaller groups abroad and their limited power. It underlines the importance of local help and knowledge in the new territory. An understanding of the host environment and in-depth knowledge of the context, as well as readily available resources, make criminal mobility all the more straightforward. Here the British accomplices had an acute knowledge of various legal loopholes. Panzuto's experience also emphasizes how it is possible to undertake criminal mobility without a friendly ethnic support system, and this may be a growing trend. Moreover, compared with other cases, this one is odd in that Panzuto used violence abroad, but not Camorra violence, and he neither established a settlement nor infiltrated the new economy as others did. He merely did what he had to do to survive. Rather than mafia association crimes, these were more impromptu, spontaneous organized crimes and financial scams, nothing that the local British police would consider really harmful or dangerous.

## The Counterfeit Market

Our general knowledge of the state of the British counterfeit market is still limited. The British authorities' definition of counterfeit crime focuses predominantly on intellectual property crime (IPC) rather than the selling and distribution of poor quality fake goods. Compared with its European counterparts, the United Kingdom has been rather slow in responding to this phenomenon as a local, national, and international problem with far-reaching consequences. The Neapolitan Camorra is a market leader in this sector and controls the sale of many fake products to an array of networks and individuals through its control of street-sellers, even in the United Kingdom. However, little is really documented.

It has taken the British authorities a long time to realize the serious and wider harm posed by the counterfeit goods market. In understanding counterfeiting crimes, they always appear to be playing catch up, although the British police now believe that "the UK leads the way in tackling IP crime" (IP2: 3). It was only in 2004 that the police started to systematically target counterfeit activities when the Intellectual Property Rights Office was established in Newport. Finally, in 2012–13, it was acknowledged that "counterfeit and pirated products impact every corner of society; from health and education to business and automotive. It is something which everyone, intentional or not, comes in contact with more regularly than they might like to believe and the impact of those occurrences can cause them physical harm, as well as harm to the local and national economy" (IP2: 5). In 2013–14, it was estimated that "the cost of IP criminality in terms of lost profits and taxes to the UK economy to be in the region of £1.3 billion per year" (IP4: 3). Loopholes to detection and enforcement remain, such as the predominant British focus on property rights and patents and not on the nature of the criminal organizations involved, which may perhaps be mafias rather than just organized crime groups: "across the UK between 250–500 groups are believed to be involved in IP crime" (IP2: 5). This focus enables the more organized Camorra and its representatives to be present in the British market undetected.

Two cases are elaborated here: members of the Secondigliano counterfeit company active in London between 1998 and 2000 and a member of the Caldarelli clan in London between 2004 and 2006. What exactly were they doing in the United Kingdom? And what was the extent of their control over street-sellers and other counterfeit outlets? Their traces are quite literally invisible, under the radar, because they were never fully investigated by British law-enforcement agencies.

## The Counterfeit Market and the Secondigliano Alliance

The Secondigliano counterfeit company had operations in the United Kingdom that were managed by a small group of businessmen and company directors. Not all these businessmen were Italians, but they lived in London, were familiar with

English culture, and traveled with ease. Because they had a good knowledge of the counterfeit sector and were friends with members of the board of directors, they became the counterfeit company's British representatives. One of them was even responsible for another European market. They imported counterfeit goods (mostly clothes but also cameras and electronic goods) into the United Kingdom and sold them to street-sellers and wholesale outlets. But this operation cannot be qualified as a Camorra clan or settlement. These sly businessmen, some with criminal records, formed part of the Secondigliano counterfeit company's extensive business network (see QN4, 3: 90–110).

In particular, toward the late 1990s and early 2000s, a trusted local manager, XK, who had a British registered company, was active in London managing the operations. He bought his goods from Naples, managed their distribution, and controlled the wholesale process through the Neapolitan street-seller network present in the United Kingdom. Some Neapolitan *magliari* were identified in London,[5] one even had a criminal record (QN4, 3: 94). XK did not employ Brits as door-to-door sellers, nor did he use violence toward local citizens. He fitted into the British business community and established an invisible and well-informed Neapolitan network that understood how to work the British counterfeit market and financial system to its favor. He felt so confident and safe in London that in 2000 he did not hesitate to hide a fugitive leader of the alliance (see QN4, 1: 172).

This is a tiny glimpse of the Secondigliano company's activities in the United Kingdom; it is a poor picture. Without exaggerating the nature of the crimes, what is clear is that the British market, like the German, Spanish, and French markets, has been targeted by the Secondigliano counterfeit company. The presence of a *magliaro* selling fake Stihl chainsaws in West Dorset (see Allum, 2012[6]), or of "a person with an Italian accent, wearing a leather coat and selling chainsaws" in Northern Ireland, might suggest this (NIA). However, if there is no political or police will to understand the wider implications of the harm caused by counterfeiting, the activities will continue. The indications are that the counterfeit market might have become saturated, which may explain its decline, but in an economic crisis citizens are more and more likely to turn to cheaper counterfeit goods—and the Camorra is just waiting.

## The Counterfeit Market and the Caldarelli Clan

Raffaele Caldarelli was arrested in London on 5 September 2006 on an EAW, as he was wanted in Naples since 2003 on charges of mafia association. In 1998, he had been sentenced to sixteen years in prison. His arrest raised the question of what was he doing in London. According to the Neapolitan judiciary, he was the leader of a small clan that had become a major player in the Neapolitan counterfeit market (GF4: 3). His presence in the United Kingdom directly linked the production country with the British market.

### THE CALDARELLI CLAN: ITS MEMBERS AND TERRITORIES

The Caldarelli clan, based in districts running parallel to via Marina, is a small family-run clan that has been able to organize more sophisticated forms of crime abroad, in particular in the United Kingdom. In Naples during the mid-1990s, Raffaele Caldarelli, also known as *Lello*, was the young leader and a close associate of the boss of the Mazzarella clan, Vincenzo Mazzarella. Some suggest that these clans were so integrated that they were in fact "one unique structure" (MMV, 12/9/2007, in PN12), whereas others say that "the Caldarelli clan is a kind of branch of the Mazzarella clan. In Camorra language, the Mazzarella clan is the mother of the Caldarelli clan" (QN6: 132).

Like many clans, it became autonomous after an internal conflict with its patrons. Lello, a once-loyal follower of the powerful Mazzarella group, split off and became a boss in his own right. He established his own criminal territory in the districts of Zona Mercato and Case Nuove, districts previously belonging to the rival Contini clan (GF4: 6). This takeover created a new conflict with the sworn enemies of the Mazzarella clan, the Secondigliano alliance. Without the help, assistance, and sponsorship of the larger Mazzarella clan, the smaller Caldarelli clan might have found its emergence, existence, and expansion more problematic.

Between 1995 and 2006, the Caldarelli clan took over the Case Nuove district, putting down firm roots. It became a recognized local criminal presence as well as an emerging player in the Neapolitan counterfeit market because it produced fake goods for its sponsors, the Mazzarella-Misso cartel. Between 2004 and 2006, Caldarelli moved to London, and once there, he extended his Neapolitan counterfeit activities. His involvement with his criminal family continued while he opened a shoe shop on the Hackney Road, from where, perhaps, he sold fake "made in Italy" shoes and bags, all carefully copied and fabricated in Naples. This shop was not an independent branch or offshoot of core Camorra activities, but a small operating cell integrated into the larger counterfeit operations with its headquarters in Naples.

The Caldarelli clan was territorial because its locus of power remained fixed in Naples, but decision making became mobile while Raffaele lived in London. From there, he tried to manage his clan. A communication chain was established to bypass the problem of the leader's absence: orders were relayed through his close relatives (QN8: 12). As he was unable to move, decisions were often made in the United Kingdom; members "would travel to London to plan ... criminal strategies" with him (SLv, 2/3/2005, in QN8: 12). And then they would return to Naples with his orders. He delegated power to them and they were his representatives (QN8: 14). His decisions were extraterritorial, as he tried to exercise power over his home territory from afar.

However, clan members in Naples soon found that Raffaele's physical distance from the home territory was too detrimental, rendering the clan's power dispersed, diluted, and remote. Although he wanted to keep absolute power to govern, a relative stepped in to become leader, believing that decisions needed to be made locally and not by a fugitive far away. The message was that those present in the local territory should "think about the district's activities," not those who lived abroad (FCv, 25/11/2005, in QN8: 28). It was believed that decisions had to be made locally and instantly, where power resided, in order to reinforce the clan's power. Raffaele did insist on his voice being respected even from London, and his leadership style did not change when he moved abroad. He remained authoritative and strong, but the distance made these qualities aloof and useless. Perhaps if this clan had been a larger clan with more resources and personnel, like the Polverino clan, things might have been different.

The organizational structure of the Caldarelli clan was an "intergenerational" family; the older and younger generations all supported, advised, and assisted the leader in his decisions. Power was both horizontal and hierarchical (FCv, 13/8/2005, in QN8: 6). Raffaele's extensive blood ties were the core of the clan's operating structure and remained stable in Naples despite his absence. His loyal foot soldiers and their families made up the periphery of the clan. They did not venture abroad, as they were firmly active and anchored in Naples. There was no resettlement or transfer of members to London seeking to reproduce the clan's traditional activities. Instead, there was a leader who took his family and perhaps two or three associates to help him function as an operating cell in a wider counterfeit network that extended out of Naples. There are no signs that Raffaele Caldarelli recruited British members in London, and he does not appear to have engaged extensively with foreign criminal groups. His main strategy was to use his Italian resources to organize his operating cell in London without being noticed or getting into trouble with other groups.

The clan contained a few strong women who were more visible than is usually the case. They had key roles at all levels, including hiding firearms, drugs, and managing the clan. In particular, they gave orders on behalf of the absent leader and were even described as "advisers" or "ambassadors" (see QN8: 14). In extreme cases, they carried firearms around the district to protect themselves (GF4: 11), showing that they were equal to their menfolk.

Survival in Naples meant having a respected internal value system, as this produced social consensus in the community. It was based on violence and power, with an operational salary system—all features that reinforced the clan's collective identity in the local territory. Although the clan controlled a limited territory, it nevertheless sought to dominate and defend it from rivals (see TN6). TV cameras in the streets and surveillance squads were used to control the district against the police and rival clans. *Omertà*, threats, and intimidation were imposed on citizens so they obeyed the clan's laws (QN8). This was more than private protection.

There were many other forms of control, all to impose the clan's values on the community: the leaders decided whether a new business could open in their district, businesses were burned down if the owner went against the clan's wishes, and members punished a man who was considered to have acted inappropriately with a child (see TN6: 24). This was a small and violent clan that imposed social and economic rules on its local community, although its political power was never made clear. In the United Kingdom, it operated as a cell that adopted an economic strategy rather than as a criminal association that behaved as a family crime enterprise, and it never used violence or intimidation toward British citizens, as this would not have helped with business.

## CALDARELLI CLAN ACTIVITIES

This clan undertook core Camorra activities, but around 2002 it developed a specialization that it exported abroad when it found new opportunities to do so. Unlike the Rinaldi clan, who took up counterfeit goods as a new commercial activity, the Caldarelli clan's counterfeiting activities were a natural extension of its Neapolitan activities. The interdependence between territories was tight because production took place in Naples and the markets and customers were abroad.

In 1995, the clan's activities in Naples were traditional Camorra activities. Salvatore Giuliano explained: "There existed a group led by Caldarelli who had total control over all the illegal activities of the district (from clandestine bets/games, to extortion rackets, to traffic in arms), and in particular, drugs" (GF4: 6). This clan was not involved in drug importation, but purely its distribution. This enabled the clan to make more money, which it could invest in new criminal activities and legitimate commercial opportunities. Indeed, Caldarelli's extended circle of relatives facilitated this extension into the legal economy, as they owned profitable commercial outlets in the city center (see SGv, 15/3/2005, in QN10).

Between 2002 and 2003 things changed. While continuing with its traditional activities in its district, the Caldarelli clan became a central player in the counterfeit sector in Naples—what *camorristi* have called the "parallel" world, for it mirrors the real world and imitates it. The production and commercialization of counterfeit goods included products such as clothes, shoes, bags, CDs and DVDs, or more important designer labels such as Louis Vuitton handbags, Prada and Hogan shoes, Lacoste T-shirts, Belstaff, and Tommy Hilfiger jackets.

Although the Mazzarella clan may have had previous contacts in this sector, when the Mazzarella-Misso-Sarno cartel decided to follow the Secondigliano counterfeit company and move into this sector, the Caldarelli clan was naturally chosen to be involved: "The decision was taken to give Raffaele Caldarelli [and his clan] the task of distributing leather material and the necessary accessories for the production of fake clothes" (QN10: 7). One of his relatives "was then given the responsibility of controlling, planning, distributing raw material and overseeing the budget for that sector" (QN10: 5). The Caldarelli clan became a vital part of the chain of an international counterfeit operation, and it was given this job for very rational business reasons: it was ideally placed to take up the challenge because the family "always did shoes" (GP) and had, as a consequence, all the necessary contacts and knowledge to move into the fake leather and clothing sector, with ease. Was Caldarelli already present in the manufacture economy? Clearly he had links to it, but he was a criminal who used his contacts and his relatives' professions to become a player in the counterfeit sector.

One *pentito* explained Caldarelli's role in Naples: "As far as the handbags are concerned, those who make them are forced to buy their primary materials (leather, lining, harnesses) solely from the Caldarelli clan. The shoes and the T-shirts were sold ready-made to the sellers. They were forced to buy the false Prada and Hogan shoes . . . they [the clan] impose the quantity and the price. They [the sellers] could buy the number of shirts that they wanted but the price was always decided by the Caldarelli clan. In this way, a real monopoly of the market for these products is established. The global profits . . . were then divided into three quotas: one went to the Mazzarella clan, one to the Caldarelli clan, and the other to the Misso clan" (GLv, 10/3/2005: 4–5).

The Caldarelli clan became a division in a larger international counterfeit operation. It controlled and oversaw the wholesale of fabrics and materials, and the full production of other items. All products were made in-house locally with no need for external input or collaboration, apart from the acquisition of raw materials. There was no need for complex transport networks from China, as all the products were "made in Italy" and sold in Naples and throughout Italy via *magliari* or shops.

Instead of having local area managers who took over the existing network of *magliari* in the United Kingdom, as the Secondigliano counterfeit company had done, Caldarelli was present and managed the business directly—selling, representing, and making investments. In this way, it can be suggested that maybe his shoe shop in London was an outlet of the Neapolitan counterfeit operation, from which there existed a continuous flow of goods and money. Or in the words of Sergio Lettieri, "he opened two shops and sold shoes," and a relative "sent him shoes every month using a courier" (SLv, 5/3/2005).

Perhaps the shop also acted as a distribution point for other Italian clothes and shoe retailers based in the United Kingdom, but these are speculations. Perhaps Caldarelli sought to control the existing network of Neapolitan street-sellers and their shops by furnishing them with "made in Italy" products. Gennaro Panzuto explains: "In England, they opened a circuit where they gave shoes to certain shoe shops. They were wholesalers selling to retailers. . . . What I know is that, as far as shoes were concerned, he was supplying them, even to small Italian shops. He was supplying everything. I have to say he was doing that and that. But he didn't threaten anybody, eh! He had good relationships" (GP).

At no point did Caldarelli cut off contact with his home territory. There was incessant communication and exchanges between the two territories and an interconnected supply and demand of money, goods, and resources. Goods and resources made with illegal money in Naples were sent to London to be sold. As with the Secondigliano company, there was a need to control the different levels of activities, but a less extensive structure was put into place because the boss could manage the transportation of goods and negotiate with Italian-British retailers directly. Moreover, there was no need to delegate responsibility to a financial adviser for local English investments, as Caldarelli could do this himself.

The profits were distributed accordingly between him and his sponsors, who always received a percentage of the profits. The smaller the group, the more hands-on and less structured the operations. No violence was recorded among this *magliari* community, but if the same methods were used as with the Secondigliano counterfeit company, it could be inferred that some form of intimidation might have been used. This smaller, less visible clan might have found it easier to control its counterfeit activity and involvement in other criminal activities such as credit card fraud, as Panzuto has suggested.

Caldarelli was arrested in September 2006, and his operations in London appear to have ceased, although his activities, methods, and contacts were never fully elucidated. A new investigation in 2014 once again mentioned London as a possible base of new operations for the Caldarelli clan (see TN25).

## CALDARELLI CLAN ACCOMPLICES

It is virtually impossible to identify Caldarelli's accomplices abroad, but he must have had some to run such an efficient, invisible organization for two years undetected. In Naples, family members played an important role, providing economic and logistical support, thus making it a true family business. The boss could count on an extensive number of accomplices who may not have had face-to-face contact with him but who were all directly involved in the clan's activities thanks to their family connections, and as a result, stood to benefit. Some relatives acted as front names (through ongoing commercial concerns in the Station district) while others produced goods that could be used in the counterfeit sector in London. Caldarelli's contacts and support system in the United Kingdom were already in place before he went on the run. In particular, he had distant relatives working there, which may explain the logistical support and useful local information he must have received to fit in so well.

Raffaele Caldarelli's time in London could be analyzed as a light economic strategy that made use of the host country to place illegal goods. The operation was not a "Camorra settlement" but a form of infiltration into the British counterfeit market. Caldarelli's experience underlines how *camorristi* can functionally exploit opportunities, contexts, and markets, as he did not explicitly leave Naples to open a local branch of Camorra activities in London, nor did he diversify his activities. But as a fugitive, he was able to come to the United Kingdom for two years and establish an illegal business completely unperturbed. He remains emblematic of the dual identity and presence of the Camorra abroad: in Naples, a criminal with fixed roots in the community; abroad, a well-to-do businessman who in 2008 had "400 million euros worth of properties" seized (*Cronache di Napoli*, 22/11/2008).

## Money Laundering

Money laundering is difficult to investigate and it takes many months of cooperation between international agencies to be able to trace money flows into bank accounts across borders and countries. It is impossible to know to what extent criminals perceive the United Kingdom and its territories as a useful center for their money-laundering activities, but the British authorities clearly believe that the country is not a primary target. The *UK Threat Assessment on Organised Crime* (2009–2010) stated that "a significant amount of the criminal proceeds generated in the UK is laundered abroad, in some cases because the risk of discovery is lower than in the UK" (SOCA: 21). However, in 2015 a Treasury and Home Office report explained that "the same factors that make the UK an attractive place for legitimate financial activity—its political stability, advanced professional services sector and widely understood language and legal system—also make it an attractive place through which to launder the proceeds of crime."[7]

One of the main attractions of the United Kingdom as a host country for *camorristi* is its multiple financial markets and its banking system. As an Italian judge explained: "There is a whole range of banking arrangements, corporate, civil, financial, which I think greatly facilitate investment here.... Both the financial and banking systems are particularly 'friendly' when it comes to allowing money to enter and then reexit, financial investment transactions that appear entirely lawful" (IJ). Indeed, it can also be suggested that Camorra clans, through third parties, have started to clean their money in the United Kingdom (MV).

*Camorristi* and their accomplices have become experts at laundering and employ the best specialists to find ways of transferring money between different bank accounts, financial institutions, and countries in order to clean it without a trace of its provenance: "Criminals move cash overseas to avoid detection by the regulated sector; to pay for goods and services; and to hide criminally acquired assets" (SOCA: 21), as was the case of the Amato Pagano clan in Montecarlo (see PN8). Many clans do not even have to leave Naples to launder money, they use an extensive community of qualified accounts and solicitors in Rome and London to do this.

Money-laundering cases involving Camorra clans in the United Kingdom have been difficult to identify, as police and financial institutions are very careful not to reveal confidential information. The case of the La Torre clan is useful because one of its protagonists, Michele Siciliano, a cousin of the La Torre brothers who lived in Aberdeen for sixteen years, explained what the clan did there. He maintains that his clan did not open a branch of core Camorra activities in Scotland, but had a few members located there who functioned as an operating base for the clan's money-laundering activities, illustrating how interconnected the clans' territories were. It also highlights that if the law-enforcement regime in a host country is unaware and unable to identify the presence of a foreign criminal clan and its money-laundering practices, the clan may have free rein, as the police don't have a clue about the Camorra.

## Money Laundering and the La Torre Clan

During the 1990s, the La Torre clan was a visible and violent presence in Mondragone, but had become an invisible and silent presence in Scotland (Allum, 2012). Having traditional local roots, the clan managed to develop a modern criminal agenda in Europe with members living permanently in Aberdeen and Amsterdam and engaging in criminal mobility. In Scotland, Antonio La Torre, brother of the boss Augusto, invested criminally acquired assets produced in Mondragone into legitimate business ventures (AC2). In this way, the clan "managed to put into place an economic system" (IPO) between 1983–2005 in Scotland, whereas in the Netherlands, members oversaw the clan's drug-importation operations. Neither authorities in Scotland or the Netherlands really suspected what this clan was doing until the Italian authorities started investigations in Naples in 1998 The clan's leader in 2003, Augusto La Torre, became a state witness, albeit not one who was considered completely trustworthy.

### THE LA TORRE CLAN: ITS MEMBERS AND TERRITORIES

The medium-sized La Torre clan was based in Mondragone, a small town northwest of Naples and west of Caserta. Today it is still called the La Torre clan, but it is no longer run directly by members of the La Torre family, as many have become *pentiti* or are in prison. Although one of the first judicial sentence against the clan dates from 1989 (AC2), the clan is believed to have existed during the 1970s under the leadership of its pater familias, Tiberio Francesco La Torre, making it more than thirty-five years old. This long-term resilience shows how the clan has managed to survive in an at times hostile environment while at the same time modernizing its criminal and financial operations.

Tiberio Francesco La Torre was the founding father of this small, traditional, family-based clan and father to Augusto and Antonio. Many of his relatives and those of his wife's family were fully involved in clan operations. Initially, blood family and intermarriage were the bonds that held the clan together and family ties were the roots in civil society, although in time, they would start to weaken. Tiberio and his sons joined Raffaele Cutolo's NCO, but in the early 1980s Tiberio consciously went over to the NF. By joining this alliance, the La Torre family joined the Bardellino-Iovine confederation and was greatly influenced by it and benefited from its protection. The La Torre clan took the side of De Falco clan against the Schiavone-Bidgnotti group in 1991, but Bardellino's efficient money-laundering system influenced the La Torre clan's European criminal vision.

Tiberio was from another era, an "old style" *guappo*, who, when the time was right in 1985, handed over the reins of the clan to his youngest son, Augusto. Antonio, his eldest son, had already left the region toward the end of 1982 to settle permanently in Aberdeen with his Scottish wife (TN16: 686). Augusto was the leader of the clan on and off between 1985 and 1997, when he was arrested and imprisoned. Antonio allegedly took over the leadership from his brother between October 1998 and March 1999, whereas previously he had always advised his brother. Whether from prison or abroad, the brothers have been able to organize the clan and its activities (see TN16).

Augusto's leadership style was authoritarian, determined, decisive, violent, and territorial. He was charismatic and had a clear criminal vision and agenda for his clan that relied heavily on his family, although he did not hesitate to violate these bonds of kinship if necessary. In Mondragone, he regularly gave orders to members and cultivated his social capital by mixing with professionals and the local political elite, as well as with the police force, to guarantee protection, immunity, and public contracts.

Decisions usually took place in Mondragone, the clan's headquarters and the La Torre family base. It was the center of the clan's activities and power. Sometimes decisions and operations were forced to become mobile when no adequate leader was free and physically present across the territory. Antonio, regardless of his distant location, filled the clan's leadership vacuum on many occasions (TN16: 657), but managing his long-distance leadership and making extraterritorial decisions was not easy for him.

During the 1980–1990s, from Aberdeen, his permanent residence, Antonio took on an advisory role, and it was often necessary for him to adopt a more assertive management style because of his physical absence. He was regularly consulted on clan-related matters, was in frequent contact with members, and gave his instructions to his trusted lieutenants who implemented his orders (see TN16: ibid). Unlike others, he did not travel back and forth, as this was too risky. Instead he gave detailed directions, controlled activities, and sanctioned threats from afar via phone.

In 1998, decision-making operations shifted to Terni, central Italy, because as part of his sentence Antonio was barred from living in Campania (*divieto di soggiorno*). From there, he managed the clan by having regular meetings with his men and was able to intimidate victims through his representatives or via phone (TN5: 13. 40). Decision-making was forced to become extraterritorial, but its success depended very much on having an army of loyal representatives available. This flexible form of leadership brought with it risks, including the possibility of rebellion by members challenging the unorthodox style of leadership. In particular, the physical absence of the leader encouraged members to seek independence: "I advise[d] him to adopt a more rigorous management style because there were some members who had started their own activities without his knowledge" said JB, his close adviser (TN5: 45). Some family members even felt the necessity to take over and ignore the brothers' wishes. Although the clan showed growing flexibility in the evolution of its power structures and activities, the territory still remained central and needed to be protected.

The La Torre family formed the foundation of the criminal organization. In the early 1980s under Don Tiberio, the clan was small, stable, hierarchical, and nuclear, with power flowing from the old patriarch. Kinship determined leadership roles, highlighting once again the importance of traditional clan values.

Power was passed down the bloodline from father to son—from Tiberio Francesco to his younger son, Augusto (the eldest away in Scotland), and then from brother to brother—Augusto to Antonio. This produced visible strength and forged a strong collective criminal identity. Blood ties created this united and cohesive clan.

A turning point came in 1985. Augusto took over the leadership and management from Don Tiberio as he retired. The clan then "gained a proper structure with a clear organizational network and paid salaries to members" (TN18: 33), as father and son "had different management styles" and Augusto turned his father's small family-run clan into a more efficiently structured business (SCv in TSMCV1: 7). As a consequence, the clan's structure was completely transformed: it went from being a hierarchical family to a generational one, from a family structure to a corporate business structure, from a family-managed clan to a Camorra-managed clan" (TSMCV1: ibid). Augusto turned it around, moved with the times, and introduced progress; he modernized the clan. One judge argued that this new organizational structure resembled "a real company" (TN5: 40) in which members had clear roles and responsibilities, making it more efficient. It was certainly more organized, but not necessarily as efficient as later clans, such as the Amato-Pagano and Polverino clans, would be.

In the late 1990s, the inner core of the family was still a vital resource in Italy but it started to weaken. This blood connection created certain obligations that ranged from looking after firearms, drugs, and money to carrying out extortions, distributing salaries, and executing punishments. Family members obeyed the requests of leaders, but this came with responsibilities, particularly when the La Torre leadership was in prison. Usually family members would take up leadership roles in crisis situations, but when they were not up to the job, trusted advisors took control. Antonio, in 1998, finding himself with his back to the wall because he did not trust his relatives, sought other unrelated supportive lieutenants to advise him.

The peripheral infrastructure was a solid support system of advisers, lieutenants, and foot soldiers, all of whom were indispensable for the criminal existence of the clan in Mondragone. The outer layer included sympathizers and accomplices who provided places to hide money, people, drugs, or whatever else was required. For example, one distant relative "would let the clan use his garage to hide stolen cars and firearms" (TN16: 651).

Augusto established a crime enterprise within the family rather than using the family as an artisanal criminal enterprise, as his father had. There was still some overlap within this new organizational structure; the traditional values of the family still prevailed, but the focus on blood ties was beginning to wane. Indeed, if family members did not behave appropriately, they too would be punished;

they no longer had privileged roles. The clan now resembled the Sicilian Mafia in terms of operational structures, roles, and activities: lieutenants took orders and implemented them with assistants, cashiers, and custodians of firearms. In time, as in other clans, the clan's organizational structure resembled that of an enterprise with two internal departments: an illegal department and a legal one. In each department there existed subdivisions. Both departments existed abroad: the illegal department in the form of drug trafficking and the legal department in the form of financial crime. In this new business-oriented organization, traditional rules and values were replaced by efficient, profit-oriented structures.

The new organizational structure consisted of an efficient clan based in Mondragone that became a business network with operating bases in Aberdeen and Amsterdam. The operations abroad were neither separate nor autonomous branches but one and the same organization: Aberdeen was a natural extension of the Mondragone clan. As Michele Siciliano explained, "They were different bases, both of the same importance. Amsterdam was important for drugs and Aberdeen was important for finance" (MS). Although foot soldiers did not travel abroad, managers did, and they directed activities even though they were not in the same location. Their operations were functional and logical extensions of the clan's legal and illegal departments in Mondragone. By extending operations beyond its borders, the clan had to be more adaptable, flexible, and mobile.

The majority of the clan's active core members lived in and around Mondragone, with a few members permanently settled in the north of Italy, Aberdeen, Amsterdam, and elsewhere. Membership figures are unclear: it is estimated by Michele Siciliano that at the height of its power, the clan had fifty to eighty members in its home territory (MS) but official figures suggested more ninety-six members in 1993-94 (Allum, 2000: 411). Members had a wide range of occupations that rooted them firmly in civil society: builders, students, bartenders, workers, butchers, cleaners, quantity surveyors, police officers, businessmen, garage workers, and shopkeepers). Based on a judicial document (TN5), the average age of members in 1996 was thirty-nine), 9 percent of them women.

In the United Kingdom, as in its other locations, members appeared as legitimate businessmen. Rather than a Camorra clan with a mass membership, there was a handful of strategic actors: a leader and his right-hand man who lived there on a permanent basis. Or in the words of Michele Siciliano, "at different moments, there were about ten people" (MS). The clan might also have recruited Italian immigrants in Aberdeen to help out. Many members visited Scotland, but they did not move there permanently: "They brought people here for short periods of time . . . over a two or three month period. . . . There were people coming up here and they were here for two weeks—holiday, almost" (GramP: 16–17). The sole purpose of the visits of these Neapolitans to Aberdeen was either to bring cash to invest in the clan's economic projects or to hide and keep a low profile. In the mid-1990s, another cousin of Antonio's who was on the run from Italian authorities joined him and Michele Siciliano in Aberdeen, benefitting from their help and the ignorance of the local community. There were also Italians across the United Kingdom whom they could count on, when and if necessary, as was the case during Michele's stay in Woking in 1992–1996. In the Netherlands, there were resident members to oversee the drug-importation business who were in contact with the leadership. In every way, members exploited the lack of understanding in host countries about this form of criminality.

The clan's strategic thinking and functional presence were evident at specific moneymaking locations. In Aberdeen, the operating cell was solely involved in transferring money from Italy (TN16, TN18). They ran legitimate businesses funded by illicitly acquired money made in Mondragone. Although not a true crime in the United Kingdom, money transfers meant the infiltration of the Scottish economy by a Camorra clan. Aberdeen was a tiny cell; members resided here as part of a looser La Torre network that also had other cells in the north of Italy and Europe. The members in Aberdeen were careful, strategic, and adopted a constant reactive approach to maintaining the operating cell. For example, when Siciliano realized the police might be on to them, he moved "because, for the first time in history, in March 1992, the English papers started writing about us, about the La Torre clan, about the activities and everything. . . . On that occasion, we split up because then if anything happened, it would happen only to him and not to me, or vice-versa, so that we could carry on. In that way someone would remain and carry on with the management of the activities" (MS).

In Mondragone and in Italy generally, recruitment was proactive and extensive; leaders were always on the lookout for new members. The former member Mario Sperlongano explained that when he "met some wild boys who showed potential to be recruited in the future for some possible job," he gave them money as an incentive for involvement with the clan (TN16: 81). Even in Terni between 1998 and 2000, Antonio recruited white-collar professionals who would facilitate the clan's activities, including banking transactions (TN5: 152).

All members showed respect for their leaders and for the hierarchy of the clan. For example, one "addressed Antonio with the 'voi' (the plural 'you'), showing him all the leader's due respect" (TN5: 115). However, time and time again it seems as if members had to be called to order: a trusted adviser often warned that when Antonio spoke, all the others had to be silent (TN5:115). Respect for the leader and for the cultural values of the clan also existed among the few members based in the United Kingdom. Michele Siciliano showed immense respect for both of his cousins, Augusto and Antonio.

In Aberdeen during the 1980–1990s, there was no recruitment process; at times, the clan had difficulties co-opting possible accomplices. On one occasion, clan members were even unable to find someone to help with the transfer of funds into a British bank account. As a former member explained: "Initially [Antonio] gave me the name of a Scottish front name, but then nothing happened so I sent the check using his name" (PSLTv, 18/2/2005, in TN16: 683). It has been suggested that Antonio did involve some local Italian immigrants in his activities and that the Augusto had recruited a British member who had never even been to Mondragone (Saviano, 2008) and paid him a regular salary. But this suggestion was not in relation to the activities in Aberdeen; the person had befriended Augusto while he was in prison abroad, and as a way of thanking him, he had been paid (MS).

Our mapping of the clan shows the fluidity of this business network, with certain members abroad (nodes 2, 8, 26, 42, 48) and others traveling between bases (nodes 1, 9, 11, 13, 17, 25, 30). Figure 6.1 is based on a 2000 Carabineri report (AC2) and covers the years when Antonio was in Scotland and then sent to Terni in central Italy as part of his parole (1983–2000). I have coded him (node 2) black because he was normally based abroad. His central position inside this criminal network reflects the great variety of contacts and relationships he had across territories. The boss, at the head of the organization, engages with nearly all the nodes of the network, a leadership strategy that does not happen in a classical hierarchical structure wherein bosses usually communicate to their advisers, who pass their orders down to other members. Important information is usually kept by the leadership at the top of the hierarchical organization. The communication between nodes in *this* network is fast and it is the leader who has direct contact with the majority of members. The drawback is that a member who turns state witness can easily explain the operational structure of the clan and its network abroad and can identify the boss and his activities.

According to Michele Siciliano, during the 1990s Mondragone women were involved in criminal activities: "On the surface, [they] were simple women, but they were women ordered by their husbands.... Affiliations and involvement are automatically formed this way. Women, yes, somehow become involved. They are involved because of their husbands. They are involved with tasks that sometimes seem unimportant, but they are not" (MS). Evidence suggests some women took on executive roles, gave orders, appointed leaders, carried out extortions, received a salary, and some even had personal drivers (see CASMCV5). The younger generation was given greater responsibility. Augusto's wife would relay messages from him in prison to his men outside, but she was also the cashier for the clan and kept arms (AC2)—roles less likely to be associated with women. In addition, women's roles in the clan made them behave in an arrogant manner, as if they were able to

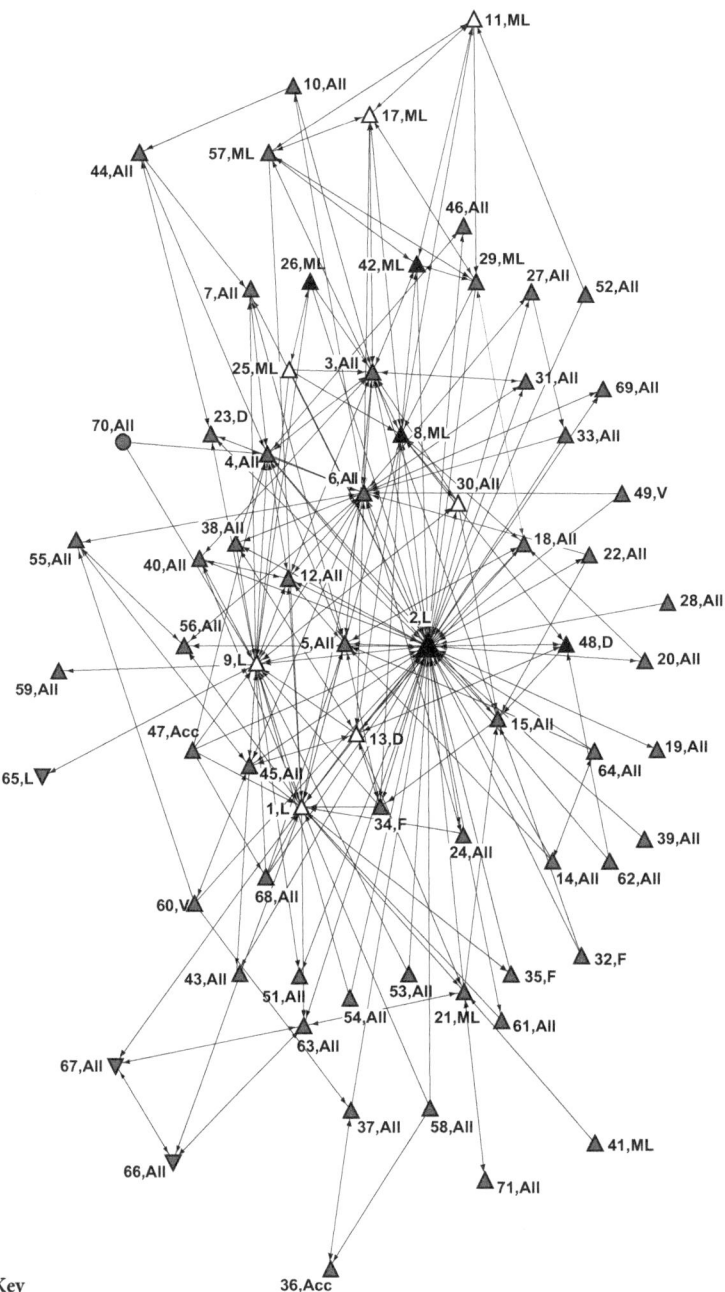

**Key**

Colors: grey (Mondragone/Italy), black (abroad), white (travels)

Shapes: △ = La Torre clan  ◯ = non-clan member  ▽ = other clan

Roles: leader (L), money laundering (ML), all Camorra activities (All), drugs (D), front name (F), accomplice (Acc), victim (V)

**FIGURE 6.1** The La Torre clan and its money-laundering network in Aberdeen (1983–2000)

do whatever they wanted and did not have to respect the basic rules of courtesy. Some women felt so powerful that they "went to this shop and took things without paying." Another "goes shopping and never pays" (PSLTv, 23/11/2003, in TN16: 646).

The clan's values have been crucial to sustaining its criminal identity and existence. Collective values and precise rules were essential to guarantee the clan's long-term survival and were its roots. However, in some instances there were signs of change and a turning away from tradition, the attachment to kin, and the use of the family as a resource. As Anna Carrino, explained, "it's all about the family . . . you are one of the family, you are not a stranger," (ACA) and therefore you can be used by the clan. In Mondragone, the blood family had a certain amount of privilege and status over the rest of civil society because of its name. But at the same time, the leaderships' disillusionment and sense of betrayal was such that they started to distance themselves from traditional values. Violence was used even against family members: when Augusto or Antonio felt that their relatives were not pulling their weight, they did not hesitate to punish them publically or downgrade their responsibilities within the clan.

The use of violence reinforced the clan's social, economic, and political power in its home territory. For example, on one occasion "the mayor of Falciano was taken and kidnapped from his home so that we could impose our conditions . . . it was Augusto himself who pointed the gun toward the mayor, talking to him in an intimate way," and "in Mondragone there were stable pre-election agreements with local politicians, in such a way as to guarantee that we would win the subcontracts" (MSv, 16/10/2003, in TN17: 58). Violence was also used extensively in Mondragone to punish members and citizens who did not respect the clan's laws; in particular, leaders would "punish members who make mistakes." Antonio once exclaimed: "I need to go and break his head, this bastard, I will go later and call him, and if he does not answer, I will get him brought to me" (TN5: 41). In the United Kingdom, there were no visible signs of physical violence among cell members or toward members of civil society: "There was no physical violence against the local, native community, but there was psychological violence to let people know that they could not refuse, yes" (MS). Physical violence was a basic value of this criminal association, but it was not used abroad in the enterprise network because it was not conducive to its economic strategy and could have drawn attention to its presence.

An important part of the clan's solidity was its basic common fund and its ability to provide a coherent welfare system—permanent care for its members inside and outside of prison. The clan had an efficient salary system and sought to provide jobs for its members and protect them from the police. This internal protections reinforced its local collective identity and sense of continuity. Indeed, the provision of salaries is one of the defining elements of Camorra clans (Coll), and the more money clans had in terms of salaries, the better organized and more efficient the clan. In this respect, the La Torre clan was very cohesive. When Antonio was in charge, he was very careful that his salary calculations should reflect "the role of the member" (TN5: 13). The financial management of the clan was looked after by a member chosen by the leader, who did the accounts and calculated the clan's expenses. This accountant would write down all the incoming funds and outgoing expenses in a payroll book (*libro paga*). This also explains why there was a sense of panic in 2001 when the payroll book went missing.

Incoming money came from extortion rackets, but also the construction business, real estate, and important public contracts. Siciliano has suggested that some money was sent back from Scotland for the common fund and salaries (MS). Outgoing money was distributed as salaries for members but also as legal assistance and salaries to members in prison (TN5: 74). Distribution decisions caused a lot of internal disagreement, particularly among the women, who often complained that they did not receive enough money. Extra money was used to repay loans on cars, for christenings, weddings, and other occasions (TN5: 82); it was a real common fund.

The common fund never moved abroad, as there was no need; *la cassa* only existed in Mondragone. But members abroad were paid regular salaries: "Augusto sent monthly payments to Antonio in Scotland; it was a salary from the clan equivalent to 4 or 5 million [lire] a month, depending on the funds. In general, it was VB who looked after sending the salary . . . On two or three occasions I looked after sending them in the post" (AMDGv, in TN16: 686). It was said that in 1995–1996 Antonio received 3 million lire a month (TN16). In Mondragone, salaries were also distributed to the wives of fugitives and some members who were not based in or from Mondragone (TN5: 16; 19). This payment reflects the attempted extension of clan roots into other territories. In addition to the common fund, the clan appropriated jobs for clan members. On one occasion, the clan sought to impose on the local hospital, a clinic, a requirement that it must employ clan members when the clan was in financial difficulty, a form of "forced employment" policy (TN5: 57–58). This did not happen abroad.

The La Torre clan in Mondragone was a family crime enterprise defined by its social features and its cultural and economic presence. In the United Kingdom, as part of the same organization, it was a business-oriented cell that was constantly in communication with its headquarters in Mondragone. This cell was part of the

La Torre's business network enterprise in Europe that infiltrated both the local, national, and European legal and illegal economy.

## LA TORRE CLAN ACTIVITIES

It was under the leadership of Augusto La Torre that the clan looked beyond its territory of origin and started to become more business and money oriented. In Aberdeen, the clan's main activity was money laundering, which it had already undertaken in Italy. As a defining feature of the clan, its activities were always intrinsically connected back to Mondragone, interlinking the clan's local territory with global markets and using Italian personnel and resources. Without Italian money, there were no foreign activities.

As with other historic clans, by the late 1990s the La Torre clan's economic activities were rationalized into two main departments made up of various interrelated subdivisions. Both the legal and illegal activities departments operated within the same organization, one feeding money into the other. The illegally acquired funds were reinvested into illegal activities, but its profits were invested into legal activities through money-laundering investments. There was an inextricable link between the two departments, and had the illegal activities not flourished, the money-laundering activities would have been rather sluggish and flat. One depended on the other, and as a consequence, the British money-laundering outfit depended very much on the money coming from Italy.

In Mondragone, the illegal department was fully active and managed two core activities run by two divisions: local extortion and international drugs importation and distribution. The clan was also involved in other related activities such as credit and loan services and arms importation. Local extortions were diverse and wide ranging, but functioned within one department. They ranged from regular monthly payments from building sites and contractors to occasional one-off extortions for special occasions, contracts, or events in town. Leaders set up different extortion rackets and sought to manage them from wherever they were, thus location and distance from the territory of origin did not seem to pose an obstacle to setting up and managing rackets.

Adopting the Bardellino model, the clan imposed on local companies their services and goods. For example, the clan imposed the mode of transport (in this case, lorries) that local wholesalers and warehouses should use. These companies were ordered to pay the clan for every journey they made. As one *pentito* explained: "It was established that for any journey, whatever its distance, the wholesaler would have to pay a sum" (PSLTv, in TN16: 649). This clearly brought heavy costs for local businesses, and also meant that the clan put down roots in its control over the territory.

The La Torre clan has been involved in drug importation and distribution into Campania/Mondragone since the 1970s and 1980s, which explains its well-organized division that had its own supply networks. Over the years, the clan's involvement and modalities have varied, but the driving factor was to distribute and sell drugs across its territory whatever way they were imported into Italy. On the one hand, the clan had its own drugs divisions, which were organized as a drugs importation network with some members present in Italy and some residents in Amsterdam to oversee and monitor the importation activities. Thus Amsterdam became the clan's center of drug-trafficking operations. On the other hand, the clan was perpetually involved in buying drugs from other wholesalers. For example, it was a customer of the De Falco clan in the 1990s (see chapter 5). Lastly, the clan also employed brokers; one such broker sought to buy drugs for the clan in the Tiro Grosso affair (see chapter 4). In addition, using similar supply channels, the clan was also involved in arms trafficking and importing arms into the region, which they sold to other clans. The headquarters of the illegal activities department was solely based in Mondragone and there was no attempt to move it abroad.

The legal activities department was based both in Italy and abroad and had the complicity of local businessmen and politicians. With time, the clan was able to develop more refined financial projects in its legal department locally and in other regions. These projects can be seen as a functional way of identifying new opportunities and markets for familiar activities, but always preserving the crucial link with Mondragone and pumping money back into the common fund.

In Mondragone, political connections were vital for success. Michele Siciliano explained that "the control of Aberdeen was very much structured only on the financial aspect, only on money laundering, on investments, on activities and then frauds. However, Mondragone was different, because in Mondragone earnings came from contracts. . . . For these contracts, the council, politics, people issuing permits to perform specific works were involved. In that case, you go and pressure people or the mayor or a politician gets involved." After sixteen years this kind of political involvement had not happened in Aberdeen, but "maybe we would have got to something like that, because wherever there is an area to invest in, a way to make money, this is the key of the organization."

Locally, the clan became involved in legal companies such as shops and waste management companies (see CASMVC5), as well as undertaking economic frauds in Campania. In the Veneto region, it was involved with food companies that imported goods to Scotland; when the companies were then declared bankrupt, the clan ended up with the goods without having to pay for them.[8] The base in Aberdeen represented the end stage of the La Torre's money-laundering operations and frauds. The clan made extensive use of the borders of Britain, Scotland, Italy, and the Netherlands to its benefit. According to investigators in Italy, there was "an extensive recycling canal between Mondragone and Great Britain, a location in which members of the clan have implanted economic [and] particularly profitable activities, certainly linked and dependent on the clan" (TN5: 14). Money made in Mondragone in this way was systematically laundered in Aberdeen.

Aberdeen was part of the clan's legal activities department: financial frauds and the recycling and reinvesting of illegal money from Mondragone into the United Kingdom. The clan employed a very simple form of money laundering. First, it transferred money from Italy to the United Kingdom. This was done either through physical cash transport or via electronic bank accounts made available to the clan. For physical cash transfers, it was usually family members who traveled to Aberdeen or even Italian immigrants living in Aberdeen. One cousin admitted: "I personally ... transferred money to Scotland." He calculated that he tried to transfer roughly 64,000 euros to Aberdeen in 2003, money made from extortions and sales of assets (PSLTv, 18/2/2005, in TN16: 683). He explained the source of the money: "the money came from the agency [a transport company] and I needed to give the sum to JK, who would give it to Antonio La Torre, who was in Scotland" (TN16: 650). On another occasion, Italian immigrants based in Scotland were asked to take "different sums of money back there. . . . I could not say how much money was taken and when" (PSLTv, 6/12/2004, in TN16: 683).

Second, Antonio La Torre invested in different financial activities. He and his cousin Michele Siciliano set up a variety of what appeared to be legitimate businesses in Aberdeen, from Italian restaurants to a fish importing business. Companies were set up with money coming from Mondragone: "We would set them up 'clean' ... in order to make 'clean' transactions and trading. Only in-depth checks could verify whether there were dirty and dodgy transactions or not" (MS). As a relative made clear: "I can say that a lot of money, made from extortions, was taken to Antonio La Torre in Scotland" (PSLTv, 18/2/2005, in TN16: 650–83). Siciliano stated that "all companies [in Scotland] were structured with the money coming from Mondragone." Companies dealing in commercial cross-border activities were set up to enable frauds to be undertaken and dirty money to be cleaned.

Antonio La Torre also tried to invest in real estate in Aberdeen. This is a classic sector chosen for money laundering because it is considered relatively easy to invest in without needing to justify the source of the money. It is alleged that Antonio La Torre, with the help of British accomplices, tried to invest in ten to fifteen apartments, bought a shoe shop, and set up various imports and exports of delicatessen food (see TN5; TN16). It was calculated that during 1998, one of the amounts transferred from Italy to the United Kingdom was 80,000,000 lire (approximately 42,000 euros) (TN5: 214). These investment opportunities were an ideal way to guarantee obscuring the origins of the clan's illegal profits made in Mondragone and laundered in Aberdeen. But as the local police in Scotland noted, they presented "no social harm" to the local community (GramP) and therefore were not considered a police problem.

The operations undertaken by the clan were pretty basic and can be analyzed as embryonic examples of how the Camorra could develop its money-laundering activities. In time, clans could become more professional, less ethnic-based, and more invisible as money-laundering activities are managed by third parties. There is a functional relationship between the clan's illegal and legal activities, between the new territory and the territory of origin, that have to be unpacked. Michele Siciliano explained in relation to Scotland: "The source was Mondragone... the funds were in Mondragone. These funds allow you to go and conduct activities somewhere else. These funds were illegal, and then, through businesses, through trading with fake invoices, they would be laundered and developed into activities that would make a lot of money."

In this way, it is unhelpful to regard La Torre's networks abroad as outposts, branches, or separate or independent units where they diversified their activities. It may be more useful to see them as one and the same organization, interconnected and interrelated in its economic activities. La Torre's business activities abroad were not an expansion strategy by one clan member to undertake traditional Camorra criminal activities in a new location in order to gain independence or colonize a new territory. Nor was it a new settlement, responding to emerging opportunities in the economy. It was the functional mobility of a clan between territories.

### LA TORRE CLAN ACCOMPLICES

La Torre's group of accomplices in Aberdeen, if there was one, has never been identified. While in Mondragone, the clan enjoyed the complicity of a variety of police officers, businessmen, white-collar professionals, and politicians whose involvement ranged from complicit and collusive to compenetrative. It has been more complicated to identify accomplices in Aberdeen because there are fewer instruments of detection at our disposal. There is no doubt that in Scotland the La Torre group benefitted from support, visible or invisible, predominantly from complicit accomplices who were not necessarily involved in, or aware of, the clan's activities. The accomplices in the United Kingdom provided logistical support, particularly when members were on the run.

Several questions could be raised here regarding attitudes toward Italian criminality in the United Kingdom. For example, La Torre gained British citizenship in 1991, but how was this possible if he had open and ongoing issues with the Italian authorities, even if he qualified by reason of his marriage? He was also given assistance when he went on the run in Scotland, and could count on people who were prepared to be front names or carry money across borders in Italy and abroad. There were Italian immigrants in Aberdeen who helped if they could: "He is a resident in the UK ... and the person responsible for transferring lire into sterling pounds" (TN5: 92). There were not an abundant number of accomplices of this kind and it is unclear if any were British. However, clan members found enough accomplices and ways to transfer money from Italy to the United Kingdom, and there was always a group available to help with logistical support and give hospitality both in Scotland and in Woking, England.

This case highlights the extensive social capital of the clan, which, though small, had an intricate web of contacts and accomplices in Italy, in civil society, and in the business and political community. Frequenting these accomplices allowed clan members to have access to information, skills, and resources that permitted them to become involved in more sophisticated forms of crime, thus blurring the lines between the legal and the illegal.

In the United Kingdom, the clan had a successful operating base that specialized in money-laundering activities, legitimate businesses in particular. Between locations, there existed a functional two-way relationship that reinforced the clan's power in Mondragone. It was a continuous relationship between different activities and particularly the illegal activities that financed the legal ones. This method of operation may be described as a move away from core activities based in one location and constrained by the territory, to more profit-orientated activities and a maximum freedom of action, possible only thanks to a local territory.

The United Kingdom is an island and may appear remote from Europe and safe from Italian mafias. But this is not the case. It is a new and welcoming environment in which the lack of understanding by the public, police, and legal system of how mafias function, together with a lack of money-laundering regulations (strategic, policy, investigative, prosecution, regulatory, and private in particular), makes it vulnerable to mafias and other criminal groups.

# Conclusion

> **You can take the man out of Naples but not Naples out of the man.**

I started this book wanting to explore the so-called criminal migration of the Camorra in Europe; I ended up discovering that it does not migrate. It travels continuously from one operational base to another. Whereas the mobility of other criminal groups might be determined by immigrant communities, strategic decisions, socioeconomic conditions, and political infrastructures, the key to understanding the Camorra's mobility lies in its territory of origin.

The cases recounted in the previous chapters explain why and how *camorristi* move out of Naples and what they do when they go abroad. Compared with other mafias, the Camorra may still be predominantly Italy focused, but it is increasingly damaging international economies with its developing European vision. In particular, the cases identified the Camorra's main features abroad, which are functionality, liquidity, invisibility, and a special trait, the interconnectedness of its territories.

This study also highlights the lack of understanding that still surrounds Italian mafias abroad, resulting in a tendency to either exaggerate or underestimate the problem. Newspapers always like a good mafia story and they will keep on getting one as long as we fail to tackle the question of Italian mafias in a clear and consistent way that focuses on the functional needs of clans, *camorristi*, and organized crime groups in general. In this conclusion, I draw out the observable features of the Camorra's functional mobility and leave the reader with some thoughts about the emerging issues.

## Functional, Liquid, Invisible

Analyzing the presence and activities of Neapolitan Camorra members and their associates in a "Europe without borders" (Van Duyne, 1993: 102) has not been a straightforward task. At times it felt like looking for a needle in a haystack because European national law-enforcement agencies do not investigate mafia association and adopt different approaches to the pursuit of organized crime. Each country uses different lenses, which may explain why, as one high-ranking police officer noted about the British authorities, there is still "a relatively low understanding and perception of this phenomenon" (BPO) and why there is still no coherent international cooperation to tackle these groups.[1]

It is difficult to make general conclusions because no two Camorra clans in Campania are the same. This heterogeneity is reflected in their operations abroad, as Judge Luca Semeraro once noted: "Paradoxically, the Camorra model, which is fragmented and very chaotic [in its territory of origin], also translates this into its foreign activities" (LS). But some of our findings on one group can be relevant for other criminal groups, and in particular, for example, the role of the territory of origin for the 'Ndrangheta, Ukrainian, and Nigerian organized crime groups.

The picture that emerges is complex, reflecting the Camorra's dynamic nature as it innovates to respond to changing local, national, and international circumstances. The mobility I have identified was based on regular cross-border crime in which it used versatile mechanisms and strategies that did not restrict it to a specific territory. It had an economic presence rather than a mafia presence. The Camorra has the formidable capacity to combine its local roots with global economic opportunities in a functional mechanism. These roots are deep and not easy to export or transplant to other locations: "In Italy, the mafias' roots in the local territory are both their strength and weakness: clearly, it is very difficult to dislodge them once they are established in the local territory but this also means that it becomes more difficult for them to establish themselves where they have no roots" (Colombié, 2012: 14).

The gardening metaphor of "transplantation" (Varese, 2011) suggests that a mafia group, like a plant, moves from one self-contained context to another, and in order to flourish its roots move with it. This is not the nature of the Camorra's movement. The Camorra's roots rarely move from its local territory. Although there is concrete evidence of some *camorristi* in Abruzzo attempting to start a clan and put down new roots using violence in a nontraditional territory between 2003 and 2011, this attempt ultimately failed (TA1).[2] Camorra associates active in other Italian regions have also been noted, but more as an economic presence with no roots (see Sciarrone, 2014). In Naples, the Camorra has a hard, solid, traditional, and embedded presence, abroad it becomes a "soft" (DNA3: 71), liquid, and invisible presence.

Clans are intrinsically linked to their local territory because, as Filippo Beatrice pointed out, "you are not a *camorrista* if you do not control a territory." Jean-Francois Gayraud reinforces this point when he states that "the *mafioso* is a territorial animal," his territory is "his 'vital space'" (2008: 224) because it provides him with "power, criminal prestige, and a form of psychological vitality" (FB). If a *mafioso* leaves his territory, he no longer has this prestige and vitality because "the strength of a mafia is its roots located in a space with invisible frontiers known to all inhabitants" (Gayraud, ibid.). Smaller clans may need the local territory more than larger clans; the latter in some instances are able to move away more freely and to appear more autonomous. But they all ultimately need the home territory as their main source of money and power. For example, the Polverino clan invested in Spain and the Di Lauro clan invested in France and the US, yet both were still so reliant on their local territory that they were prepared to fight wars with their rivals.

Clans have had the ability to develop their global activities in relation to their local power base and markets. Activities and locations are developed not only in terms of the new settings (new economic opportunities, low detection of organized crime, relaxed culture, etc.) and territory of origin but also because of the interdependency that exists between old and new territories. As a consequence, what all clans have in common, when and if they move abroad, is their capacity to connect their different territories in a commercial cycle; they establish a functional interdependency between their territories.

A reciprocal link is established by clans between their headquarters in Naples and the new host country. This is no one-way movement away from the homeland to set up an independent or semiautonomous Camorra settlement or franchise and there is no expanding into virgin economies without experience; rather, we see a functional calculation once abroad about how to make territories and markets work for the benefit of the clan in Naples, even if it appears chaotic.

The further away from Naples clans travel, the more liquid they become, while retaining their essential solidity at home. The significance of Naples is fully apparent. Increasing liquidity, a result of functional calculations, is a dangerous development because it is predominantly economic, invisible, and violent only toward Neapolitan Italian communities, whereas a clan's relationship with the host society is completely normal.

The basic conditions of capitalism, modernity, and globalization create the incentives and opportunities for Camorra clans, once in Europe, to make money and elaborate strategies to extract the necessary goods, resources, and labor from their territories. But, surprisingly, clans do not instinctively go abroad to open new local branches in the way successful legitimate businesses would; they do not adopt global or transnational business strategies to expand their portfolio of activities. This is because the territory of origin remains fundamental to their criminal existence and it is why they seek to continuously interconnect their territories.

## The Clans: Their Members and Territories

Our cases have shown that Camorra clans have a crime-family enterprise structure in Naples, whereas abroad they become network enterprises. Isaia Sales talks of the *"vicolizzazione"* of the city clans to highlight that their power stems from their presence in their *vicolo*, their street (IS). Indeed, it is from the local territory that the Camorra takes its resources, strength and power, it is the local territory that it exploits and dominates to make its regular money—from extortion rackets to subcontracts. Giovanni Messina reiterates how vital this territory is for a *camorrista*: "The connection to the territory must always exist. It must exist because without this connection to the territory, you are a *nobody*." He goes on to say, "I got to the point where mentioning my name was enough" to control the local territory and ensure racket money (GM).

Tom Behan argues that "the extent of the Camorra's international links is severely restricted by its need to maintain power and influence through territorial control" (1996: 128). The military, economic, and political strengths of a clan at home may explain its potential abroad. Indeed, it is the powerful clans with extensive social capital, territory, members and alliances, such as the Polverino clan, the Secondigliano alliance, the Amato-Pagano clan, the Casalesi clan, and the Contini clan, that have the capacity for long-term survival abroad. But perhaps those clans that have less territory to control, such as the Nuvoletta clan, may also have more of a need to look elsewhere—abroad—for flourishing investment opportunities (GB).

Behan's argument for the Camorra's essential ties to its home territory is apt: "Once they move abroad, major criminals do not wield the same influence they enjoyed at home; in particular they lack the political protection which often enables them to avoid arrest" (1996: 128). Nevertheless, although attempting to take over a new territory is a challenge, and one that may be considered not worth the investment, survival is possible by other means, such as simple organized crime activities or more sophisticated forms of money laundering, without putting down roots abroad. The lack of incentive or ability to colonize a territory does not mean a lack of activity; the absence of roots does not represent an obstacle for the Camorra, but only a different way of engaging with territory abroad, a more efficient way.

The Camorra's presence in host countries takes different shapes that vary greatly from clan to clan and from market to market. This presence abroad is more limited than is often described by the media and newspapers. There were no real "settlements," "imitation mafia groups," or "new hybrid groups" (Sciarrone and Storti, 2014). There were no extensive settlements, but rather loose business networks that infiltrate the new setting, its markets and economies. These networks could be described as "operating cells" and "bases" for Camorra clans. Therefore, there were no autonomous groups with sophisticated business strategies. Even the La Torre clan established in Aberdeen since 1983 had not sought independence. Perhaps the Zaza clan could be defined as "independent," but it had few if any members in situ and resembled more an economic strategy than a criminal clan. (In addition, it was difficult to study Michele Zaza's link with Naples once he was in France.) The De Falco clan's cell in Spain was essential to the clan in Casal di Principe and might have started to contaminate the local territory, but it was not a settlement, it was a tiny one-man cell. The territory in Casal di Principe once lost meant that Nunzio operated as an autonomous broker in drug-trafficking networks. The Secondigliano alliance imposed its violence on the Neapolitan *magliari* network but did not develop deep roots in its new territories. The Annunziata-Aquino family, the Gala subgroup, and the Stolder clan had key individuals in functional places who traveled often. The question remains whether these groups will ever seek or want to become truly independent in Europe.

DTS, Gennaro Panzuto, the De Falco cell (after 1992), and the Di Tommaso team did not have predominant mafia features or strategies abroad. They all adapted to circumstances, contexts, and necessities differently. The notion of "liquidity" is useful to explain different organizational manifestations and activities: it is believed that one person from the De Sena clan was active in La Seyne-sur-Mer, France, in 2007; two members of the La Torre clan appeared in Aberdeen, United Kingdom; a group of fifteen to twenty members of the Amato-Pagano clan were active in Spain in 2004–2005.

Thus the internal organization of the Camorra changed from solid in Naples to liquid abroad. In Naples, Camorra clans are considered "fluid," "fragmented," and "horizontal" (DNA1: 63) compared with their Sicilian and Calabrian counterparts; nevertheless they have fixed and embedded roots. In Naples, the Camorra is a stable criminal association; its secret society dimension predominates and its organizational structure is still primarily a family-crime enterprise. Its power is territorial and is defined by its traditional internal value system, behavioral codes, structures, activities, and strategies.

To use the term "clan" to describe the Camorra's organizational structure abroad is imprecise because not one Camorra clan transplanted itself abroad or replicated its internal value system, behavior, and management structures (common fund and salary system) permanently. Instead there were small (two or three individuals or associates) or medium (more than ten members) groups located abroad and traveling between the home and host territory. Abroad, no Neapolitan clans with firm roots at home control or have power over extensive aspects of new territories. Indeed there are very few traditional foot soldiers abroad, but rather managers, brokers, accountants, solicitors, and businessmen. The personnel varied.

Clans "appear little more than plastic organizations that can be molded in many different ways" (Williams, 2001: 65). The operating structures abroad became networks that functioned in different markets and engaged with other networks and alliances: "Modern organised crime...abroad can be characterised as a fluid network of many autonomous buyers, brokers, financiers, middlemen, and distributors from different groups, ethnicities, nationalities, and countries that come together to make deals by capitalizing on each other's special ties and strengths" (Schneider, 2009: 344).

The emerging organizational structures abroad are open, flexible, versatile, and loose networks rather than the tight family-based formal hierarchical clans found in Naples. It is often argued that the chosen market dictates the organizational structure, particularly in relation to drug trafficking (see Calderoni, 2012: 35). In relation to the Camorra, markets influence some of the organizational structures, but in general, their operations abroad are loose networks, regardless of their market. For example, even the counterfeit sector in 2014 has now many detached networks that perpetually change and evolve. "Some sociologists conclude that network-based organizations are [more] capable of superior performance than are more traditionally structured hierarchical organizations, especially in terms of adaptability to changes in their environment" (Williams, 2001: 67).

Neapolitan groups are "network enterprises" characterized as "loose, temporary," "pervasive, intangible, ubiquitous, invisible, everywhere, nowhere," and able to coexist, adaptable, dynamic, flexible (see Williams, 2001: 63–67). When abroad, the stable, traditional clans transform themselves into fluid, economic networks that engage and interact with markets and other business networks (such as Moroccans, Colombians, Chinese, or Venezuelans). They become international "criminal cooperatives" (the Fijnaut group, quoted in Klerks, 2001: 57). Neapolitan clans have understood that social ties abroad need to be adaptable, as they are more conducive to business than those in traditional, stable, and hierarchical organizational structures. However, even within a network enterprise, Camorra bosses seek order, control, and dominance. For example, the drug networks of the Amato-Pagano clan and the Polverino clan had a clear leader to whom everyone answered.

Our limited material did not provide systematic examples of clans or leaders enforcing their reputation or power over a new setting or imposing their internal value system on citizens abroad. Diego Gambetta's statement that "it does not follow that a lasting reputation can grow out of thin air" (1993:45) appears well founded, and may suggest why some bosses do not seek to exert their violence and power abroad. Petrus van Duyne noted this when he wrote: "The leader of a crime-family does exert authority in his home country *and* in Europe where his relatives obey his orders. Does not that constitute a transnational authority?

No, it is only the same authority over his own relatives in several countries, because the authority follows the family. The migration of the family to several countries means the spatial spreading of the authority. Only further integration in the receiving country can lead to mixing with indigenous crime groups and new (multiethnic) power-building (1996: 373).

Bosses control only those who recognize their power, although this might slowly be changing. We see few examples of power spreading beyond the boundaries of recognized collective identity and nationality; not one clan leader truly had "transnational authority" within European civil society. Nunzio De Falco in Granada supposedly developed a relationship with local drug dealers, but this was probably based on business transactions rather than authority, and the same was suggested of Raffaele Amato. Little is known of the Secondigliano counterfeit company's use of violence against natives, but it was clearly used against Neapolitan *magliari*, who acknowledged the company's power. Gennaro Panzuto was fully integrated into the local criminal underworld in Preston—roguish businessmen knew he was a *mafioso* on the run and used his reputation and violence to intimidate rivals and customers. These are visible examples, but what about the invisible ones? Moreover, are bosses really that concerned that they do not dominate the new territory, or exercise power in the new setting? Surely for them it is more important to go unnoticed, stay below the radar, and get on with their financial activities in relative peace.

In Naples, the main organizational unit of Camorra clans is the core, nuclear, blood family. Around this family unit, there is an extended family structure and loyal followers who are lower-level clan members and foot soldiers. Compared with the Sicilian Mafia and the Calabrian 'Ndrangheta, the role of the family in the Camorra is presented by many academics as less significant. It is true that Raffaele Cutolo's NCO was not based on a tight-knit family structure, but this should not overshadow how crucial the blood family is for Camorra clans. The blood family is the basis of its organizational structure and what enables its solidity and rootedness in the local territory. Without tight blood families, Camorra clans are weaker, less effective, and less efficient in the internal management of their organizations and their business operations across their territory. Even with the new younger generation of leaders who are particularly violent and trigger happy, the family remains key.

Hierarchy within the clan is based on blood ties. Three different types of clan structures based on the family were identified in Naples (see table 7.1): the patriarchal/traditional family, the intergenerational clan, and the "generational" family (Gribaudi, 1999). There does not appear to be one predominant family type, although the patriarchal model has given way to the intergenerational and generational models that appeared in the mid-1980s.

**TABLE 7.1** Family structures in the Camorra (1980–2015)

| FAMILY STRUCTURE | GROUPS |
| --- | --- |
| Patriarchal/traditional family (1980s) | La Torre clan (until 1982), Zaza clan, Antonio Bardellino |
| Intergenerational family (1990s–) | Polverino clan, Misso clan, Piccirillo clan, Caldarelli clan, Annunziata-Aquino family |
| Generational family (1990s–) | Licciardi clan, Amato-Pagano clan, De Falco clan, Rinaldi clan, Tedesco clan, Stolder clan, Nuvoletta clan, Mazzarella clan, La Torre clan |

In Europe, not one clan sent members abroad to open a new branch. In the majority of cases, it was the boss who initially moved abroad, out of necessity rather than for strategic expansionist reasons. Generally, bosses and their business associates move abroad. The lower-level members, the foot soldiers, commute between Naples and the host country, whereas the military arm and killers remain in Naples and do not travel abroad. The personnel remains the same with few foreign members and few Neapolitan killers traveling. The average age of members involved in activities abroad is higher (thirty-five to forty years) than that of the younger inexperienced foot soldiers, who remain at home to police the territory.

Once forced abroad, members make functional decisions about their activities that are relevant to the location. Going abroad turns them into international players. Although they are less feared than the Russian Mafia and Calabrian 'Ndrangheta, they nevertheless are able to operate as an invisible, liquid, economic network. The concept of "functional mobility" stresses the importance of both the local context and the new global location. It stresses the need to understand the interplay of dynamics, organization, logics, strategies, tensions, needs, and pressures of the clan in both contexts.

Functional mobility underlines how behavior and activities abroad are different from those found in Naples: "In their territory of origin, Mafia groups tend to control the territory, manage the local economy, influence political decisions, infiltrate public contracts, command the main criminal markets. Out of their territory of origin, this penetration can take very different forms, rarely a real and true control of the territory similar to that of the territory of origin" (TS). Some distant associates may have been sent or told where to move by the clan and then eventually called on, but this is difficult to document.

Mobility in different activities varied. For acquisitive crime, small groups of foot soldiers move abroad and one member emerges as the leader. The counterfeit goods world saw extensive recruitment from and use of the existing *magliari* network; smaller clans use *magliari* as outer layers of the group, specifically to sell fake goods. When it comes to drugs, usually there are key Camorra members resident in the host country; they are assisted by local native brokers and their Neapolitan couriers who travel between host and home territory. The leader tends to be present to manage and oversee the transactions. In money laundering, the boss and other often-shady individuals associated with the clan travel, but they become invisible because many are respectable businessmen with no criminal records, or they employ respectable accountants in situ to deal with their business deals.

On this basis, I identified five categories of mobility (see table 7.2): commuters, seasonal commuters, regular visitors, occasional visitors, and residents abroad. Commuters are criminals who continuously travel back and forth between Naples and the host countries. I found that drug couriers and money-laundering accomplices travel frequently (so much so that some wives complain). Seasonal commuters are criminals who went abroad for a couple of months and then return to Naples, as was the case for acquisitive crime. Regular visitors are individuals who return to Naples at frequent intervals. Occasional visitors are Neapolitans living abroad who may return home and who help out when they do so.

Thanks to the Schengen agreement, *camorristi* can now travel at will, according to how convenient and functional it is for their activities in Naples. A leader's presence in his territory is vital, whereas his absence may be fatal. Even a boss such as Giuseppe Polverino or Raffaele Amato, who were both on the run from the law or in danger of being shot by rival clans, risked returning to Naples to keep an eye on their territory, like feudal lords surveying their fiefdom. Their presence was a *"quiet dictatorship"* (Di Meo, 2008: 64, my emphasis). Those who could not return or who delegated their powers to others often found themselves in difficulties. Nunzio De Falco tried to control Casal di Principe from Spain, but even with help of competent and loyal associates, this proved a losing battle. Michele Zaza appears to have become less powerful after he left Naples and no longer controlled a set territory, although his nephews carried on his activities.

**TABLE 7.2** Types of Camorra mobility (1980–2015)

| CAMORRA MOBILITY | VISITS TO AND FROM NAPLES | TYPE OF CRIME |
| --- | --- | --- |
| Commuter | More than 4–5 times a month | Drug trafficking/money laundering/CF |
| Seasonal commuter | 2–3 months abroad and return | Acquisitive crime/CF |
| Regular visitor | 2–3 times every 6 months | Drug trafficking/money laundering/CF |
| Occasional visitor | Once every 6 months | Complicity |
| Resident abroad | Never | n/a |

For members and associates who travel back and forth to Naples, there is an extensive transport network of goods and money. Each activity requires specific resources. For counterfeit activities and drug importation there is a continuous coming and going of people, goods, and cash; for simple, acquisitive crime, there is a movement of people and stolen goods; and for money-laundering activities, it is predominately the physical movement of cash (people traveling) or its transfer through bank accounts.

Illegal activities undertaken in host countries make it possible to identify the clan's general money flow: where the money is produced, where and how it transits, and where it is finally recycled and invested. All illegal money made from counterfeit goods and drug importation usually goes back to Naples to contribute to the common fund and pay members. Money laundering is secondary to keeping the clan afloat.

The French weekly *Le Point*,[3] quoting Europol, suggested that there were three phases of financial development in groups active abroad: (1) criminal groups send money home, (2) criminal groups invest in host country, and (3) criminal groups become autonomous and independent. For the Camorra, I identified only the first two phases. The general trend is for all money made illegally in host countries to go back to Naples and into the common fund of the clan. But money made illegally in Naples is also invested abroad in different financial and money-laundering activities.

The real capacity to invest abroad depends not only on having substantial amounts of money but also on being able to count on willing, loyal, cooperative, and knowledgeable enablers who are familiar with the local context. What becomes apparent when studying these different clans is the type of support systems that they have at their disposal. Communities abroad surround, protect, and can conceal a Camorra presence. This is the most interesting part of the network, and yet it is an aspect that cannot be seen or identified. We can make out only a few aspects of it: the boss is not at the center of a clan, as he would be in Naples, but of a fluid network enterprise made up of various layers and contacts: an inner core of trusted associates resident in the host country and some locals (mostly Italian), and some traveling advisers who are perpetually on the move.

There is no standard rule that is applicable to understanding how a Camorra clan functions abroad. However, by examining a clan in its territory of origin we can discern why, how, and what it moves abroad.

## Camorra Clan Activities

Whereas the internal organizational structure and behavior of our different Camorra clans change and adapt to their new setting, their activities in general do not. Apart from territorial activities such as extortion, which very few clans undertake abroad,[4] their main activities are an extension and continuation of Neapolitan activities that they have already perfected.

In general, clans do not diversify their activities from one territory to another, they do not become involved in new activities, but rather their structures alter to become more efficient and functional. Fundamentally, clans are not interested in installing a fixed and solid mafia organization abroad, but solely in making money out of their host territory with the resources at their disposal.

Clans already have the needed skill sets; they do not learn new skills or venture into unknown, virgin markets where they have to test local conditions. They transpose their Neapolitan skills abroad, whether for drug importation or money laundering. For example, in the 1980s, Michele Zaza was "the king of cigarette smuggling" in Naples, and when he moved permanently to Nice in 1988, he carried on these activities, becoming involved with an international contraband network. He might have had some small counterfeit activities on the side but more importantly, sought to reinvest his money in Nice and elsewhere in France, as he did in Naples. Some British law-enforcement officers have asked whether the Camorra transpose "a successful business plan" to new locations (LP), but this is an oversimplification of the picture. It is not just a question of implementing a global business plan.

When they move abroad, *camorristi* do not necessarily have a thought-out plan, but rather set about using the resources available to them, whether these are moneymaking opportunities, family networks, judicial loopholes, or cultural stereotypes. They target the countries where their activities can best be fulfilled. They do not undertake extortion or private protection rackets in host countries, and this is because they do not control the local territory. I found scarce evidence of Neapolitan Camorra clans involved in markets where they had little or no local knowledge, resources, or contacts. Camorra clans are interested in supplying Italian and Neapolitan markets, particularly in the case of drug importation, whereas the 'Ndrangheta has become an international player in the drugs market and is involved with the British and European drugs market. The Camorra's involvement abroad is predominantly a criminal and economic presence, but not a social one.

The Camorra's criminal activities abroad involves organized crime, as opposed to mafia association crime. Three main categories of criminal activities in host countries were identified (table 7.3): acquisitive crime, organized crime, and financial crime. In all, the Camorra's organizational structure becomes liquid and invisible, more difficult to detect. *Camorristi* adapt to new contexts and seek to fit in, both in the legal and illegal markets and environments.

A clan's, or an individual's, relationship with a host country does not form overnight. It takes time and local knowledge of the host country and its language,

**TABLE 7.3** Type of crimes Camorra clans are involved in abroad

| TYPE OF CRIME | SPECIFIC CRIMES |
| --- | --- |
| Acquisitive crime | Theft, robbery, fraud |
| Organized crime | Production and sale of fake goods |
| Organized crime | International drug trafficking |
| Financial crime | Laundering and investing money |

and often depends on a prevailing infrastructure and resources. An existing support system can often be transformed into an operational base, although this can involve risks and expenses.

Using Dean, Fahsing, and Gottschalk's (2010) phases of business development in a legitimate company (establishing, expanding, consolidating, positing), it is possible to highlight the phases of relocation of a Camorra clan from one location to another, and in this way understand what variables are significant for its long-term development in the new chosen host country or market. For the four main activities identified, the phases of development were very different. This variation underlines not only the importance of the conditions in the host country but also the nature of its infrastructure and institutional structures, the complexities of the chosen market, and the type of Camorra organization and its roots in Naples. In terms of development, acquisitive-crime activities had very basic dynamics. The gangs of thieves and roaming bandits have little contact with the host territory, no ties, links, input, or investment, and no attempt to settle. These roaming bandits are marginal to the main Camorra activities. They may be in the south of France one day and in the south of Spain the next. A Camorra member belonging to a small or peripheral clan in Naples encounters difficulties in establishing more sophisticated Camorra activities abroad, and so turns to acquisitive crimes with the support of local contacts or networks. Here we usually find reliance on contacts, and visits and settlement, but the settlement was neither permanent nor long term. These activities were not planned in advance; they were more ad hoc, but they needed a certain amount of organization to be successful.

The development of drug importation and distribution was different. Here a pattern, a thought-through development process, involves an attempted investment in the host territory. The essential variables remain the existing networks in the host country, established contacts with sellers from South America or North Africa, the support of the local clan in Naples, an efficient structure, and an attempt to establish a base. This is not really expansion, but rather consolidation. The development of money-laundering activities follows a similar pattern. Settlement means a fixed operational base in the host country, but the most important *camorristi* who settled abroad were constantly traveling back to Naples. Here the pattern of behavior is one of trying to fit in and become invisible, like liquid that seeps into everything and is then detectable only consequentially.

Expansion into the international counterfeit sector was not attempted from scratch, unlike drug-importation clans, who had to go through a delicate phase of identifying and developing contacts within the local market and among sellers. For drug clans this phase can be tricky and potentially dangerous, it can easily go wrong and may result in an aborted settlement. For the counterfeit market, it was more a question of taking over an established network of *magliari* and of certain individuals taking over existing structures. This process can be analyzed as a form of colonization of the *magliari* network and an expansion of activities, using violence to impose the clan's agenda in the new territory, but decisions were made in Naples.

The choice and use of host countries by Camorra clans is always functional in relation to their activities and power base in Naples. Not all host countries are used to the same end. Once abroad, members identify the countries that can help their clan's economic activities (see table 7.4). Geographic location and opportunities are both parts of the functional calculations of Camorra clans. For example, associates of clans, brokers, were involved in transnational drug networks in France and Germany because these networks were functional parts of the route for importing cocaine or hashish into Italy. As Spain and the Netherlands are the two main entry points for drugs into Europe, many Camorra clans have associates who reside there to monitor their overseas operations. But, they do not sell their drugs to locals.

Do Camorra players infiltrate the local political process abroad, as they do in Naples and Campania? In Naples, clans have social, criminal, economic, and political power. In host countries, they have acquired criminal and economic power, but as yet there is very little systematic evidence of social or political power (corruption of officials or infiltration of the political process). Some examples were uncovered. From the accounts of some *pentiti*, in Spain clans tried to corrupt officials, specifically police officers and customs and excise officers; for example, the Polverino clan (PN15: 108). In France, Michele Zaza in 1988 managed to co-opt customs representatives. Local politics provides some examples, but these remain poorly investigated and documented, although there are small signs that Camorra

**TABLE 7.4** Functional use of host countries

| TYPE OF CAMORRA CRIME | FUNCTIONAL USE OF HOST COUNTRY |
| --- | --- |
| Acquisitive crime | Goods/victims |
| Counterfeit goods | Market/customers |
| Drug trafficking | Importation network/market |
| Money laundering | Investment opportunities |

associates are trying to infiltrate the local political process in Spain, Germany, and France, which could be the gateway to new moneymaking opportunities.

Understanding which activities the Camorra is involved in abroad may seem an intricate or even an impenetrable task, but identifying the main specialties of Camorra groups at home helped us to understand what activities they undertake abroad and helped explain their strategies, thinking, and planning.

## Camorra Clan Accomplices

We identified two distinguishable layers of accomplices: (1) a natural support system among relatives, friends, and immigrant communities, and (2) a *borghesia camorrista* (Camorra middle class) (De Gennaro and Pizzuti, 2009), professionals that include public administrators, technical consultants, bank employees, bankers, solicitors, lawyers, accountants, academics, and businessmen. They are the dark side of the Camorra's "social capital" in Naples and the invisible arm of clans.

The first layer is discernible and not necessarily criminal. More often than not, they act out of genuine friendship without any self-interested agenda. The second layer functions, to use the term favored by *camorristi*, as an "above suspicion" network. The network consists of a blurred grey zone of professionals that help clans cover their tracks or provide information that places clans at an advantage, without which they would encounter difficulties in undertaking many activities, especially those in the economic sphere. These professionals not only provide protection but also teach *camorristi* certain key skills, in particular how to invest money efficiently and how to identify economic and legal loopholes. They are a vital ingredient for Camorra activities in both contexts.

If the Camorra prospers in Naples, it is to a large extent due to the existence of this complicit class, and the same can be said for the Camorra in Europe. Accomplices are always present and they make a difference. If some clans are more successful criminal tourists abroad than others, it is because of this Camorra middle class who continually cooperates with them in their criminal projects. Thanks to accomplices, *camorristi* gain access to practical formalities, extensive networks, excellent knowledge, and relevant information.

The longer Camorra associates are present abroad, the more they become integrated in the local fabric and the more they extend their contacts into the local professional class, those white-collar professionals who can undertake economic transactions to clean the clan's money. So far the professional class of facilitators called on by clans abroad is essentially Neapolitan Italian, especially when it comes to counterfeit goods, drug trafficking, and money laundering. For example, the Amato-Pagano clan employed an Italian financial consultant. But we see signs of the growing involvement and full awareness of foreign accomplices. The Polverino clan, for example, appears to have taken on Spanish associates (including accountants) when Neapolitan business associates were arrested in 2011.[5] Another growing trend is the employment by clans of third-party financial advisers based in European capitals. These professionals launder the clans' money without clan members having to physically move, which means it is practically impossible to detect their presence in host countries. Clans become clients investing abroad, not criminals laundering illicit profits.

In Naples, women are the unrecognized "reserve army" (Arsovska and Allum, 2014) of Camorra clans: they are foot soldiers, accountants, accomplices, and support system all in one. There is evidence of women being fully involved at all levels of Camorra activity abroad, apart from acquisitive crime. They play a significant supportive role but never seek autonomy and remain in Naples predominantly. Among other things, they are front names of companies in Spain, money transporters, drug couriers, threat enforcers, message carriers, and homemakers, looking after the domestic aspects of their men's criminal mobility. Without the full involvement and complicity of these women, as seen in our cases, Camorra operations abroad would have been severely compromised, but more systematic and in-depth research is required to document their role.

The accomplices identified in all activities abroad demonstrate features of complicit-collusive-compenetrative behavior. By frequenting *camorristi* they are constantly teaching them skills and providing resources and knowledge for how to do business in Naples and in new contexts. However, it is clear that the general motives of possible accomplices still needs further research.

## The Journey Continues

Important debates emerge from this ongoing research into Camorra activities abroad. Methodology is important when carrying out this kind of interdisciplinary and cross-border research, but so are the underlying assumptions about the reality being studied and the language used to describe and analyze it. The creation of "truths" and "norms" by journalists and academics, especially about organized crime and mafias abroad, can be dangerous; they show how little we know, leading to exaggeration or underestimation. A good example of this is the recent findings of Transcrime (2013) on Italian mafias in Europe, reported in British newspapers in August 2014. The picture that emerges is of an active Camorra in Aberdeen. The investigation was in the late 1990s, early 2000s, yet presented as current fact. An Italian member of the European Parliament makes a statement that the Camorra is active in Aberdeen. The British press picks it up and publishes headlines such as: "Is Aberdeen Really the New Home of Feared Mafia Group? EU Report Says Camorra 'Controls' Catering, Food Retail and Property in the Scottish City," "Mafia Strongholds Found in Aberdeen and London, Claims EU," and "Mafia Tightens Grip on Aberdeen."[6]

The Italian press then publishes articles in Italy stating that the Camorra is active in Aberdeen in 2014. That may be the case, but no current data or established facts prove it. Yet this version of events has now become an established "truth." The same can be said about academic research. Academics establish their narratives by focusing on specific variables while excluding others, which they then present as "the truth." This interpretation becomes an accepted fact at the cost of other possible explanations.

To what extent is the analysis of criminal mobility developed in this book useful and applicable to other mafias and organized crime groups? It is clear that no single explanation or model explains criminal mobility. For example, Albanians in New York do not engage in the type of criminal mobility described here, and neither has the Calabrian Mafia. Indeed, it has recently been argued that the 'Ndrangheta's presence in the north of Italy has changed from infiltration to putting down roots, especially in the economy and in local politics. Possibly Camorra clans could develop in this way.

I do not pretend to hold the truth about Camorra mobility, but I propose an alternative explanation based on variables as yet ignored in other models. Adopting a general structure and agency approach allowed the development of the notion of "functional mobility," which was able to capture organizational structures, activities, and accomplices in both the territory of origin and the new setting; it identified the interconnection between territories as central to understanding how the Camorra functions abroad.

The innovative aspects that emerged were thus the spatial/temporal dimension of criminal mobility, the clans' functional approach to their local and international commercial activities, and the interconnectedness of their territories. These dimensions provide new insight into the more visible features of Camorra mobility—though I acknowledge there may well be imperceptible levels of clan members, activities, and accomplices that are not caught by this approach or by the material available. I believe that future studies on transnational organized crime groups, but also terrorist groups, need to take into account not only the international level of analysis but also the local-national levels and how territories interconnect, so that we understand better the evolving international crime community and the mobility of Mexican, Nigerian, and Russian criminal groups, for example.

On the other hand, this book makes clear that international law-enforcement communities need to study the dynamics of criminal groups both in their local and international contexts and urgently need to think more in terms of the functional mobility of criminal groups. This, however, requires a cooperative international approach (in particular, intelligence sharing) rather than the isolated nationalistic ones that still predominate. Perhaps a renewed look at how to tackle terrorist groups collectively after the Paris terrorist attacks in October 2015 might also influence the way European policymakers think about mobile criminals and *mafiosi*; it must not, though, be a distraction. There also needs to be more understanding at the local level of transborder phenomenon that often exist under the radar. Sovereignty and lack of political will remain obstacles to this type of proactive international cooperation.

What do we really know about Italian mafias in Europe today? We have a lot of media speculation but we know very little about the concrete presence and precise activities of Italian mafias in Europe. The same can be said about North and South America. There exists no European mechanism for registering or identifying *mafiosi* with criminal records in Italy and their activities abroad, no European mapping system to identify the general movement and zones of interests of various groups. No mechanism exists for registering crimes, criminal records, or convictions, which means that convicted criminals can travel around without necessarily being flagged, and can even establish new businesses (which they can also do under a false identity or with the complicity of third parties). A form of "regime shopping" is systematically taking place across the world, whereby mafias move where they know they will be relatively safe and can undertake their moneymaking and laundering activities undisturbed. We see no violent Camorra clans abroad, but rather the investment of Camorra money.

Can the fight against the criminal mobility of mafias and other organized crime groups be improved? Or do we accept the existing system, which allows these groups to take advantage of globalization to the detriment of nation-states that are not organizing against criminal transborder groups. The EU, Eurojust, and Europol's remit of activities are increasing in terms of tackling transnational organized crime groups,[7] but because they are supranational bodies they still have limited powers when it comes to imposing systematic and coherent cooperation within member states. In addition, there also exist extensive bilateral and multilateral agreements which means that there is an interest in tackling these issues. So the fight against transnational organized crime is taking place at EU and international levels with a lot of positive results, but the question of mafias is still perceived to be purely Italian (Allum, 2012; Allum, 2013).

If mafia association were recognized in all EU countries as a crime, it might reduce the mafias' foreign projects. It is clear, however, that declaring mafia association to be a crime is often seen as problematic for countries without the same history, culture, and past as Italy.[8] The crime is based on the group's association and its capacity to impose its violent methods and rules to commit crime, to corrupt individuals and civic institutions, and to control a specific territory. Many do not understand or recognize the power of the organized crime association, which has to be proved with solid evidence and beyond a reasonable doubt.

Mafia association is becoming an international problem as *mafiosi* travel abroad. Surely just because clan members cross a border, their association and criminal projects do not cease to exist. Yet the absence of mafia association legislation in Europe would appear to suggest so. The boss Domenico Rancadore was convicted in Italy for mafia crimes; in the United Kingdom his crimes have hardly been recognized.[9] Is this justice?

Why is it not possible to consider "mafia association" like membership in an international terrorist group and introduce it as a universal and recognizable international crime? Wherever the crime is committed, prosecution in another country would become possible against members, associates, and accomplices. Under current circumstances, the message is that it is acceptable to commit crimes in one country and launder the proceeds in another. An "association" law might reduce the ease with which Italian mafias and other groups now conceal criminal activities abroad and manipulate judicial loopholes and incoherencies. Can European states really wait for another Duisburg massacre, a shootout between 'Ndrangheta members in Germany in 2007, to realize the damage Italian mafias are doing abroad? More worrying is their invisible financial presence in the legal economy, the extent of which is still unclear. Is it best not to know because our legal economies depend on this criminal money? I suggest that we need to know because legal economies and companies are undermined and challenged by mafia money.

Italian mafias have a dual identity: their organizational structures change but their activities extend to other countries and remain much the same.[10] The Camorra in Europe does not behave as it does in Naples, rather it seeks to fit in undetected and become part of the scene in order to make more money. To the untrained eye, it often presents itself as a simple form of organized or financial crime, or even an investment in the economy, which is not perceived as particularly harmful. As Saint Exupéry once said in *The Little Prince*, "What is essential is invisible to the eye." The danger the Camorra poses abroad becomes invisible, off the police radar and off the political agenda. It is not a policing or political priority, yet Camorra activities continue to undermine the legal economy as a form of "outlaw capitalism" (Venkatesh, 2008: 37).

A covert threat means, in effect, no threat at all. And this is what the *mafiosi* are counting on. As the DNA's *Annual Report* stated in 2013, "it is not the [mafia] association that is being, let's say, exported, but the mafia method" (DNA4: 107). In other words, it is the Camorra money, mentality, use of intimidation, corruption, bullying, and harassment that these criminal groups are starting to reproduce in Europe in order to influence behavior and business.

Recent investigations in Rome in December 2014, called "Mafia Capital," have uncovered a system of corruption between criminals, politicians, and businessmen. It has been described as a "mafia" not for its control over a set territory but for its control over public state contracts and business deals. It is this "mafia method" that *camorristi* are transporting with them to Europe in their acquisitive crimes, counterfeit-goods scams, drug trafficking, and money-laundering activities. If the rest of Europe continues to ignore these signs and voices, believing that it is purely an Italian problem, they might be in for a big surprise. I hope it is not too late.

# Notes

**INTRODUCTION**

1. Nunzio De Falco was arrested in 1995 and extradited in 2000. In 2003, he was given a life sentence for the murder of the priest Don Diana.

2. Michele Zaza was extradited in March 1994 to stand trial for mafia association and drug trafficking, but died in Rome later that year.

3. *Il Mattino*, 25/2/1992, M. Jouakim, "Cosi la Camorra conquista l'Europa: Un'allarmante mappa tracciata della Criminalpol," 25; and 25/2/1992, M. Jouakim, "La Camorra export: Droga e riciclaggio: Cosi le mani sull' Europa," 28.

4. *Libération*, 16/12/2006, "90 trafiquants de drogue interpellés en Europe," http://www.liberation.fr/monde/2006/12/16/90-trafiquants-de-drogue-interpelles-en-europe_60462 (accessed 3/1/2010).

5. These countries were chosen because they are the core of Western Europe and the countries I am most familiar with (linguistically and culturally), but also because of my academic training.

6. Article 416-bis of the Italian criminal code was introduced in 1982 and defines the membership of a mafia-type criminal association ("mafia association") in the following terms: "when those belonging to the [mafia] association exploit the potential for intimidation which their membership gives them, and the compliance and *omertà* which membership entails and which lead to the committing of crimes, the direct or indirect assumption of management or control of financial activities, concessions, permissions, enterprises and public services for the purpose of deriving profit or wrongful advantages for themselves or others" (quoted in Seindal, 1998: 20).

7. In 1994, it was estimated that there were 132 clans in Campania: 79 in Naples city and its province, 29 in the province of Caserta, 13 in the province of Salerno, 7 in the province of Avellino, and 4 in the province of Benevento (see CD3).

8. Police and judicial figures are used here to give a general idea of the dimensions of the phenomenon.

9. Individuals who imposed prices between farmers and the market in Naples.

10. For example, the Nuvoletta, the Bardellino, the Zaza, the Giuliano, the Alfieri, the Galasso, the Fabbrocino, and the Vollaro clans.

11. This was an internal split of the Di Lauro clan.

12. Even the family of members in prison receive a regular salary and have their lawyers' fees paid.

13. The period from the late twentieth century onward, also called "a new era," "information society," "consumer society," "post-modernity," "post-modernism," "post-industrial," "post-capitalist" (see Giddens, 1990: 1–2).

14. These three concepts seem to fit coherently into my general structure/agency framework (see Allum, 2006) (inspired by Giddens, 1984). It is for this reason that a grounded theory approach was used rather than applying an established theoretical approach to the material. This approach enabled the study to go beyond the judicial narrative and understand, on the one hand, the context (structure), and on the other, the logics, culture, and thinking of *camorristi* (agency) in order to draw out a clear picture of their Camorra mobility in Europe.

15. Discussion with an undergraduate student, Adam Tiepi (2012), who developed the same idea about the Calabrian 'Ndrangheta as Bianchi and Rio (2013), who also used this expression to describe the relationship between '*ndrine* in the north of Italy and Calabria. Without a close relationship to the mother group in Calabria, the '*ndrine* in the north has little hope of success (see pp. 26–27). It is an interesting idea but does not really work for the Camorra because it suggests ultimate independence, and from our evidence, the umbilical cord has never fully been cut.

16. I do not study the invisible layer of associates who can be sent, such as door-to-door sellers, *magliari*, or relatives retiring abroad, or the second generation of Neapolitans who now live abroad permanently.

17. As opposed to "solid" modernity in Naples, characterized by heavy organizational structures and traditional values. The liquidity perspective on mafias has been used by others (see CD2; Lamberti, 2009; Forgione, 2009; Beatrice, 2013). This perspective was expanded within a more general structure/agency framework of society and behavior. It captures the subtleties and complexities of Camorra mobility abroad without being normative or prescriptive. This general framework enables a flexible macroanalysis while concurrently examining diverse forms of individual criminal behavior in wide-ranging contexts.

18. One clan in Spain appeared to have moved explicitly to set up a business and stay there, but members soon returned to Naples.

19. Spanish and Italian police have noted that this may start to happen in Spain and the United Kingdom, but as yet there is no concrete evidence.

20. The terms "accomplice" and "complicity" in this book are used from a sociological perspective to describe any person who helps a *camorrista* or their associates. This does not necessarily entail a blameworthy or criminal act as such, but any form of emotional, social, economic, or political support (see Sciarrone for definition and elaboration of these terms and concepts, 2011: 35–39).

21. Some situations have evolved, but I have tried to note this where possible.

22. Forgione in *Mafia Export* stated that he identified *mafiosi* in more than one hundred cities in Europe (2009: 239–294), but his methodology had its limitations: for example, he did not clearly define who or what he was identifying and counting—were they associates, members, or crimes? What is interesting to note but also perhaps a bit dangerous is how the figures given by Forgione have been accepted by many as correct and a given, without much engagement about how he arrived at them. Europol's 2013 *Threat Assessment, Italian Organised Crime* (Europol2) did not give such a figure, demonstrating perhaps how complicated this task is, as there do not exist the proper instruments to measure and calculate their presence in Europe.

23. European and Italian judicial documents, police files, in-depth interviews with insiders and specialized observers (see bibliography), and extensive field visits to the different districts of the clans were undertaken in Naples. For the sixteen clans that were studied, over one hundred judicial and police documents were collected and analyzed.

24. The figures used for numbers of clan members must be handled with care. They are only used to give a general overview, not a precise figure. I have figures from 1988 *Carabineri* documents (AC1–1 and AC1–2 and Allum, 2000) and from various other sources, but I stress again that they are used to give a sense of the size of the clan. In some cases, how the figures are reached can be questioned.

25. The German, British, Dutch, and Italian police forces as well as the British, French, and Italian judiciaries. Some were more helpful than others: the German police engaged positively with this project, whereas the Dutch police refused on several occasions to enter into a dialogue about the situation in the Netherlands. I was unable to access the German, Dutch, and Spanish judiciary and I was unable to talk with the British Crown Prosecution Service representative in Rome.

26. Those located in the United Kingdom, Spain, and France. The Dutch liaison police officer based in Rome refused to be interviewed.

27. The French, Italian, Spanish, and British Home Offices.

28. For example, the European Parliament, Eurojust, the United Nations Office on Drugs and Crime, the United Nations Interregional Crime and Justice Institute, and from various bodies interested in specific crimes. For example, for counterfeit goods, the Union des Fabricants (UniFab) in France and the Intellectual Property Office in the United Kingdom.

29. In some of my case studies, it may appear that one source has been predominantly used and no others. This is because the specific details or anecdotes come from one specific document; still, I have systematically double-checked events and interpretations using other documents not necessarily referenced.

30. Gennaro Panzuto (11 April 2011, Naples), Michele Siciliano (20 December 2011, Rome), Giovanni Messina (25 April 2012, Naples), Anna Carrino (30 October 2012, Rome), and Rosa Amato (27 December 2012, Naples). All gave consent to their interviews being used in this study. I thank them once again for their time and explanations, which were extremely useful.

## CHAPTER ONE. LOCAL MOTIVES, GLOBAL CHOICES

1. *La Repubblica*, Napoli, 12/6/1984, "A Napoli si scantena la guerra di Camorra sono quattro gli uccisi," at http://ricerca.repubblica.it/repubblica/archivio/repubblica/1984/06/12/napoli-si-scatena-la-guerra-di.html (accessed 2/5/13).

2. He was arrested in 1989 in Uruguay and extradited to Italy in 1991. *La Repubblica*, 23/12/1989, "Preso in Uruguay il boss che sa tutto sul caso Cirillo," http://ricerca.repubblica.it/repubblica/archivio/repubblica/1989/12/23/preso-in-uruguay-il-boss-che-sa.html (accessed 1/12/12). However, for various reasons he was freed and returned back to Paraguay, where he died in 2015, aged seventy-five.

3. For definitions of the terms "mafia" and "mafia association," see the introduction, p. 4, and note 6.

4. A recent exception to this may be the case of Pasquale Scotti, a former member of the NCO, arrested in Brazil on 26 May 2015. See *The Guardian*, 26/6/15, "Mafia Boss Pasquale Scotti Arrested in Brazil after 31 Years on the Run," http://www.theguardian.com/world/2015/may/26/italian-mafia-boss-pasquale-scotti-arrested-brazil (accessed 26/6/15).

5. *Formia Libera*, 18/9/12, "De Angelis guidava da formia un impero da 80 milioni di euro, cosa c'e negli atti," http://www.formialibera.it/wordpress/de-angelis-guidava-da-formia-un-impero-da-80-milioni-di-euro-cosa-ce-negli-atti/ (accessed 24/9/12).

6. "Push factors" as defined by Morselli, Turcotte, and Tenti (2011) are "forces which drive criminal groups away from a setting," and pull factors are "forces which draw criminal groups to a setting" (166).

7. In other words, he was condemned for belonging to a Mafia type association.

8. "Conditional freedom" can be conceded to criminals rather than spending time in prison.

9. He was arrested in 1996 in Amsterdam for possession of firearms and mafia association and extradited back to Italy. In 2005, he was arrested in the United Kingdom and extradited back to Italy to serve thirteen years.

10. *Scotland on Sunday*, 6/10/1996, "Restaurant Owner Arrested on Italian Mafia Charges."

11. *Divieto di soggiorno*: whereby an individual is forced to live in a specific location away from his hometown for a set period of time.

12. Giuseppe Polverino was sentenced to twenty years in prison for Camorra association in 2012.

13. *Libero Quotidiano*, 3/9/2010, "Arrestato in Spagna camorrista del clan di Polverino," http://www.liberoquotidiano.it/news/480637/Arrestato_in_Spagna_camorrista_del_clan_di_Polverino.html (accessed 24/1/13).

14. *Cronache di Camorra*, 5/10/2008, "Le rivelazioni di Gennaro Panzuto," http://cronachediCamorra.blogspot.fr/2008/10/le-rivelazioni-di-gennaro-panzuto.html (accessed 28/4/2011).

15. *Daily Star Sun*, 18/1/2009, "UK on Alert over Mafia Turf Wars," http://www.dailystar.co.uk/news/latest-news/66269/UK-onalert-over-Mafia-turf-wars (accessed 6/6/2011).

16. Pietro Licciardi was sentenced to eight years in prison for his involvement in counterfeit activities in 2011.

17. Raffaele Caldarelli was convicted in 2006 for Camorra association.

18. *Il Corriere del Mezzogiorno*, 27/1/2010, "Preso in Spagna 'Paoluccio l'infermiere': Parcheggiava lo scooter sul marciapiede," http://corrieredelmezzogiorno.corriere.it/napoli/notizie/cronaca/2010/27-gennaio-2010/preso-spagna-paoluccioinfermiereera-dei-super latitanti-camorra-1602359269144.shtml27/1/2010 (accessed 20/4/13).

19. Such as Gelsomina Verde, who had nothing to do with the Camorra, apart from being the former girlfriend of a clan member. She was tortured and burned before being killed in 2005 at the age of twenty-two.

20. *Il Mattino*, 19/7/1994, 26, "Droga, mafia e . . ."

21. *Il Mattino*, 19/7/1994, 1, "Morto il re del contrabbando, Michele Zaza stroncato da un infarto."

22. DTS was convicted in France for car trafficking in 2009 and for Camorra murder in Italy in 2013.

23. Alfonso Annunziata was sentenced to sixteen years in prison for international drugs trafficking in 2009.

24. I tried to find the records of this case, but the archives of the Magistrates' Court had moved and I was told that there would be very little detail in the judge's verdict and explanation, which would also be difficult to locate.

25. See *The Mirror*, 25/5/2007, "Sopranos in Our Suburbs," http://www.mirror.co.uk/news/uk-news/sopranos-in-our-suburbs-477528 (accessed 7/7/2011).

26. *Daily Star Sunday*, 18/1/2009, "UK on Alert over Mafia Turf Wars," http://www.dailystar.co.uk/news/latest-news/66269/UK-on-alert-over-Mafia-turf-wars (accessed 6/6/2011).

**CHAPTER TWO. FUNCTIONAL MOBILITY**

1. We can see a different dynamics in Naples city, where members of certain clans will physically move to a new district to colonize it for their clan and take it over. This does not happen abroad.

2. Also known as "a star network." This network is organized with spokes that connect and refer to one hub at the center.

3. Overall, it was the clan that benefited from this presence abroad, although there were also many examples when it was only the boss and his family who benefitted, in particular in relation to financial investments.

4. The British definition of the term "acquisitive crime" "covers all household and personal crime in which items are stolen, and can be split into household and personal acquisitive crimes. *Household acquisitive crime*: Burglary, attempted burglary in a dwelling, theft in a dwelling, theft from outside a dwelling, theft and attempted theft of and from vehicles, theft of a pedal cycle. *Personal acquisitive crime*: Snatch theft, stealth theft, attempted theft from the person, other theft of personal property and other attempted theft of personal property, robbery and attempted robbery. Although acquisitive crime includes robbery, because of the use of threat or force when depriving an individual of their property, robbery is considered to be a violent crime" (see HO1:26).

5. The Dutch police define the term "property crime" thus: "Domestic and industrial burglaries, shoplifting, cargo theft, car theft, robberies and ram raids, skimming and handling of stolen goods (DP1: 141).

6. In 2001, this would be roughly the equivalent of 47,000 euros.

7. The UniFab is an international organization based in France that seeks to protect intellectual property, http://www.unifab.com/en/our-association/history.html (accessed 25/9/12).

8. *La Repubblica*, 22/10/12, "I falsi bruciano 110 mila posti di lavoro Contraffazione, mercato da 13,7 miliardi," http://www.repubblica.it/economia/2012/10/22/news/contraffazione_tasse_lavoro-45053155/?ref=search (accessed 4/11/12).

9. See "law," p. 3, http://www.reatisocietari.it/new/images/il%20delitto%20di%20contraffazione%20di%20marchi.pdf (accessed 20/9/12).

10. *Il Mattino*, 15/5/93, "Nizza Connection."

11. "ICT piracy" is defined as the illegal copying and distribution of CDs, DVDs, films, games, software, and other products, resulting in infringement of copyright (DP1: 192). The report did not analyze the counterfeiting of other items (such as electrical goods, clothes, etc.) apart from counterfeit money.

12. *La Depeche*, 6/7/11, "La mafia napolitaine arnaque dans nos campagnes," http://www.ladepeche.fr/article/2011/07/06/1122891-la-Mafia-napolitaine-arnaque-dans-nos-campagnes.html (accessed 1/12/12).

13. Roughly speaking, they suggest that a DVD costs 0.20 euros but is sold at 45 euros, whereas cannabis costs 1.52 euros and is sold at 12 euros.

14. In 1997–1998, Spain and the Netherlands accounted for 63 percent of all European seizures, http://www.drugscope.org.uk/resources/faqs/faqpages/where-do-drugs-come-from (11/5/11).

15. The different cocaine routes identified in judicial documents: (1) South America into Naples port, (2) South America into Spain, then on to Naples, (3) South America into Amsterdam, then into Naples, (4) Croatia into Naples.

16. Some clans still insist on not selling drugs in their districts because of the stigma attached.

## CHAPTER THREE. CAMORRA CLANS IN GERMANY AND THE NETHERLANDS

1. Petra Reski, "Le mafie al Nord e in Europa: Infiltrazione o radicamento?" https://www.youtube.com/watch?v=lje-4v-Ouzs (accessed 10/11/14).

2. Twenty-six Italian-dominated groups were identified, with a total of 270 Italian Organized Crime suspects (139 new ones identified); 31 percent were homogenous, consisting of exclusively Italian nationals, 69 percent were heterogeneous, consisting of individuals from at least one more nation, and 23 out of 26 groups conducted their illegal activities with some kind of international connection (see BKA-NS for 2013).

3. For example, in 2013 it was reported that there were 11 so-called "Mafia investigations" undertaken by the BKA: 6 had links to the 'Ndrangheta, 3 to the Camorra, 2 to the Apulia (see BKA-NS, 2013).

4. Raffaele Giuliano elaborates: "Peppe was also a cigarette smuggler and gave money to my brothers. . . . This money was given as a form of compensation for the protection that my family gave him and other smugglers (see chapter 5, Di Tommaso brothers).

5. Likewise, 36 percent of imported European counterfeit goods were detected at Dutch borders in 2008 (UNODC2: 179).

6. The Dutch police started to investigate and look into Italian mafias in May 2013 by collecting information from academics working in this area. But they still do not fully and openly engage with academics on this topic.

7. L'Alleanza di Secondigliano is also called the *Cupola di Secondigliano*. The term "alliance" was given in order "to express the notion of 'coalition' that exists between the various criminal clans and families" (see TN19: 9).

8. For the Secondigliano alliance, as far as America, Brazil, Australia, Czech Republic, Spain, Portugal, and Turkey (see QN4, 3: 1).

9. In 2013, twenty-six members (QN14).

10. Like many other bosses, Gennaro Licciardi, head of the Licciardi clan, lost a brother, Antonio, who was killed by the NCO during the first Camorra war in the 1980s (LGv, 06/3/2003: 3).

11. His nickname was "the monkey" because he was so agile and good at jumping around buildings when he was a burglar in his youth.

12. See, for example, the marriages of Michele Mazzarella and Marianna Giuliano, Giuseppe Missi and Assunta Sarno, Erminia Giuliano and Patrizio Bosti, Amelia Stolder and Carmine Giuliano, Rosa Stolder and Salvatore Stolder (see Brancaccio, 2011b), Rosa Nuvoletta and Raffaele Lubrano, Enrico Maisto and Rosa Orlando, Luigi Sciorio and Rosetta Orlando (see Allum, 2006).

13. The exact number of his siblings remains unclear: minimum 8, maximum 11 (LB).

14. The advantages of the alliance abroad were: first, that they had more men and thus more control over economic activities, and second, more possible front names and accomplices.

15. *La Repubblica*, 6/2/2005, "Una rete d'affari in mezzo mondo ha scatenato i 'balcani' di Napoli," http://www.repubblica.it/2005/a/sezioni/cronaca/napolitre/balcan/balcan.html (accessed 1/9/2010).

16. The usual division was 30 percent Mallardo, 30 percent Contini, 40 percent Licciardi.

17. Mainly the leadership of the Secondigliano alliance and the Mazzarella/Misso cartel.

18. *La Cronaca di Napoli*, 6/10/2010, "Incastrato il magliaro del clan Rinaldi," 3.

19. We can define them as real ideologies.

20. *La Repubblica*, 12/10/2007, "Preso in Germania il boss del racket," 2, http://ricerca.repubblica.it/repubblica/archivio/repubblica/2007/10/12/preso-in-germania-il-boss-del-racket.html?ref=search (accessed 12/12/12).

21. PG had a criminal record in Italy but not in Germany (QN4, 1: 52–53).

22. Why Como? Probably because it was where one of the Licciardi members had spent some time (an obligatory residence order) and thus became familiar with the new territory and invested there.

23. *La Repubblica*, 11/8/2008, "Ville, donne e soldi: La dolce vita dei narcos di Scampia," http://ricerca.repubblica.it/repubblica/archivio/repubblica/2008/08/11/ville-donne-dollari-in-costa-brava-la.html?ref=search (accessed 21/8/2015).

24. They also both imported drugs from Spain.

25. *Metropolis*, 04/01/2008, "Camorra: Arrestato a Fiumicino boss Alfonso Annunziata," http://www.metropolisweb.it/Notizie/Campania/Cronaca/camorra_arrestato_fiumicino_boss_alfonso_annunziata.aspx (accessed 21/3/2012).

26. Scampia is a modern but run down and neglected suburb north of Naples (with a population of about 80,000 people) particularly renowned for its drug piazzas where clan members sell their drugs to clients. The expression "Scampia of the Vesuvius" suggests similar conditions near Boscoreale and Torre Annunziata where groups can sell their drugs.

27. *La Repubblica*, 30/9/2005, "False fatture per miliardi di lire in ventisei patteggiano la pena," http://ricerca.repubblica.it/repubblica/archivio/repubblica/2005/09/30/false-fatture-per-miliardi-di-lire-in.html (accessed 23/3/12).

28. Domenico Verde would become one of Giuseppe Polverino's right-hand men in his hashish importation network in Spain in 2006.

29. The Maglio trial saw the main leaders of the Camorra clans of the 1990s on trial together with many local and national MPs (including the former minister Antonio Gava, who was acquitted) who were accused of having a corrupt relationship (see Allum, 2006).

30. Twenty-four members in 1997 (Scribani, 1997); twenty-five in 2011 (QN13).

31. *Il Giornale di Napoli*, 16/3/2006, "Annunziata-Aquino: Cocaina dalla Colombia, 21 arresti, blitz del Ros di Napoli: latitante Alfonso Annunziata" and *Il Giornale di Napoli*, 16/3/2006, 3, "La cosca gestita dal ras latitante e dai due scalatissimi nipoti."

32. *Il Giornale di Napoli*, 16/3/2006, "La cosca gestita dal ras latitante dai due scalatissimi nipoti."

33. It has also been suggested that he owned property in Amsterdam, as did other members (TNI).

34. They also imported from Spain. The case of SG, who was arrested in 1993 on the Spanish-French border with his caravan full of drugs, is a good example of the type of couriers they used in the 1990s (see TN8: 69, 70).

35. See *Metropolis*, 7/8/2007, "Il boss Carmine Aquino lascia il carcere."

36. *Il Mattino*, 20/5/1997, "Assolto il boss Raffaele Stolder," 30. See also CAN2.

37. The drugs markets of Poggiomarino, Scafati, Boscoreale, and Boscotrecase.

38. Three drug hoards were intercepted in Kassel and Fussen between 2002 and 2003 (TTA1).

39. A guarantor is a person from the buying group who would be used to make sure that there was no double-dealing.

40. *La Repubblica*, 13/12/2004, "Napoli, operazioni anticamorra arrestato il boss Luigi Di Biasi," http://www.repubblica.it/2004/l/sezioni/cronaca/napoli2/zona/zona.html (accessed 10/5/14).

## CHAPTER FOUR. CAMORRA CLANS IN FRANCE

1. *La Repubblica*, 11/8/2010, "Il boss viveur di Cosa nostra dalla Francia al carcere 41 bis," http://palermo.repubblica.it/cronaca/2010/08/11/news/il_boss_viveur_di_cosa_nostra_estradato_dalla_francia-6214973/?rss (accessed15/5/14).

2. *Le Point*, 27/09/2010, "Arrestation en France d'un boss de la mafia calabraise en cavale," http://www.lepoint.fr/societe/arrestation-en-france-d-un-boss-de-la-mafia-calabraise-en-cavale-27-09-2010-1241755_23.php (accessed 15/5/14).

3. *La Repubblica*, 8/11/13, "'Ndrangheta, arrestato in Francia latitante per traffico di droga," http://www.repubblica.it/cronaca/2013/11/08/news/_ndrangheta_arrestato_in_francia_latitante_per_traffico_di_droga-70484652/ (accessed 15/5/14).

4. *Nice Matin*, 16/4/14, "Antonio Lo Russo, le boss de la mafia italienne, arrêté à Nice," http://www.nicematin.com/nice/antonio-lo-russo-le-boss-de-la-mafia-italienne-arrete-a-nice.1699939.html (accessed 15/5/14).

5. *Historia*, July 2003, "Dossier: Mafias et pouvoirs," http://www.historia.fr/rubrique/dossier-mafias-et-pouvoirs (accessed 25/9/2010). *L'Express*, August 2002, "Mafia: Les nouveaux parrains," http://www.lexpress.fr/informations/mafia-les-nouveaux-parrains_648940.html?xtmc=Mafia_2002&xtcr=3; *L'Express*, August 2010, "La mafia ne connait pas la crise," http://www.lexpress.fr/actualite/societe/la-mafia-ne-connait-pas-la-crise_913490.html (accessed 25/9/2010); *L'Express*, July 2015, "Mafias comment elles détruisent la planète," http://www.lexpress.fr/actualite/societe/environnement/mafias-comment-elles-detruisent-la-planete_1699506.html (accessed 25/7/15). *Le Point*, July 2011, "La mafia en France," http://www.lepoint.fr/societe/la-mafia-en-france-21-07-2011-1357336_23.php (accessed 25/7/2011).

6. Pietro Grasso, National Antimafia Prosecutor of the DNA (2005–2013), Rome. *Le Figaro*, 16/11/2011, "Pietro Grasso: La France, cible de la mafia," http://www.lefigaro.fr/actualite-france/2011/11/16/0101ww6-20111116ARTFIG00623-pietro-grasso-la-france-cible-de-la-mafia.php (accessed 6/10/2012). *Le Figaro*, 19/3/14, "60.000€ en faux-billets saisis à Paris," http://www.lefigaro.fr/flash-actu/2014/03/19/97001-20140319FILWWW00431-60000-de-faux-billets-saisis-a-paris.php (accessed 25/7/14). The production of fake coins is perceived by the French authorities as a Neapolitan specialty. November 2014 in Campania saw arrests of the Gruppo Napoli, a gang of counterfeiters who

produce fake euros and flood Europe with them. These are not Camorra clans, although they pay them a tax in order to operate. See *Il Fatto Quotidiano*, 26/11/14, "Euro falsi a Napoli: 56 arresti. Coinvolta mamma della bimba morta a Caivano," http://www.ilfattoquotidiano.it/2014/11/26/napoli-euro-falsi-56-arresti-coinvolta-mamma-bimba-uccisa-caivano/1234193/ (accessed 27/11/2014).

7. See, for example, *Var Matin*, 18/9/12, "Un an de prison pour les Napolitains voleurs de montre à Cannes," http://www.nicematin.com/cannes/un-an-de-prison-pour-les-napolitains-voleurs-de-montre-a-cannes.994442.html (accessed 25/9/12).

8. ilgiornale.it, 20/9/2013, "Camorra, guerra tra clan Maxiblitz nel napoletano: 23 finiscono in manette," http://www.ilgiornale.it/news/Camorra-guerra-clan-maxiblitz-nel-napoletano-23-finiscono.html (accessed 8/9/13).

9. *La Cronache di Napoli*, 5/2/2008, "Nel miro dei scari pur il ras Tedesco."

10. *La Repubblica*, 20/9/10, "Guerra tra clan, 23 arresti nel Napoletano," http://napoli.repubblica.it/cronaca/2010/09/20/news/guerra_tra_clan_23_arresti-7242144/ (accessed 29/9/2010).

11. *Var Matin*, 25/3/11, "Armes et voitures: Traffic à la sauce Napolitaine," http://archives.varmatin.com/article/toulon/armes-et-voitures-trafic-a-la-sauce-napolitaine.489456.html (accessed 30/3/2012).

12. GA was Contini's representative and board member who had previously looked after the American market (TN15).

13. *Le Progress*, 6/7/2011, "Des Napolitains écroués à Lyon pour association de malfaiteurs," http://www.leprogres.fr/rhone/2011/07/06/des-napolitains-ecroues-a-lyon-pour-association-de-malfaiteurs (accessed 12/2/13).

14. In 2014, it was estimated that in Naples cigarette smugglers pay five or six euros per box to the local clan.

15. *Le Figaro*, 6/3/12, "La mafia calabraise investit la Côte d'Azur," http://www.lefigaro.fr/actualite-france/2012/03/05/01016-20120305ARTFIG00376-la-mafia-calabraise-investit-la-cote-d-azur.php (accessed 12//12/12).

16. La Provence.com, 6/1/2010, "Drogue: Alain Chaffard condamné à 12 ans," http://www.laprovence.com/actu/region-en-direct/255000/drogue-alain-chaffard-condamne-a-12-ans.html (accessed 5/4/10).

17. *Il Mattino*, 4/2/14, "Napoli, camorra. Clan Zaza, attività illecite in tutta Italia: 29 arresti nella capitale," http://247.libero.it/rfocus/19750249/1/napoli-camorra-clan-zaza-attivit-illecite-in-tutta-italia-29-arresti-nella-capitale/ (accessed 10/2/14).

18. Between 1979 and 1982, he was arrested eight times for importing contraband cigarettes.

19. Under the rota system, each organized contraband group had their allocated time slot to unload their cigarettes in Naples (see Behan, 1996).

20. Newspapers regularly report that "Zaza left an empire" to his Mazzarella nephews and a cousin. See *La Repubblica*, 4/6/2006, "Bar devastati e gang in azione la nuova faida di Napoli Ovest," http://ricerca.repubblica.it/repubblica/archivio/repubblica/2006/06/04/bar-devastati-gang-in-azione-la-nuova.html (accessed 13/11/12). "He left his nephews, the Mazzarellas, he left this situation (PM).

21. *Il Mattino*, 1/12/1984, 15, "E intanto manette al 'vice' di Zaza."

22. *Le Soir*, 13/5/93, "Mafia napolitaine piegée sur la Cote d'Azur, le parrain de la Camorra arreté," 16, http://archives.lesoir.be/mafia-napolitaine-piegee-sur-la-cote-d-azur-le-parrain-_t-19930513-Z06R61.html (accessed 1/12/12).

23. See Giuseppe Di Cristina and Tommaso Buscetta, both of whom indicated that "Michele Zaza as the coordinator of the contraband of (foreign produced) cigarettes in the districts of S. Lucia and San Giovanni a Teduccio, was constantly in contact with the *mafiosi* Nunzio La Mattina and Tommaso Spadaro" (in Gay, 1996: 4).

24. *Il Mattino*, 13/5/93, "La scalata di Michele 'O Pazzo,' dalle bionde alla costa Azzurra."
25. *Il Mattino*, 19/7/94, "Morto il re del contrabbando."
26. The investigation was called "Tiro Grosso" and included the collaboration of the French and Italian authorities. The French and Italian prosecuted different parts of the network.
27. *L'Express*, 16/3/2011, "10 ans ferme pour un membre présumé de la Camorra," http://www.lexpress.fr/actualite/societe/justice/10-ans-ferme-pour-un-membre-presume-de-la-camorra_972721.html (accessed 10/2/13).

**CHAPTER FIVE. CAMORRA CLANS IN SPAIN**

1. *Il Mattino*, 21/6/2009, "Patto tra camorra, mafia e 'ndrangheta. El pais: La Spagna diventa Cosa nostra," http://www.ilmattino.it/italia/cronacanera/patto_tra_camorra_mafia_e_n_039_drangheta_el_pais_la_spagna_diventa_cosa_nostra/notizie/62999.shtml (accessed 13/6/13).
2. See *Il Mattino*, 13/9/12, "Rifiuti di Camorra sepolti in Spagna," http://www.ilmattino.it/napoli/citta/rifiuti_di_camorra_sepolti_in_spagna_scatta_l_039_indagine_della_guardia_civil/notizie/219223.shtml (accessed 13/6/13).
3. Gomez and Gurrieri identified the following Camorra activities in Barcelona: drug trafficking to Italy, in particular cocaine, and money recycling (2001: 65).
4. See World Tourism Organization, "Tourist Highlights 2014 (UNWTO)," 6, http://www.e-unwto.org/content/r13521/fulltext.pdf (accessed 1/12/14). In 2012, the number of tourists was 57.5 million, and in 2013, 60.7 million.
5. See *Typically Spanish*, 24/1/2008, "Major Bank Robbery Gang Broken Up in Spain," http://www.typicallyspanish.com/spain-archive/national/Major_bank_robbery_gang_broken_up_in_Spain.shtml (accessed 15/6/2013).
6. Called in Italian *uno scippo*, see glossary.
7. Some Rolexes were even sold in the US using fake warranties. See *La Repubblica*, 1/2/2006, "Quel gioielliere pestato dalla sporca dozzina," (accessed 21/11/2015).
8. They do see fake documents as an issue, but not other fake goods such as clothes, electronic goods, etc.
9. *Europa Press*, 27/7/2011, "Desmantelada la mayor red de falsificación vinculada a la Camorra," http://www.europapress.es/sociedad/sucesos-00649/noticia-desmantelada-mayor-red-falsificacion-vinculada-Camorra-20110727103947.html (accessed 1/9/2013).
10. Ibid.
11. A. Smith, *The Florentine*, 12/5/2005, "Organized Crime Still a Force in the South" http://www.theflorentine.net/articles/article-view.asp?issuetocId=1555 (accessed 6/2/14).
12. The Ministry of the Interior identified 24 members in the Caserta region and 179 in the Naples region. It is not very clear how they came to these figures.
13. *La Repubblica*, Napoli, 23/11/2010, "Camorra: Operazione DIA, 4 arresti per favoreggiamento clan Casalesi (2)," http://napoli.repubblica.it/dettaglio-news/18:45/3876881 (accessed 6/2/13).
14. Francesco Schiavone and Francesco Bidognetti became the two main leaders of the Casalesi clan.
15. His fellow leaders, Schiavone and Bidognetti, believed that he had given them up to the police when they were arrested in 1990.
16. An overview of the Casalesi clan in TN3: 141 members, average age 39, all men, and TN4: 86 members, all men, average age 46.
17. Perhaps there was still a reservation about prosecuting women.

18. Giuseppe De Falco was murdered in the company of his lover, Caterina Mancini, on 5 March 1992. It was the first time that a woman had been murdered during a Camorra war, and her murder was symbolic, a clear message to Giuseppe De Falco's wife to keep quiet or else. It was also common knowledge that Vincenzo De Falco had a lover and a child in France.

19. It is also believed that the clan trafficked from the Netherlands.

20. Col. Mario Cinque, 3/5/2011, http://www.9online.it/primopiano/2011/05/03/arresti-clan-polverino-i-dettagli-delloperazione/Arresti clan Polverino: i dettagli dell'operazione—30.6. (3 maggio 2011) (accessed 15/5/2011).

21. He was under "controlled freedom" (*libertà controllata*), which meant that he had to comply with certain conditions (such as no driving license, no passport, etc.).

22. *Il Mattino*, Omicidio Candela, quattro arresti. I pm: "Il boss latitante ordinò il delitto in un summit in Spagna," 25/2/2016, http://www.ilmattino.it/napoli/cronaca/xxx-1572984.html (accessed 21/2/2016).

23. This is not unusual for clans. The same has been said for the Moccia clan. To avoid wire taps, discussion are often held in the open air.

24. The use of this new technology that has no roots, no physical location, is a feature of liquidity.

25. There appeared to be some activity in the Netherlands as well.

26. Once Giuseppe Polverino was arrested in 2011, some of his relatives moved to Spain to continue his activities. See *El Mensual de 20 Minutos*, 14; Octubre 2013, "El capo que solo perdió una vez al poker," http://www.20minutos.es/especial/el-mensual-20minutos/pdf-octubre-2013 (accessed 12/1/14).

27. In the Annunziata-Aquino family, where there existed a kind of intransigence toward flexibility, autonomy, and independence, this was considered a big problem, but here it proved rather successful.

28. *El Mensual de 20 Minutos*, 14/10/13, "El capo que solo perdió una vez al poker."

29. *La Repubblica*, 19/2/2012, "Soldi del narcotraffico ai terroristi islamici," http://ricerca.repubblica.it/repubblica/archivio/repubblica/2012/02/19/soldi-del-narcotraffico-ai-terroristi-islamici.html?ref=search (accessed 23/1/13).

30. *Il Mattino*, 5/6/13, "Vino imposto dal clan Polverino: Così la camorra arriva a tavola," http://www.ilmattino.it/napoli/cronaca/vino_imposto_dal_clan_polverino_cos_la_camorra_arriva_a_tavola_video/notizie/288216.shtm (accessed 5/12/13).

31. *El Mensual de 20 Minutos*, 14/10/13, "El capo que solo perdió una vez al póker," 24–27.

32. See *Il Mattino*, 29/7/2014, "L'uomo scappa in ginocchio, il killer lo insegue e lo uccide: Ergastolo," http://www.ilmattino.it/NAPOLI/CRONACA/l-39-uomo-scappa-in-ginocchio-il-killer-lo-insegue-e-lo-uccide.-ergastolo-il-drammatico-video/notizie/822222.shtml#fg-slider-auto-75408 (accessed 29/7/14).

33. Whereas in the late 1990s, the clan sold hashish at 5,000,000 euros per kilo to other clans.

34. Livorno, which was abandoned after their goods had once been seized.

35. The article in *El Mensual de 20 minutos* suggested that he was able to co-opt Spanish accountants only after his Neapolitan associates and advisers had been arrested in 2011. As a reaction, the clan sought help and advice elsewhere among natives in Spain, http://www.20minutos.es/especial/el-mensual-20minutos/pdf-octubre-2013 (accessed 12/1/14).

36. We believe that it could be more than two, as there are traces of the clan in the Netherlands, but this is still relatively uninvestigated.

37. *La Repubblica*, 15/6/2015, "Camorra a Milano, scacco al clan Nuvoletta: 10 arresti, sequestri per 13 milioni," http://milano.repubblica.it/cronaca/2015/06/10/news/camorra_milano_nuvoletta-116530669/ (accessed 12/8/15).

38. He died in 2013.

39. *Europa press*, 18/10/11, "Desarticulado un entramado de blanqueo de capitales de la mafia italiana en Tenerife," http://www.europapress.es/sociedad/sucesos-00649/noticia-amp-desarticulado-entramado-blanqueo-capitales-mafia-italiana-tenerife-20111018144332.html (accessed 10/1/13).

40. Blog de Wordpress.com, 25/10/11, "CONEXIONES DEL PP CON LACAMORRA NAPOLITANA," http://corrupcionencanarias.wordpress.com/2011/10/25/conexiones-del-pp-con-la-camorra-napolitana/ (accessed 27/9/13).

41. Diariodeavisos.com, 19/10/2011, "Golpe a la Camorra en Tenerife," http://www.diariodeavisos.com/2011/10/golpe-a-la-Camorra-italiana-en-las-americas/—(accessed 27/9/13).

42. *El Dia.Es*, 19/10/2011, "Trece detenidos por blanquear dinero a mafiosos italianos en el Sur de Tenerife," http://eldia.es/2011-10-19/sucesos/1-Trece-detenidos-blanquear-dinero-mafiosos-italianos-Sur-Tenerife.htm (accessed 27/9/13).

43. See *Antena 3 Television*, 19/10/11, "Detenidos en Tenerife trece miembros en la mafia italiana," http://www.antena3.com/noticias/sociedad/detenidos-tenerife-trece-miembros-mafia-italiana_2011101900121.html (accessed 27/9/13).

44. *Il Mattino*, 13/1/13, "Il boss in fuga dalla faida si rifugiano a Tenerife," http://m.ilmattino.it/m/mattino/articolo/inchieste/243996 (accessed 25/3/13). See also Infooggi.it, 05/11/2011, "Il diritto di Sapere, Mariano Rajoy e quella foto inopportune," http://www.infooggi.it/articolo/mariano-rajoy-e-quella-foto-inopportuna/19979/ (accessed 24/3/13).

## CHAPTER SIX. CAMORRA CLANS IN THE UNITED KINGDOM

1. The examples are not easy to find but there are other clan members and associates who were active in the United Kingdom, such as, according to the flying squad in Naples, a *camorrista* who was arrested in London in 2002 and who worked in a pizzeria.

2. Level-1 crimes: "Local issues—usually the crimes, criminals and other problems affecting a basic command unit or small force area. The scope of the crimes will be wide ranging from low value thefts to great seriousness such as murder. The handling of volume crime will be a particular issue at this level" (NCIS: 8).

3. To show how inconsistent these figures are, in 2011 it was estimated that there were about one hundred members (QN13: 9).

4. *La Repubblica*, 22/3/12, "Pentito accusa il Primario Iannelli da lui favori al clan," http://napoli.repubblica.it/cronaca/2012/03/22/news/pentito_accusa_il_primario_iannelli_da_lui_pavori_al_clan-32019945/ (accessed 13/5/12).

5. One Neapolitan police officer noted that many Neapolitan *magliari* were so well integrated into British society that they often went to the English National Football Stadium in London, Wembley Stadium.

6. See also https://www.youtube.com/watch?v=rf-unuPGifM (accessed 21/3/2016).

7. *The Guardian*, 15/10/2015, "UK Banks at High Risk of Exposure to Laundered Money, Says Report," http://www.theguardian.com/money/2015/oct/15/report-uk-banks-high-risk-aiding-money-laundering (accessed 18/11/15).

8. *Il Mattino di Padova*, 13/4/2006, "La camorra firma una megatruffa in Veneto," http://ricerca.gelocal.it/mattinopadova/archivio/mattinodipadova/2006/04/13/MCDPO_MCD01.html (accessed 10/4/2010).

## CONCLUSION

1. However, I note recent interest by Europol, which has set up a special unit on Italian mafias and which produced in 2013 the publication "Threat Assessment—Italian Organised Crime" (see Europol2: https://www.europol.europa.eu/content/threat-assessment-italian-organised-crime).

2. *Il Mattino*, 6/2/2014, "Ecco la camorra in Abruzzo: 31 arresti. 'Pericoloso gruppo dedito allo spaccio,'" http://www.primadanoi.it/news/italia/546919/Ecco-la-Camorra-in-Abruzzo-.html (accessed 21/3/14).

3. *Le Point*, 21/7/11, "La mafia en France," http://www.lepoint.fr/societe/la-mafia-en-france-21-07-2011-1357336_23.php (accessed 12/3/12).

4. Although one of the Stolder brothers mentioned that he undertook extortions in France (see CAN2).

5. *El mensual de 20 minutos*, Octubre, 2013, "El capo que solo perdió una vez al póker," 24.

6. Daily Mail, 21/8/2014, http://www.dailymail.co.uk/news/article-2730494/Is-Aberdeen-really-new-home-feared-Mafia-group-EU-report-says-Camorra-controls-catering-food-retail-property-Scottish-city.html (accessed 21/8/2014); *Daily Express*, 20/8/14, http://www.express.co.uk/news/uk/501585/Mafia-Stronghold-Gang-Aberdeen-Scotland-SNP-London-EU-Europe (accessed 21/8/2014); *The Scotsman*, 21/8/14, http://www.scotsman.com/news/mafia-tightens-its-grip-on-aberdeen-1-3516206 (accessed 21/8/2014).

7. For example, Europol has more powers (among others, joint investigation teams and coordination of meetings) and there are some important EU initiatives (European arrest warrant; European evidence warrant; Council Framework Decision 2001/500/JHA of 26 June 2001 on money laundering, the identification, tracing, freezing, seizing, and confiscation of instrumentalities, and the proceeds of crime; and EU Directive of 15 February 2014 on the freezing and confiscation of proceeds of crime). But each member state has to want to adopt and implement them.

8. Some argue that implementing Italian antimafia legislation would have perverse effects on the nature of democracy and the rule of law, but does this approach not ignore the victims and the harm mafias do?

9. *Daily Mail*, 21/3/2014, "The Godfather of Uxbridge: Blood-Soaked Past of Mafia Don Posing as 'Mr Suburbia' Who Beat Deportation Because It Would Violate His Human Rights," http://www.dailymail.co.uk/news/article-2586578/The-Godfather-Uxbridge-Blood-soaked-past-Mafia-don-posing-Mr-Suburbia-beat-deportation-violate-human-rights.html (accessed 1/12/2014).

10. Apart from extortion, which remains *the* territorial activity of Naples.

# Works Cited

**PRIMARY SOURCES**

(The sources are listed by country under the name of the institutions that produced them.)

## *Italy*

*Direzione Distwrettuale Antimafia, Napoli (District Antimafia Prosecution Service, Naples)*

PN1  Richiesta di applicazione di misura cautelare nei confronti di Aceto Orlando + 55, 9598/R/95 N.R. Mod. 21, 1995.
PN2  Richiesta di applicazione di misura cautelare della custodia in carcere e contestuale richiesta di sequestro preventivo nei confronti di Cesarano Ferdinando + 69, 12396/96 N.R. Mod. 21, 1996.
PN3  Richiesta per l'applicazione di misure cautelari nei confronti di Allegro Fabio + 42, Procedimento penale n. 12234/R/94 R.G. notizie di reato, 22/10/1996.
PN4  Richiesta di applicazione di misura cautelare a carico di Addeo Giuseppe Salvatore + 39. Proc. n. 57/09/97 R.G. Mod. 21.
PN5  Richiesta di applicazione di misure cautelari nei confronti di Gaetano Bocchetti + 40, Proc. n. 2504/R/97-DDA, 1997.
PN6  Richiesta di emissione di ordinanza applicativa di misura cautelare nei confronti di Vincenzo Licciardi + 96, Proc. n. 57523/00/R, 4/6/2003.
PN7  Richiesta di applicazione di misura cautelare personale nei confronti di Alfano Emilio + 41, Proc. n. 64007/r04 R.G. Mod. 21, 9/5/2005.
PN8  Richiesta di applicazione della misura della custodia cautelare in carcere nei confronti di Abete Mariano + 113, Proc. n. 19964/05, 2005.
PN9  Fermo di indiziato di delitto nei confronti Antonio Bianco + 33, Proc. n. 52613/2005 RGNR, 6/11/2006.
PN10  Richiesta di rinvio a giudizio nei confronti di Aquino Carmine + 60, Proc. n. 81633/2001 R.G. Mod 21, 9/11/2006.
PN11  Decreto di fermo indiziato di delitto nei confronti di Mazzarella Gennaro + 20, Proc. n. 66184/04 Mod. 21, 25/11/2006.
PN12  Decreto di fermo di indiziato di delitto nei confronti di Vincenzo Candurro + 30, Proc. n. 60455/02 Mod. 21, 24/1/2007
PN13  Indagini su di un'organizzazione internazionale promanante da alcuni Clan Napoletani, Proc. n. 54548/2008 RGNR, 9/12/2008.
PN14  Procedimento penale n. 54548/2008 del Registro Generale della Procura di Napoli—Richiesta di scambio informativo preliminare tra autorità giudiziarie. Art. 18 Convenzione O.N.U. sul Crimine Organizzato, Riferimento per Eurojust n. 4991/2008, 15/12/2008.
PN15  Decreto di fermo del Pubblico Ministero a carico di Caputo Carmine + 10, Proc. n. 21944/2009, 27/1/11.
PN16  Decreto di fermo del Pubblico Ministero a carico di Caputo Carmine + 10, Decreto di Sequestro Preventivo, Proc. n. 21944/2009 R.G. notizie di reato, 4/3/11.

PN17 Richiesta di applicazione di misura cautelare personale a carico di Aieta Antonio + 102, 7982/05 R.G. notizie di reato, 19/12/11.

*Tribunale di Napoli (Naples Tribunal)*

TN1 Ufficio del G.i.p, Decreto di applicazione della misura della sorveglianza speciale e di sequestro dei beni a carico di Zaza Michele + 6, 153/83 R.G. notizie di reato, 10/1/1985.

TN2 Ufficio del G.i.p, Ordinanza di custodia cautelare in carcere nei confronti di Agizza Antonio + 100, N.9086/R/92 RGPM notizie di reato, 19/9/1994.

TN3 Ufficio del G.i.p, Ordinanza custodia cautelare in carcere contro Abbate Antonio + 142, N.3615/R/93Reg.PM, N. 4458/95 A Reg. GIP, 27/7/95.

TN4 Ufficio del G.i.p, Ordinanza custodia cautelare in carcere nei confronti di Baldascino Antonio + 85, Reg. N. 2667/96. A Reg. GIP.N. 291/96, n. 3615/R/93, 11/10/1996.

TN5 Ufficio del G.i.p, Ordinanza custodia cautelare in carcere contro Massimo Alfiero + 42, 7141r96 R.G. notizie di reato, 7/6/2002.

TN6 Ufficio del G.i.p, Ordinanza di custodia cautelare in carcere contro Caldarelli Raffaele + 6, N. 2504/97 RGPM, 1/7/2002.

TN7 Ufficio del G.i.p, Ordinanza di applicazione di custodia cautelare nei confronti di Alteri Roberto + altri, N. 3020/2002 Pm, 2002.

TN8 Ufficio del G.i.p, Ordinanza di custodia cautelare in carcere e di parziale rigetto nei confronti di Addeo Giuseppe Salvatore + 39, N. 5709/97 R.G. notizie di reato, 14/3/2003.

TN9 Ufficio del G.i.p, Ordinanza di applicazione e di parziale rigetto di misure coercitive personali e reali nei confronti di Divano Luciano + 23, Reg. PM. 4743/02 RG GIP N. 46/03 R.O.C.C. 24/1/2003.

TN10 Ufficio del G.i.p, Ordinanza di custodia cautelare in carcere nei confronti di Alfonso Annunziata + 32, N. 81633/01 RGPM, 30/6/2003.

TN11 Ufficio del G.i.p, Ordinanza di applicazione e di parziale rigetto di misure coercitive personali nei confronti di Licciardi Vincenzo + 96, Proc. n. 57523/00 RGNR, 5/7/2004.

TN12 Ufficio del G.i.p, Ordinanza in materia di misure cautelari personali a carico di Alfano Emilio + 42, N. 64007/04 RGPM, 2/3/2006.

TN13 Sentenza nei confronti di Albano Giovanni + 19, N. RG. 27448/04+33891/04 notizie di reato, 27/10/2006.

TN14 Ufficio del G.i.p, Ordinanza di custodia cautelare in carcere e di rigetto di misura cautelare contro Acosta Perez Roberto Arturo + 112, N. 52594/2002 RGNR, 16/11/2006 ("Tiro Grosso" operation).

TN15 Sentenza nei confronti di Licciardi Vincenzo + 49, NRG 57523/00, notizie di reato 48380/04, 30/10/2007.

TN16 Il Giudice per le indagini preliminari, Procedimento a carico di Alfiero Luigi + 60, N. 33360/03 RGNR, 28/3/2007.

TN17 Sentenza nei confronti di Alfano Emilio + 38, N. 81633/01 R.G. notizie di reato, 15/10/2007.

TN18 Sentenza nei confronti di La Torre Augusto + 4, N. Reg Sent. 426/08, 18/2/2008.

TN19 Sentenza nei confronti di Abbatiello Paolo + 36, N. 11931/06 RGNR, 21/10/2009

TN20 Sezione del giudice delle indagini preliminari, Procedimento penale nei confronti di Affinito Ciro + 56, n. 31751/04 RGNR, 29/6/2010.

TN21 Sentenza contro Amato Raffaele + 51, n. 50426/09 RGPM, 20/5/2010.

TN22  Sentenza nei confronti di Abete Mariano + 6, N. 10585/10 + 20702/10 RGNR, 22/10/2010.
TN23  Ufficio dei Giudici per le Indagini preliminari, Procedimento penale n. 21944/200 a carico di Anna Albino + 83, 9/2/11.
TN24  Ufficio dei Giudici per le Indagini preliminari, Procedimento penale n. 8730/06 R.G.N.R., nei confronti di Baccante Vincenzo + 23, Nel proc. n. 8730/06 RGNR, 11/1/2012.
TN25  Ufficio del G.i.p, Ordinanza di applicazione di misure cautelari personali e contestuale decreto di sequestro preventivo contro Luciano Mazzarella + 66, Nr 36019/10 RG,Noti, 7/1/14.

*Corte d'Assise di Napoli (Assize Court of Naples)*
CAN1  Sentenza nei confronti di Bocchetti Gaetano + 32, N.43/01 del Reg Sent, 19/5/2003.
CAN2  Sentenza nei confronti di Raffaele Stolder + 2, Sezione II, 19/5/1997.

*Corte d'Appello di Napoli (Court of Appeal, Naples)*
CApN1  Decreto n. 21/81 su Zaza Michele, nato Procida (NA) 10/4/1945 in atto detenuto in Francia, 15/12/92 (sezione Misure di Prevenzione).

*Tribunale di Santa Maria Capua Vetere (Santa Maria Capua Vetere Tribunal)*
TSMCV1  Sentenza nei confronti di Augusto La Torre + 23, RG 286, 6–7/5/94.

*Corte d'Assise di Santa Maria Capua Vetere (Assize Court of Santa Maria)*
CASMCV1  Sentenza nei confronti di Abbate Antonio ed altri, 9/98, 1998.
CASMCV2  Sentenza nei confronti di Giuseppe Andreoli + 32, RG 10/99, 1/3/2000.
CASMCV3  Sentenza nei confronti di Santoro Mario + 3, RG 7/98, 5/1/2001.
CASMCV4  Sentenza nei confronti di Nunzio De Falco, RG 3/01, 23/1/2003.
CASMCV5  Sentenza nei confronti di Barbato Angelo + 11, 1/10/2010.

*Tribunale di Nocera Inferiore (Nocera Inferiore Tribunal)*
TNI1  Sentenza emessa nei confronti di Annunziata Alfonso per i reati di traffico internazionale di stupefacenti, R.G. 288/2005, 28/5/2009.

*Tribunale di Torre Annunziata (Torre Annunziata Tribunal)*
TTA1  Sentenza nei confronti di Casillo Aniello + 3, 81633/01 RGNR, 28/1/2010.

*Tribunale di Palermo (Palermo Tribunal)*
TP1  Mandato di Cattura nei confronti di Giovanni Abbate + 365, N. 2289/82 Reg Gen. Uff. Istruz. 29/9/1984.

*Tribunale di L'Aquila (Aquila Tribunal)*
TA1  Ufficio del G.i.p, Ordinanza a carico di Baldassarre Nazzareno + 83, N. 657/2012 RGNR, 20/1/14.

*Squadra Mobile, Questura di Napoli (Flying Squad, Naples)*
QN1  Informativa di Reato nei confronti di Licciardi Maria + 2, n. 02988/S M S 1, 17/1/1998.

QN2   Indagine relativa alla faida Mazzarella-Alleanza di Secondigliano, n. 5290, Prot/U=98, Napoli, vols. 1–2, 1/7/98.

QN3   Indagini relative alle Organizzazione Camorristiche denominate clan Mazzarella, clan Formicola, clan Rinaldi, clan Reale, clan Altamura, gruppo D'Amico, operanti nella zona di Giovanni a Teduccio della città di Napoli, Prot. 2615 U./2000, vols. 1–2, 7/3/2000.

QN4   Informativa di Reato a carico di Aiello Carmela + 64, nr. 02002/Sq. Mob. Sez.3 a, Prot. n. 4734/U/02, vols. 1–3, 22/5/2002.

QN5   Comunicazione notizia di reato ex art. 347 c.p.p. redatta a carico di Annunziata Alfonso + 22, Nr._____/03/U/QU.NA/S.M./1ª C.O./1°, 8/1/2003.

QN6   Procedimento penale n. 66184/04, Indagini relative all'esistenza di un'Associazione di Stampo Camorristico facente capo a Mazzarella Gennaro, Prot. n. 9516/U/06, 27/9/2006.

QN7   Proc. n. 19281/06 RGNR, "Operazione Almeria," nei confronti di Di Giorgio Vincenzo + 23, 28/4/2006.

QN8   Scheda 1, Capi d'imputazione e fonte di prove, Raffaele Caldarelli, 2006.

QN9   Indagini sull'associazione a delinquere di stampo camorristico denominata gli Scissionisti, operativa in Napoli quartiere Scampia e nei comuni di Melito, Mugnano e Casavatore, Prot. n. U/3/2007, PP. 19964/05/21, 2007.

QN10   Verbale di Esecuzione del fermo del PM effettuato nei confronti di Ottaviano Paolo e contestuale verbale di arresto in flagranza di reato per i reati di cui all'art. 461 bis, 648, 747, c.p nei confronti di Rinaldi Francesco + 1, del 21/10/2008.

QN11   Fermo a carico di Mattera Luca + 2, del 13/12/2008.

QN12   Scheda di Vincenzo Licciardi, Ministero degli Interni (2011) (http://www.interno.it/mininterno/export/sites/default/it/assets/files/15/0915_scheda_Licciardi.doc, accessed via Internet 1/12/12)

QN13   Situazione della criminalità organizzata nella provincia di Napoli, Overview Camorra Clans 2011, Napoli (e-mail correspondance, 10/6/2011).

QN14   Dati Aggiornati al mese di Dicembre 2013. Case-study clans (e-mail correspondence, 9/6/2014).

QN15   Mappa criminalità, Napoli (e-mail correspondence, 9/6/2014).

*Squadra Mobile, Questura di Caserta (Flying Squad, Caserta)*

QC1   Polizia di Stato, Centro Interprovinciale, Squadra Mobile, Criminalpol Campania-Molise, Oggetto: "Operazione Goya," Prot. n. 123/I/94/Criminalpol, 18/2/1995.

*Squadra Narcotici, Questura di Roma (Drug Squad, Rome)*

QR1   Rapporto Giudiziario di denuncia a carico di Bono Giuseppe + 159 ritenuti responsabili di associazione per delinquere di tipo Mafioso e finalizzata al traffico delle sostanze stupefacenti, vols. 1–2, del 7/2/1983, Roma.

*Arma dei Carabinieri, Naples (Italian Military Police, Naples)*

AC1   Legione Carabinieri di Napoli, Gruppo Napoli I, Gruppo Napoli II; *Rapporto sul fenomeno della Camorra*, Dicembre 1988, vols. 1–2 (AC1–1 + AC1–2).

AC2   Regione Carabinieri Campania, Comando Provinciale di Caserta, Nucleo Operativo, n. 471/53–1998 di prot. Informativa circa la denuncia a carico di La Torre Augusto + 73, del 18/9/2000.

AC3 Carabinieri di Napoli, Oggetto: Insediamento dell'Organizzazione denominata clan Rinaldi nella città d'Amburgo, Esiti della Cooperazione di Polizia Italo-Tedesca, 2010.
AC4 Mappatura della Criminalità Organizzata, Elenco dei clan nel Capoluogo, 2013.

*Guardia di Finanza / Nucleo Polizia Tributaria di Napoli (Finance Police, Naples)*

GF1 Overview of the Zaza clan, 1985.
GF2 Procedimento penale n. 43915/R/02 D.D.A. - Operazione "L'ORO DI NAPOLI," Comunicazione di notizia di reato ex art. 347 c.p.p. redatta nei confronti di Missi Giuseppe + 44, Prot. n. /GICO/4^/4970 C.O, 29–30/11/2004.
GF3 Comunicazione notizia di reato a carico di Aristo Federico + 13, Procedimento Penale n. 1672/06, 2006.
GF4 Informativa riepilogativa dell'attività di Indagine condotta sul clan Caldarelli, Prot. GICO/2, Proc. P 8536/06 RGNR, nei confronti di R. Caldarelli + altri 2006 (limited access).

*Verbali d'Udienza, Napoli (Statements Made in Court Naples)*

TNv1 Verbale d'udienza, 8/3/10, Messina Giovanni, proced. 44/10 RG.
TNv2 Verbale d'udienza, 9/3/10, Messina Giovanni, proced. 44/10 RG.
TNv3 Interrogatorio, Dario Tedesco, 9/3/10, Rogatoria.
TNv4 Interrogatorio, RI, 9/3/10, Rogatoria.

*State Witness Statements in Court/Trial Transcripts*

CSv   Carmine Schiavone (Casalesi clan)
GGv   Gaetano Guida (Licciardi clan)
GQv   Giuseppe Quadrano (De Falco clan)
AdTv  Alberto Di Tella (De Falco clan)
LGv   Luigi Giuliano (Giuliano clan)
SGv   Salvatore Giuliano (Giuliano clan)
CGv   Carmine Giuliano (Giuliano clan)
RGv   Raffaele Giuliano (Giuliano clan)
CAv   Carmine Alfieri (Aflieri clan)
MTv   Massimo Tipaldi (Nuvoletta clan)
GLv   Gennaro Lauro (Giuliano clan, then Mazzarella clan)
SLv   Sergio Lettieri (Caldarelli clan)
SIv   Salvatore Izzo (Nuvoletta clan)
FCv   Francesco Capuozzo (Vatiero-Cardarelli clan)
AFv   Antonio Formicola (Formicola clan)
PAv   Pasquale Avagliano (Giuliano clan)
FAv   Francesco Amen (Rinaldi clan)
DVv   Domenico Verde (Polverino clan)
SCv   Salvatore Conte (La Torre clan)
GMv   Giuseppe Missi (Misso clan)
MMv   Michelangelo Mazza (Misso clan)

*Direzione Nazionale Antimafia, Roma (National Antimafia Directorate, Rome)*

DNA1 Relazione Annuale sulle attività svolte dal Procuratore Nazionale Antimafia e dalla Direzione Nazionale Antimafia nonché sulle dinamiche e strategie

della criminalità organizzata di tipo mafioso nel periodo 1 luglio 2009–30 giugno 2010.
DNA2 Relazione Annuale sulle attività svolte dal Procuratore Nazionale Antimafia e dalla Direzione Nazionale Antimafia nonché sulle dinamiche e strategie della Criminalità Organizzata di tipo mafioso nel periodo 1 luglio 2010–30 giugno 2011.
DNA3 Relazione Annuale sulle attività svolte dal Procuratore nazionale Antimafia e dalla Direzione Nazionale Antimafia nonché sulle dinamiche e strategie della criminalità organizzata di tipo mafioso nel periodo 1 luglio 2011–30 giugno 2012.
DNA4 Relazione Annuale sulle attività svolte dal Procuratore Nazionale Antimafia e dalla Direzione Nazionale Antimafia nonché sulle dinamiche e strategie della criminalità organizzata di tipo mafioso nel periodo 1 luglio 2012–30 giugno 2013.

*Direzione Investigativa Antimafia, Roma (Antimafia Investigation Directorate Rome)*

DIA1 Informativa riassuntiva complessa circa le indagini effettuate sull'organizzazione camorrista denominata dei "Casalesi" nell'ambito del procedimento penale 3615/R/93; 125/NA/H3/19/6^ di prot.828, 4/11/1994.
DIAa Audizione del Direttore davanti al Parlamento Europeo, "Commissione speciale sul Crimine Organizzato, la Corruzione e il Riciclaggio di Denaro" (CRIM), 19 Giugno 2012.

*Divisione Gabinetto (General Affairs Office)*

DIAb III Reparto, Nota "La Collaborazione tra le forze di polizia italiane e tedesche nella lotta alla 'Ndrangheta e alle altre Organizzazioni Criminali."
DIAc Relazione del Ministero dell'Interno al Parlamento sull'attività svolta e sui i risultati conseguiti dalla Direzione Investigative Antimafia, 2 semestre 2014, Roma http://www1.interno.gov.it/dip_ps/dia/semestrali/sem/2014/2sem2014.pdf.

*Ministero dell' Interno (Ministry of the Interior), Dipartimento della Pubblica Sicurezza*

MI1 Rapporto Annuale sul Fenomeno della Criminalità Organizzata per il 1993 (published April 1994).
MI2 Rapporto Annuale sul Fenomeno della Criminalità Organizzata per il 1994 (published April 1995).
MI3 Commissione Rogatoria Internazionale nr 50/90 del 5/11/1991 emessa dal Sig. Sampieri, Giudice Istruttore di Marsiglia/Francia nei confronti di Giuseppe Liguori ed altri accusati di violazione alla legislazione sugli stupefacenti ed altro, 10/12/1991.
MI4 Indagini su una vasta associazione criminale, di natura mafiosa, operante sul territorio nazionale con collegamenti all'estero ed in particolare con il Nord e Sud America, 30/10/1982.
MI5 Rapporto sulla Criminalità in Italia. Analisi, prevenzione, contrasto, 2007, L'andamento generale della criminalità (Abstract), http://www1.interno.gov.it/mininterno/export/sites/default/it/assets/files/14/0902_ABSTRACT_rapporto_sicurezza_2006.pdf (accessed 5/11/13).
MI5-1 Full report. Rapporto sulla Criminalità in Italia. Analisi, prevenzione, contrasto, 2007, L'andamento generale della criminalità (full report) http://www1.interno.gov.it/mininterno/export/sites/default/it/assets/files/14/0900_rapporto_criminalita.pdf (accessed 5/11/13).

MI6 Statistiche Relative all'elenco aggiornato dei cittadini italiani residenti all'estero per il 2007 (AIRE). http://infoaire.interno.it/stat_note.htm (accessed 2/11/14).

*Ministero dello Sviluppo Economico (Ministry for Economic Development), Dipartimento per l'Impresa e l'Internazionalizzazione, Direzione Generale per la Lotta alla Contraffazione*

MSE1 La contraffazione come attività gestita dalla criminalità organizzata transazionale, il caso Italia, 2012, UNCRI. http://www.unicri.it/in_focus/files/contraf_unicr2.pdf (accessed 4/5/13).

MSE2 La contraffazione in cifre: la lotta alla contraffazione in Italia nel quadriennio 2008–2011, Roma Luglio 2012. http://www.uibm.gov.it/iperico/Report_Iperico_2012/Iperico2012.pdf (accessed 20/9/12).

*Presidenza del Consiglio dei Ministri (Cabinet office)*

PCM La Relazione Annuale al Parlamento su droga e dipendenze 2015: un percorso condiviso con istituzioni e società civile. http://www.politicheantidroga.it/attivita/pubblicazioni/relazioni-al-parlamento/relazione-annuale-2015/presentazione.aspx (accessed 21/9/15).

*Camera dei Deputati (Italian Parliament) Commissione Parlamentare d'Inchiesta sul Fenomeno della Mafia e sulle altre Associazioni Criminali Simili*

CD1 Relazione sulla Camorra (Relatore, Luciano Violante), 21/12/1993.
CD2 Relazione Annuale sulla 'Ndrangheta (Relatore, Francesco Forgione), 19/2/2008.
CD3 Clans camorristi in Campania, doc n. 2642, Commissione Antimafia, 9/3/1994

*Istituto Nazionale di Statistica (National Institute for Statistics)*

ISTAT Noi Italia, 100 statistiche per capire il Paese in cui viviamo, 2012, ISTAT, Roma. http://noi-italia2012.istat.it/ (accessed 14/7/13).

## France

*Parquet de Marseille, Juridiction Inter-régionale Spécialisée (Interregional Prosecution Team, Prosecution Service, Marseille)*

PM1 Fiche de suivi d'affaire, 2/12/9.

*Tribunal de Grande Instance de Marseille (Marseille Tribunal)*

TGIM1 Réquisitoire de Renvoi devant le Tribunal Correctionnel et de non lieu Partiel contre Sanoukian Marius + 50, 11/3/1991.
TGIM2 Appel des Douanes n. 7733, 18/6/1991.
THIM3 Appel du Parquet, n. 7733, 19/6/1991.

*Cour d'Appel d'Aix-en-Provence (Court of Appeal, Aix-en-Provence)*

CAAP1 Réquisitoire de Renvoi devant le Tribunal Correctionnel, contre MB +1, Parquet: 04/1303556, 19/5/2005.
CAAP2 Réquisitoire Définitif de non-lieu Partiel, de Réqualification, de Disjunction, de mise en accusation devant la cour d'assises et de renvoi devant le tribunal correctionel contre Romera Jean + 10, Parquet: 03/130259.2006.

250  WORKS CITED

CAAP3　Réquisitoire de Réqualification, de non-lieu Partiel, de renvoi partiel devant le tribunal correctionnel, de maintien de détention, de maintien sous contrôle judiciaire, de poursuite de l'information contre Chris de Velde + 17, Parquet: 07/000024, 9/6/2009 et 5/11/2009.

CAAP4　Réquisitoire Définitif de non-lieu Partiel, de Requalification, et de Renvoi devant le Tribunal Correctionnel, contre Deligey Philippe + 8, Parquet 08/14600, 19/11/10.

CAAP4–1　Document 1654 of case file: Colonna Francese del Gruppo Tedesco.
CAAP4–2　Interrogation, FC, 13/1/2009.
CAAP4–3　Interrogation, PD, 16/4/2009.
CAAP4–4　Interrogation, AT, 9/3/2009.
CAAP4–5　Interrogation, AT, 17/4/2009.
CAAP4–6　Interrogation, AT, 19/5/2009.

CAAP5　Réquisitoire Définitif de non-lieu Partiel, de Requalification, et de Renvoi devant le Tribunal Correctionnel, contre Giuseppe D'Angeli + 5, Parquet 08/000050, 9/7/12 (GOMORRAH).

*Ministère de l'Intérieur (Ministry of the Interior)*

MIF　Direction Générale de la Police Nationale, Direction Centrale de la Police Judiciaire (SIRASCO), "Impact des mafias italiennes en France," 27 juin 2011.

*Assemblée Nationale (French National Parliament)*

AN1　Rapport n. 3251 de la Commission d'Enquête sur les moyens de lutter contre les tentatives de pénétration de la mafia en France; Président: M. F. D'Aubert; B. M. Gallet (rapporteur), 27/1/1993.

*Union des Fabricants Français (French Union of Manufacturers)*

UniFab1　Rapport contrefaçon et criminalitéorganisée, 3 édition, 2005, http://www.google.co.uk/url?sa=t&rct=j&q=&esrc=s&source=web&cd=1&ved=0ahU KEwjP_J--rKXLAhUL83IKHcCuCHcQFggfMAA&url=http%3A%2F%2F www.iccwbo.org%2FData%2FDocuments%2FBascap%2FWhy-enforce%2 FLinks-to-organized-crime%2FRapport-Contrefacon-Criminalite- Organisee%2F&usg=AFQjCNGVB9pEXTqca9G-1f2SEbi6N5J4OA& sig2=kYGDAo2vHr2GybG-_EPHmw (accessed 6/12/2012).

UniFab2　Rapport sur l'impact de la contrefaçon vu par les entreprises en France, Avril 2010, Paris. http://www.ladocumentationfrancaise.fr/var/storage/ rapports-publics/104000186/0000.pdf (accessed 6/12/2012).

*Tribunal de Première Instance, Monaco (Tribunal of Monaco)*

PMTPI1　Ordonnance de Requalificatoin et de Renvoi devant le Tribunal Correctionnel contre Tufano Antonio, Dossier JI B4/08, 9/6/2008.

**Germany**

*Bundeskriminalamt (BKA) (Federal Criminal Police Office)*

BKA-NS　Organised crime—National Situation Reports, 2000–2013. http://www.bka. de/nn_195184/EN/Publications/AnnualReportsAndSituationAssessments/ OrganisedCrime/organisedCrime__node.html?__nnn=true (accessed 2010–2015).

BKAa　Polizeiliche Kriminalstatistik. Berichtszeitraum: 1987–1990. Total number of Italian suspects including gender and age. Retrieved 13/12/2013.

## United Kingdom

*Police*

NCIS  National Criminal Intelligence Service 2000. "The National Intelligence Model." http://www.intelligenceanalysis.net/National%20Intelligence%20 Model.pdf (accessed 15/9/15).

SOCA  Serious and Organised Crime Agency, "The UK Threat Assessment on Organised Crime, 2009–10."http://www.twolittlegirls.org/ufiles/2009-10_UKTA_NPM.pdf (accessed 6/5/2012).

*Home Office, London*

HO1  User Guide to Home Office Crime Statistics. https://www.gov.uk/government/uploads/system/uploads/attachment_data/file/116226/user-guide-crime-statistics.pdf (accessed 1/10/14).

HO2  Richard Ridley, Powerpoint presentation, Thames Valley Police, Meeting on Organised Crime, 27 September 2013.

*Intellectual Property Crime Group, Newport*

IP1  IP Crime Annual Report, 2010–2011. Newport: IP office. http://www.ipo.gov.uk/ipcreport10.pdf (accessed 4/5/2013).

IP2  IP Crime Annual Report, 2012–2013. Newport: IP office. http://www.ipo.gov.uk/ipcreport12.pdf (accessed 4/5/2013).

IP3  Intellectual Property Office website, http://www.ipo.gov.uk/ipenforce/ipenforce-crime.htm (accessed 23/6/11).

IP4  IP Crime Annual Report, 2013–2014. Newport: IP office. https://www.gov.uk/government/uploads/system/uploads/attachment_data/file/374283/ipcreport13.PDF (accessed 1/12/14).

*Northern Ireland Assembly*

NIA  "Public Accounts Committee Official Report" (Hansard). "Memorandum to the Committee of Public Accounts from the Comptroller and Auditor General for Northern Ireland: Combating Organised Crime." 22 April 2010. http://archive.niassembly.gov.uk/record/committees2009/PAC/100422_MemorandumonCombattingOrganisedCrime.htm (accessed 7 September 2013).

*High Court of Justice, Queen's Bench Division, Divisional Court, London*

HCJ1  Lord Justice Laws, Mr. Justice Tomlinson. Case between Raffaele Caldarelli and Court of Naples, 12/7/2007.

HCJ2  Case Nos: CO/9716/2008; CO/8464/2008; CO/8965/2008. Before Lord Justin Toulson and Mr. Justice Forbers. Between The Queen on the Application of Raffaele Caldarelli and City of Westminister Magistrates Court, the Court of Naples, 27/1/2009.

## Spain

*Gobierno de Espana, Ministerio Del Interior (Ministry of the Interior)*

S1  Balance 2010 de la lucha contra el crimen organizado y principales ejes de la Estrategia española 2011–2014. http://www.interior.gob.es/documents/10180/1209187/Balance+2010+de+la+lucha+contra+el+crimen+organizado+y+principales+ejes+de+la+Estrategia+espa%C3%B1ola+2011-2014.pdf/a89955b0-e29e-4609-a166-78f04a469498 (accessed 15/11/15).

S2   El Crimen Organizado en Espana, Comparecencias lucha contra, 2 November 2010. http://www.lamoncloa.gob.es/Documents/7feb-6f0c-bal_crimen_organizado_noviembre_presentacion.pdf (accessed 8/12/15).

## The Netherlands

*Politie (Police)*

DP1   "National Threat Assessment, 2008." Organized Crime, 2009. Zoetermeer: IPOL dept.

DP2   De 'Ndrangheta in Nederland Aard, criminele activiteiten en qwerkwijze op Nederlandse bodem, 2011. KLPD: Driebergen.

*Klynveld Peat Marwick Goerdeler (accounting firm)*

KPMG   Project Sun: A Study of the Illicit Cigarette Market in the European Union, 2013. http://www.kpmg.co.uk/email/06Jun14/OM014549A/PageTurner/index.html#1 (accessed 1/9/14).

*Organised Crime Monitor*

OCM1   "Organised Crime in the Netherlands." Third Report of the Organised Crime Monitor, 2005 (summary). https://english.wodc.nl/images/ob252_summary_tcm45-81965.pdf (accessed 25/5/2013).

## Europe

*European Commission*

EC1   Summary of Community Customs Activities on Counterfeit and Piracy, Results at European Borders—2006. http://ec.europa.eu/taxation_customs/resources/documents/customs/customs_controls/counterfeit_piracy/statistics/counterf_com m_2006_en.pdf (accessed 23/5/12).

EC2   A Report on the Global Illicit Drug Markets, 1998–2007. Edited by Peter Reuter and Franz Trautmann. Brussels, 2009. http://ec.europa.eu/justice/anti-drugs/files/report-drug-markets-short_en.pdf (accessed 15/7/13).

EC3   Report on EU Customs Enforcement of Intellectual Property Rights, Results at EU Borders—2010. http://ec.europa.eu/polska/news/documents/120206_statistics_2010.pdf (accessed 23/5/12).

*European Parliament*

EP1   "International Organized Crime in the European Union." Note, DG for Internal Policies, Policy Department, Justice, Freedom, and Security. Brussels, 2011. http://www.europarl.europa.eu/document/activities/cont/201206/20120627ATT47775/20120627ATT47775EN.pdf (accessed 23/5/12).

*Europol*

Europol1   "EU Organised Crime Threat Assessment, 2011." https://www.europol.europa.eu/sites/default/files/publications/octa_2011_1.pdf (accessed 5/4/12).

Europol2   "Threat Assessment, Italian Organised Crime, June 2013." https://www.europol.europa.eu/sites/default/files/publications/italian_organised_crime_threat_assessment_0.pdf (accessed 7/8/2013).

*European Court of Human Rights*

ECHR1   Enea vs. Italy, 74912/01, 17/9/2009. http://hudoc.echr.coe.int/sites/eng/pages/search.aspx?i=001-94072#{%22itemid%22:[%22001-94072%22]} (accessed 3/4/14).

*European Monitoring Centre for Drugs and Drug Addiction*

EMCDDA1   "Cocaine: a European Union Perspective in the Global Context." EMCDDA, Europol, Lux: EU publications, April 2010. http://www.emcdda.europa.eu/publications/joint-publications/cocaine (accessed 15/1/11).

EMCDDA2   "The State of the Drugs Problem in Europe, 2010." Lux: EU publications. http://www.emcdda.europa.eu/publications/annual-report/2010 (accessed 14/5/12).

EMCDDA3   Country Profile—Spain. http://www.emcdda.europa.eu/html.cfm/index5174EN.html?pluginMethod=eldd.countryprofiles&country=ES (accessed 13/11/15).

## Switzerland

*Istituto Federale della Proprietà Intellettuale (Swiss Federal Institute of Intellectual Property)*

ISFPI   Judicial Information. https://www.ige.ch/it/info-giuridiche/settori-giuridici/contraffazione-e-pirateria.html (accessed 20/9/12).

## International

*International Monetary Fund*

IMF   "Mutual Evaluation Report: Anti-Money Laundering and Combatting the Financing of Terrorism. Germany, 19/2/2010. http://www.fatf-gafi.org/media/fatf/documents/reports/mer/MER%20Germany%20full.pdf (accessed 24/5/12).

IMF2   "Spain: Report on the Observance of Standards and Codes—FATF Recommendations for Anti-Money Laundering and Combating the Financing of Terrorism." Country Report No. 07/70. pp 21. February 2007. https://www.imf.org/external/pubs/ft/scr/2007/cr0770.pdf (accessed 1/12/15).

*United Nations Office for Drugs and Crime*

UNODC1   *World Drug Report 2010.* http://www.unodc.org/documents/wdr/WDR_2010/World_Drug_Report_2010_lo-res.pdf (accessed 2/4/11).

UNODC2   "Globalization of Crime: A Transnational Organized Crime Threat Assessment, 2010." Vienna. www.unodc.org/documents/data-and-analysis/tocta/TOCTA_Report_2010_low_res.pdf (accessed 10/5/11).

UNODC3   "The Transatlantic Cocaine Market, 2011." Research paper. https://www.unodc.org/documents/data-and-analysis/Studies/Transatlantic_cocaine_market.pdf (14/5/12).

UNODC4   *World Drug Report 2012.* http://www.unodc.org/documents/data-and-analysis/WDR2012/WDR_2012_web_small.pdf (15/7/13).

UNODC5   *World Drug Report 2005*, vol. 1, *Analysis.* https://www.unodc.org/pdf/WDR_2005/volume_1_web.pdf (13/11/15).

*United Nations Interregional Crime and Justice Research*

UNCRI   Contraffazione: Una diffusione globale, una minaccia globale, lancio del rapporto delle Nazioni Unite sui legami tra contraffazione e crimine organizzato, 6 December 2007.

*Interviews*

ACa—Anna Carrino, former member of Bidognetti clan, Rome, 30/10/2012.
ACb—Alessandro Colletti, Independent researcher, 2012–2015, discussions.
BKA1—Bundeskriminalamt Wiesbaden, police officer, December 2010, email correspondence.
BKA2—RP Karlsruhe, Landespolizeidirektion, DS/OK, German police officer, February 2011, email correspondence.
BPO—High-ranking police officer, ACPO, London, 20/5/2012.
BRIF— Brigade de Recherche et d'Investigations Financière du SRPJ de Toulouse, France, 13/8/2012, e-mail correspondence.
CD—Charles Duchaine, Judge, Juridiction Interrégionale Spécialisée (JIRS), Marseille, 12/8/2011.
EGP—Giap Parini, University of Calabria, 25/6/2011.
FB—Filippo Beatrice, National Antimafia Directorate (2009–2014), Naples, 21/2/2011.
FR—Franco Roberti, Head Prosecutor of Salerno (2010–2013) and National Antimafia Prosecutor (DNA, Rome) (2013–), Naples, 27/11/2010.
GB—Giuseppe Borrelli, Deputy Prosecutor (DDA) Catanzaro (2009–2014), 15/11/2012, e-mail correspondence.
GM—Giovanni Messina, former member of De Sena clan, Naples, 25/10/2011.
GP—Gennaro Panzuto, former member of Piccirillo clan, Naples, 4/4/2011.
GramP—Grampian police officers, 26/5/2010, telephone interview.
IJ—Italian judge working in Europe, 2/6/2010, discussions.
IPO—Italian police liaison officer working in Europe, 10/5/2010, discussions.
IS—Isaia Sales, Professor of Criminology, Naples, 26/3/2012.
JM—Jon Murphy, Association of Chief Police Officers, Lead on Organised Crime (2008–2010) London, 9/11/2009.
LB—Luciano Brancaccio, University of Naples, 2013–2015, discussions.
LP—International Office, Lancashire Police, 13/4/2011, e-mail correspondence.
LS—Luca Semeraro, Judge, Perugia, 24/9/2012, e-mail correspondence.
MdG—Marco Del Gaudio, Antimafia Prosecutor (DDA), Naples, 15/11/2013;
MS—Michele Siciliano, former member of La Torre clan, Rome, 20/12/2011.
MV—Maurizio Vallone, Director of the Naples Antimafia Investigation Directorate (DIA) (2009–2013), Naples, 21/12/2011.
NB—Nicolas Bessone, Procruteur Adjoint, Toulon, France, 4/8/2011.
PF—Pierpaolo Filippelli, Antimafia Prosecutor (DDA), Naples, 19/4/2011.
PM—Paolo Mancuso, Head Prosecutor of Torre Annunizata, Naples, 12/4/2011.
PZ—Pasquale Zafino, Polizia di Stato, Squadra Mobile, Naples, 4/11/2011.
RB—British Banker's Association London, 18/5/2012.
RC—Raffaele Cionti, Italian police liaison officer, Polizia di Stato, Madrid, Spain, 22/11/2010, e-mail correspondence.
RM—Raffaele Marino, Head Prosecutor of Nola, Naples, 12/4/2011.
SG—Sliviana Giusti, Antimafia Investigation Directorate, Naples, 4/11/2011.
SM—Solange Marouchini, Judge, Paris, France, 16/12/2010.
SqM1—Squadra Mobile, e-mail correspondence, 14/12/10.
SqM2—Squadra Mobile, e-mail correspondence, 10/6/14.

TS—Tommaso Solazzo, Antimafia Investigation Directorate, European Dept, International office (2009–2013), Rome. 25/1/2012, 1/3/13, email correspondence.

VdO—Vincenzo D'Onofrio, Antimafia Prosecutor (DDA), Naples, 23/2/2011.

*Other Oral Contributions*

AA   Alfonso Annunziata, Processo ad Antonio Gava ed altri (Carmine Alfieri + 101), Radio Radicale.it,15/11/2000, http://www.radioradicale.it/scheda/336355/processo-ad-antonio-gava-ed-altri-carmine-alfieri-101 (accessed 8/7/13).

ACap   "Le Mafie al Nord: Incontro con Anna Canepa," 15/5/2015, Radio Radicale.it, http://www.radioradicale.it/scheda/442161/le-mafie-al-nord-incontro-con-Anna-Canepa.

Coll   Alessandro Colletti, "Mafia and Welfare in Campania," Conference paper, "Transnational Organized Crime: Italian Connections," The American University of Rome, Rome, November 24, 2012.

MdP   Michele del Prete, "The Neapolitan Camorra," Presentation at workshop on "Italian Mafias in the UK" (organized by the University of Bath), 18/5/2012, London.

Trib   Information provided on sentence of Angeli court case from anonymous source, Marseille, April 2014.

## SECONDARY SOURCES CITED

Abadinsky, Howard. 1990. *Organized Crime*. Chicago: Prentice Press.

Allum, Felia. 2000, *The Neapolitan Camorra: Crime and Politics in Post-War Naples (1950-1992)*, A thesis submitted for the degree of Doctor in Philosophy, Government Department, University of Brunel (http://bura.brunel.ac.uk/handle/2438/5085, accessed 1/12/2013).

———. 2006. *Camorristi, Businessmen and Politicians: Organized Crime in Post-War Naples*. Leeds: Maney Publishers.

———. 2012. "Italian Organized Crime in the UK." *Policing* 6 (4): 354–359.

———. 2013. "Italian Organized Crime in the UK: Continuing the Debate." *Policing* 7 (2): 227–232.

———. 2014. "Understanding Criminal Mobility: The Case of the Neapolitan Camorra." *Journal of Modern Italian Studies* 19(5): 583–602.

Arlacchi, Pino. 1988. *Mafia Business: The Mafia Ethic and the Spirit of Capitalism*. Oxford: Oxford University Press.

Armao, Fabio, 2003, "Why Is Organised Crime so Difficult to Define?" In *Organised Crime and the Challenge to Democracy*, edited by Felia Allum and Renate Siebert. London: Routledge.

Arsovska, Jana. 2015. *Decoding Albanian Organized Crime: Culture, Politics, and Globalization*. Berkeley: University of California Press.

Arsovska, Jana, and Felia Allum. 2014. "Introduction: Women and Transnational Organized Crime." *Trends in Organized Crime* 17 (1–2): 1–15.

Aubry, Gilles. 2009. "Organisations criminelles et structures répressives: Panorama français." *Cahiers de la Sécurité: Les Organisations Criminelles* (January–March): 25–40.

Bauman, Zygmunt. 2000. *Liquid Modernity*. Cambridge: Polity Press.

Beatrice, Filippo. 2009. "La Camorra Imprenditrice." In (a cura di) edited by Gabriella Gribauldi, *Traffici criminali. Camorra, mafie e reti internazionali dell'illegalità* Torino: Bollati Boringheri.

———. 2013. *Beyond the Statistics*. ECPR Standing Group on Organised Crime Newsletter, January 2013. http://www.academia.edu/2530405/ECPR_Standing_Group_on_Organised_Crime_Newsletter_January_2013 (accessed 5/2/2013).
Becucci, Stefano. 2004. "Old and New Actors in the Italian Drug Trade: Ethnic Succession or Functional Specialization?" *European Journal on Criminal Policy and Research* 10 (4): 257–283.
Behan, Tom. 1996. *The Camorra*. London: Routledge.
Bianchi, Dorina, and Raffaele Rio. 2013. *L'impero della 'Ndrangheta, radiografia di un' organizzazione criminale in continua espansione*. Rome: Giulio Perrone.
Bianchini, Roger Louis. 1995. *Mafia, argent et politique: Enquête sur des liaisons dangereuses dans le Midi*. Paris: Seuil.
Borgatti, Stephen Peter. 2002. *NetDraw: Graph Visualization Software*. Harvard: Analytic Technologies.
Brancaccio, Luciano. 2011a. "Magliari, imprenditori e camorristi: Il mercato del falso a Napoli." In Sciarrone, *Alleanza nell'ombra*.
———. 2011b. "Il Sommerso e l'economia da svelare, il ciclo della contrafazzione e la cultura del lavoro," presentazione all'Anteprima del festival NAPOLI, 28/5/2011.
Brancaccio, Luciano, and Vittorio Martone. 2014. "L'espansione in un'area contigua: Le mafie nel Basso Lazio." In *Mafie del nord, strategie criminali e contesti locali*, edited by Rocco Sciarrone, Rome: Donzelli.
———. 2015. "Mercati violenti e gruppi di Camorra." In *Affari di Camorra: Famiglie, imprenditori e gruppi criminali*, edited by Luciano Brancaccio and Carolina Castellano. Rome: Donzelli.
Calderoni, Francesco. 2012. "The Structure of Drug Trafficking Mafias: The 'Ndrangheta and Cocaine." *Crime, Law and Social Change* 58: 321–349.
Calvi, Fabrice. 1993. *L'Europe des parrains: La mafia à l'assaut de l'Europe*. Paris: Grasset.
Campana, Paolo. 2011. "Assessing the Movement of Criminal Groups: Some Analytical Remarks." *Global Crime* 12 (13): 207–217.
Capacchione, Rosaria. 2008. *L'Oro di Napoli*. Milano: BUR futuropassto.
Castells, Manuel. 2000a. *The Rise of the Network Society*, vol. 1, *The Rise of the Network Society*. Oxford: Blackwells.
———. 2000b. *End of Millennium*, vol. 3, *The Information Age: Economy, Society and Culture*. Oxford: Blackwells.
Ciconte, Enzo, 1992. *'Ndrangheta dall'Unità ad oggi*. Laterza: Roma-Bari.
Colombié, Thierry. 2012. *La French Connection: Les entreprises criminelles en France*. Nantes: OGC.
Dean, Geoff, Ivar Fahsing, and Peter Gottschalk. 2010. *Organized Crime: Policing Illegal Business Entrepreneurialism*. Oxford: Oxford University Press.
De Gennaro, Giacomo, and Domenico Pizzuti. 2009. *Dire Camorra oggi: Forme e metamorfosi della criminalità organizzata in Campania*. Napoli: Alfredo Guida Editore.
Di Meo, Simone. 2008. *L'impero della Camorra: Vita violenta del boss Paolo Di Lauro*. Roma: Newton Compton.
Falcone, Giovanni, and Marcelle Padovani. 1993. *Men of Honour: The Truth about the Mafia*. London: Warner.
Fijnaut, Cyrille, Franck Bovenkerk, Gerben Bruinsma, and Henk van de Bunt. 1998. *Organized Crime in the Netherlands*. The Hague: Kluwer Law International.
Forgione, Francesco. 2009. *Mafia Export: Come 'Ndrangheta, Cosa Nostra e Camorra hanno colonizzato il mondo*. Milan: Baldini Castoldi Dalai.

Gambetta, Diego. 1993. *The Sicilian Mafia: The Business of Private Protection*. Oxford: Oxford University Press.

Gay, Luigi. 1996. *L'atteggiarsi delle associazioni mafiose sulla base delle esperienze processuali acquisite: La Camorra, relazioni tenute nell'incontro* 284: "I delitti di criminalita' organizzata: Profili criminologici, sostanziali e processuali." Consiglio superiore della magistratura, Rome.

Gayraud, Jean-Francois. 2008. *Le monde des mafias: Géopolitique du crime organisé*. Paris: Odile Jacob poches.

Giddens, Anthony. 1984. *The Constitution of Society: Outline of the Theory of Structuration*. Cambridge: Polity Press.

———.1990. *The Consequence of Modernity*. Cambridge: Polity Press.

Gomez, Ramon Macia, and Salvatore Gurrieri. 2001. "Il caso di Barcellona e il contesto Spagnolo." In *Omicron, l'influenza della criminalità straniera sulla struttura degli interessi e dei comportamenti criminali: Le grandi aree metropolitane nell'Europa Mediterranea* (Barcellona, Parigi, Milano). Commissione Europea, Bruxelles. http://www.unige.ch/formcont/files/3614/3921/7104/17-Omicron.pdf.

Gómez-Céspedes, Alejandra. 2012. "Spain: A Criminal Hub." In *Corruption and Organized Crime in Europe: Illegal Partnerships*, edited by Philip Gounev and Vincenzo Ruggiero. London: Routledge.

Gounev, Philip, and Tihomir Bezlov. 2010. *Examining the Links between Organised Crime and Corruption*. Centre for the Study of Democracy. European Commission, Belgium.

Gribaudi, Gabriella. 1999. *Donne, uomini, famiglie: Napoli nel novecento*. Napoli: L'Ancora del Mediterraneo.

Ianni, Francis A. J. 1974. *Black Mafia: Ethnic Succession in Organized Crime*. New York: Simon and Schuster.

Jamieson, Alison. 2000. *The Antimafia*. London: Macmillan.

Keh, Douglas, and Graham Farrell. 1997. "Trafficking Drugs in the Global Village." *Transnational Organized Crime* 3 (2): 90–110.

Kelly, Robert. 1982. "Field Research among Deviants: A Consideration of Some Methodological Recommendations." *Deviant Behavior* 3 (3): 219–228.

Klerks, Peter. 2001. "The Network Paradigm Applied to Criminal Organisations: Theoretical Nitpicking or a Relevant Doctrine for Investigators? Recent Developments in the Netherlands." Connections, INSN. http://citeseerx.ist.psu.edu/viewdoc/download?doi=10.1.1.129.4720&rep=rep1&type=pdf.

Lamberti, Amato. 2009. "Se anche la Camorra è 'liquida': *Corriere del Mezzogiorno, dossier, osservatorio sulla Camorra e sull'illegalità*." 25 June.

Massari, Monica. 2001. "La criminalità mafiosa nell'Italia centro-settentrionale." In *Mafie nostre, mafie loro: Criminalita' organizzata italiana e straniera nel centro-nord*, edited by Stefano Becucci and Monica Massari. Milan: Edizioni di Comunita.

Moran, Nathan. 2008. "The Activities of Transnational Organized Crime." In *Organized Crime, from Trafficking to Terrorism*, edited by Frank G. Shanty. Santa Barbara, CA: ABC-CLIO.

Morselli, Carlo, Martha Turcotte, and M. Tenti. 2011. "The Mobility of Criminal Groups." *Global Crime* 12 (13): 165–188.

Mueller, Gerhard. 1999. "Transnational Crime: An Experience in Uncertainties." In *Organized Crime: Uncertainties and Dilemmas*, edited by S. Einstein and M. Amir. Chicago, IL: The Office of International Criminal Justice.

Nicaso, Antonio, and Lee Lamothe. 2005. *Angels, Mobsters and Nacro-Terrorism: The Rising Menace of Global Criminal Empires*. Ontario: Wiley.

Paoli, Letizia. 2003. *Mafia Brotherhoods: Organized Crime, Italian Style.* Oxford: Oxford University Press.
Paoli, Letizia, and Cyrille Fijnaut. 2006. "Organised Crime and Anti-Crime Policies." In *Developments in European Politics*, edited by Paul M. Heywood, Erik Jones, Martin Rhodes, and Ulrich Sedelmeier. London: Palgrave Macmillan.
Perakyla, Anssi. 1997. "Reliability and Validity in Research Based on Transcripts." In *Qualitative Research: Theory, Method and Practice*, edited by David Silverman. London: Sage.
Queralt, Joan. 2013. *La Gomorra di Barcellona: Sull'altra riva del Mediterraneo.* Urbino: Editori Internazionali Riuniti.
Rawlinson, Patricia. 2000. "Mafia, Methodology, and Alien Culture." In *Doing Research on Crime and Justice.* New York: Oxford University Press.
Reski, Petra. 2015. In *Dialoghi sulle Mafie*, edited by Simona Melorio and Marcello Ravveduto. Soveria Mannelli: Rubbettino Editore.
Roberti, Franco. 2008. "Organized Crime in Italy: The Neapolitan Camorra Today." *Policing, a Journal of Policy and Practice* 2 (1): 43–49.
———. 2012. "Legalità e lotta ai poteri criminali in Campania." In *Per un contrasto Europeo al crimine organizzato e alle mafie: La risoluzione del Parlamento Europeo e l'Impegno dell'Unione Europea*, edited by S. Alfano and A. Varrica. Milan: Franco Angeli.
Robinson, Jeffrey. 1994. *The Laundrymen: Inside the World's Third Largest Business.* London: Simon and Schuster UK.
———. 2000. *The Merger: The Conglomeration of International Organized Crime.* New York: Overlook Press.
Rowan, John. 1976. *The Power of the Group.* London: Davis-Poynter.
Ruggiero, Vincenzo. 2000. "Transnational Crime: Official and Alternative Fears." *International Journal of the Sociology of Law* 28: 187–199.
Sales, Isaia. 1988. *La Camorra, le Camorre.* Rome: Riuniti.
———. 1995. "La cultura della Camorra." In *Per amore del mio popolo, Don Peppino Diana, vittima della Camorra*, edited by G. Fofi. Napoli: Tullio Pironti.
Sands, Jennifer. 2007. "Organized Crime and Illicit Activities in Spain: Causes and Facilitating Factors." *Mediterranean Politics* 12 (2): 211–232.
Saviano, Roberto. 2008. *Gomorrah: Italy's Other Mafia.* London: Macmillan.
———. 2012. *Le combat continue: Résister à la mafia et à la corruption.* Paris: Robert Laffont.
Savona, Ernesto. 1999. *European Money Trails.* Amsterdam: Harwood.
Schneider, Stephen. 2009. *Iced, the Story of Organized Crime in Canada.* Ontario: Wiley and Sons.
Sciarrone, Rocco. *1998. Mafie vecchie, mafie nuove, radicamento ed espansione.* Rome: Donzelli.
———, ed. 2011a. *Alleanze nell'ombra, mafie ed economie locali in Sicilia e nel Mezzogiorno.* Rome: Donzelli.
———. 2011b. "Mafie, relazione e affari nell'area grigia." In *Alleanza nell'ombra.*
———, ed. 2014. *Mafie del nord: Strategie criminali e contesti locali.* Rome: Donzelli.
Sciarrone, Rocco, and Luca Storti. 2014. "The Territorial Expansion of Mafia-Type Organized Crime: The Case of the Italian Mafia in Germany." *Crime, Law and Social Change* 61 (1): 37–60.
Seindal, Rene. 1998. *Mafia: Money and Politics in Sicily, 1950–1997.* Denmark: Narayana Press.
Soudijn, Melvin R. J., and Sander Huisman. 2010. "Criminele expats: Britse criminelen in Nederland en nederlandse criminelen in Spanje." (Criminal expats: British

criminals in the Netherlands and Dutch criminals in Spain). *Tijdschrift voor Criminologie* 52 (2): 186–200.
Transcrime. 2013. "Gli investimenti delle mafie." Realizzato dall'Università Cattolica del Sacro Cuore (Centro Interuniversitario Transcrime) per il Ministero dell'Interno (PON Sicurezza, 2007–2013).
Treverton, Gregory F., Carl Matthies, Karla J. Cunningham, Jeremiah Goulka, Greg Ridgeway, and Anny Wong. 2009. *Film Piracy, Organized Crime and Terrorism.* Santa Monica, CA: Rand.
Van Duyne, Petrus. 1993. "Implications of Cross-Border Crime Risks in an Open Europe." *Crime, Law and Social Change* 20 (2): 99–111.
———. 1996. "The Phantom and Threat of Organized Crime." *Crime, Law and Social Change* 24 (4): 341–377.
———. 1997. "Organized Crime, Corruption and Power." *Crime, Law and Social Change*, 26 (3): 201–38.
Varese, Federico. 2011. *Mafias on the Move: How Organized Crime Conquers New Territories.* Oxford: Oxford University Press.
Venkatesh, Sudhir. 2008. *Gang Leader for a Day.* London: Penguin.
———. 2013. *Floating City: Hustlers, Strivers, Dealers, Call Girls, and Other Lives in Illicit New York.* New York: Alan Lane.
Vessia, Aldo, 1988. "Relazione sull'Amministrazione della Giustizia nell'Anno 1987." *Assembea Generale della Corte*, 13 January.
Von Lampe, Klaus. 2012. "The Practice of Transnational Organized Crime." In *The Routledge Handbook of Transnational Organized Crime*, edited by F. Allum and S. Gilmour. London: Routledge.
Williams, Phil. 2001. "Transnational Criminal Networks." In *Networks and Netwars: The Future of Terror, Crime, and Militancy*, edited by John Arquilla and David Ronfeldt. Santa Monica: Rand. http://faculty.cbpp.uaa.alaska.edu/afgjp/padm610/networks%20and%20netwar.pdf.
Williams, Phil, and Rod Godson. 2002. "Anticipating Organized and Transnational Crime." *Crime, Law and Social Change* 37 (4): 311–355.
Willian, Philip. 2005. "Camorra Factions Vie for Control of Naples Drug Market." *Jane's Intelligence Review* 17 (2): 42–43.

# Index

Page numbers followed by f, t, m, and n indicate figures, tables, maps, and notes.

Abadinsky, Howard, 45–46
Acquisitive crime, 10
  Camorra's functional mobility and, 43–48, 45t, 219–20, 221, 234n4
  definitions, 234n4
  functional use of host countries, 224, 224t
  in Germany, 65–66
  in Netherlands, 65
  phases of development of, 222–25, 223t
  types of involvement in, 46–48
Acquisitive crime, and De Sena clan in France, 106–14
  accomplices, 113
  activities, 112–13
  members and territories, 104–9, 110f, 111
Acquisitive crime, in Spain, 137–39
  Misso clan and, 138, 139f, 140
Acquisitive crime, in United Kingdom, 181–82
  Piccirillo clan and, 182–88
Africa
  counterfeit goods and, 18, 114
  drugs and, 56, 143–44, 223
Alfieri, Carmine, 79, 84
Alfieri Confederation, 25, 94
  drug trafficking in Germany, 91–92
Altamura-Reale clans, 69
Amato, Raffaele, 218, 220
  drug trafficking and, 58
  motivations for leaving Naples, 30, 33, 36
Amato-Pagano clan, 5, 88, 167, 215, 216, 225
  acquisitive crime, 46
  drug trafficking, 56, 58, 217
  known as *gli Spagnoli*, 30
  money laundering, 62
Ammaturo, Umberto, 19, 21, 26, 28
*Angels, Mobsters and Narco-Terrorism* (Nicaso and Lamothe), 14–15
Annunziata, Alfonso, 233n23
  drug trafficking, 36, 92–94, 96–97, 99–100, 101
Annunziata-Aquino family, 58, 216
  drug trafficking, 56, 96–103
Aquino, Carmine, 96, 97, 100

Aquino, Raffaele, 96, 100, 101
Aubry, Gilles, 106
Austria, 2, 87, 148
Avagliano, Pasquale, 60–61

Bardellino, Antonio, 2, 19, 21, 154, 155
  drug trafficking in Germany and, 91–92
  drug trafficking in Spain and, 146–49
  money laundering and, 61, 173
  motivations for leaving Naples, 25, 28, 35, 38–39
Bardellino-Iovine Confederation, 26, 36, 146–48, 154, 156, 198
Bauli Spa fraud, 103, 104
Bauman, Zgymunt, 166
Beatrice, Filippo, 81, 213
Behan, Tom, 41, 215
Belgium, 2, 100, 129, 134
Bidognetti, Francesco, 146, 149
Bosti, Patrizio, 70, 87
Brancaccio, Luciano, 40
Buscetta, Tommaso, 5

Caldarelli, Raffaele, 27, 37, 38, 190–96, 233n17
Caldarelli clan, in United Kingdom, 190–91
  accomplices, 195–96
  activities, 193–95
  members and territories, 191–93
Calvi, Fabrice, 122
Camorra
  accomplices, 8, 225–26, 232n20
  clans in and around Naples, 13m
  continuation of perfected activities, 221–22
  criminal activity development phases, 222–25, 223t
  data collection about, 9–14, 11t, 12t
  emerging issues, 226–30
  family structures and blood ties, 218–19, 219t
  financial development phases, 221
  functional mobility, 6, 8, 212–15, 213, 219–20
  functional mobility, categories of, 220–21, 220t
  history of, 4–5

261

Camorra *(continued)*
  interconnectedness of territories, 212
  interdependency of territories, 6, 8, 40, 92, 193, 214
  liquidity of, 6, 215–18
  network structure of, 6–8
  presence in Europe, 1–3
  use of term, 4
  *see also* Pull factors; Push factors
Canepa, Anna, 41
Carrino, Anna, 205
Car trafficking, in France, 109, 110*f*, 111, 112
Casalesi clan, 21, 25, 149–50, 153–56, 215
Castells, Manuel, 60
Caterino, Raffaele D'Urso, 108
China, counterfeit goods and, 52–53, 67, 87, 114, 116–18, 141, 142–43
Cigarettes, Zaza clan and contraband, in France, 106, 119, 121–31
  accomplices, 130–31
  activities, 127–30
  members and territories, 121–25, 126*f*, 127
Cima, Roberto, 105
Cionti, Raffaele, 136
Cocaine. *See* Drug trafficking
Common fund, of clans, 5, 216, 221
  De Falco clan, 153
  De Sena clan, 112
  methods of sending monies to Naples, 88
  Nuvoletta clan, 175
  Piccirillo clan, 186
  Polverino clan, 160, 163, 166–67
  Secondigliano alliance and, 115, 143
  social cohesion and, 153
Commuters, functional mobility and, 220, 220*t*
Contini, Eduardo, 69–70, 72
Contini clan, 19, 27, 62, 69, 73, 83–84, 87, 90–91, 118, 145, 191, 215
Cosa Nostra, 4–5, 54, 122, 124, 128, 158, 173
Counterfeit goods
  Camorra's functional mobility and, 43*t*, 48–53
  Camorra's specific interests in, 10, 52–53
  economic value and impact of, 49, 51
  European market for, 50–51
  functional use of host countries, 224, 224*t*
  motivations for leaving Naples providers of, 33–34
  phases of development of, 222, 224
Counterfeit goods, in France, 114–31
  cigarettes, 106, 119, 121–31
  city clans and, 116–19
  drug trafficking and, 119–21

  Secondigliano alliance and, 114–16
Counterfeit goods, in Germany and Netherlands, 66–69
  clan accomplices, 89–91
  clan activities, 82–89, 86*t*
  clan members and territories, 69–82, 74*f*, 76*f*, 78*f*
Counterfeit goods, in Spain, 140, 140*t*
  city clans and, 141–43
  Secondigliano alliance and, 140–41
Counterfeit goods, in United Kingdom, 188–89
  Caldarelli clan and, 190–96
  Secondigliano alliance and, 189–90
Crimaldi family, 107
Cutolo, Raffaele, 4–5, 29, 183, 218
Czech republic, 2

D'Alessandro clan, 132
D'Avino, Fiore, 122
Dean, Geoff, 223
De Falco, Antonio, 146
De Falco, Giuseppe, 146, 148, 157, 240n18
De Falco, Mario, 146
De Falco, Nunzio, 1, 12, 218, 220, 231n1
  drug trafficking in Spain and, 146–50, 151*f*, 152–53, 154–57, 160
  money laundering and, 155
  motivations for leaving Naples, 25–26, 33, 36
De Falco, Vincenzo, 240n18
  drug trafficking in Spain and, 146–49, 152, 155, 156
  motivations for leaving Naples, 25–26
De Falco clan, 56, 107, 167, 198, 216
De Falco clan, drug trafficking in Spain and, 145, 146
  accomplices, 156–57
  activities, 153–56
  members and territories, 146–50, 151*f*, 152–53
*Dépêche, La*, 51
De Sena clan, 30, 216
De Sena clan, and acquisitive crime in France, 106–14
  accomplices, 113
  activities, 112–13
  members and territories, 104–9, 110*f*, 111
De Tommaso brothers, 138, 139*f*, 140, 216
Diana, Don Peppe, 146, 153, 231n1
Di Fiore family, 107
Di Lauro, Cosimo, 30
Di Lauro clan, 5, 30, 67, 90, 114–15, 214

INDEX    263

Di Mauro, Paolo, 19, 27–28, 83
Drug trafficking, 2, 10, 217
  Camorra's functional mobility and, 43*t*, 54–59, 57*t*
  couriers for, 58–59
  in France, 119–21, 131–35
  functional mobility and, 220
  functional use of host countries, 224, 224*t*
  phases of development of, 223
  phases of involvement in, 55–56
  Rinaldi clan and, 83
  types of involvement in, 56–58, 57*t*
  in United Kingdom, 180
Drug trafficking, in Germany and Netherlands, 83, 91–95
  clan accomplices, 103–4
  clan activities, 99–103
  clan members and territories, 93–99
Drug trafficking, in Spain, 143–46
  De Falco clan and, 145–57, 151*f*
  Polverino clan and, 145–63, 164*f*, 165–72

Economic opportunities, as pull factor for mobility, 22, 23, 23*f*, 35–36
Eurojust, 116, 228
European Arrest Warrant (EAW), 37, 38, 94, 190
Extortion rackets/*pizzo*, 7, 41, 44, 59, 65, 73, 215
  Calderelli clan, 19
  De Falco clan, 148, 153–56
  De Sena clan, 107–8, 112
  La Torre clan, 200, 203, 206–7, 209
  Licciardi clan, 83
  Nuvoletta clan, 93, 95, 102, 177, 179
  Piccirillo clan, 182, 185, 186
  Polverino clan, 158–59, 162, 165, 167
  Rinaldi clan, 27
  Secondigliano alliance, 82–83

Fabbrocino, Mario, 21, 124
Fahsing, Ivar, 223
*Faida di Scampia*, 28, 30. *See also* Gang activity, as push factor mobility
Falcone, Giovanni, 62
Falsone, Giuseppe, 105
Familiar networks, as pull factors for mobility, 22, 23*f*, 31–35
Fijnaut, Cyrille, 2
Financial crime. *See* Money laundering
Firearms trafficking
  in France, 111–12
  in Germany, 91–92, 93, 94

Forgione, Francesco, 232n22
France, 1–3, 105–6, 106*t*, 214
  acquisitive crime in, 106–14
  Camorra's functional mobility in, 42*t*, 48, 49, 50–51, 51, 54–55, 58, 61
  counterfeit goods in Germany and Netherlands, 114–31
  data collection in, 9
  drug trafficking and, 119–21, 131–35, 144
Franco, Giovanni, 105
Frizzero clan, 182–83
Fucito, Silvana, 83
Functional mobility, 6, 48–53
  acquisitive crime and, 43–48, 45*t*, 219–20, 221
  counterfeit goods and, 43*t*, 48–53
  drug trafficking and, 43*t*, 54–59, 57*t*
  dual identity of clans and, 41
  emerging issues and, 227–28
  extortion and, 43*t*
  familiar skills and crimes and, 40–41
  money laundering and, 41, 43*t*, 59–63
  *see also* Mobility of criminals

Gala, Giuseppe, 92–95, 97, 98, 102–4
Gala subgroup, 92, 98, 99, 102, 216
Gambetta, Diego, 217
Gang activity, as push factor mobility, 22, 23*f*, 28–31, 29*f*
Gayraud, Jean-Francois, 213–14
Generational family structure, 72, 77, 95, 147, 161, 182, 192, 200, 218–19, 219*t*
Germany, 2, 64–65, 65*t*
  acquisitive crime, 65–66
  Camorra's functional mobility in, 42*t*, 48, 54, 59
  counterfeit goods, 66–91, 74*f*, 76*f*, 78*f*, 86*t*
  data collection in, 9
  drug trafficking, 83, 91–104
Giddens, Anthony, 6
Gionta clan, 144–45
Giuliano, Guglielmo, 84
Giuliano, Luigi, 28, 46, 49, 79, 87, 127
Giuliano, Raffaele, 61, 66
Giuliano, Salvatore, 193
Giuliano clan, 47, 83, 138, 145
Globalization, effect on clans, 5–6, 41–42, 48, 60, 214–15, 228
Godson, Rod, 31
Gómez-Céspedes, Alejandra, 137
*Gomorrah* (Saviano), 3–4
Gottschalk, Peter, 223
Grasso, Pietro, 106

264   INDEX

Heroin. *See* Drug trafficking
Holland. *See* Netherlands

Iacolare, Corrado, 17
Ianni, Francis A. J., 46
*I Magliari* (film), 75
Intergenerational family structure, 96, 183, 192, 218–19, 219*t*
Iovine, Mario, 26, 105, 146, 149, 152–53

Jamieson, Alison, 24
Judicial and police activity, as push factors for mobility, 22, 23–28, 23*f*, 25*t*

Kelly, Robert, 12

Lamothe, Lee, 14–15
La Torre, Antonio, 233n9
  motivations for leaving Naples, 26, 32, 35, 37, 38
  in United Kingdom, 197, 198–200, 202–3, 205–6, 209–11
La Torre, Augusto
  motivations for leaving Naples, 26
  in United Kingdom, 197, 198, 200, 202–3, 205–7
La Torre, Tiberio Francesco, 26, 32, 37, 198–200
La Torre clan, 9, 37, 56, 61, 62, 132, 147, 162, 171, 216
La Torre clan, money laundering in United Kingdom, 197–98
  accomplices, 210–11
  activities, 207–10
  members and territories, 198–203, 204*f*, 205–7
Law enforcement, weak, as pull factor for mobility, 22, 23, 23*f*, 36–39, 39*t*
Leather jackets. *See* Counterfeit goods
*Libération*, 2
Licciardi, Antonio, 236n10
Licciardi, Gennaro, 69–70, 79, 184, 236n10
Licciardi, Maria, 71, 79
Licciardi, Pietro, 27, 34, 70, 73, 75, 79, 84, 85, 91, 142, 234n16
Licciardi, Vincenzo, 91
Licciardi clan, 52, 66, 75, 141
  counterfeit goods, 69–70, 72–73, 77, 82–88
Liguori, Giuseppe, 30
Lo Russo, Antonio, 105
Los Angeles, CA, Zaza and, 121, 123, 128

"Made in Italy" concept, 142–43, 191, 194–95.
  *See also* Counterfeit goods
Mafia, defined, 4

Mafia/Camorra association, 9, 23, 145, 213
  A. La Torre and, 26
  Ammaturo and, 26
  Bardellino and, 25
  Caldarelli and, 190–91
  counterfeit market and, 52
  as crime under Italian Penal Code 416 bis, 17, 37, 231n6
  emerging issues and, 222, 228–30
  N. De Falco and, 148
  Panzuto and, 187–88
  pull factors for leaving Naples, 36–38
  V. De Falco and, 25–26
  Zaza and, 125, 131, 231n2
*Mafia Export* (Forgione), 232n22
Mafia methods, spread to Europe, 229–230
  Nuvoletta clan and, 178
  Polverino clan and, 159, 166, 169
  Rinaldi and, 27
  Secondigliano alliance and, 84, 116
*Magliari* community (door-to-door sellers)
  Camorra's functional mobility and, 53
  in France and, 115–18
  in Germany and Netherlands, 71, 74–75, 79, 80–82, 84–86, 90
  in Spain, 141, 142–43
  in United Kingdom, 190
Mallardo, Francesco, 70, 72
Mallardo clan, 29, 69, 84
Mancini, Caterina, 240n18
Mancuso, Paolo, 29–30, 121, 122
Marouchini, Solange, 122
Martone, Vittorio, 40
Mazzarella, Ciro, 121, 124
Mazzarella, Vincenzo, 70, 191
Mazzarella clan, 30, 48, 50, 117, 118, 138, 140, 142, 145, 191, 194
Mazzarella-Misso Cartel, 67, 117, 184, 194
Mazzarella-Zaza family, 19, 121
Messina, Giovanni, 30, 108, 112, 215
Misso clan, 47, 66, 117, 138, 139*f*, 140, 194
"Mobile banditism." *See* Acquisitive crime
Mobility of criminals, motives for, 16–39
  economic opportunities, as pull factor, 22, 23, 23*f*, 35–36
  familiar networks, as pull factor, 21, 22, 23*f*, 31–35
  fear of gang activity, as push factor, 22, 23*f*, 28–31, 29*f*, 39*t*
  judicial and police activity, as push factor, 22, 23–28, 23*f*, 25*t*

overview of, 16–21, 18t, 19t, 20t
weak law enforcement, as pull factor, 22, 23, 23f, 36–39, 39t
see also Functional mobility
Money laundering, 2, 10, 220
  Camorra's functional mobility and, 41, 43t, 59–63, 221
  forms and patterns of, 60–62
  functional use of host countries, 224, 224t
  as integral to Camorra's activities, 60
  phases of development of, 222–25, 223t
  Zaza and, 127, 128–30
Money laundering, in Spain, 172, 176f
  Nuvoletta clan and, 172–79
Money laundering, in United Kingdom, 196–97
  La Torre clan and, 197–211, 204f
Moran, Nathan, 60
Mueller, Gerhard, 59

'Ndrangheta, 4–5, 7, 16–17, 31, 54–56, 64, 119, 168, 180, 213, 218, 219, 222, 227
Netherlands, 2, 64–65, 65t, 144
  acquisitive crime, 65
  Camorra's functional mobility in, 42t, 46–47, 51, 55–56, 57, 59
  counterfeit goods, 66–68
  data collection in, 9
  drug trafficking, 91–104, 144
Nicaso, Antonio, 14–15
*Nuova Camorra Organizzata* (NCO), 4–5, 69
  motivations for leaving Naples, 17, 24–25, 28–29
*Nuova Famiglia* (NF), 4–5, 69
  motivations for leaving Naples, 19, 21, 24–26, 28–29
Nuvoletta, Angelo, 174
Nuvoletta, Aniello, 17
Nuvoletta, Lorenzo, 28, 61, 121, 158, 162
Nuvoletta clan, 7, 25, 88, 102–3, 132, 158–59, 215
  drug trafficking in Germany, 91–92
  see also Gala, Giuseppe; Polverino, Giuseppe
Nuvoletta clan, money laundering in Spain and, 172–73
  accomplices, 179
  activities, 177–79
  local politics and, 179
  members and territories, 173–75, 176f, 177
Nuzzo, Nicola, 107

Operation Green Sea, 129–30
Organized crime, phases of development of, 222–25, 223t

Orsini, Vincenzo, 80
*Outilleurs Napolitains* scam, 51, 116–19
"Outlaw capitalism," 1, 229

Panzuto, Gennaro, 23, 27, 82, 136, 216, 218
  Camorra's functional mobility and, 47, 48
  motivations for leaving Naples, 34, 37–38
  United Kingdom and, 182–88
Paoli, Letizia, 2, 4
Parmalat products, 102–3, 104
Pascarella, Raffaele, 80–81
Patriarchal/traditional family structure, 146, 195, 200, 218–19, 219t
Petty crime. See Acquisitive crime
Piccirillo, Ciro, 182–83
Piccirillo, Rosario, 182–83
Piccirillo clan, acquisitive crime in United Kingdom and, 7, 72, 182
  accomplices, 187–88
  activities, 186–87
  members and territories, 182–86
Pizza Connection, 128
*Point, Le*, 105, 221
Polverino, Giuseppe, 19, 170–71, 220, 233n12
  drug trafficking in Spain and, 157, 158–63, 166
  motivations for leaving Naples, 26, 33, 36
Polverino clan, 46, 58, 88, 214, 215, 217, 224, 226
  money laundering and, 62, 173, 174–75
Polverino clan, drug trafficking in Spain and, 145–46
  accomplices, 170–72
  activities, 167–70
  members and territories, 158–63, 164f, 165–67
Portugal, 2, 56, 141, 144
Presteri, Maurizio, 38
Pre-trial arrests. See Judicial and police activity, as push factors
Pull factors, for mobility, 6, 233n6
  economic opportunities, 22, 23, 23f, 35–36
  familiar networks, 22, 23f, 31–35
  weak law enforcement, 22, 23, 23f, 36–39, 39t
Push factors, for mobility, 6, 233n6
  fear of gang activity, 22, 23f, 28–31, 29f
  judicial and police activity, 22, 23–28, 23f, 25t

Rancadore, Domenico, 37, 229
Regular visitors, functional mobility and, 220, 220t

Residents abroad, functional mobility and, 220, 220*t*
Rinaldi, Antonio, 70, 72
Rinaldi, Gennaro, 27, 72
Rinaldi, Salvatore, 27
Rinaldi, Vincenzo, 69, 70, 72
Rinaldi clan, 30, 34, 68
    counterfeit goods and, 68–72, 77–82, 78*f*, 88–89
    drug trafficking and, 83
    money laundering and, 62
Roberti, Franco, 5, 61, 122, 144
Robinson, Jeffrey, 5
Rognoni-La Torre law (1982), 17–18, 146
Rolex watches. *See* Acquisitive crime
Rosi, Francesco, 75
Ruggiero, Vincenzo, 8
Russian Mafia, 218, 219

Sacca, Dario, 129
Salaries, paid by clans, 5, 70, 73, 82, 153, 186, 193, 200, 203, 205–6, 216
    clans lacking, 95, 99, 115
    paid to families of imprisoned members, 111, 175, 230n12
    *see also* Common Fund
Sales, Isaia, 40, 215
Saviano, Roberto, 3–4
Schengen agreement, 6, 42, 58, 120, 220
Schiavone, Carmine, 66
Schiavone, Francesco, 146, 149
Schiavone-Bidgnotti Confederation, 147, 149, 157, 198
Sciarrone, Rocco, 8
Secondigliano alliance, 61, 94, 215, 216, 218
    counterfeit goods in France, 114–16
    counterfeit goods in Germany, 67–91, 74*f*, 76*f*
    counterfeit goods in Spain, 140–41
    counterfeit goods in United Kingdom, 189–90
    Piccirillo clan and, 184–85, 186
Semeraro, Luca, 213
Siciliano, Michele, 8, 152
    La Torre clan and money laundering, 201–2, 203, 208, 209
    motivations for leaving Naples, 26, 32, 37
Silvestro, Pasquale, 80
Simeoli family, 174
Social capital, of clans, 4, 19, 108, 184, 215, 225
    Bardellino and, 148
    De Falco clan and, 149, 156
    La Torre clan and, 198, 210

Polverino and, 161, 170
Secondigliano alliance and, 89–90
Zaza and, 122–23, 130
South America, 17–18, 20–21, 50, 228
    drug trafficking and, 54–59, 92, 99–100, 102, 104, 128, 131, 132–34, 143–44, 155
Spain, 1, 136–79, 137*t*, 214
    acquisitive crime, 137–40, 139*f*
    Camorra's functional mobility in, 42*t*, 47, 54–59, 62
    counterfeit goods, 140–43, 140*t*
    data collection in, 9
    drug trafficking, 143–72, 151*f*, 164*f*
    money laundering, 172–79, 176*f*
    as preferred camorra destination, 136–37, 172
    weak law enforcement in, 37, 38–39
Sperlongano, Mario, 202
*Staffetta* system, drug trafficking and, 59
Stolder clan, 99, 216

Tiro Grosso affair, 131–34, 208, 239n26
Tortora, Rolando, 105
Transcrime, 9, 226

UniFab (Union des Fabricants Français), 49, 50, 235n7
United Kingdom, 2, 180–81, 181*t*
    acquisitive crime and, 181–88
    Camorra's functional mobility in, 42*t*, 49, 51, 54
    counterfeit goods, 188–96
    data collection in, 9
    money laundering, 196–211, 204*f*
    weak law enforcement in, 37–38, 197

Vallone, Maurizio, 36–37, 41–42
Value system/ideology, of clans, 4–5, 81, 98–99, 102, 111, 115, 127, 153, 165–66, 185, 193, 216–17
Van Duyne, Petrus, 217–18
Vanelli-Grassi group (*i girati*), 5
Varese, Federico, 35
Venkatesh, Sudhir, 1
Verde, Domenico, 26, 157, 162–63, 166, 168
Verde, Gelsomina, 233n19
Vessia, Aldo, 54
*Vicolizzazione*, 215
Von Lampe, Klaus, 22

Waste management, 4, 53, 106, 137, 208
Williams, Phil, 31
Willian, Philip, 54

Women
    in Annunziata-Aquino family, 97–98
    in Caldarelli clan, 192
    in De Sena clan, 109, 111
    in La Torre clan, 203, 205
    in Piccirillo clan, 185
    in Polverino clan, 165
    as "reserve army," 226
    in Rinaldi clan, 79–80
    in Secondigliano alliance, 70, 71, 75, 79
    in Zaza organization, 124, 125

Zagaria, Vincenzo, 146
Zaza, Ciro, 28, 106

Zaza, Michele, 1, 12, 19, 90, 106, 173, 216, 220, 222, 224, 231n2
    birth, death, and family of, 121–23
    Camorra's functional mobility and, 46, 50
    money laundering and, 61
    motivations for leaving Naples, 28–30, 32, 35
Zaza, Michele, contraband in France and, 106, 121–31
    clan accomplices, 130–31
    clan activities, 127–30
    clan members and territories, 121–25, 126*f*, 127
Zaza, Salvatore, 29–30, 122
Zaza clan, 115, 216